OLD AND NEW BIRMINGHAM.

"Ask Britain who gives her the spear and the shield,
The helmet, the sword—her defence in the field?
Ask Science (from Science the tribute is due)
Who gives her the lever, the wedge, and the screw?
Ask Ceres (for Ceres the claim will allow)
Who gives her the sickle, the scythe, and the plough?
'Tis Birmingham!"

—William Hamper

OLD AND NEW BIRMINGHAM:

A HISTORY OF

THE TOWN AND ITS PEOPLE.

BY

ROBERT K. DENT.

VOLUME I

"So describe,
That you shall fairly streets and buildings trace,
And all that gives distinction to the place."
—CRABBE.

WITH A NEW INTRODUCTION BY DOROTHY H. McCULLA

Republished by
EP Publishing Limited
1972

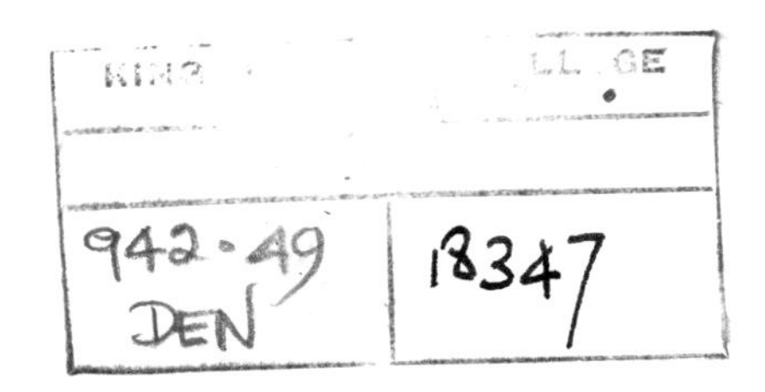

Publisher's Notes

This volume is a reprint of the first 23 chapters of 'Old and New Birmingham' covering the period up to 1760.

Volume II includes chapters 24 to 60 and covers the period 1760–1832.

Volume III includes chapters 61 to 68 and the 10 chapters comprising part 2, and covers the period 1832–1880.

The work was originally published in weekly numbers between 1878 and 1880 by Houghton and Hammond, Scotland Passage, Birmingham.

Facsimiles of some of the original covers for this work are reproduced at the end of each volume.

This volume has been reproduced from Birmingham Public Library copy number 242137. The six small corrections mentioned in the original errata have been corrected in this reprint.

East Ardsley, Wakefield
Yorkshire, England

ISBN 0 85409 782 1

Please address all enquiries to EP Publishing Ltd.
(address as above)

Reprinted in Great Britain by
Scolar Press Limited, Menston, Yorkshire

TO

SAM: TIMMINS, ESQ., J.P., F.S.A.,

WHOSE LABOURS THE DEPARTMENT OF ARCHÆOLOGY
ENTITLE HIM TO REPRESENT

OLD BIRMINGHAM;

AND TO

JOSEPH CHAMBERLAIN, ESQ., M.P.,

WHO HAS, BY HIS CONSTANT EFFORTS FOR THE WELFARE OF
THE TOWN, RENDERED

NEW BIRMINGHAM

FAMOUS AND PROSPEROUS,

THIS HISTORY OF

"OLD AND NEW BIRMINGHAM"

IS DEDICATED, AS A TOKEN OF THE SINCEREST ADMIRATION AND RESPECT,

BY THE

AUTHOR AND PUBLISHERS.

"The said towne of Brymyncham ys a verey mete place."

INTRODUCTION

by Dorothy H. McCulla
Local Studies Librarian, Reference Library, Birmingham

It was indeed fortunate for Birmingham, the town too busy turning the wheels of the world to write about itself, that Robert Kirkhope Dent chose to record its history.

After John Hammond heard Dent deliver a lecture called 'Old and New Birmingham' he suggested that the material should become the subject of a book. The idea grew and flourished in the mind of Robert Dent and during his spare time, which was limited, when it is considered he worked as a librarian until nine o'clock in the evening, he examined every document and record in an effort to produce a readable general history of the town especially compiled to inform and interest its busy inhabitants. This spare time work, undertaken during the years 1877 to 1878 resulted in this work, 'Old and New Birmingham', which was an immediate success.

Robert K. Dent was not born in Birmingham but he had an intense love and veneration for the town of his adoption: symptoms in common with many famous citizens. In fact he was born in Tamworth in 1851 and grew up to be a studious boy, more interested in reading than playing cricket. Young Dent used to tramp some seven miles from his home to visit his uncle, who had charge of a library in Lichfield, just to browse among the books. The historical plays of Shakespeare thrilled him beyond measure and must have stimulated his interest in history.

In the year 1866, Robert K. Dent came to Birmingham, where at the age of fifteen he became a junior assistant at the newly opened Free Library. His talent for story-telling was revealed in 1867 when he won the prize of a guinea's worth of books offered by Beeton's magazine for the best story. The subject he chose at the age of sixteen was 'Guy Fawkes'. For six years he worked in the library and he often recalled 'those enquiring customers' who required him to serve as many as seventy volumes of patents at one time! During the latter years of his service he worked as a cataloguer under John Mullins, the Chief Librarian.

In order to gain further knowledge of books he went to work for William Downing, the antiquarian bookseller, in 1872. Meanwhile the newspapers and literary magazines were busy printing articles from his pen. He wrote many articles for the Birmingham Daily Mail, under the signature 'Delta', until in October 1877 in competition with 33 applicants, he learned that he had been given the post of Chief Librarian of Aston Manor Public Library, where he worked until 1911. It must have been during his first year of office as Chief Librarian that 'Old and New Birmingham' was born. On 1st June 1878 the issue of the work commenced in weekly, monthly, and half-yearly parts. The numbers were advertised for sale as weekly numbers, price one penny, monthly parts, price sixpence, and half-yearly sections, price three shillings.

The prospectus for the work, dated 1878, defines the purpose of the publication as:

> . . . but as yet, no work has been published on the subject, sufficiently attractive in style and appearance to excite, among the masses of Birmingham men and women an interest in the history of their town. To meet this want Messrs. Houghton and Hammond are now issuing in Weekly Numbers, Monthly Parts and Half-yearly Sections, an Illustrated Serial, under the title of 'Old and New Birmingham', compiled and edited by ROBERT K. DENT; a work which will give in a popular form the story of the rise of the great hardware village, from the 'one street', with its 'one paroch church', of Leland's time, to its present position, as the metropolis of the midlands. . . .

Large paper copies are advertised in the prospectus as being especially suited for collectors as:

> 'To those who are interested in our old town, and have leisure and opportunities of searching for old prints and literary curiosities illustrative of its history, no occupation can possibly be more fascinating than to ADDITIONALLY ILLUSTRATE any work on the History of Birmingham.
>
> 'OLD AND NEW BIRMINGHAM' will, the Publishers believe, be found specially suited for this purpose, and they are therefore issuing a limited number of copies on LARGE PAPER, royal 4to size, the illustrations being printed from the original wood blocks.
>
> In this form it will also be found a desirable book for collectors.'

A final reference to the prospectus should be made to record the comments of prominent people and the popular press to the first issues of the work:

> 'It has told me much I did not previously know.'—COUNCILLOR MARTINEAU.
>
> 'The idea is excellent.'—JOSEPH CHAMBERLAIN, ESQ., M.P.
>
> 'Deserves a hearty welcome in all Birmingham homes.'—DAILY POST, MAY 22ND, 1878.

Plans, prospect views, profuse illustrations and apt quotations patiently extracted from

Aris's Gazette newspaper and facts stored by an enquiring mind are employed by the story-teller to set and sketch the scenes as they are presented to the reader in progression, from the Domesday Survey until the times of Joseph Chamberlain; some 886 years of achievement. Each period is treated as a whole, within the main sequence of history and the chapters which help to link the periods together are those devoted to the appearance of the town. The reader therefore becomes pleasantly enveloped in the atmosphere created for him as his attention is focussed so completely on each phase.

This is how Dent introduces the reader to the history of the General Hospital:

'When the year 1765 was drawing to a close and the first touch of the coming winter led men to think of the poor, and especially of the sick poor, by whom the icy hand of winter is always most keenly felt, an advertisement appeared in Aris's Birmingham Gazette, Nov. 4th, 1765, as follows:

'A General hospital, for the Relief of the Sick and lame, situated near the Town of Birmingham, is presumed would be greatly beneficial to the populous Country about it, as well as that place. A Meeting therefore of the Nobility and Gentry of the Neighbouring Country, and of the Inhabitants of this Town, is requested on Thursday, the 21st Instant, at the Swan Inn, at Eleven in the Forenoon, to consider of proper Steps to render effectual so useful an undertaking.'

The survey of the town in 1760 ends with a few poetical descriptions in praise of Birmingham, the following verses were delivered from the stage of the theatre, presumably the King's Theatre which once occupied part of the site of New Street Station, by Mr. Brodin:

'Thus blest with every Grace the Powers can give,-
May Birmingham long flourish and e'er live.'

After using the above quotation Mr. Dent cannot resist making the following comment:

'With this prayer, which every man and woman of Birmingham should echo to-day, we close the present survey of the town.'

It is time some tribute is paid to the illustrations used in the work, especially the excellent wood engravings by George H. Bernasconi and H. Dugard.

Henry Dugard was a wood engraver working at No. 45 Bull Street in the 1870s. George Henry Bernasconi was born in Bedford Square, London. He was endowed with the same artistic talent as his father and grandfather. Photography also interested him, indeed he was one of the first men in the country to discover the means of enlarging a photograph.

In 1866, he came to Birmingham to work as an artist in Mr. Thrupp's photographic gallery. Later on he went into partnership with Langford; the firm became Bernasconi and Langford, artists and designers, 29 Bennett's Hill. Mr. Bernasconi produced cartoons for various magazines, these drawings became so popular with the general public that soon they became weekly features of the magazines.

As the Chief Librarian of Aston Manor Public Library Robert Dent was responsible for the forming of a remarkable Reference library and for the publication of penny catalogues of the various classes of literature in the library, but most successful of all was the introduction of a series of free lectures on local history which became quite a feature of Aston life. In 1894 Dent compiled another history of the life and growth of Birmingham entitled 'The Making of Birmingham'. The text was brought up to date and had more continuity in which the more important aspects of the town's history were treated equally instead of the sketchy, sometimes gossipy accounts given in 'Old and New Birmingham'. However, it must be remembered that this first history compiled by Dent was merely a glimpse into Birmingham's past. It was not a scholarly work, produced to promote argument, indeed it was not the author's intention that it should do so. 'Old and New Birmingham' was written to interest the masses of men and women in the history and achievements of their town—Birmingham.

The writer's great feeling for the subject stimulates and yet embarrasses the modern reader, who has become so conditioned to the cold, clinical, academic approach to history. Indeed, it is to be regretted that just a little of the Victorian enthusiasm is sadly lacking from most of the histories of towns and industries written to-day.

Robert Dent was a member of the Library Association of the United Kingdom from 1881 and a member of the Library Association Council for over 25 years. In 1895 he was instrumental in forming the Birmingham and District Library Association and for 18 years he acted as its Hon. Secretary. He was a proud member of the Central Literary Association and a member and past President of the Midland Arts Club. In his life-time it was said that no ancient stone was ever upturned or discovery made relating to the past history of Birmingham that Dent did not observe and carefully examine. He was present when the stones of the old Priory of St. Thomas were unearthed on the site now known as Lewis's store, Bull Street. He was a very interested spectator when the catacombs of Christ Church were searched for the body of John Baskerville in 1893. In a letter to Walter Powell, City Librarian of Birmingham, he affirmed his belief in the identity of William Shakespeare. The letter was written to try and persuade Mr. Powell to give a paper on Shakespeare at a meeting of the Birmingham and District Library Association in 1902 as:

> 'Why not a short sensible shut-up to the Bacon cackle? You could do it like smoke, for the simple reason that any person who really *knows* the Elizabethan literature knows how utterly impossible it is that any one but Shakespeare wrote the plays that are acknowledged as his.'

As well as the numerous guide books and contributions to magazines Robert K. Dent was responsible for the following works; the list also includes two works produced in collaboration with Joseph Hill:

Houghton's Guide to Birmingham. ?1885.

Allday's Gossiping guide to Birmingham. 1893.

John Baskerville: a memoir by R. Straus and R. K. Dent. 1907.

City of Birmingham. History and description of the Public parks, gardens and recreation grounds. 1916.

Historic Staffordshire, by R. K. Dent and J. Hill. 1896.

Memorials of the Old Square, by J. Hill and R. K. Dent. 1897.

Although 'Old and New Birmingham' was published over 90 years ago it still remains a useful work of reference which is in constant use in the Local Studies Department of the Reference Library, where letters, telephone messages and people arrive hourly to learn more about a place called Birmingham. When the information given therein is double checked it is rarely proved to be incorrect. The reprinting of this work insures its availability to students of Birmingham history for the years to come and is a tribute to a remarkable librarian, Robert K. Dent.

Two tributes paid to Edmund Burke by Samuel Johnson and faithfully recorded by Boswell seem to describe both the writer and the book:

> 'He does not talk from a desire of distinction,
> but because his mind is full.'
>
> 'Take up whatever topick you please he is ready
> to meet you.'

JULY 1972

Photo. by H. J. Whitlock & Sons

MR. ROBERT K. DENT

PREFACE.

I DARE not hope that this book will satisfy the requirements of the antiquary, or of those learned in the ancient history of our town, as the space at my disposal—in order to bring the entire history within the compass of a popular volume—does not allow of my entering upon the *minutiæ* of local archæology. But I have endeavoured to omit nothing of interest from the early history of the town I love so well, and have striven to present an accurate picture of *old* Birmingham, as well as of the Birmingham of to-day.

I have also endeavoured to weave into the story of the town some account of those who have helped to make her what she has become. The lives of William Hutton and John Baskerville, of Matthew Boulton, James Watt, and Joseph Priestley, are as much a part of the history of the town as the story of the rise of her institutions.

It has been my aim to preserve, as far as it is practicable, the chronological sequence of the events in our local history, endeavouring to keep the various portions of the story abreast, so to speak, and to give as completely as possible the picture of each period by itself,—rather than to trace out the entire history of each of the various institutions separately. How far I have succeeded it will be for the reader to judge.

I need scarcely say that the work could not possibly have been accomplished without the kind assistance of those who possess original documents, or rare books and prints, who have generously placed these valuable materials at my disposal. The cordial manner in which the authors of the many valuable works on the history of various local institutions, etc., have permitted me to make use of those storehouses of local history has also greatly encouraged me, and I here tender to them my grateful thanks for the incalculable assistance I have received therefrom.

My thanks are due to Mr. W. Bates, B.A., Mr. J. T. Bunce, Dr. J. A. Langford, and Mr. Sam: Timmins, for permission to quote from their various works relating to Birmingham, and I have also to acknowledge my indebtedness to the works of William Hutton, W. Hawkes Smith, and J. Toulmin Smith, and to the "Hints for a History of Birmingham," by Mr. James Jaffray. Many rare and valuable books, prints, MSS., pamphlets, and broadsides have been very kindly lent to me by Mr. Alderman Avery, Mr. W. Bates, B.A., Mr. W. Franks Beale, Mr. R. Birbeck, Mr. W. Buncher, Mr. W. Downing, Mr. Joseph Hill, Mr. J. Hitchman, Mr. Joseph Lander, Mr. Oliver Pemberton, Mr. Sam: Timmins, and Mr. J. Wilson, and to these my sincerest thanks are due, as also to Mr. J. D. Mullins, and Mr. C. E. Scarse, for their great kindness in permitting me to make use of the Birmingham books in the libraries under their superintendence.

I should be wanting in gratitude if I did not also acknowledge here the thanks I owe to the publishers, Messrs. Houghton and Hammond, for the manner in which they have entered into the work, and also for the great kindness and consideration which has rendered its publication one of the pleasantest experiences of my life.

R. K. D.

Aston, November 25th, 1879.

CONTENTS.

CHAPTER.		PAGE.
i.	The Manor and its Lords - -	3
ii.	Deritend, its Chapel and its Martyr Worthy	11
iii.	Birmingham in the Sixteenth Century	17
iv.	Aston Hall and its Owners - -	19
v.	The Battle of Birmingham - -	32
vi.	Birmingham in Transition - -	44
vii.	Appearance of the Town—1660-1700	54
viii.	A peep into the Old Town Books -	57
ix.	The Church in Prosperity and the Church in Danger - -	60
x.	A Picture of Birmingham in 1730-31 -	64
xi.	The Free Schools and Charities of Birmingham in the Seventeenth Century	71
xii.	Samuel Johnson in Birmingham -	79
xiii.	Aris's Birmingham Gazette and the appearance of the Town in 1741-1750	83
xiv.	The Story of a runaway Apprentice -	92
xv.	The Churches and Sects of Birmingham in 1720-1760 - - -	99
xvi.	How our Ancestors Travelled - -	103
xvii.	The Old Prison of Birmingham -	109
xviii.	Local Manufactures in the Eighteenth Century - - - -	111
xix.	John Baskerville - - -	114
xx.	Birmingham in 1760 - - -	119
xxi.	The General Hospital - -	125
xxii.	William Hutton in Birmingham -	132
xxiii.	The Story of Soho - - -	138
xxiv.	Public Life and Events in 1760-1775 -	141
xxv.	The Lamp Act - - -	156
xxvi.	Poet Freeth and the Birmingham Book Club - - - - -	163
xxvii.	The Churches and Sects of Birmingham in 1760-1780 - - -	169
xxviii.	The Birmingham Triennial Musical Festivals, first period from 1768 to 1799 - - - -	176
xxix.	The first History of Birmingham -	181
xxx.	Public Life and Events in 1775-1790 -	185
xxxi.	The Birmingham Library - -	197
xxxii.	Appearance of Birmingham in 1790 -	203
xxxiii.	A few old Birmingham Worthies -	210
xxxiv.	What led to the Riots of 1791 - -	220
xxxv.	The Fourteenth of July and its Events	226
xxxvi.	The Second Day of the Riots -	232
xxxvii.	The Third Day of the Riots - -	235
xxxviii.	The End of the Riots - - -	244
xxxix.	After the Riots - - -	247
xl.	The Theatre in Birmingham from 1775 to the burning of the New Street Theatre in 1792 - - -	257
xli.	The Story of Soho, Part II. -	265
xlii.	A Second Chapter of Local Worthies -	272
xliii.	Public Life and Events—1790-1800	293
xliv.	Churches and Sects in Birmingham—1791-1812 - - -	306
xlv.	Appearance of the Town at the commencement of the Nineteenth Century - - - - - -	308
xlvi.	Intellectual and Literary Activity of the Town at the close of the Eighteenth Century - - - -	313
xlvii.	Amusements of the People, including the History of the Birmingham Theatre, 1795-1810 - - -	318
xlviii.	Public Life and Events—1801-1810	327
xlix.	Local Trade and Commerce—1765-1810	337
l.	More about Travelling - - -	344
li.	The First Campaign in the Struggle for Freedom—1811-1820 - -	349
lii.	The Churches and Sects in Birmingham—1811-1820 - - - -	360
liii.	Local Charities, Chiefly Medical -	364
liv.	Public Life and Events—1811-1820 -	367
lv.	Amusements of the People, including the History of the Theatre Royal from 1811 to 1820 - - -	380
lvi.	The First Philosophical and Artistic Societies of Birmingham - -	387
lvii.	The Churches and Sects in Birmingham—1821-1830 - - - -	391
lviii.	The Birmingham Political Union and the Struggle for Parliamentary Reform—1828-1832 - - -	396
lix.	Public Life and Events—1821-1830 -	415
lx.	Birmingham in 1832 - -	425
lxi.	The Theatre in Birmingham—1821-1830 with Notices of other Amusements of the People - - - -	431
lxii.	Birmingham Triennial Musical Festivals, Second Period from 1802-1829	437
lxiii.	Education in Birmingham—1801-1840	442
lxiv.	The Birmingham Railways -	447
lxv.	Political History—1833-1840, including the History of the Bull Ring Riots of 1839 - - - - -	450
lxvi.	The Churches and Sects in Birmingham—1831-1840 - - - -	462
lxvii.	Public Life and Events—1831-1840	469
lxviii.	Amusements of the People, including the History of the Theatre Royal from 1831 to 1840 - - -	482

PART II.

CHAPTER.		PAGE.
i.	Municipal History of the Borough	491
ii.	Political History—1841-1879	529
iii.	Public Life and Events—1841-1879	550
iv.	The Churches and Sects of Birmingham—1841-1879	574
v.	Education, Literature, and Literary and Scientific Societies in Birmingham—1841-1879	589
vi.	Charitable Institutions—1841-1879	600
vii.	The Triennial Musical Festivals, Third Period, 1834-1879	605
viii.	Amusements of the People—1841-1879, including the History during that period	608
ix.	Local Trade and Commerce—1841-1879	613
x.	Public Buildings and Appearance of the Town—1841-1879	616

LIST OF ILLUSTRATIONS.

Westley's Plan of Birmingham in 1731, to face p. 96
William Hutton's first visit to Birmingham, to face p. 104
Facsimile of Rothwell's Coaching Bill, to face p. 105
Bradford's Plan of Birmingham, 1751, to face p. 145
Allin's Cabinet of Curiosities - to face p. 292
Lower end of New Street (about A.D., 1800), to face p. 309
Old View of the Moat from Lower end of Moat Lane - - - - to face p. 313
Interior of the Society of Artists' Rooms, to face p. 389

	PAGE.
The Council House. *Vignette Title.*	
Monuments of the Bermingham Family -	5
The "Propper Chappell" of Deritend	9
Portrait of John Rogers -	13
The "Old Crown House," Deritend	16
Birmingham, in 1640	20
Aston Hall. *(East Front)*	24
Long Gallery, Aston Hall	25
Great Staircase, Aston Hall -	28
Portrait of Charles I.	29
Aston Church	33
Portrait of Prince Rupert	37
The Old Ship Inn, Camp Hill	41
St. Martin's Church (Old View)	45
Stratford House, Camp Hill	49
Old Meeting House	52
Market Cross	55
The Welsh Cross	58
North prospect of St. Philip's Church	61
Interior of St. Philip's Church -	65
Westley's East prospect of Birmingham	69
Free Grammar School	73
The Old Workhouse	77
The Blue Coat School	81
Dr. Johnson	82
The Old Square -	85
St. John's Chapel, Deritend	89
The New Meeting House -	93
John Wesley	101
The Old Prison, Peck Lane	104
St. Bartholomew's Church -	106
John Baskerville	115
The General Hospital	118
Theatre Royal, New Street	123
The House in the Old Square	127
St. Mary's Church	131
The Soho Manufactory	135
Watt's House, Harper's Hill	139
John Ash, M.D., founder of the General Hospital	143
The Canal Office	151
The Moat	154
Poet Freeth	159
St. Paul's Chapel	162
William Hutton -	167
St. James's Chapel, Ashted -	174
The General Hospital, showing the two wings -	175
Facsimile of a Letter, written by Hutton at the age of seven	182
"Hockley Abbey" -	183
Old Windmill, Holloway Head -	187
Birmingham Old Library, Union Street	191
"Old Smithy," in Digbeth	195
"Old Tripe House," Digbeth	199
Stained Window in St. Paul's Chapel	202

	PAGE.
The Freeth Circle - - - - -	207
Joseph Priestley, LL.D. - - - - -	211
"A Birmingham Toast, July 14th, 1791." -	215
The Attack on the Old Meeting House, July 14th, 1791 - - - - -	223
Houses destroyed by the Rioters, July, 1791 -	231
Houses injured or destroyed during the Riots, July, 1791 - - - - - -	239
Old Caricature Print of the Riots - -	250
Livery Street (Union) Meeting House. Old Meeting House, rebuilt 1792-96. New Meeting House, rebuilt 1802 - -	254
The Old Court of Requests - -	255
Portrait of John Collins, Author of "The Brush"	259
,, Matthew Boulton - -	266
,, James Watt - - - -	267
Bingley House. Residence of Charles Lloyd.	274
Portrait of Charles Lloyd (the elder) - -	278
Watt's House, Heathfield - - - -	286
The Old Post Office - - - - -	287
The Loyal Association - - - -	291
Christ Church, New Street - - - -	295
Christ Church. Medal, commemorating the Laying of the First Stone - - -	299
Hen and Chickens, New Street - -	307
The Nelson Statue, High Street - -	310
Old House in the Bull Ring - -	314
Section of Old Map, showing the district round St. Martin's, Old Mill Pool, etc. - -	319
Old View of the Bull Ring - - -	322
The Public Office, Moor Street - -	330
Old Houses removed to make way for the Public Offices - - - - - - -	335
Old St. Martin's Parsonage - - -	338
Old View of Temple Row West, from Colmore Row - - - - - - - -	343
St. Philip's Church - - - - -	346
Statue of Thomas Attwood - - -	351
Portrait of George Edmonds - -	354
St. George's Church, from Great Hampton Row	359
Bust of the late Rev. John Angell James -	362
Penn's Lane, adjoining the scene of Mary Ashford's Death - - - - -	370
Plan of the scene of Mary Ashford's Death -	374
Portraits of Abraham Thornton and Mary Ashford - - - - - - - -	375
Portrait of Mary Ashford, in the dress she wore at the dance - - - - - -	378
Old View of the Top of New Street, showing the Society of Artists' Rooms - - - -	383
"Romeo Coates" - - - - -	386
Holy Trinity Chapel, Bordesley - - -	392
St. Peter's Church, Dale End - -	394
View of the Ruins of St. Peter's after the fire -	399
Wesleyan Chapel, Cherry Street - -	402
The Gathering of the Unions on Newhall Hill -	407
Lord John Russell. From a pen and ink sketch	418
The Reformers' Medal - - - - -	419
Old View of Digbeth, from the end of Mill Lane - - - - - - -	423
Portrait of late Dean Hook - - -	427
,, Alfred Bunn - - -	432
The Town Hall - - - - - -	435
Botanical Gardens, Edgbaston - -	439
The Free Grammar School - - -	443
Birmingham and Edgbaston Proprietary School	448
New Royal Hotel, New Street - - -	451
Bishop Ryder's Church - - -	455
Interior of St. Chad's Cathedral - -	458
Springhill College - - - - -	463
Interior of the Market Hall - - -	466
Old View of the Town Hall, from Hill Street	471
Interior of the Town Hall - - -	474
Monument to Joseph Sturge - -	479
St. Philip's Church, from the East end - -	483
Interior of the Theatre Royal - -	487
The late G. F. Muntz, M.P. From an old print - - - - - - - -	493
Insanitary Houses : A court in John Street	495
Insanitary Houses : No. 2 court John Street -	498
Insanitary Houses : No. 1 court Steelhouse Lane	499
Joseph Chamberlain, Esq., M.P. - -	506
The Right Hon. John Bright, M.P. -	510
The Exchange - - - . - -	511
Statue of the Late Prince Consort, by Foley	514
Statue of James Watt in Ratcliff Place - -	522
Statue of Dr. Priestley in Congreve Street -	523
The Elkington Challenge Shield, in the Corporation Art Gallery - - - -	527
New Line of Street—Colmore Row and Ann Street - - - - - -	530
The Union Club House, Colmore Row - -	535
Illumination of St. Philip's Church -	539
Exterior of St. Martin's Church as re-built in 1875 - - - - - - - -	543
Interior of Saint Martin's Church - -	547
Great Western Arcade - - - - -	551
Portrait of George Dawson, M.A. - -	554
The Church of the Messiah - - -	559
Wycliffe Chapel - - - - -	562
Queen's College - - - - - -	567
Sir Josiah Mason's Science College - -	570
Views in Aston Lower Grounds - - -	575
The Council House - - - - -	583
Sir Josiah Mason's Orphanage - - -	591
Handsworth Old Church - - -	602
Edgbaston Old Church - - - - -	607
Stratford House - - - - -	622

"OLD AND NEW BIRMINGHAM" PORTRAIT GALLERY.—No. 1

ALDERMAN AVERY.

PHOTOGRAPHED BY WHITLOCK.

BIRMINGHAM: HOUGHTON AND HAMMOND, SCOTLAND PASSAGE.

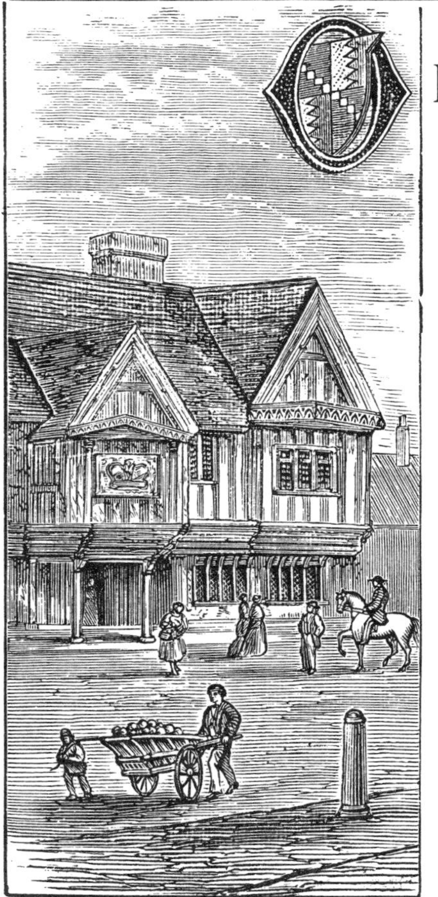

OLD AND NEW BIRMINGHAM.

INTRODUCTORY.

In the far west of America there have grown up within the memory of thousands now living, great and populous cities, abounding in handsome buildings, with thoroughfares which have already taken rank among the "streets of the world," —cities which twenty years ago were not thought worthy of the briefest notice in the gazetteer or geography, which were in fact little better than rude backwood settlements, selected by the emigrant settler on account of their natural advantages. The history of such a city will naturally be brief, and easily traced out. Extending over only half a lifetime, its beginnings will be within the memory not merely of "the oldest inhabitant," but of many who cannot lay claim to that proud distinction. But where the growth of a great town has been the work of centuries, rather than of decades, where it has existed as a small town or village for some hundreds of years,—as is the case with many of the large towns and cities of England, the tracing out of its early history is a matter of greater difficulty, and is in some cases almost an impossibility The little village or town, having existed for so long a period before it became of sufficient importance to excite any interest in its history, its origin and early history are not unfrequently shrouded in dense obscurity, which the most painstaking research fails to dispel.

Such, to a considerable extent, is the case with the town of which we are about to write; and although we shall find here and there a ray of light thrown on our path by the labours and researches of the worthy historians who have preceded us, we shall be able to give but a brief outline of the early history of that little Warwickshire village which has, by the industry and ingenuity of its inhabitants, so outgrown its ancient limits as to take high rank among the great cities of the empire, and has become famous all over the world, as the home of the arts, the birthplace of many of the most useful inventions which have blessed mankind, and one of the great centres of intellectual and political liberty.

"Boston State-House," says the most delightful essayist of our time, "is the hub of the solar system. . . . Cockneys think London is the only place in the world. . . . It is quite as bad with smaller places. . . . The axis of the earth sticks out visibly through the centre of each and every town or city."* We fear our love and veneration for Birmingham—the old and the new alike—may lead us into a similar weakness, one of which almost every good citizen of Birmingham is guilty, for one of the most notable traits in the character of Birmingham men and women is their attachment to, and love of, the town of their birth or adoption. We must crave the forgiveness, therefore, of outsiders who may read these notices of Old and New Birmingham, if in our records of its history we may seem to them to be guilty of the Bostonian error of supposing our town to be the centre of the universe, or of ignoring the fact that there are, up and down our world, greater cities than that of which we write—cities which can boast of an antiquity which makes the earliest records of our own seem to be but things of yesterday, and which may point to a history beside which our own annals may appear but as "small beer chronicles" and simple village records. But we are conscious of these facts, and it is for this reason that we would warn all who seek for chronicles filled with the records of brilliant pageants and pompous ceremonials, the doings of courts and the fortunes of court favourites, that in turning over these pages they will be wofully disappointed. Royal visits to Birmingham have been few and far between, and have not always conduced to the happiness and comfort of the royal visitors; no decrees or edicts, so far as we are aware, have ever been "given at our Court at Birmingham," and no building now standing, or that ever has stood, in the great hardware village, has at any time been used as a palace of royalty.

But if the reader be interested in the history of industrial progress, in "the story of our lives from year to year," in this busy hive of workers,—if he has any desire to trace the growth of Birmingham from the little village of one street, as Leland saw it in the beginning of the sixteenth century, to the great midland metropolis of the last quarter of the nineteenth century, then we will endeavour to fulfil his expectations.

We shall try to picture the town, both by pen and pencil, as it was in its infancy, to look upon it in its lusty youth, when the stern supporters of Cromwell and his Parliament were fighting against their king and his courtiers,—in its early manhood, when Samuel Johnson, then unknown to fame and unable to obtain an entrance into the inner world of letters, first made his abode here, and spent his leisure hours in translating Lobo's *Voyage to Abyssinia*,—and to journey hither and thither through the old streets and into the old places of resort, now into the church and among the tombs, anon into the theatres and other places of amusement and recreation, here in the tavern club among the old newsmongers, politicians, and scribblers, and there amid the din of anvils and hammers, watching the stout workmen as they help to lay the foundations of Birmingham's future greatness, by their cunning handicraft, which even in Camden's day was

* Oliver Wendell Holmes: *Autocrat of the Breakfast Table.*

heard of as far away as London and even Ireland. As we pass out of the eighteenth century we shall find ourselves now and then among the men who helped to gain for us our political freedom, and to secure for our town a voice in the councils of the nation. We shall stand once more amid the throng on Newhall Hill, as they solemnly promise to sacrifice themselves, their homes, and their families on the altar of freedom; we shall not forget to pay a visit to the great Soho factory, where Boulton and Watt and their associates are engaged in the production of that which kings strive most to possess—Power; and we shall watch the growth of the new Borough, one long series of triumphs over injustice and social inequality, over vice, and wretchedness, and ignorance, until the name of Birmingham has become almost synonymous with good government, and the greatest of English statesmen point thereto, as an example which other towns would do well to imitate.

CHAPTER I.

THE MANOR AND ITS LORDS.

The Domesday Survey—Etymology of the Name—The Story of the Berminghams—Appearance of the Town in the twelfth century—St. Martin's Church—The Monuments—Appearance of the finished mediæval church.

"RICHARD holds of William [Fitz-Ausculf] four hides in *Bermingham.* The arable employs six ploughs; one is in the demesne. There are five villeins and four bordars, with two ploughs. Wood half a mile long and four furlongs broad. It was and is worth 20s." In this brief passage, translated from the great Domesday Book of William the Conqueror, we have the first mention of the place which in after ages was to be known not merely as 'the Toyshop of Europe,' but as the great hardware manufactory of the world—which should supply many of the most indispensable articles of daily use, not merely to the cities of the Continent, but to the emigrant in the bush and the backwoods; to the half-savage inhabitant of the heart of Africa, and the islander of the South Seas—a great hive of toilers whose handiwork should go forth to the ends of the earth.

"A hide," says Hutton, "was as much as a team could conveniently plough in a year, perhaps about fifty acres. I think there are not now more than two hundred ploughed in the parish." Speaking of the "wood half a mile long and four furlongs broad," he observes,—"What difference subsisted between half a mile and four furlongs, in ancient times, is uncertain; we know of none now. The mile was reduced to its present standard in the reign of Queen Elizabeth: neither are there the least traces of those woods, for at this day it is difficult to find a stick that deserves the name of a tree, in the whole manor." Let us hope the next generation of Birmingham men and women may find matters improved in this particular, and that the youthful trees recently planted in various parts of the borough may, in years to come, afford pleasant shade, and help to beautify our streets, and thus restore something of the old pleasantly-wooded appearance to our town.

The etymology of the name of the town has at all times been a bone of contention among local antiquaries, from Hutton downwards. According to Dr. Langford, there are at least one hundred and forty different ways of spelling the word. William Hutton, misled by the common corruption of the name into Brommigeham, or Brummagem, believed the original to have been *Bromwych;* "*Brom,* perhaps, from broom a shrub for the growth of which the soil is extremely favourable; *Wych,* a dwelling, or a descent." This, he supposes, may have been its only name for many centuries, until, "a series of prosperity attending it, its lord might assume its name, reside in it, and the particle *ham* ["Bromwych's home"] would naturally follow. This very probably happened under the Saxon Heptarchy, and the name was no other than *Bromwycham.*" But the original name was not Bromwych, nor even Bromwicham, but Bermingeham or Bermingham, as we have seen from the entry in Domesday Book. Dugdale supposes the name to have been given to the place by its original owner, and this supposition is borne out by a modern authority, Mr. E. A. Freeman, the able historian of the Norman Conquest. In a letter published in the *Athenæum*, Sept. 8, 1855, he says, "The word Birmingham is so thoroughly Saxon in its construction that nothing short of positive historical evidence would warrant us in assigning any other than a Saxon origin to it. The final syllable, *ham*, means a home or residence, and *Berminghas* would be a patronymic or family name, meaning the Berms (from Berm, a man's name, and *ing* or *iung*, the young, progeny, race, or tribe). The word dissected in this manner, would signify the home or residence of the Berms; and there can be little question that this is its true meaning." It is probable, as Dr. Sebastian Evans suggests, that the corruption of the name into "Brummagem" arose from the old local pronunciation of the g soft, as in "singe," and similar words.

Hutton labours hard to show that the town was of considerable importance even in the time of the ancient Britons, and both Hamper and Dr. Whitaker attempted to identify it with the Roman station *Bremenium,* but there is much of fancy and imagination and but little of fact in the picture of Birmingham as a flourishing and important 'hardware village' supplying both Britons and Romans with weapons of warfare and implements of agriculture. That one of the great Roman roads passed near to the place is certain enough, and a memorial of the fact still remains in the name of Icknield Street, and some traces of the road remain in Icknield Port Road, and more perfectly in Sutton Park. But the real history of our town does not commence until a much later period than that of the Roman occupation of Britain. It was in Edward the Confessor's days, according to Dugdale, the freehold of one Ulwine, but after the Norman invasion (as we have already seen from the Survey) it was the property of William Fitz-Ausculf, who had his home at Dudley Castle. It was, as we have also seen, rated for four hides, valued at twenty shillings, and held of Fitz-Ausculf by "Richard." "Whether the before specified Richard," says Dugdale, "was paternal ancestor to those who afterwards assumed this place for their sirname, I cannot positively affirm; but certain it is, that the Paganells (who immediately succeeded W. Fitz-Ausculf in the enjoyment of Dudley Castle and the substance of all other his lands) passed it away, with other fair possessions, to be held by military service: for in 12 Henry II. (1166) amongst the knights' fees then certified by Gervase Paganell, it appears that Peter de Bermingham held nine of him, *de veteri feoffamento;* so that it is thereby clear that the father of the same Peter, whose name was William, if not his grandfather, became first enfeoft thereof in Henry I. time."

Peter de Bermingham was steward to Gervase Paganell, Lord of Dudley, and had a castle here,

The ancient seat of the Lord Birmingham.
From Westley's Map, 1731.

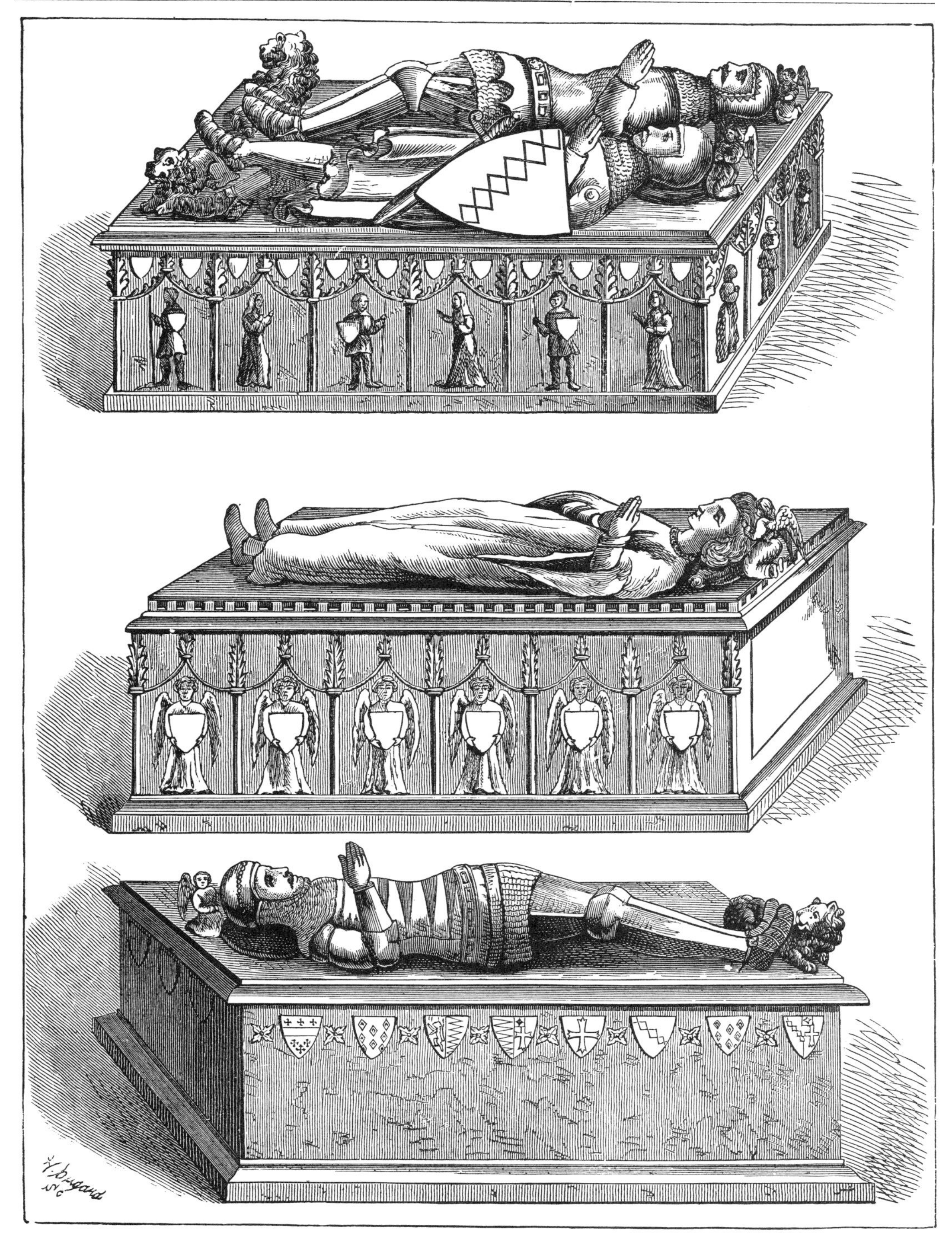

MONUMENTS OF THE BERMINGHAM FAMILY. *(See page 10.)*

which according to Dugdale, "stood scarce a bow-shoot from the church south-westwards." The moat which surrounded this castle is shown in Westley's map of the town published in 1731, although it does not appear in the "Prospect" engraved in Dugdale's Warwickshire, in 1656, from which our first view of the town is taken. The site is still indicated in the names of Moat Row and Moat Lane in that locality.

During the lifetime of Peter de Bermingham, a weekly market on the Thursday was established in the town by grant of King Henry II., as also of Gervase Paganell. This privilege was confirmed to Peter's son and successor, William de Bermingham, whose uncle was supposed to be instrumental, under Richard Strongbow, in the reduction of Ireland, in the reign of Henry II., and was rewarded with an estate in that country, and the title of Earl of Lowth.

William de Bermingham was succeeded in the year 1246 by his son William, who married the daughter of the eminent Thomas de Astley. In 34 Henry III. (1250) he had a charter for a four-days' fair to be held annually here, beginning on the eve of Ascension Day (Holy Thursday). In the rebellion raised by Simon de Montfort against Henry III., this William de Bermingham joined his father-in-law, Thomas de Astley, and was slain in the battle of Evesham, in the year 1265. For the part the lord of Birmingham had taken in this rebellion, his lands (including the Manor of Birmingham, then valued at £40) were confiscated, and given to Roger de Clifford, as a reward for his faithful service. The lands thus forfeited were, however, redeemed by the son of the rebel, the third William de Bermingham, who in 11 Edward I. (1283) obtained a charter of free warren throughout all his demesne lands here, as well as in his other estates. In the 25th year of the same king's reign (1297), he was, according to Dugdale, in the service of the king in Gascony, under the conduct of the Earl of Lincoln and John de St. John of Basing (a great baron), where, intending to relieve Bellagard, then besieged by the Count of Arras, the said earl and baron divided their forces, the Lord St. John leading the van through a wood; and, being encountered by the enemy, was over-powered with numbers, and so routed, himself, with Sir William de Bermingham and eight more knights, and many esquires, taken prisoners, and carried in triumph to Paris.

William de Bermingham died, and was succeeded by his son, the fourth William, in 1306, who was knighted in 1317.

In a suit betwixt this William de Bermingham and certain inhabitants of King's Norton, for the recovery of market tolls from the latter, the lord of Birmingham alleged in justification of his cause, that *his ancestors had a market in the town before the Norman Conquest.* "In 11 Edward II." [1317], says Dugdale, "this William was a knight; after that, finding no more of him by that title, I have adventured to conclude the next mentioned William to be his son." This fifth William de Bermingham raised troops under Edward II., in the year 1324, "four hundred foot soldiers within this county, excepting the towns of Warwick and Coventre, and [armed] them for the defence of the realm; and likewise the same year knights, esquires, and other men at armes to attend the king into Gascoin."

In 1326 (after the deposition of Edward II.) he had the custody of Dudley Castle; and in the following year, the first of Edward III., was for the first and only time summoned to Parliament by the title of Lord William de Bermingham.

The fifth and last of the Williams was succeeded (before or about the year 1340) by Sir Fouk de Bermingham, of whom the first mention discovered by Dugdale is, that in the above named year he lent 48 marks to Sir Baldwin Frevill, of Tamworth Castle, in return for which he had five mills in that ancient borough, in lease for one year. In the year 1344 he was retained by Thomas, bishop of Durham, to attend the King in his French expedition. Latterly he was returned member for Warwick in several Parliaments.

To him succeeded John de Bermingham, who was, in succession, returned member for the counties of Warwick, Bedford, and Buckingham. He died without issue, and his widow, Elizabeth, married the Lord Clinton, and held the lordship of Birmingham in dower till her death, in the year 1423.

We must now pass over a period during which the fair estate of Birmingham was held by comparative strangers, until the year 1500, when Edward, the last of the Berminghams, succeeded his grandfather, at the age of three, (being born in 1497).

Edward Bermingham could not but be proud of the noble possessions which had thus fallen to him after a lapse of many years. They then included not merely the manor of Birmingham, but also large estates in Oxfordshire, Bucks, and Worcestershire. But "being contemporary with that ambitious man, John Dudley, afterwards Viscount L'Isle, (more commonly known by those greater titles which he sometimes had, viz., Earl of Warwick and Duke of Northumberland), he was strangely wrested out of this lordship; for the said John, having possest himself of Dudley Castle, and observing Bermingham a fit ornament for so noble a seat, but being the principal residence of such a family as had for some hundreds of years enjoyed it, not likely to be purchased from the then rightful owner, conspired by a wicked stratagem to work him out of it."*

It was but a repetition of the old story of Ahab and his greedy desire for the vineyard of Naboth, and when an unscrupulous Ahab finds himself unable to gratify his selfishness by ordinary means, he is not slow to avail himself of more desperate and unlawful measures. John Dudley, seeing that there was no hope of his becoming the purchaser of Edward Bermingham's estate, "did set on some of his agents to lodge in Bermingham, and to learn when Master Bermingham was to ride out from home; which being accordingly done, they so contrived their business, that one of their plot should ride leisurely before, so that they might soon, keeping but an ordinary pace, overtake him; whereupon they watcht an opportunity to strike into Master Bermingham's company, as travellers, with whom they soberly rode for a while, but being come up to their confederate, forthwith set upon him for his purse, so that the villain thus seemingly rob'd, makes pursuit after them, and likewise after Master Bermingham, as one of the pack; who, being thereupon apprehended and prosecuted, apparently saw his danger."* The plot was therefore to make Edward Bermingham a criminal, the perpetrator of a crime which was punishable by death. Not that it was intended that he should suffer the penalty of the law,—*that* would not have fallen in with the conspirator's base design. He, good man, anxious to save poor Edward Bermingham's life, was to appear as the condemned criminal's friend, on condition that the fair estate which he so coveted should be given up to him, as the reward of his mediatorial efforts on his friend's behalf.

In order to give the better colour to the transaction, the estates were yielded to the King, and ratified by special Act of Parliament, which Dugdale gives, as follows:—

"WHERE Edward Byrmingham, late of Byrmingham in the Countie of Warwick Esquire, otherwise callid Edward Byrmingham Esquire, ys and standyth lawfully indettid to our sovereing Lord the Kynge in diverse grete summes of money; And also standyth at the mercy of his Highness, for that the same Edward ys at this present convicted of Felony; our seide sovereign Lord the Kynge, ys contentid and pleased, that for and in recompence and satisfaction to his grace of the seyde summes of money, to accept and take of the seyde Edward, the Mannour and Lordship of Byrmingham, otherwise callid Byrmincham, with the appurtenances, lying and being in the Countie of Warwick, and all and singular other lands and tenements, reversions, Rents, Services, and hereditaments of the same Edward Byrmingham, set lying and beying in the Countie of Warwick afforeseyde. Be yt therefore ordeyned and enacted, by the

* Dugdale.

* Ib.

authorities of this present Parliament, that our saide sovereine Lord the Kynge, shall have hold and enjoy to him his heirs and assignes, for ever, the seide Mannour and Lordship of Byrmingham (&c.) In which Act there is a Reservation of £40 per An. to the said Edward, and Elizabeth his Wife, during their Lives."

It was not the design of the wily Dudley to seize upon the injured man's possessions at once. He allowed nine years to elapse before the grant was made from the Crown to himself, in the thirty-seventh year of the reign of Henry the Eighth, December 21, 1545; but the ill-gotten possessions were enjoyed only for a brief space, for in the first year of the reign of Queen Mary, being attainted, he lost his head on the scaffold, and all his estates passed to the Crown.

Having thus brought to a conclusion our story of the lords of the manor, we will retrace our steps a little, and take a peep at Birmingham as it appeared during the lordship of the Bermingham family.

"If we survey Birmingham in the twelfth century," says Hutton, "we shall find her crowded with timber, within and without; her streets dirty and narrow, but much trodden. The inhabitant became an early encroacher upon her narrow streets, and sometimes the lord was the greatest. Her houses were mean and low, but few reaching higher than one story, perhaps none more than two; composed of wood and plaister—she was a stranger to brick. Her public buildings consisted solely of one, *the Church.*"

Little is known of the early history of the mother church of Birmingham. "The materials for any history at all," says Mr. Bunce, "are very scanty. There is no known record of the foundation or consecration of the Church in existence, nor any trace of such record. In Domesday there is no mention of either a Church or priest in Birmingham, which quite disposes of Hutton's fanciful conjecture that the building dates as far back as Saxon times. Until lately, it was believed that no fragment even of Norman architecture was preserved to justify the supposition that a Norman Church once occupied the site; but in the course of demolishing the late building, a few pieces of stonework, evidently Norman, were found built into a wall."*

There is therefore some ground for presuming that a small Church, sufficient for the accommodation of the village population, existed in the days of the Norman rule. The building which was removed to make way for the present handsome Church, is supposed by Rickman and others to have been erected in the latter part of the thirteenth century. The earliest mention of a Church in Birmingham appears in the Inquisition taken on the death of Roger de Someri, in 1290. It is also mentioned in the Norwich Taxation, at about the same period, and valued at £5 per annum.

There exists no documentary evidence as to the founders of the Church, but it was in all probability erected by one of the lords of Birmingham, whose residence was "scarce a bowshoot" therefrom. The principal benefactors to the Church were the Clodshales, lords of Saltley, who founded chantries, the services in which continued until the suppression of religious houses and endowments by Henry the Eighth, at which date they were valued at £11 16s. 3d. Trivial as this endowment would seem, compared with the immense revenues Henry seized elsewhere, it was not too small to escape, and "the Clodshale Chantries went the way of the great foundations of Tintern, of Rievaulx, and of Fountains: the Mass was unsung, the priests dispossessed, and the lands passed to the Crown."† They were afterwards disposed of by the Crown, to various persons,—to the Throckmorton family, William Morice, of Chipping Ongar, Essex, John Nethermill, of Coventry, and several others.

Among other Church property belonging to St. Martin's, seized by Henry VIII., was the Chantry founded by the Gild of the Holy Cross, an asso-

* J. T. Bunce: History of Old St. Martin's, Birmingham.
† *ib*, p. 4.

THE "PROPPER CHAPPELL" OF DERITEND, IN THE FOURTEENTH CENTURY.

ciation of Birmingham men for various religious, charitable, and educational works, of which the reader may find further particulars, (as well as of 'the Gild called Lench's Trust,' and other similar societies), in the late Mr. Toulmin Smith's "Memorials of Old Birmingham: Men and Names," and in his very valuable "History of English Gilds." The endowments belonging to this Gild thus seized were returned to the town in the reign of Edward VI., for the purpose of establishing a Grammar School, of which we shall have to speak hereafter.

A few words are necessary respecting the monuments, of which there now remain four, reposing on altar tombs. Our engraving is taken from that contained in Dugdale's "Antiquities of Warwickshire," made before the year 1656, and thus represents them in an almost perfect condition; but they have since suffered much from rude and careless hands, and exist only as ruins of what they once were. The first, as will be seen from the engraving, consists of two figures on one tomb. The nearest, bearing a shield charged with a bend lozenge, is supposed to be the third William de Bermingham, who was made a prisoner by the French at the siege of Bellagard, in the year 1297. It is a common error to suppose the cross-legged attitude to indicate that the person thus represented had visited the Holy Land as a Crusader. "It had probably," says Mr. Bloxam, in a description of the monuments, "a symbolic though now esoteric meaning."

The further effigy on the same tomb is assigned by the authority quoted above to the middle of the fourteenth century, and supposed to be the fifth William de Bermingham. "These two statues cut in freestone," says Dugdale in his MS. notes, "doe lye thus upon a raysed tombe, scarce two foote high, in the south ile of the Church."

The second altar tomb represented in our engraving, bears the recumbent figure of an ecclesiastic, in alabaster, assigned by Bloxam to the latter part of the fifteenth century, (*temp.* Henry VII.). Dugdale says, "This monument of alabaster, of one of the Berminghams, a priest, standeth close to the wall at the foot of the last."

The lowest figure in the engraving represents a high tomb of alabaster, bearing the recumbent figure of a knight, sculptured in alabaster, and clad in plate armour. "This faire monument of alabaster," says Dugdale, "standeth in the same ile towards the chancel, and was erected (as I suppose) for Sir John Bermingham, Knt., who married Elizabeth, the daughter and heir of William de la Plaunche." If the reader desires a fuller description of these interesting monuments, we would refer him to that which was written by Mr. M. H. Bloxham at the time of their restoration, in 1846, and published in the *Midland Counties Herald*, from which it is reprinted in Mr. Bunce's "History of Old St. Martin's."

Of the appearance of the finished Mediæval Church, with the various chantries previously mentioned, Mr. Bunce says:—

"It consisted of nave and chancel, both lofty and nobly proportioned; north and south aisles, extending almost as far eastward as the chancel itself, and with the clerestory windows of the nave rising well above them; and a tower and spire at the north-west corner, the tower opening by a bold and lofty arch into the north aisle, and by another arch into the nave. Beneath the south aisle, at the west end, was a crypt, and another crypt, larger and capable of use as a priest's chamber, existed beneath the chancel. The internal dimensions of the Church were of importance. Its length from the west end of the nave to the east end of the chancel, was probably about 113 feet; its breadth, from wall to wall of the aisles, 65 feet; its height over 60 feet; while the tower and spire rose above the body of the fabric to a height of 200 feet. Besides these general outlines, some details help us to form some idea of the building and its appearance. Internally it was probably covered with paintings —scenes from the life of St. Martin, the patron, and patterns of various descriptions in colour;

remains having been found of both these kinds of decorations. There were three altars—the high altar in the chancel; on the south side, the altar of the Blessed Virgin, in Clodshale's chantry; on the north side, the altar, probably, of St. Katherine, in the chantry of the Guild of the Holy Cross. These altars would be 'served' by several priests—the Rector of the Church and at least one assistant, for the high altar; two priests for the Clodshale chantries; and one, if not more, for the chantry of the Guild. The floors were no doubt completely laid with encaustic tiles, of which a few specimens were found in the course of demolition; the windows were filled with stained glass, large remains of which existed in Dugdale's time, and some even in Hutton's; and probably in the Clodshale chantry, and in the chancel, on either side, were the monuments of the lords of Birmingham and other benefactors, reposing on altar tombs. When these details are combined into a mental picture, and heightened by the spectacle of worship, the solemn strains of the Mass, the priests in their vestments, the lighted candles on the altar, the clouds of incense rising in the chancel, the gleam of colour from wall, and window, and roof, and floor, with the great picture of the Last Judgment above the chancel arch,—it will be seen that Mediæval St. Martin's was a Church not unworthy of a town destined to become one of the greatest communities in the kingdom, and one to which Birmingham may look back with pride."

CHAPTER II.

DERITEND: ITS CHAPEL AND ITS MARTYR-WORTHY.

The Building of Deritend Church—Appointment of a Minister—Agreement with the Monks of Tickford—John Rogers, Translator of the Bible, and first Protestant Martyr of the reign of Queen Mary—Appearance of the town in the fourteenth century—The "Old Crown House."

As the fourteenth century drew towards its close, and the new doctrines of John Wycliffe and his followers began to be circulated, and when those manuscript copies of the scriptures which the great reformer caused to be made found their way into many of the towns and villages in the midlands, the inhabitants of the hamlets of Deritend and Bordesley became "moved by the spirit that breathed through the teachings of Piers Plowman and Wyclif, and had grown thoroughly dissatisfied with being dependent for their religious services upon Aston Church and its Vicar."* For these hamlets, although in the lordship of Birmingham, were (and are still) in the parish of Aston; and the great distance at which they were situated from their parish church often prevented the inhabitants from joining in the public worship of God, especially in the winter time, when "the flooding of the streams, and the obstructions often . . . threatening and happening in the other ways between the aforesaid parish church of Aston, and the far-off towns or hamlets of Deritend and Bordesley, (as a document to which reference will be more particularly made hereafter quaintly sets forth)—rendered a journey to church by no means uneventful, and gave the villagers many good reasons for spending the Sunday at home. This was an unsatisfactory state of affairs to people who evidently did *not* believe themselves to be "farthest from God when the Church they were near," (whether they believed or not that the "infants dwelling in the said towns or hamlets for want of the rite of baptism might perish for ever," as the 'Agreement' urges), and they determined to build a church for themselves by the side of their own river Rea, where they might meet, from week to week, to worship God, without fear of accident by

* Toulmin Smith: "Birmingham Men and Names."

flood or field,—and perhaps in a purer form, more in accordance with the teachings of the parson of Lutterworth, than that used by Sir John Shobenhale, perpetual vicar of Aston. "The new church was begun," says Toulmin Smith, "according to trustworthy tradition, in the year 1375." It was somewhat smaller than the present building, but certainly not so ugly. A plain, modest little church, such as may be found to-day in hundreds of English villages, standing at the end of the hamlet, nearest Birmingham, almost opposite the "mansion house of tymber," close to the banks of the brooklet, forming a pretty picture of rustic comfort and simplicity such as could not fail to charm the traveller as he passed through it on his way to Birmingham, and did so delight the old antiquary Leland that he declared it to be "a pretty street as ever I entred."

Having built a church, it was next necessary to obtain a minister. The Rectorial appropriators of the parish of Aston were the Monks of Tickford (or Tykeford), near Newport Pagnell, and an agreement was made between them and the Vicar of Aston on the one hand and the Lord of Birmingham and thirteen inhabitants of the hamlets of Deritend and Bordesley* on the other, (with the consent of the Bishop of Lichfield and Coventry, Sir Robert Stretton—who by some authorities is believed to have been a Birmingham man), whereby the aforesaid parishioners (for the reasons already quoted from this 'Agreement') "shall have *and may appoint*, at their own charges, one chaplain fit to administer and discharge, before God and the parishioners dwelling in the aforesaid towns or hamlets of Deritend and Bordesley, divine services; which are always and forever henceforth to be celebrated in a certain Chapel in honour of John the Baptist, there lately built within the lordship of Deritend aforesaid." The very important privilege thus accorded to the people of Deritend, of appointing their own Chaplain, has been exercised from that time until the present day, and thus rendered them entirely independent of the vicar of Aston, both in the choice of a pastor after their own hearts, and in the adoption of a form of worship more in accordance with the doctrines which they appear to have accepted; and in this little church,—and probably from this very clergyman,—John Rogers, the first Protestant martyr of the troublous times of Queen Mary, and the coadjutor of Miles Coverdale in the translation of the Bible, received his earliest religious teaching.

John Rogers was born in the hamlet of Deritend somewhere about the year 1500. The honour of having given birth to the first martyr of the reign of Mary, and the editor of the first printed English Bible, was originally claimed for Birmingham by Anderson in his Annals of the English Bible, and this claim has since been substantiated by our own historian, Mr. Toulmin Smith.

Rogers was educated in the University of Cambridge, "where," says the Martyrologist Fox, "he profitably travailed in good learning, at length was chosen and called by the merchant adventurers to be their chaplain at Antwerp in Brabant, whom he served to their good intention many years." At Antwerp he became acquainted with William Tyndale and Miles Coverdale, who were both at that time exiled from their native land by their religious convictions. In John Rogers the two Reformers recognised one who from his learning and ability would be of great assistance to them in the work of translating the Bible into the English language. "In conferring with them the Scripture," says Fox, "he came to great knowledge in the gospel of God, insomuch that he cast off the heavy yoke of popery, perceiving it to be impure and filthy idolatry. . . . He, knowing by the Scriptures that unlawful vows may lawfully be broken, and that matrimony is both honest and honourable among all men, joined himself in lawful matrimony, and so went to Wittenberg in Saxony, where he, with much soberness of living, did not only greatly increase

* "Geoffry Boteler, Robert o' the Grene, John Smyth, William Jeffe, Thomas Holdon, William Couper, William Dod, Adam Bene, Richard Bene, Simon Huwet, Richard of Broke, Robert Flaumvile, and Thomas Chattok."

in all good and godly learning, but also so much profited in the knowledge of the Dutch tongue, that the charge of a congregation was orderly committed to his care."*

After the accession of Edward the Sixth in 1547, Bishop Ridley invited Rogers to return to England, to which invitation he would seem to have immediately responded, as appears from a preface to Melancthon's work on the "Weighing of the Interim," signed by Rogers and dated August 1st, 1548. In 1550 he was presented to the vicarage of St. Sepulchre's, and the rectory of St. Margaret Moysey, both of which churches were destroyed in the great fire of 1666. In 1551 he was appointed a Prebendary of St. Paul's by Bishop Ridley, and was soon after elected by the Dean of the College of St. Paul's to the professorship of Theology. On the accession of Queen Mary he was called to preach at St. Paul's Cross the first sermon after the Queen's proclamation, and although he knew the danger to which his opinions exposed him under the new *régime*, yet he had the courage to proclaim them openly, avowing his continuance in the Protestant faith as steadfastly as he had done under royal and episcopal favour, and exhorting the people constantly to remain in the same, and to "beware of all pestilent popery, idolatry, and superstition."* For this sermon he was immediately summoned to appear before the Privy Council, and he there defended his conduct with so much ability, that he obtained a temporary dismissal, but was recalled ten days later, to answer again for the same sermon. The result of this examination was that he was commanded to remain a prisoner in his own house.

He remained in this seclusion for six months, "till at length," Fox tells us, "through the uncharitable procurement of Bonner, bishop of

JOHN ROGERS.

* JOHN FOX: Acts and Monuments of the Church, edited by the Rev. John Cumming, D.D., 1875.—iii. 1.

* ib. iii, 2.

London, who could not abide such honest neighbours to dwell by him, he was removed from his own house to the prison called Newgate, where he was lodged among thieves and murderers." Twelve months passed away before he was removed from his prison house for examination, and during this period he was debarred from all companionship, even that of his books. He was refused intercourse with his family, and, as it would appear, kept without any knowledge of them whatever. On the 22nd of January, 1555, he was examined before the Privy Council, and once more made a bold stand for the truth, and seems to have been quite a match for his enemies, who again ordered him back into prison, but recalled him for a final examination on the 28th of the same month, pronounced sentence of excommunication, and handed him over to the judgment of the secular power. On Monday, the fourth of February, 1555, he was awaked early, and warned to prepare himself immediately for the fire. So soundly did he sleep even in the hour of imminent peril, that, says Fox, "he scarce, with much shogging," could be awaked. Being told to make haste, he replied, "then if it be so, I need not tie my points." He begged to be allowed to speak for a few minutes with his wife before his execution, but this request was cruelly refused. "So he was brought into Smithfield by Master Chester and Master Woodrooffe, then sheriffs of London, there to be burnt; where he showed most constant patience, not using many words, for he could not be permitted; but only exhorting the people constantly to remain in that faith and true doctrine which he before had taught, and they had learned, and for the confirmation whereof he was not only content patiently to suffer and bear all such bitterness and cruelty as had been showed him, but also most gladly to resign up his life, and to give his flesh to the consuming fire, for the testimony of the same."*

Thus bravely perished John Rogers, a man whom Birmingham should be proud to enrol among her worthiest sons. Why has he remained so long without a memorial in his native town?

Let us now once more glance at the growth of the town, in the fourteenth century, through the eyes of our quaint old historian, Hutton.

"If," he says, "we behold her in the fourteenth century, we shall observe her private buildings multiplied more than improved; her narrow streets, by trespass, become narrower; her public buildings increased to four, two in the town and two at a distance—the Priory, of stone, founded by contribution, at the head of which stood her lord; the Guild, of timber, now the [old] Free School; and Deritend Chapel, of the same materials, resembling a barn, with something like an awkward dovecot at the west end, by way of steeple."

Mr. J. T. Bunce, writing of the same period, says, "In the 14th century Birmingham was but a small place, a sort of country and town in union. The Church was probably somewhat above the centre of the town, standing on a green hill—sandstone rock below—sloping boldly from the brow at present occupied by High Street and New Street, to the actual site of the Church, and thence falling somewhat abruptly down to the present site of Smithfield, then occupied by the Manor House, or dwelling of the lords of Birmingham. Not far from the Church, at the end of what is now Edgbaston Street, stood the rectory house or parsonage, a clear stream running by it, forming, lower down, the moat of the Manor House, and thence passing on to fall into the Rea. There was probably a fringe of houses along the sides of the Bull Ring, in the upper part of which stood the Old Cross. Further in this direction there would be nothing but the Guild Hall, on the site of the present Grammar School, and the Priory, on the site of the Old Square, and including in its lands the streets now known as the Upper and Lower Priory. To the west, from the line of St. Martin's, might be seen Edgbaston Church, with the ancient home of the Middlemores; to the north east, Aston Church;

*ib. iii. 15

and to the south, St. John's Chapel, Deritend, with a cluster of houses dotted near it, the chapel being built because the inhabitants of this distant part of Aston could not get to their parish church in winter, on account of the floods. Digbeth constituted the road between Birmingham and Deritend, and was probably lined with houses built of timber framing, filled in with plaster, and having on the ground floor the open shops in which the smiths—then the chief artificers—had their hearths. It is possible, though not certain, that a few houses were dotted along Moor Street, and perhaps on the site of the narrow streets now running off from the opposite side of the Bull Ring. There would be houses in Spiceal Street, and perhaps one or two in St. Martin's Lane; and these would be all. Beyond the lines above indicated, there would be nothing but fields close to the town, and open unenclosed country beyond. The roads leading in each direction were mere footpaths most of them—excepting the main road through the town from Camp Hill to Hockley, and thence on to Wolverhampton—and the rest horse roads, very narrow, and deeply sunken between high banks."

Prominent among the buildings on the banks of the Rea, in the Deritend portion of the town, rose the fair "Mansion House of tymber," which remains to this day as the "Old Crown House." This house, which was built in the latter part of the fourteenth century, still remains, in very fine state of preservation, having been restored to something like its ancient appearance by the late owner, Mr. J. Toulmin Smith, about fifteen years ago. It was built, like most houses of that period, chiefly of timber, and consisted, on the ground floor, of a large Central Hall, with smaller rooms on each side. On the upper floor there were originally four rooms, but the portion of the "Great Chamber" which projects very prominently beyond the rest of the wall over the entrance was subsequently made into a separate room, and has for many years borne the name of "the Callorye Chamber;" probably so called from its having in earlier times been separated from the remainder of the Great Chamber by a balustrade.

In a town like Birmingham, in which so few remains of antiquity exist, such a house as the "Old Crown" cannot fail to interest us, by the associations which cluster round it. For little less than five hundred years,—as Toulmin Smith remarks, in his interesting history of this house—no one has gone out of Birmingham towards Warwick and Coventry, or come into the town from the Warwick and Coventry Road, without his eyes falling on that fair "Mansion House of tymber" now called the Old Crown House. By far the most interesting apartment in the building is that which is called the Gallorye Chamber. In it, according to tradition, Queen Elizabeth once passed a night, and standing in its latticed, overhanging window, one cannot but recall memories of the principal events of our past history during the five hundred years through which this house has remained, amid the destruction which has left but little of the old town standing. As we look through the eastern lattice, we think of Prince Rupert, and of the gallant struggle which our ancestors made to prevent his entering the town,—of his manifestation of his "Burning Love to England in Birmingham's flames;"—of Shakespeare, who may perhaps have journeyed past the mansion of timber into Birmingham, during those early days of Warwickshire rambling, before he sought for fame and fortune in the metropolis;—of old Leland, riding through as pretty a street as ever he entered, into Birmingham;—of the fire which blazed half a mile away from here on that 14th of July, 1791, when the infuriated "Church and King" rabble, failing in their endeavours to take the life of that devoted disciple of philosophy, Joseph Priestley, set fire to his dwelling, and destroyed his invaluable philosophical library, the whole road, almost as far as the house in which we stand to take our survey, being filled with the burnt papers;—as we look through the western lattice,

we think of the little village we have been endeavouring to describe—of the old lords of the manor—of the second William de Bermingham, as he passed out to join his father-in-law in the rebel army of Simon de Montfort—and of Edward Bermingham, as he rode forth on that ill-fated journey which cost him his inheritance;—we think of the "one street" of Leland's time, and as we pause in our reverie our eye rests upon the "restored" Church of St. Martin, and brings forcibly to our mind the contrast between the quaint old village and the great modern city, and we are at once recalled from our day-dream to the matters-of-fact of our story.

As an illustration of the diversity of callings pursued by Birmingham men, even in the infancy of the town, the following extract is given by Nash in his History of Worcestershire, from the Churchwardens' ledger of Halesowen:—"1498, *paid for repeyling the organs, to the organ-maker at Bromwicham, 10s.*" Remarking on this entry, Hutton says, "Birmingham then, we find, discovered the powers of genius in the fine arts, as well as in iron. By '*the* organ-maker,' we should suppose there was but one. It appears that the art of acquiring riches was as well understood by our fathers as by us; while an artist could receive as much money for tuning an organ, as would purchase an acre of land, or treat near half a gross of Lord Abbots."*

CHAPTER III.

BIRMINGHAM IN THE SIXTEENTH CENTURY.

Leland's Itinerary—Camden's description of the town—The Spanish Armada—Queen Elizabeth at Kenilworth—Shakespeare in Birmingham.

WE now come to the first authentic contemporary picture of Birmingham, as seen by a stranger, and the first literary notice of the town at all, if we except the brief note in Domesday. In the reign of King Henry the Eighth, John Leland made his famous Itinerary of Britain, and during the year 1538 passed through Birmingham, and records his impressions of the place as follows:—

"I came through a pretty street or ever I entred into Bermingham towne. This street, as I remember, is called Dirtey. [Deritend.] In it dwell smithes and cutlers, and there is a brooke that divideth this street from Bermingham, and is an Hamlett or Member, belonginge to the parish therebye.

"There is at the end of Dirtey a propper chappell, and mansion house of tymber* hard on the ripe,† as the brooke runneth downe; and as I went through the ford, by the bridge, the water ran downe on the right hand, and a few miles below goeth into Tame, ripa dextra. This brooke, above Dirtey, breaketh in two armes, that a little beneath the bridge close again. This brooke riseth, as some say, four or five miles above Bermingham, towards Black Hilles.

"The beauty of Bermingham, a good markett towne in the extreame parts of Warwikeshire, is one street going up alonge, almost from the left ripe of the brooke, up a meane hill, by the length of a quarter of a mile. I saw but one Parroch Church in the towne. There be many smiths in the towne that use to make knives and all mannour of cuttinge tooles, and many loriners that make bittes, and a great many naylors. Soe that a great part of the towne is maintained by smithes, who have their iron and sea-cole out of Staffordshire."†

Of the "propper chappell and mansion house

* The "Old Crown House." † Bank.

* Alluding to another extract from the same ledger: "*Paid for bread and ale, to make my Lord Abbot drink, in Rogation week, 2d.*" Hutton adds, "What should we now think of an ecclesiastic accepting a twopenny treat from a country churchwarden?"

† LELAND: second edition, by Thomas Hearne, M.A., Oxford, 1745. iv., 108.

of tymber" we have already spoken. The "one street" consisted, of course, of Digbeth, and the lower part of High Street, with a few narrow offshoots on either hand, and a part of Spiceal Street on the western side of the church. This early picture of the busy aspect of the town is interesting, not only as showing the antiquity of Birmingham as a manufacturing community, but also in preserving for us a record of an almost extinct local trade—that of general cutlery. The "knives and all mannour of cuttinge tooles" made in Birmingham now-a-days cut but a poor figure in our local trade returns, and the Birmingham artizan would spurn the knife that had not a Sheffield brand on it. But the fire-arms that have made Birmingham known all over the world do not find a mention in Leland's entry, neither do the buttons, or the countless other useful and indispensable articles, which are now turned out by millions from the "toyshop of the world."

We have no further notice of Birmingham until 1586, in which year Ben Jonson's well-beloved teacher, William Camden, published his "Britannia." He came to Birmingham from Kenilworth, through Solihull (which he spells "Solyhill"), where he saw nothing remarkable but its church, but as he passed through the same pretty street, and past the same fine old "mansion house of timber," as his predecessor Leland, and came into "Bremicham," he found it "*swarming with inhabitants, and echoing with the noise of anvils,*" adding, that "here are great numbers of smiths." As he entered the town, he noticed that the lower part was "very watery," but observes, that "the upper part rises with abundance of handsome buildings; and it is none of the least honours of the place that from hence the noble and warlike family of Bremichams in Ireland had their original and name."

After this there is another blank, during which we find no records of the town or of its people. Doubtless, however, the latter went about their work as usual, making, perhaps, more and more weapons of warfare, which were not destined to remain long unused. In 1588 came alarming rumours of a threatened Spanish invasion, followed quickly by tidings of the equipment of an Invincible Armada, which was even then on its way to England, to crush the power of the glorious queen, and once more to replace the yoke of the Popedom on the necks of a newly-liberated people. The alarm flashed forth through the length and breadth of the land on beacon fires, which

"Sprang from hill to hill,
Till the proud peak unfurled the flag o'er Darwin's rocky dales,
Till like volcanoes flared to heaven the stormy hills of Wales,
Till twelve fair counties saw the blaze on Malvern's lonely height,
Till streamed in crimson on the wind the Wrekin's crest of light."

These "answering points of fire" would doubtless rouse the inhabitants of the little hillside Warwickshire town, and from the crest of the "meane hill" which o'ertopped St. Martin's, the blazing beacon-fire would flash the news along to the swart toilers in the "sea-coal mines" of Staffordshire, and while

"The fisher left his skiff to rock on Tamar's glittering waves,"

and

"The rugged miners poured to war from Mendip's sunless caves,"

the "many smiths," the "loriners that make bittes," and the "great many naylors" of Birmingham, would not be behind their toiling brethren in the manifestation of their patriotism; and it would indeed ill accord with the traditional love of liberty which has ever characterized Birmingham men if, amid the ranks at Tilbury which listened to the inspiriting words of the "Virgin Queen," there were not some of those stalwart workmen whose resounding anvils William Camden had heard a few months earlier, and whose sons so gallantly withstood the Cavaliers at Camp Hill fifty years later.

The remembrance of this stirring period of English history makes us the more regret that there is no direct light thrown by the historian on the doings of our townsmen during those years which elapsed between Camden's visit in 1586, and the "Battle of Birmingham" in 1643. For during that period many interesting events happened. In 1575 Queen Elizabeth was the guest of the proud Earl of Leicester at Kenilworth, and the fame of that splendid pageant could not fail to reach the ears of Birmingham men, and perhaps some of them may have even witnessed those "princeleye pleasures" so elaborately described by Gascoigne and Laneham. "The preparations for this celebrated entertainment," says Mr. Charles Knight, "were on so magnificent a scale, the purveyings must have been so enormous, the posts so unintermitting, that there had needed not the flourishings of paragraphs (for the age of paragraphs was not as yet) to have roused the curiosity of all mid-England." *

During the same period the matchless dramas of the bard of Avon were produced, and even in Birmingham, albeit there was not at that time a single shop in the town at which even a Bible or an almanack might be bought, there might perhaps have found their way a few of those entrancing little sixpenny quartos of the "Midsommer Nights Dreame," "The Tragicall Historie of Hamlet, Prince of Denmarke," the "Merrie Wiues of Windsor," "The Lamentable Tragedie of Romeo and Ivliet," or other of those now excessively rare little pamphlets of which a few may be seen in our Shakespeare Memorial Library. Perhaps even the great poet himself may have read in Camden's "Britannia" of the busy little town "swarming with inhabitants and echoing with the noise of anvils," and may have travelled from Stratford to see the town and to note the humours of the busy throng, some of whom he may have immortalized in those merry groups of workmen and citizens which figure in his Roman and English Historical Plays. The prototype of the merry quibbling cobbler in the first scene of *Julius Cæsar* may have been found, perchance, in "the street called Dirtey," and the poet may have met Kit Sly in the kitchen of the "Old Leather Bottel" or other of the quaint old taverns which were dotted along the same "pretty street." Perhaps the poet may have passed through the town to see the sites of some of the incidents of the historical plays; "through Coventry" to Birmingham, and thence "to Sutton Coldfield to-night;" to the "plain near Tamworth," where Richmond's army encamped before the Battle of Bosworth Field; perhaps to Bosworth Field itself. He may at least have visited *some* of these places, and would scarcely be likely to miss the opportunity of seeing Birmingham on his way.

* CHARLES KNIGHT: "William Shakspere, a Biography."

CHAPTER IV.

ASTON HALL AND ITS OWNERS.

The Holte Family at Duddeston—Inventory of furniture, etc., at Duddeston Hall—Sir Thomas Holte obtains the title of Baronet—Description of Aston Hall—Edward Holte's marriage and its consequences—Visit of Charles I. to Aston—Death of Edward Holte—The Siege of Aston Hall—A dark deed—Death of Sir Thomas Holte—Aston Church.

DURING the year 1618 Birmingham people, looking across north-eastward, where rose the graceful spire of Aston Church, saw rising among the trees of the well-wooded park the noble outline of that hall which the newly-created baronet of Duddeston Manor House, Sir Thomas Holte, was building for himself.

The Holte family had resided in or near Birmingham since the close of the 13th century, the first of whom any mention is found being Sir Henry Holte. The name is of Saxon origin, the early bearers of it using the prefix "atte." The word Holte signifies a grove, or woody place. With the earlier members of the family, however, we have not here to do; ours is not a

BIRMINGHAM IN 1640.

From the "Prospect" in Dugdale's Warwickshire, 1656.

family history, except in so far as the history of a family illustrates that of the town.

The first member of the Holte family of whom there exists any monument at Aston is William, the thirteenth from Sir Henry, the first known bearer of the name. He died in 1514, and was buried in the north aisle of the church, under an altar tomb, bearing his effigy, life-size, clad in a suit of mail armour. The fourteenth, Thomas Holte, was a "learned lawyer," and Justice of North Wales in the reign of Henry the Eighth. He lies buried by the side of his father, his tomb being covered by a monumental brass, laid in the floor, containing portraits of himself and his wife, with the following epitaph :

"Thomas Holte here lyeth in grave ; Ihu for thyn passyon,
On him thou have compassyon, and his soolle do save."

The following particulars from an "Inventory of all the goodes and catells movable and unmovable, plate, juells, and houshold stuffe of Thomas Holte, esquire, decessed" (given in Davidson's "History of the Holtes of Aston," to which we are indebted for most of the particulars relating to the family), will help to give the reader some idea of the size and appointments of the Manor House of Duddeston at this period. Of sleeping apartments there were thirteen, "the chambur over the buttrie, the chappell chambur, the maydes' chambur, the great chambur, the inner chambur to the great chambre, [*sic.*] the yatehowse chambur, the inner chambur to the same, the geston chambur, the crosse chambur, the inner chambur, the clark's chambre, the yeomen's chambre, and the hyne's chambre." Beside these there was "the hawle, the plece, the storehouse, the galarye, the butterye, the ketchyn, the larder howse, the deyhowse, the bakhowse, the bultynge howse, and the yeling howse ;" also a chapel, of which the furniture was as follows :

"Inprimis a canabe, a pixe, and the sacrament thereof.................... xiij*s*. iiij*d*.
"Item ij corporas cases ij pillos for the same, iij frunts, ij pere of vestments, a cope, ij candlesticks, a surples, a masbok, iij altr clothes, ij cruets, a pere of censes, iij torches, iij carpyt quissions, iiij carpets, and a challes .... viij *li*
"Item in the boddy of the chappell a frunt for an alter, a cloth for the same, a pentyd table, and ij bolles xs.
Sum ...... ix *li* iij*s*. iiij*d*.

"The principal bed chambers," says Mr. Davidson, "were hung with splendid hangings, those of the great chamber being 'of gaye colors, blewe and redde ;' one of the beds in the same room being 'wrought with gildinge and fyne bise,' and having 'a tester of satten, blewe and redde ; with cuverleyd of sarsnet of the same collor.' In the same room were also 'ij long satten quissions, a quission of yellow and blewe for the cheyre, and a quission of tynsoll for the cupborde.'" The total value of the furniture in this richly adorned room is set down in the inventory at £13 14s. 4d. The other apartments were furnished in the same luxurious style, and evidences the possession of considerable wealth. His son and successor, Edward Holte, was born in 1541, and was therefore only about four years old at his father's death. He married Dorothy, daughter of John Ferrers, Esq., of Tamworth Castle, a descendant of the famous Marmion

——"Lord of Fontenaye,
"Of Lutterward and Scrivelbaye
"Of Tamworth tower and town."

He died February 3rd, 1592, and his lady survived him only a little more than two years, being buried on the 20th of December, 1594. His eldest son, Thomas, who succeeded to the estate, was born in 1571, and had therefore just reached manhood at the time of his father's decease. In the year 1599, he served the office of Sheriff for the county, and in April, 1603, was a member of a deputation to welcome King James to England, and on the 18th of the same month received the honour of knighthood. But SIR THOMAS HOLTE had not yet reached the summit of his ambition, and an event of grave national importance afforded the ambitious knight the means of gratifying his still unsatisfied desire after worldly distinction. The province of

Ulster was in a state of rebellion, and there seemed to be no means of reducing it to obedience, except by increasing the already heavy burden of taxation. But the sagacity of James I. was equal to the occasion. He offered a title of baronetcy to every gentleman possessed of an annual income of £1,000, whose ancestors, for two generations at least, had borne arms, the principal condition being, however, that he should maintain, for the defence of Ireland, "and especially for the security of the Province of Ulster, . . . thirty foot soldiers in the King's army, after the rate of 8d. sterling per day," for three years, the whole amounting to £1,095. The royal arms of Ulster—the red hand—was also assigned to the baronets thus created, from whence has arisen the gruesome notion of a "bloody hand" in heraldry, erroneously supposed to denote the presence of the stain of murder on the family escutcheon. The popular estimate of the cost of a baronetcy having been £1,000 is not, as we have seen, so wide of the mark. Twelve months after the creation of the new order Sir Thomas Holte obtained this dignity, and, immediately afterwards, commenced the work of enclosing the park at Aston, preparatory to the erection of a new family mansion, more in keeping with his increased dignity and wealth, having received a considerable accession of property by his marriage with Grace, daughter of William Bradburne, Esq., of Hough, Derbyshire.

The erection of the noble hall at Aston was commenced in April, 1618. He came to reside in his new mansion in 1631, although, as the inscription over the entrance sets forth, it was not completely finished until 1635. The building appropriately crowned the principal eminence in the park, and was approached from the Lichfield Road, through a noble avenue of elms and Spanish chestnuts. Like most buildings of its class which were erected at that period, it consists of a centre and two wings, a compliment to the Queen after whom the style is called, being emblematic of the initial letter of her name. The name of the architect of this noble mansion is not known, but it is not impossible that it may have been one of the works of Inigo Jones. At each side, a little in advance of the main building, but connected therewith by a wall, are small buildings of two stories, intended as lodges for the falconer or gamekeeper, and gardener. The two wings, which may be said to form the top and bottom of the letter E, each contain two large embayed windows to the front, and are surmounted by lofty towers with closed ogee roofs of a dome-like character. In the centre of the main building is a similar, but more massive, tower, surmounted by a double ogee roof. On either side of the tower are two curved gables, those nearest the tower rising above the cornice and balustrade which surmounts the projecting portion of the front; the other two surmount the more embayed portions on either side. The doorway consists of a semicircular arch, with two fluted columns on square bases, supporting an entablature, above which is an ornamental panel containing the following inscription:

SR THOMAS HOLTE OF DVDDESTON IN THE COVNTIE OF WARWICK KNIGHT
AND BARONET BEGAN TO BVILD THIS HOVSE IN APRILL IN ANNO DOMINI
1618: IN THE 16TH YEARE OF THE RAIGNE OF KING IAMES OF ENGLAND &c.,
AND OF SCOTLAND THE ONE AND FIFTIETH AND THE SAID SR THOMAS HOLTE
CAME TO DWELL IN THIS HOVSE IN MAY IN ANNO DOMINI: 1631: IN THE
SEAVENTH YEARE OF THE RAIGNE OF OVR SOVERAIGNE LORD KING
CHARLES, AND HE DID FINISH THIS HOVSE IN APRILL ANNO DOMINI 1635:
IN THE ELEVENTH YEARE OF THE RAIGNE OF THE SAID KING CHARLES.
LAVS DEO.

Above the inscription is a shield, on which are emblazoned quarterly the arms of Holte, Castells, Maidenach with Grimsarwe, and Willington.

"If the east front of Aston Hall may be designated as grand," says Davidson, "the southern view may, with equal propriety, be termed beautiful. The more prominent feature is the projection in the centre, containing the windows in the Chapel, and the large one in the Great Drawing Room. On each side, on the ground floor, is a colonnade of four arches, having plain circular pillars, with capitals and bases. These pillars support semicircular arches with dripstones, and ornamented on the faces and reveals with sunk panels. Adjoining the Great Drawing Room, and over the east colonnade, are the King's Bed Room and Dressing Room, the latter having been partitioned off from another room, the remaining portion also serving as a dressing room to the first floor room as seen from the east front. These two dressing rooms, and that part of the colonnade over which they are placed, did not form a portion of the original building, as the bracket of an oriel window may be seen, partially hidden by the roof of the colonnade; and the places where the junctions have been effected are distinctly visible on the exterior of the building."

Over the western colonnade, and adjoining the Great Drawing Room, is Lady Holte's Drawing Room, the wall of which still bears traces of the cannonading in 1643, the besiegers' battery having been erected, as is supposed, on a small eminence about 240 yards from the Hall, exactly opposite this room. Many of the balls passed entirely through this room to the Great Staircase; one of them shattering a massive oak standard and lodging in the adjoining wall, as shown in our engraving of the staircase. Further westward over the same colonnade is the vestibule to the Long Gallery.

On the western front are five rooms on the ground floor, and the whole of the lower portion of this wall was formerly mantled with ivy. Above these five rooms is the Long Gallery, without which no Elizabethan mansion of an important character was considered complete. The northern end of the building contains, on the ground floor, the Servants' Hall, Kitchen, and Housekeeper's Room, and on the first floor the Blue Room, Chinese Room, and Lady Holte's Bed Room and Boudoir. The centre of this side projects slightly beyond the Long Gallery. This is the least interesting side of the Hall, and has been disfigured by the alteration and modernization of many of the windows. Beyond this, on the northern side of the Hall, are the stables and out-offices.

In the above description of the external appearance of the building we have sufficiently indicated the position of most of the rooms; it will not therefore be necessary to make further reference to the less important of them. The principal apartments requiring special notice are the Great Hall, the Chapel, the Great Drawing Room, the Long Gallery, and King Charles's Bed Room. The Great Hall is 47 feet long by 24 feet wide, and has four large windows, two on each side of the entrance, deeply set in the walls. The ceiling is richly decorated with bosses, grotesque heads, flowers, etc.; and a broad cornice, interspersed with various animals (including the elephant, lion, unicorn, griffin, stag, etc.) is carried round the room. The lower portions of the walls are wainscotted, with the exception of four compartments (on each side of the door leading to the Saloon, opposite the entrance, and in the north-west and south-west corners), flanked by pilasters, each containing a picture,—those on each side of the Saloon being landscapes, and those in the two corners full-length figures of Roman Emperors. On the north side of the apartment is the fireplace; the back of the grate bears the Royal Arms and the initials C.R., and the compartments on each side the Holte Crest, with the initials H. and W. Over the chimney-piece are the following verses:

> IF SERVICE BE THY MEANE TO THRIVE,
> THOV MVST THEREIN REMAINE,
> BOTH SILENT FAITHFVL IVST AND TRVE,
> CONTENT TO TAKE SOME PAINE;
>
> IF LOVE OF VERTVE MAY ALLVRE,
> OR HOPE OF WORLDLY GAINE,
> IF FEARE OF GOD MAY THEE PROCVRE,
> TO SERVE DOE NOT DISDAINE.

From the south-west corner of the Hall we enter the vestibule leading to the Great Staircase;

but before ascending to the upper apartments we pass through the Chapel Passage and enter the Gallery of the Chapel. This gallery was the seat appropriated to the family, and is raised a few feet above the level of the chapel. It is very commodious, extending along the whole of the north side; the front was covered with velvet, and all the cushions were of crimson. The books contained therein were Watson's folio Bible, and seventeen Prayer Books: two folio editions published by Baskett, covered with velvet; one by Bill, in blue Turkey; one large quarto, by Baskett, also in blue Turkey; twelve in calf, marked with the name of Sir Lister Holte; and an octavo printed by Baskerville. The chapel was lighted by two windows in the south wall, both of which were afterwards stopped up, but have of late been reopened; but of the alterations we shall have to speak hereafter, in our notice of the present condition of the building. The walls are wainscotted; the floor of the building contained large seats on the eastern and western sides for the domestics, the centre being unappropriated. The communion table (of oak) was placed between the two windows, and was covered with a velvet cloth.

ASTON HALL.

Returning from the Chapel we ascend the Great Staircase, which is very similar in design to the famous one at Crewe. It is divided into numerous landings, and to each flight is an ornamental compartment divided by square high standards, richly carved, and surmounted with vase-like terminations, boldly carved, and capped with an Ionic volute. The fourth landing (by which we

"OLD AND NEW BIRMINGHAM" PORTRAIT GALLERY.—No. 2.

GEORGE DIXON.

PHOTOGRAPHED BY THRUPP.

BIRMINGHAM: HOUGHTON AND HAMMOND, SCOTLAND PASSAGE.

LONG GALLERY, ASTON HALL.

arrive at the first floor) bears traces of the attack in 1643, to which we shall refer more particularly hereafter. The staircase continues upward to the top of the house, where a door leads out to the leads over the Long Gallery. Another door leads to a gloomy corridor in the roof, called "Dick's Garret," from a domestic of that name who is said to have hung himself there from one of the low rafters of the roof.

But we cannot stay to explore these lonely regions further, and so return to the first landing, and enter the Great Drawing Room, which is over the Chapel. "This splendid apartment, which is 39 feet by 23 feet, is lighted from the south by two noble mullioned windows, of three divisions and nine lights each, and from the portion of the wall in which they are placed projecting a little beyond the main line of the building, advantage has been taken to introduce a small window of two divisions and six lights on each side, thus adding materially to the effect. A large north window looking into the quadrangle has long been stopped up. The walls are panelled to within about a yard of the cornice, which is bold, but plain. The most peculiar feature of the decoration of the room, however, is an ornamented stone frieze placed between the cornice and panelling. It contains, under shallow semicircular-headed openings, placed at alternate distances round the room, bold figures in military costumes of different times and nations, ranging from the polished Roman to the rude Highlander; and from the mail-clad mediæval warrior to the courtly knight of the Elizabethan era. Four of these figures are displayed on the west, three on the south, three on the east, and one on the north, walls. The portions of the frieze between the figures are covered with decorations in low relief, similar to those in the ceiling. There is a general resemblance between this room and the large one at Crewe, though the details and the figures in the latter are much bolder. The ceiling is ornamented with one of those indescribable patterns peculiar to the period. It consists of three large centre oval compartments, flanked by the same number, of a similar description, on each side, every oval containing a smaller one ornamented with appropriate Elizabethan scroll work, the centres containing a cherub's head; and each of the circles formed at the junctions of the principal ovals is filled with a grotesque head. The chimney-piece is especially worthy of notice. It reaches nearly to the cornice, and is divided into two parts by bold entablatures, each being supported by graduated pilasters; the upper ones, moreover, rest on bases supported by grotesque heads. The centre of the upper part is left perfectly plain. On the upper entablature are placed scroll ornaments, enriched with shells; at equal distances on the scrolls being placed shields—Holte; Holte quartering Castells, Maidenach with Grimsarwe, and Willington; and Holte impaling Bradbourne. A door in the east wall, close to the fire-place, opens into King Charles's Bed Room, and one on the opposite side leads through Lady Holte's Drawing Room to the Long Gallery. . . . This Gallery—perhaps, with the exception of those at Hardwicke and Hatfield, the finest in England—is 136 feet in length, by 18 feet in width, and 16 feet high. It is lighted by five large mullioned windows, of four lights and twelve divisions each, the centre window slightly projecting. At the north end is a large oriel, in one of the compartments of which is a small shield, in stained glass, charged with the Family arms impaling Newton, and similar to the one in the east window of the north aisle of the Church. The walls are covered with oak panelling, divided, by pilasters having capitals, into thirteen compartments. These pilasters are divided into three stages—the lower, or base, being boldly moulded and ornamented. The second has numerous projecting bevelled blocks placed perpendicularly and horizontally, and surrounding a boldly carved acorn; while the third, or upper, is fluted in minute divisions, and finished with a capital. The rows of panels are eight in number, each containing a semicircular arch supported by pilasters, all in low relief, similar to those so often seen in pulpits of the Jacobean era. A shallow cornice, or frieze, covered with ornaments, also in low relief, is carried round the room. The ceiling is decorated with two rows of ornaments, formed of squares, having semicircular projections, the centres being occupied with graceful devices, of which the principal feature is the cornucopia. The chimney-piece is of marble, and by far the most important in the house, and is in the centre of the east wall. Its principal features are broad entablatures and cornices, supported by grotesque Caryatides, and divided into two principle portions, the upper one, again, being also divided into two compartments, containing oblong panels of grey marble surrounded by scroll-work. The lower portion is supported by graduated pilasters with sculptured heads, in a fine style of art. Three shields, charged similarly to those in the Great Drawing Room, are placed on the upper part of the chimney-piece. The fire-place has hand-irons, for supporting logs of wood."*

The total number of rooms (including out-houses, etc., and the Chapel,) is 103. "It was evidently the architect's intention," observes Mr. Davidson, "to bring prominently forward in the internal construction, the Entrance Hall, the Great Drawing Room, the Long Gallery, and the Staircases, as, after these, every other portion is comparatively small, and plain in the decoration; and the traditionary custom of having the chief rooms on the upper floor has been observed."

We now return to the story of the noble owner of Aston Hall. He had a family of fifteen children, the eldest of whom, Robert, died young. The story of the second, Edward, who was born in 1600, is full of sadness, yet of sweetness also. He married one of the daughters of Dr. John King, Bishop of London,—King James's "King of Preachers"—and thereby so provoked the ire of the haughty Baronet that he threatened to disinherit him, and was only prevented from this act of cruelty by the interposition of King Charles, who either at this time, or a little later, appointed the offending heir of Aston his Groom of the Bedchamber. The royal letter to Sir Thomas is given by Davidson, from the original, which was then in the possession of the late C. Holte Bracebridge, Esq. It runs as follows:

"Charles R.

"Trusty and well beloved, Wee greet you well. Wee have taken knowledge of a marriage between your sonne and a daughter of the late Bishop of London, and of your dislike thereof, soe far expressed as to threaten a disinheritance of your sonne: of whom wee have also heard very well, as having many good parts that make him able to doe us service, and fitt rather to bee cherished of all good encouragements, than oppressed with a heavy hand. Whereas is no greater cause of offence against him, and the interest wee have in all our subjects, and especially in families of the best qualitie, giveth Us cause to interpose in this, where a severe proceeding against your sonne would endanger the overthrow of your house, whereof there are so many examples, and leave that tytle of honour which must descend upon him by our late father's gratious grants, contemptable, when it should fall upon one, deprived by your act of the state and means to support it. For the match, We consider and may well hope that a blessinge and many comforts will follow the daughter of a soe reverend and good a man, whose other children are in soe hopeful wayes and soe well disposed; and an alliance with them cannot be a disparagemente,—and what inequalitie you may thinke of betweene your sonne and her, for estate or otherwise, Wee will be ready to supply our grace and assistance, in giving him advancement and impartinge our favour to him in such wayes as his good parts are capable of. Wee doe therefore recommende it to you that you doe not only forbeare any act against your sonne in respect of his match, but that you restore him into your former favour and good opinion, wherein Wee doubt not that our mediation upon grounds of much reason and indifference will soe far prevail with you, that Wee shall have cause to accept graciously your answer, which Wee expect you return unto Us with all conveniency. Given at our Courte at Hampton, the 7th day of August, in the third yeare of our reigne."

But even the royal intercession was of no avail in restoring him to favour. The proud, unyielding baronet still refused to forgive his exiled son.

In October, 1642, that son, probably for the first time since his marriage, spent two nights under his father's roof, for, on the evenings of Sunday and Monday, the 16th and 17th of that month, King Charles, whose army was marching from Shrewsbury towards Banbury, (to relieve Banbury Castle,) staid at Aston Hall, as the guest of Sir Thomas Holte. The room in which he slept during that

* A. Davidson: History of the Holtes of Aston, pp. 62-4.

brief visit has already been indicated in the description of the building, and to this day, notwithstanding the numberless objects of interest in the museum which now occupies the hall, the little empty recess in King Charles's chamber attracts the closest attention, and has, perhaps, greater interest (even for the radical artisans of the midland metropolis,) than any other portion of the noble mansion which has now become their own.

"That Sabbath evening," says Davidson, "was a memorable season in the annals of Aston Hall. We see, in imagination, the last rays of the setting sun glancing athwart those mosque-like minarets whose metalled roofs yet retained their pristine freshness. We see the royal standard, as it proudly

GREAT STAIRCASE: SHOWING THE INJURIES SUSTAINED DURING THE CANNONADING.

floats from the highest turret, as if in defiance of all gainsayers. We hear the clash of arms, the loud flourish of martial music, the joyous ringing of the old church bells, the glad acclaim of a loyal assemblage, who raise the shout which erst greeted the ear of the Jewish king; and we look on the sombre, pensive countenance of him, in whose honour all this demonstration is made, as he courteously acknowledges the deferential obeisances of the assembled throng. In that retinue of attendants on the monarch, we likewise behold one, who, with sorrowful face and averted eye, casts around him furtive glances as the cavalcade proceeds, and is anxiously longing to see if the man who is so prodigal of his affections towards his sovereign has any feeling of regard towards a son, whom, for eighteen years, he has viewed with unmitigated hatred. And, as no ray of compassion became from the eye of the old man, we can well imagine that utter sinking of spirit which came over 'the noblest, the best, and the bravest,' of all who ever bore the name of Holte. Go, old man! hug thy patents and commissions—produce thy pardon from thy sovereign, duly signed, sealed, and delivered, and defy the world to charge thee with crime—rejoice in thy noble mansion and thy broad domains—but remember! there is a canker at the root of all thy greatness, so long as that gallant son of thine—in so few days to shed his blood in thy royal master's cause—remains unforgiven for the magnanimous crime of having made her whom he so truly loved his wife."

CHARLES I.

Edward Holte was wounded at the battle of

Edge Hill—only seven days after that Sunday on which he had first looked upon his father's house after nearly twenty years' exile. He recovered, however, and still remained faithful to his royal master; but died on the 28th of August in the next year, 1643, from a fever contracted while he was engaged in the defence of Oxford. He was buried in the cathedral of that city, close by the monument of an earlier Bishop King (of Oxford), grand-uncle of his wife's father.

Returning to Aston, we find the residents at the hall in some alarm at the state of affairs in Birmingham, to which we shall more particularly refer in the next chapter. Fearing that the people who had been so cruelly treated by Prince Rupert and the Cavaliers might possibly be led to avenge themselves upon one who was now so well known as a friend of the King, and a trusty supporter of his cause in the war against the Parliament—for he assisted the royal cause with his purse, although too far advanced in years to render any assistance in actual warfare—Sir Thomas applied to Colonel Leveson, Governor of Dudley Castle, for a guard of soldiers in order to protect the hall from the possible attacks of his Birmingham neighbours; and on the 18th of December, forty musketeers were lodged in his house. Did the old man ever think, during those days and nights of peril, of that brave son whose death his anger had in all probability accelerated, and who otherwise might have rendered valuable assistance in defending his beloved home, had he been permitted to dwell under its roof? Did he think of the valorous services of his son Edward at Edge Hill, where

> "in *his* Royal Master's cause and war,
> "*His* ventured life brought off a noble skarre;
> "Nor did his faithful services desist,
> "Till Death untimely struck *him* from the list."*

There came a time, during those dark December days, when the presence of such a son would have been an arm of strength for the old man to lean upon, for on the 26th of the month, probably in the midst of the stately festivities of Christmas, the Parliamentary forces (1,200 in number) commenced their attack upon the Hall. It is the opinion of Mr. Davidson that the array thus brought against the Hall could not have consisted of regular troops, as in that case the small number of the beseiged—forty foot soldiers and the household of Sir Thomas—could not have defended the place for any length of time. It is probable, that they consisted of an undisciplined concourse of townsmen, who had not forgotten the cruelties perpetrated on the preceding Easter Monday and Tuesday, and had determined, with the assistance of a few gunners and other regular soldiers, to revenge themselves upon the loyal old baronet of Aston. The siege continued three days, and at the end of that time the defenders surrendered their forces, having lost twelve of their own men, and inflicted a loss of sixty on the enemy. The marks of the cannonading are still visible on the outer wall, while within, the handsome staircase bears evidence, in a shattered pillar and other considerable damage, to the skill of the gunners in their dangerous craft.

The Hall was plundered by the besiegers, many of the family papers were destroyed, and Sir Thomas was imprisoned. His household goods were twice confiscated, and other sums were forced from him; altogether, the damage he sustained through his loyalty to his Sovereign was estimated by Collins at about £20,000.

We have thus far seen that, excepting Sir Thomas Holte's loyalty to his Sovereign, there was but little in his character worthy of admiration. Mr. Davidson's estimate is that, as far as the baronet's actions serve as a test, "he appears to have been proud, obstinate, and revengeful." Of his pride, the costly mansion he has left behind him, and the purchase of the title of Baronet at a cost of over a thousand pounds, are sufficient evidences. Of his obstinacy we need look no further for an example than the incident we have just described, in which he so

* "An Elegy on the Death of Mr. Edward Holte," by his brother-in-law, Dr. King, Bishop of Chichester: *v.* Hannah's Edition of his Poem, p. 105.

hopelessly defended his mansion at the cost of several lives, when the overpowering number of the besiegers should have shown him at once the futility of such a proceeding. And in the sad story of poor Edward Holte, exiled from his home and left in penury, dependent upon the charity of a brother-in-law, for the simple offence of loving a true and noble woman, and making her his wife, we have surely such an instance of mingled pride and revenge as has seldom been equalled.

But of his cruel vengeance, if a tradition for which there is much corroborative evidence is to be believed, there is an even worse example on record. The most probable version of the story is that he was on one occasion returning from hunting, and, in the course of conversation, laid a wager as to the punctuality of his cook, who on this fatal occasion was, for once, behind time. The baronet, enraged at the jeers of his companions, is said to have rushed into the kitchen, and seizing a cleaver which lay at hand, clove the poor cook's head in twain. This tradition has been associated by the ignorant with the so-called "bloody-hand" in the arms of the family, but we have already pointed out the erroneous nature of the supposition that the Ulster badge denoting baronetcy has anything to do with murder. But there is sufficient evidence to prove that this terrible story has not been invented to explain the presence of the supposed stain of murder in the coat of arms, for in 1606 Sir Thomas Holte, by his attorney, preferred a bill against one William Ascrick, for having "open, publicly, maliciously, and in the hearing of divers persons," uttered "with a loud voice, these false, fictitious, scandalous, and opprobrious words in English, respecting the said Sir Thomas, viz.: 'Sir Thomas Holte tooke a cleever, and hytt hys cooke with the same cleever uppon the heade, and clave his heade, that one syde thereof fell uppone one of his shoulders, and the other syde on the other shoulder; and this I will veryfy to be trewe.'" The damages were laid at £1000. The defendant, by a quibble, pleaded not guilty; but a verdict was returned for Sir Thomas, with damages to the amount of £30, with one shilling costs. But when we take into consideration the fact that Sir Thomas, in 1625-6 obtained from Charles I. a royal pardon, "so ample," says Mr. Davidson, "That every crime of thought, word, or deed, prior to the 27th of March then last past (the day of the death of King James), is entirely remitted," and that not merely every crime, but every *suspicion* of crime is included therein, we cannot but come to the same conclusion as the historian of the Holtes, "that a very strong degree of probability rests in favour of the opinion that the poor cook's head was cloven in twain, as charged in the libel."

Sir Thomas out-lived all his children except one, his eldest daughter Grace, who married Sir Richard Shuckburgh. He died at the age of 83 (December, 1654), and was buried with his ancestors in Aston Church, where a handsome monument sets forth, in Latin, his many virtues, and even claims some reflected honour towards himself from the position of his disowned son Edward as chamberlain to Charles the First! Hutton says, in his quaintly cynical manner, of the founders of the Gilds, "When a man of fortune had nearly done with time, he began to peep into eternity through the windows of an abbey; or if a villain had committed a piece of butchery, or had cheated the world for sixty years, there was no doubt but he could burrow his way to glory through the foundation of an abbey." Perhaps Sir Thomas Holte may have had some qualms of conscience on the score of his cruelty to his son and his servant, and may have thought that a little posthumous kindness to the poor and infirm at his gates might perchance equalise the balance a little. He therefore provided in his will for the erection of an Almshouse (which virtuous act is duly set forth on the before-mentioned tablet), which still remains an asylum for the poor, in which they may spend the end of their days in peace, while the family out of whose bounty it was erected is known in Aston no more.

Sir Thomas was succeeded by his grandson Robert, the elder son of the unfortunate Edward, but the story of his life, and of his successors, need not be told in these pages. We shall have something to say of the decadence of this noble family at a later period of our story.

Opposite the principal entrance gates to Aston Park is the fine old church, which was originally built by the prior and monks of Tickford, Newport Pagnel, in the year 1253. The east end of the chancel was added in the reign of Edward II., and the fine tower, with its tall and graceful spire, was erected in the reign of Henry VI. Beside the Holte monuments there are several altar tombs, the finest being that erected to the memory of Walter de Arden, A.D. 1407. A more detailed account of this church and of the village of Aston will be given later on, in the chapters devoted to the history of the suburbs of Birmingham.

CHAPTER V.

THE BATTLE OF BIRMINGHAM.

The Royalists harassed by the people of Birmingham—"Sent to Coventry"—Discipline of the Royalist troops—Prince Rupert opposed at Camp Hill—Defeat of the townsmen—Loss of Royalist officers—The sacking and burning of the town—Tracts relating to the battle.

Our last chapter has somewhat overstepped the bounds of the period it was destined to cover. It will be necessary, therefore, for us to retrace our steps, and take a glance at the doings of our townsmen in the year 1642.

A few days before the memorable Battle of Edge Hill, which was fought on the 23rd of October, in the above-mentioned year, King Charles I. passed through Birmingham on his march from Shrewsbury (on which occasion, as stated in our last chapter, he was the guest of Sir Thomas Holte, at Aston Hall); and the day after he left the town, the inhabitants seized his carriages containing the royal plate and other valuables, and removed them to Warwick Castle. They also harassed the royal party in many ways; attacking small parties of them whenever they appeared, and sending them as prisoners to Coventry. "Hence," says Hutton, "the proverbial expression to a refractory person, *Send him to Coventry.*" Nor did they merely exhibit their preference for the Parliament party, by harassing the royalists, but afforded material assistance to the former, by supplying them with arms; having sent, according to the "*Letter from Walshall,*" fifteen thousand swords for the Earl of Essex's forces, and "not only refused to supply the King's forces with swords for their money, but imprisoned diverse who bought swords, upon suspicion that they intended to supply the King's forces with them."

The apologists and partizans of the royalists have endeavoured to represent the soldiers as being restrained from all acts of violence or oppression, and rigorously punished when detected therein. "There was not," says Clarendon, in his *History of the Rebellion,* "the least violence or disorder among the common soldiers in their march which 'scaped exemplary punishment, so that at *Bromwicham,* a town so generally wicked, that it had risen upon small parties of the King's, and killed or taken them prisoners, and sent them to *Coventry,* declaring a more peremptory malice to his Majesty than any other place, two soldiers were executed for having taken some trifle of no value, out of a house, whose owner was at that time in the rebel's army." How far this representation, and that of the "Worthy Gentleman," who wrote from "Walshall," are borne out by facts, may be judged from the ensuing narrative.

Early in the spring of 1643, Prince Rupert received orders from his royal master to proceed, with a detachment of 1,200 horse, and between

600 and 700 foot, to open a communication between Oxford and York. According to Clarendon, the King ordered him to march towards Lichfield; "in his way thither," he says, "he was to march through *Bromwicham*, a town in Warwickshire before mentioned, and of as great fame for hearty, wilful, affected disloyalty to the King, as any place in England."

ASTON CHURCH.

The inhabitants of Birmingham had already had cause to fear an attack upon their town, from the "divers troopes of Robbers and Plunderers" with which "these parts of the country had began to be much infested;"* they therefore resolved to arm themselves, and "to maintaine two Captaines for the better Disciplining and ordering of their men to that end." But while they were engaged in making preparations for defence, news came that Prince Rupert, with near two thousand men, "with 4 Drakes and 2 Sacres," was marching through Warwickshire in the direction of Birmingham. The inhabitants, however, hoped he

* "Prince Rupert's Burning Love," *see p. 40.*

might pass them by, but as they supposed his design was to enter Staffordshire, they felt that there was little ground for the hope. It was about three o'clock on Easter Monday afternoon, when the prince, with his army, reached Birmingham. There was a small company of foot belonging to the "rebels" stationed in the town, also a troop of horse, from the garrison at Lichfield, but the entire force did not amount to more than two hundred, and the prince did not suppose they would attempt resistance at such odds, so sent his quarter-masters to demand lodging and offer protection; assuring them, (according to the "*Letter from Walshall*,") that if they would quietly receive his Highness and his forces they should suffer no injury. "But," says Hutton, "the sturdy sons of freedom having cast up slight works at each end of the town, and barricaded the lesser avenues, rejected the offer and the officers." Soldiers and citizens joined to oppose the progress of the prince's forces, "and from their little works, with mettle equal to their malice, they discharged their shot upon him." * The royalist pamphleteer of Walsall says that "when his forces drew neare they set up their Colours, and sallyed out of their workes, and gave fire upon them, and with opprobious speeches reviled them, calling them *Cursed doggs, develish Cavaliers, Popish Traytors*, and this was done not by a few of them, but by almost all of them with great shouts and clamours." They fought bravely, and succeeded twice in beating off the prince's army at the entrance of the town, but, notwithstanding that they had an excellent position for defence, were compelled at length to yield, being overpowered by force of numbers, the prince's army being in the proportion of ten to one. But although he succeeded in silencing the townspeople's fire he was still unable to enter the town, for the inhabitants had blocked up the deep and narrow way between Deritend and Camp Hill with carriages, so that he was compelled to alter his route, and his men had to "force the waies over the medowes . . . and so by incompassing them that did defend the out-worke, caused them to draw inward, to other workes there in Digboth, which worke they defended to the adversaries losse." * They kept up a running fire through the town, but were again silenced by the enemy, and put to flight, and "with breaking through houses, over garden waies, escaped over hedges and boggy medowes, and hiding their armes, saved most of them." † "The Cavaliers," says another account, "rode up into the Towne like so many Furyes or Bedlams, the Earle of *Denbigh* being in the Front, singing as he rode, they shot at every doore or window where they could espy any looking out, they hacked, hewed, or pistolled all they met with, without distinction, blaspheming . . [and] cursing most hideously." ‡

* Clarendon.

Discovering a troop of horse (of the Parliamentary army) which was under the command of Captain Greaves, at the northern end of the town, the Earl of Denbigh pursued them some two miles out of town, up Shirland lane, in the manor of Smethwick, when, says the writer of the first narrative in the *True Relation*, § "Captain Greaves observing his time, betwixt two woods, faced about and charged the pursuers most valiantly, as they themselves confesse, and drove them backe againe: in which charge Denby was slaine immediately, and the rest fled, and so we escaped with safety; onely Captaine Greaves received one shot in the face, and a cut in the arme, but not mortall: in the pursuit of that troope God made a way for all our souldiers, saving some two or three, to escape most with their armes, which they threw away and hid in pits and ditches as they could, whereof the most, I thinke, the cavaleeres found not, and not one Captaine or Officer was hurt or taken prisoner, nor any considerable man, but most poore fellowes, and malignants, because they could meet with no better, and all are released saving two of the best, though of no

* "A True Relation," etc. [R. G.'s narrative], *see p. 37.*

† Ib., *see p. 37.*

‡ "Prince Rupert's Burning Love," *see p. 40.*

§ Supposed to be R. Porter, a sword-blade manufacturer, of Birmingham, *see next page* great quality, some redeemed themselves for 2d., 12d., and 8d. apiece, and some one or twofor 20s."

Provoked at the continued resistance of the inhabitants, and still more enraged at the loss of several distinguished officers of his army, Prince Rupert gave orders to his soldiers to set fire to the town. "His wrath is said to have kindled in Bull Street," says Hutton, "and consumed several houses near the spot, now No. 12." The writer of the pamphlet entitled *Prince Rupert's Burning Love, etc.*, says "they used all possible diligence in every Street to kindle fire in the Towne with Gunpowder, Match, Wispes of Straw, and Besomes, burning coales of fire &c. flung into Straw, Hay, Kid piles [*i.e.* piles of wood fuel], Coffers, Thatch, and any other places, where it was likely to catch hold; . . . yea, it is confidently related, that they shot fire out of their Pistolls, wrapping lighted Match with powder or some other ingredients in formes of slugs, or bullets in brown Paper, which themselves confessed was the Lord *Digbies* devise, that English Firebrand; and lest any should save any of their goods they had left, or quench their flames, they stood with their drawne swords and Pistols, about the burning Houses, shooting and indeavouring to kill every one that appeared to preserve goods, and quench the fire." Eighty-seven houses are said to have been thus destroyed, besides stables and other outbuildings, and between three and four hundred persons were left homeless.

Not content with thus setting fire to the town, they also pillaged and plundered the town to a considerable extent, "picking purses and pockets, searching in holes and corners, Tiles of houses, Wells, Pooles, Vaults, Gardens, and every place they could suspect for money and goods." One Thomas Peake, a miser, was said to have been robbed of nearly £1,500. Altogether, the pamphleteer above quoted estimates that they took away from the town about £3,000 in money, spending the last night of their occupation of the town in the most shameless rioting, drunkenness, and debauchery. Yet withal Vicar says, in his *God in the Mount*, "that in the plundering and burning of the Town, the greatest losse was to the malignant partie of that Town who inhabited among them, most of the honest and godly men there, having by God's mercy and good providence carryed and conveyed away their best goods into *Coventry* before the Cavaliers came to their Town."

Some time after this the royalists caused the Blade-mill of one Mr. Porter to be destroyed, on account of the disloyalty of its owner, in making sword-blades thereat for the service of the Parliamentary army only. This Mr. Porter would appear to be the "R. P." whose signature is appended to the first of the two narratives in the "True Relation of Prince Rupert's Barbarous Cruelty against the Towne of Brumingham," for he says therein, "The malignants . . . have since pulled down my Mill, and pretend that Prince Rupert so commanded." If it be the same, this old Birmingham sword-cutler could not only make these implements of warfare, but also knew well how to use them, for he says in his narrative that he himself was in Captain Greaves' troop which so valiantly withstood and vanquished their pursuers near Smethwick, in which engagement the Earl of Denbigh lost his life.

We have thus endeavoured to re-tell the story of the Battle of Birmingham from the pamphlets and other contemporary records thereof, but as there may be among our readers some who are desirous of perusing these curious old pamphlets themselves, we have here reprinted them verbatim.

The first in chronological order is that to which we have just referred, containing two narratives, the first signed "R. P. [? R. Porter] *Coventry, April* 8, 1643," and the second "R. G." It is entitled:

A TRUE
RELATION
OF
PRINCE RUPERT'S
BARBAROUS CRUELTY
AGAINST THE
TOWNE OF BRUMINGHAM,

To which place on Monday Apr. 3, 1643, he marcht with 2000 horse and foot, 4 Drakes, and 2 Sakers; where after two houres fight (being twice beaten off by the Townsmen, in all but 140 Musqueteers) he entered, put divers to the Sword, and burnt about 80 Houses to ashes, suffering no man to carry away his goods, or quench the fire, and making no difference between friend or foe ; yet by God's providence the greatest losse fell on the malignants of the Town.

And of the Cavaliers were slaine divers chiefe Commanders, and men of great quality, amongst whom was the Earle of Denbigh, the Lord John Stewart : and as themselves report, the Lord Digby.

LONDON :
Printed for John Wright in the Old-baily,
April 12, 1643.

A TRUE
RELATION,
&c.

SIR,

THOUGH I can write you but the same lamentation which I believe you have already heard, yet I cannot be silent to acquaint you of the truth as neere as I can ; If Coventrey had sent us what helpe it might, I beleeve the enemy durst not have assaulted us, but in regard they had been in danger of cutting off by the way, in case they had been sent, I must excuse them, though it be to our owne suffering. We with the Captaines were sensible, that if the Cavaliers came, we were not likely to withstand them, they being neere 1500, and we not above 150 Musketiers, with a Troope of Horse of Captaine Greaves, which did no good but in their flight, as hereafter you will heare ; but in regard the generall desire of the Towne, especially of those that bore Armes, would have them stand it out, and not march away with their Armes, as we might in time, and that both they, and the malignant would have reviled, and curst the Captaines and Majestrates of the Towne if they had left them, made the Captaines and better sort content to stay and trie the issue, rather than be so perpetually reproacht. And though the same fall hard on our side in loosing the Towne and some Armes, and about 80 Houses burnt to ashes, with all that therein was, and some fifteen men, and two women lost their lives, yet their gaine was nothing at all, yea, they count it greate losse and curse the time that ever they medled with us, for I beelive they lost as many ordinary men as we, besides three men of great quality, which they much lament, whereof two of them were Lords, as we have great cause to thinke, the one the Earle of Denby that's sure, the other Lord we something doubt of his name, but we heare by divers of the Cavaliers it is Digby, sure we are he is wounded ; and it is as sure that some of their Collonels say it was a man of greater ranke, and more considerable then Denby ; the other a chiefe Commander : Denby pursued Captaine Greaves Troope some two Miles out of Towne being at their heeles, before our Troope departed, among whom I went away, and Captain Greaves observing his Time betwixt two woods faced about, and charged the pursuers most valiantly as they themselves confesse, and drove them backe againe : in which charge Denby was slaine immediately, and the rest fled, and so we escaped with safety ; onely Captaine Greaves received one shot in the face, and a cut in the Arme, but not mortall ; in the pursuit of that troope God made a way for all our souldiers, saving some two or three, to escape most with their armes, which they threw away and hid in pits and ditches as they could, whereof the most, I thinke, the cavaleeres found not, and not one Captaine or Officer was hurt or taken prisoner, nor any considerable man, but most poore fellowes, and malignants, because they could meet with no better, and all are released saving two of the best, though of no great quality, some redeemed themselves for 2d. 12d. and 8d. apiece, and some one or two for 20s. Prince Rubert being enraged that he should take never a prisoner of so great a company, and of those not to raise 20*l.* when he himselfe had undergon so great a losse ; and of those that were slaine [of our side were most poore malignants, some three young men of ordinary quality that bare Armes, and John Carter, and that in their flight ; for but one was slaine,] and one lightly shot in the flesh ; in the enterance for pillage they spared none, friend or foe they lighted of, yet for the most part those that did most against them escaped best, the same I may say of the fire, though they intended to burne the Towne utterly, as may be known by their laying lighted match, with powder, and other combustible matter at the other end, which fired in divers places, and divers was found out and prevented, so that we may truely say, that the flames, sword, pilledgers, but especially the prison, made a difference betwixt those that feared God, and those that feare him not. But this is remarkable in their vilenesse, that all these houses saving two were fired in cold blood, at their departure, wherein they endeavoured to fire all, and in the flames they would not suffer the people to carry out their goods, or to quench it, triumphantly with reproaches rejoyced that the Wind stood right to consume the Towne, at which present the Lord caused the Winds to turn, which was a token of his notice of their insultation.

For pillage I heare but of little I lost, having obscured the things I had of any valew ; and for fire, God did marveliously prevent, both to me and many others, whereat the malignants are so enraged that they have since pulled down my Mill, and pretend that Prince Rupert so commanded, and threaten to pull downe my house and divers others, which I thinke they dare not, lest they build it up againe, the County having sent them admonition of their insolency.

Prince Rupert with Hastings kept their rendezvow this day, within two miles of Lichfield, as we credibly heare, what their designe is we know not. I believe they can doe no good at Lichfield ; I hope their cruelty in our sufferings will provoke this unwilling kingdome to jealousy for the Parliament. I pray you when you have read this, shew it to Mr. B. and Mr. E. not onely to acquaint them with the newes, but of my being in health, with all my Company, wherein I have great cause to rejoyce in the Lord, and so I rest,

Your loving friend,

Coventry, April 8, 1643. R.P.

SIR,

BEING by my promise ingaged unto you, I am now to make relation of a most barbarous massacree of our townesmen of *Bermingham,* and of the enraged cruelty of Prince *Rupert* and his inhumane Cavaliers : Sir, thus it was, about three of the clocke one Munday in the afternoone, he had with neere two thousand horse and foote, foure Drakes and two Sakers, set against the towne, playing with his ordnance, and endeavouring to force his way, with foote and horse, were twice beaten off with our musqueteers at the entrance of *Derrington,* at which many of their men fell, the townes-men held them in play above an houre, we had not above one hundred and fourtie musquets and having many entrances into the towne they were many too few, *Coventry* men had withdrawne their forces three daies before, all but Captaine *Castledownes* Dragooneers, a Troope of horse of Master *Perkes* commanded by Captain *Greaves* being in the Towne, not fit for that service, made escape when the adversaries began to incompasse the Towne, and force the waies over the medowes, and fired the Towne in two places, and so by incompassing them that did defend the out-worke, caused them to draw inward, to other workes there in Digboth, which worke they defended to the adversaries losse, but being the enemy brake in at the Millone* they were forced to leave that worke also, and so put to shift for themselves, with breaking through houses, over garden waies, escaped over hedges and boggy medowes, and hiding their armes, saved most of them, the enemy killed none, as I here in fight unlesse some three or foure, Mr. *Carter,* and Samuell *Elsmore,* being of them, some with their armes defended themselves stoutly till death, they persued the rest in fields and lanes, cutting and most barbarously mangling naked men to the number of fifteene men, one woman, another being shot, and many hurt, many men sore wounded, and Mr. *Tillam* the surgeon standing in his dore to entertaine them, was most cruelly shot, having his leg and thigh bones broken, they pillaged the Towne generally, their owne friends sped worst, and one tuesday morning set fire in diverse places of the Towne, and have burnt neere a hundred dwellings the Welch end, Dale

PRINCE RUPERT

* Is this a mis-print for *Mill-lane?*

end, and More street end, Humphrey *Rans*, the Bell, and diverse houses thereabout, many other fires they kindled, but they did not burne, they left kindled matches with gunpowder also in other places, intending nothing lesse then utterly to destroy the Towne, but by Gods providence they whose hurt they chiefly intended by Gods hand is much prevented, the Cavaliers lye about *Clanke* beyond *Wosall*, are joyned with *Hastings* forces, and intend to set on the Close at *Lichfield*, where I feare not but they will have enough ; your Father's house stands, but hath lost much, Mr. *Roberts* Mr. *Porters*, and mine be safe, but are threatned to be pulled downe, and they pretend Prince *Ruperts* warrant, but however its their envy to God's overruling providence hath turned the mischiefe so much on the heads of those that might with their timely helpe have prevented this mischief ; I am much grieved at the losse of your brother, and many other friends, three being my honest worke-men, whose lives I would I had redeemed with mine estate. The Cavaliers have lost thirty men at least, of which there be three or foure chiefe men Earles and Lords, I beleeve you have heard them named the Earle of *Denby*, the Lord John *Stewart*, some say the Lord *Digby*, thirty are said to be buried and many carried away wounded, this did so much enrage them, that they appeared more like Devills then men, lamenting more their losse, then boasting of their gaine, which was much in goods and in money, its thought above two-thousand pound, thirteene hundred being taken from Mr. *Peake*, Mr. *Jennens* lost much, the which men if they had parted with little before, our fortification had beene such as they could not have entred, which went on well for the time. So wishing you to have comfort in our God, who is able to turne the rage of men to his praise, and sweeten this bitter cup by some other comfort, I conclude and rest,

Yours to command,

R.G.

I could wish I might heare how the City stands affected with our losse, for a little reliefe from them, might much comfort many poore people, which have lost all, and are left well nie naked and harbourlesse : it would much encourage all to stand out in the cause, that are but indifferent, a helpe to ease the better party of, the burthen of the which will be otherwaies too great for us ; I would move some friends if you thinke fit, I have already put on the worke of contribution in this City.

FINIS.

The second is that of the royalist of Walsall :

A

LETTER

WRITTEN FROM

WALSHALL,

BY A WORTHY GENTLEMAN TO HIS FRIEND IN OXFORD,

CONCERNING

BVRMINGHAM.

Printed in the Yeare M.DC.XLIII.
(A MS. Note adds "April 14th.")

A

LETTER

WRITTEN FROM WALSHALL BY A WORTHY GENTLEMAN TO HIS FRIEND IN OXFORD,

CONCERNING BURMINGHAM.

SIR,

HEARING of the approach of Prince *Rupert* his Highnesse, and coming according to my duty to attend him, In my way I heard of the miserable destruction of *Burmingham* by fire ; which I must confesse tooke the deepest Apprehensions with me of any one accident since the beginning of these unhappy distractions, as presenting to my view a picture of the present estate of *Germany*, and as by a prospective shewing me (not very farre off) the Scene translated from thence hither. This sad thought drew me to a more narrow enquiry of the causes of the burning of the Towne, and whether it was done by authority or no. And I found that the Inhabitants of that Towne were they who first stirred up those of *Coventry* to resist the King, and that about 300 from thence went into *Coventry* to defend it against the King's Forces, that from thence they sent 15000 Swords for the Earle of Essex his Forces, and the ayd of that Party, and not onely refused to supply the King's Forces with Swords for their money, but imprisoned diverse who bought swords, upon suspicion that they intended to supply the King's forces with them. That afterwards when His Majesty marched that way with His Army, out of his princely goodnesse and in hope that His Grace and favour would prevayle with them to turne good subjects, he gave expresse order that they should not be plundered, and because some were plundered (though but a few and very little taken from them) there was exemplary Justice done by the hanging of two Officers, and they had a speciall protection granted to them. Yet so little use did they make of the King's Clemency, that the King's Army was no sooner removed from thence but they stayed all the Carriages which did not move the same day with the King's Army, amongst which was some of the King's Plate and diverse goods of great value, and therein they were so hearty and zealous that at their owne charges they carried them to *Warwicke* Castle before the king was out of that Shire.

And they have still continued upon all occasions violently to oppose the King, and to ayd those who have taken up armes against him. Insomuch that they made fortifications about the Town, and sent out parties to plunder the King's friends.

And when his Highnesse upon Munday last sent one to them to take up his quarter at *Burmingham*, who assured them that if they would quietly receive his Highnesse and his forces they should suffer no injury, But otherwise they must expect to be forced to it, they refused to give him Entrance, and prepared themselves with all their strength to resist him ; and when his forces drew neare they set up their Colours, and sallyed out of their workes, and gave fire upon them, and with opprobious speeches reviled them, calling them *Cursed doggs*, *develish Cavaliers*,

Popish Traytors, and this was done not by a few of them but by almost all of them with great shouts and clamours. This could not but incense the souldiers, and the Prince to make his passage into the Towne was forced to give orders for firing a house or two; but they retiring and flying, upon his entrance into the Towne he immediately gave order for quenching of the fire which was done accordingly, and no more hurt was done on Munday. But yesterday his Highnesse being to march from thence, and fearing what those great provocations might worke with the Souldiers, he gave expresse command that no souldier should attempt to fire the Towne. And after his departure thence some souldiers (as yet unknown) having fired the Towne in diverse places, he immediatly sent to the inhabitants of the Towne, to let them know it was not done by his command, and therefore wished them to quench it, but the wind being high and the fire encreased, it could not be so soone extinguished as was to be desired!

One thing more I heard of at this taking of *Burmingham*, which made some Impression with me, which was the death of a minister killed presently after the entry of the souldiers into the Towne. But it is alleadged that he told the souldier who killed him, that the King was a Perjured and Papisticall King, and that he had rather dye then live under such a king, and that he did and would fight against him; and in his pocket after his death were found some papers sufficient to make mee to beleeve the man was either mad, or one of the new Enthusiasts. It burdens my modesty to repeat them, but the truth (which you will desire to know) extorts them from mee, some of them were to this effect, that the 28 of March last he had a comfortable Kisse from Mris. E. with some moystnesse, and another day a cynnamon Kisse from another woman, and another from one of 14 yeares old, with much more such like stuffe which I blush to write.

And surely whatsoever the Principles of these teachers may be, the conclusions made by their Disciples is very strange. One of the best sort of their prisoners here being discoursed withall concerning his taking up armes against the King, and demanded how he could take up armes in that manner considering his oaths of Allegiance and Supremacy, peremptorily answered, he never did nor never would take those oaths.

Sir, this I thought fit to write to you, while the memory of the businesse is fresh; and though it may be accompanied with these circumstances, yet it much troubles his Highnesse that this Accident should now fall out, he well knowing that they who are the great *Boute fieus* and Incendiaries in the State, will be apt to calumniate him for the firing of this Towne, which he never Commanded or Countenanced, and the actors of which he is most desirous to punish, and is most carefull to find out. And this narrative now made you may be confident is true, comming from

Your most humble and
faithfull Servant.

Walshall, April 5, 1643.

FINIS.

The third, which certainly bears the palm for comprehensiveness of title, is quaintly entitled,

PRINCE RVPERT's
BURNING LOVE TO
E N G L A N D,
DISCOVERED IN
BIRMINGHAM's FLAMES.
OR,
A more Exact and true Naration of *Birmingham's* Calamities, under the barbarous and inhumane Cruelties of P. Rupert's forces.
Wherein is related how that famous and well affected Town of *Birmingham* was

Unworthily opposed,
Insolently invaded,
Notoriously robbed and plundered,
And most cruelly fired in cold blood the next day.
} *By Prince* Rupert's Forces.

Together with the Number of Prince *Rupert's* Forces, his considerable Persons slaine, or mortally wounded; their many abominable Carriages in and after the taking of the Town. The small Strength which *Birmingham* had to maintaine their defence, the Names of their men slaine; the number of houses burned, and persons thereby destitute of habitation; with divers other considerable passages.

Published at the request of the Committee at *Coventry*, that the Kingdom may timely take notice what is generally to be expected if the Cavaliers insolencies be not speedily crushed.

A righteous man regardeth the life of his Beast, but the tender mercies of the wicked are cruell. Prov. xii. 10.

London: Printed for *Thomas Vnderhill*, 1643.
[A MS. Note adds, "1st of May."]

A
TRUE RELATION
OF THE INHUMANE CRUELTIES EXERCISED BY THE CAVALIERS
At *Birmingham*, in Warwickshire.

TO correct the many false Reports already spread abroad, and to prevent all false narrations for future, concerning the late surprisall and spoyling of the Towne of *Birmingham*, in the County of *Warwick*. This ensuing Relation of Passages, hath beene collected from the severall Informations of divers trusty and Intelligent Inhabitants of *Birmingham*, who were eye witnesses of, and sufferers under many the said calamities of that Towne, so farre as the truth of such turbulent distracted Occurrents can be yet discovered.

The Towne of *Birmingham* perceiving that for their

faithfull affection to King and Parliament, they had derived the hatred of Popish and prophane Malignants upon themselves; and that since the Noble Lord *Brookes* death, these parts of the Country began to be much infested with divers Troopes of Robbers and Plunderers, whereby their persons and estates were much indangered, resolved to Arme themselves and estates, and to maintaine two Captaines for the better Disciplining and ordering of their men to that end: But whilst they were beginning to make some slight mounds and Breast-works for defence the week before Easter last, information came that Prince *Rupert* with 1500 or 2000 men with 4 Drakes and 2 Sacres was upon his march at *Stratford* upon *Avon* and about *Henly* some 10 miles distant from *Birmingham*, where these forces hovered about 4 dayes, pillageing the Country extreamly (as their manner is) *Birmingham* hoped they might passe by them, but afterwards perceiving on Saturday night, that it was probable their designe was toward *Staffordshire*, and that they would take *Birmingham* in their way; The Minister of *Birmingham* entreated the Captaines and chiefe of the Towne, by no meanes to thinke of such an impossible defence of themselves against 2000, themselves having scarce six score Musqueteers in all the Towne, but rather to march away with all their Armes, and so secure their Armes and persons, though their goods were hazarded, as a thing farre more safe and rationall, which motion the Captaines and chiefe of the Town readily imbraced, but the middle and inferior sort of people, (especially those that bore Armes) would by no meanes be drawn to leave the Towne, and so they all resolved to stand upon their own guard, otherwise the chiefe of the Towne and the Captaines must have departed as Cowards, with great Contempt many scornes and curses.

On *Easter* Monday Prince *Rupert's* Forces approached to the Towne about 2 or 3 o'Clock in the Afternoone, at one end, presently assaulted it with great fury, discharging their Musquets and great pieces onely about 100 Musketiers opposing them (the rest hiding themselves) which were also divided into severall ends of the Town, and not many in any one place, a good while the Musketiers kept them off their Works, and drove them back till they fired a thatched house, and burnt 2 or 3 houses at Towns end and their Horse also broke into the fields and came in at the backsides of the Town through Lake-meadow, which forced the Towns-men to retreat back into the Towne to charge them, when they came up, when they slew some very considerable man who was presently stripped of his rich garments, and wrapped in a gray coat, and a woman of theirs suborned to lament for him as her husband, they called him *Adam a Bell*, but this losse so enraged them that they presently burnt 2 or 3 houses to the ground, where they conceived he was *shot*; then they broke in so forcibly upon the few *men* in the *town* that they were forced to scatter and fly for their *lives*. It is very remarkable that none of them were slaine or hurt whiles they stood upon their Guard (as is credibly averred) till they scattered and were so singled out. The Cavaliers rode up into the Towne like so many Furyes or Bedlams, the Earle of *Denbigh* being in the Front, singing as he rode, they shot at every doore or window where they could espy any looking out, they hacked, hewed, or pistolled all they met with, without distinction, blaspheming, cursing, and damming themselves most hidiously. Discovering a Troope of Horse, which was under the command of Captain *Greaves* at the further end of the Towne facing them, they pursued after them, who after a little flight wheeled about, and most stoutly charged them through, and the Captaine received five small wounds (which are now almost well:) In which charge the Ea. of *Denbigh* was knockt off his horse, laid for dead, and his pockets rifled (though his wounds not so mortall as to die presently) the rest of his horse were chased till they came neere their own Colours, which was excellent Service, for meane while most of the Townes foot escaped away.

After which Captaine *Greaves* retreated, and so advanced to *Lichfield*. Their Horse rode desparatly round the Town, leaping hedges and ditches (wherein one is reported to breake his neck) to catch the Townes-men; no madmen could ride more furiously. They slew in their frenzy as we are informed, about 14 in all, *viz. John Carter*, junior, *William Knight*, Glasier, *William Billingsley*, junior, *Joseph Rastell*, *William Turton*, Cutler, *Thomas* the Ostler at Swan, pistolled comming officiously to take their Horses, *Richard Hunt* Cobler, *Henry Benton* Labourer, *Samuel Elsmore* Cutler, *William Ward* Cutler, *Richard Adams* Cobler, *Widdow Collins*, *Lucas* his Wife, and one Mr. *Whitehall* a Minister, who hath bin long Lunatick, held Jewish opinions, and had layn in Bedlam and other prisons (some say) 16, some 22 yeares, and was lately come out; they comming to him asked him if he would have quarter, he answered to this (or like purpose) he scorned Quarter from any Popish Armies or Souldiers, whereupon they supposing him to be Mr. *Roberts* Minister of *Birmingham*, did most cruelly mangle and hack him to death, and found certain idle and foolish papers in his pocket, which they spared not to divulge (as they thought to the Roundheads infamy) and so went insulting up and down the Towne that they had quartered their Minister, out of whose bloody hands the Lord's gracious providence delivered him a little before the Towne was assaulted, and (blessed be God) hee is neither slain nor hurt. All the considerable men escaped out of their snare, some 40 (they say) were taken prisoners, whereof scarce 20. of their own Towne, all inferior men, most of them their own favourers, and since for trifling sums of money they are released all, save 2 or 3 (as unworthy to be kept.)

Having thus possessed themselves of the Towne, they ran into every house cursing and damming, threatning and terrifying the poore women, most terribly, setting naked Swords and Pistolls to their breasts, they fell to plundering all the Towne before them, as well Malignants as others, picking purses, and pockets, searching in holes and corners, Tiles of houses, Wells, Pooles, Vaults, Gardens and every place they could suspect for money and goods, forcing people to deliver all the money they had. It is credibly believed they took from one *Thomas Peake* a Councellor 1500 or 1300 *li.* at least, for he afterwards deeply professed that they had but left him in money 15d. q; and it was commonly known he had about

THE OLD SHIP INN, SAID TO HAVE BEEN PRINCE RUPERT'S HEAD QUARTERS.

the said sums lying cankering and rusting by him for these many Yeares, and yet to this day he would never voluntarily lend or give the least summe for the Relief of God's Ch: and the Land in the present saddest distresses, who being under *Oneals* hands (as we are credibly informed) when tidings of their Minister's death was brought to him, replied (thinking thereby to curry favour) that it had bin well if he had bin killed 7 yeares agoe. They have had divers great Summes also from others, who have shewed small love to *King and Parliament*; tooke much money to protect people's Houses, and afterwards betrayed them, and set them on fire. It is conceived they had 3000*l.* in money from the Towne. They beastly assaulted many Women's chastity, and impudently made their brags of it afterwards, how many they had ravished; glorying in their shame, especially the *French* among them, were outragiously lascivious and letcherous. They broke the Windowes, spoyled the goods they could not take away, and carried with them all the chiefe goods in the Towne, some having little left, some nothing but bare walls, some nothing but cloathes on their backs, and some stripped to their very shirts and left naked. That night few or none of them went to Bed, but sate up revelling, robbing, and Tyrannizing over the poore affrighted Women and prisoners, drinking drunke, healthing upon their knees, yea drinking Healths to Prince *Ruperts* Dog.

Nor did their rage here cease, but when on next day they were to march forth of the Towne, they used all possible diligence in every Street to kindle fire in the Towne with Gunpowder, Match, Wispes of Straw, and Besomes burning coales of fire &c. flung into Straw, Hay, Kid piles, Coffers, Thatch, and any other places, where it was likely to catch hold; many of which attempts were successlesse and found after their departure, yea, it is confidently related, that they shot fire out of their Pistolls, wrapping lighted Match with powder or some other ingredients in formes of slugs, or bullets in brown Paper, which themselves confessed was the Lord *Digbies* devise, that English Firebrand; and lest any should save any of their goods they had left, or quench their flames, they stood with their drawne swords and Pistols, about the burning Houses, shooting and indeavouring to kill every one that appeared to preserve goods, and quench the fire, domineering at the flames, *Where's your Coventry now? Where's your God Brookes now? You may see how God fights against you*, &c. And when some of the Town (whose purses had dearely purchased some interest among them) diswaded them from further fiering, one of their owne men confessed that every *Quartermaster* was sworne to fire his owne Quarter, and that they durst not but doe it. By all which it notoriously appeares, that their full intention was, and that by command (let them pretend what excuse they can) to burne downe the whole Towne to the ground, and doubtlesse would have done it, had not the Lord been the more mercifull: the houses burned, were about 87. besides multitudes of Barnes, Stables, and other back buildings, belonging both to these dwelling Houses and to others that escaped the flames. Persons unfurnished and fallen into extreme distresse by this fire, 340, and upwards. So that many are quite undone by these barbarous cruelties, which are so much the more cruell, in as much as all these (except five or six Houses) were burnt in cool blood, the next day after they had sacked the Towne. And yet for all this the Souldiers told the Inhabitants, that Prince *Rupert* dealt mercifully with them: but when they came back againe with the *Queenes Army*, they would leave neither Man, Woman, nor childe alive. Such are the Cavaliers mercies. This Towne (as is thought) was the first Towne in the Kingdom, that was generally plundered when the King marched from *Shrewsbury*, before *Keynton* battell and the first that in cold blood was barbarously fyred: However Prince *Rupert* hath got himselfe eternall honour, by conquering so mighty an enemy as 100. Musketiers, with so small an army as 2000. men. Since their departure Prince *Rupert* hearing that some in *Birmingham*, cursed him for his Cruelties, had designed (as one of their owne Party informed) two Troopes of Horse to fire the rest of the Towne. Whereupon some of the Towne petitioning him not to doe it, he replyed he would not if they rebelled not againe, nor returned to their vomit. Sithence they have caused one Mr. *Porters* Blademill in the Towne, to be pulled downe, wherein swordblades were made and imployed, onely for the service of the Parliament, and so they were informed (which cost erecting about 100*l.*) threatning if it were not pulled downe, the rest of the Towne should be burnt. For now they begin to be great Agents in Fire-Workes.

On their part it is probably believed there fell three very considerable Men, *viz.* Earle of *Denbigh* who died not long after of his Wounds, another as is supposed, was Sir *William* AYRES. The third as yet not knowne.

Certainely two Coffins were made in *Birmingham*, while the Earle of *Denbigh* was alive; and many common Souldiers are supposed to be slaine, some suspected to be buryed in the Breast-workes ditch they entred, which they laid flat, and charged that none should meddle with it upon paine of death, and when they came into the Towne, they cursed at the Round-heads, and swore *they shot, as if they had been shooting at Sparrowes, scarce ever missed Man or Horse.* They tooke away two Cart load of wounded Men, about 12 in a Cart, when they went away. Now they have made *Birmingham* a woful spectacle to behold, a thorow Faire for Thieves and plunderers; the rich are wofully wasted and spoyled multitudes, almost quite beggered, and undone; it is thought 20000*l.* cannot repaire their *losses*, their own Malignant neighbours rage at the well-affected, like mad men, their minister is driven from home, debarred from all imployment and deprived of all his maintenance; besides his many losses by fire and plundering, and till those parts be cleared small hopes of his safe returne, being so much maligned and threatned by the Cavaliers, and the domineering anti-guard left in *Birmingham*. The People that are left are fed with such rayling Sermons as one *Orton* Curate to *Parson Smith* the ancient Pluralist can afford them, rankly tempered with the malignancy of his owne distempered Spirit. And all well-affected People are forced to be absent from their habitations, to their excessive charge in this their low estate, for feare of surprizalls, large summes being proffered to apprehend them, especially those of better ranke. Yet they desire to bear all these crosses patiently and profitably take with joy the spoyling of all their goods, knowing in themselves that they suffer in a good cause, and that they have in Heaven a farre better and more enduring substance.

Let all the Kingdome well consider *Birminghams* calamities and conclude what all are like to feele unlesse they maturely bestirre themselves to shake off the Cavaliers more then *Egyptian* yoke.

FINIS.

The passage from Vicars's "*God in the Mount*,"* relating to this event, (from which we have already quoted in our narrative), is as follows:—

"April the 8th came certain intelligence to *London* from *Brumingham* of the cruell slaughter of diverse of the inhabitants of that honest Town, and that about eighty of their dwelling houses were burnt downe by that barbarous and butcherly Prince of *Robbers*, and his accursed Cavaliers. But yet withall, that his filching Forces got little by their so inhumane barbarity: for, God fought for those poore unarmed inhabitants, who were for the most part, Smiths, whose profession or trade was to make nails, sythes and such like iron commodities; and that with such iron-weapons as they had they so knocked the Earl of *Denbigh* that he received his deaths wound in his furious pursuit of some of them, and immediately after dyed of those his wounds: And with him also (as it was credibly informed) the Lord *Digby* that arch-traitor to the Common wealth of *England* was sorely wounded in the same fight. And this also was noted and credibly informed thence as a remarkable providence of the Lord. That in the plundering and burning of this Town the greatest losse was to the malignant partie of that Town who inhabited among them, most of the honest and godly men there, having by Gods mercy and good providence carryed & conveyed away their best goods into *Coventry* before the Cavaliers came to their Town."

The Old Ship Inn, Camp Hill, is said to have been the head quarters of Prince Rupert during the attack on the town, and the last proprietor of the inn, previous to its demolition, published a little book on its history and age, containing many curious and interesting details, which were well worth preserving. Whether this house was "Prince Rupert's Head Quarters" or not, there can be no doubt it is a very old one, and was probably a roadside inn three centuries ago. It was formerly known as "The Anchor."

* Jehova-Jireh. God in the Mount; or, England's Remembrancer. By John Vicars. London, 1641. p. 296.

There is yet another pamphlet relating to the civil war troubles in the vicinity of Birmingham which we do not remember to have seen reprinted or referred to in any previous history of the town. It would seem to refer to the period at which the people of Birmingham harassed the royalist troops, and seized the king's carriages, but we cannot find any mention elsewhere of such a battle near Birmingham. The copy of the tract from which we have taken our reprint is in the valuable collection of Warwickshire books, prints, and MSS. formed by the late Mr. Staunton, of Longbridge, Warwickshire, now in the Birmingham Reference Library. It is not improbable that this exceedingly rare little pamphlet of eight pages is unique.

A TRUE
RELATION
OF A
GREAT AND CRUELL
Battell fought by the Lord *Willoughby* of *Parham* with 800. Horse and Foot who were going to the L. Generall, against Prince *Robert* with 9. Troops of Horse, and 300. Foot, neer Brumegum in *Warwickeshire, October the 17.*

Declaring also the manner of the L. *Willoughbies* obtaining the Victory, killing about 50. of the Cavaleers, and taking 20. prisoners, *with the losse of* 20. men.

Sent in a Letter from His Excellencie to the House of Commons, and read in the said House, October 18.

Printed for *Richard West* October 20.

A RENOWNED
VICTORIE
OBTAINED
By the Lord *Willoughby of Parham*, against Prince Rupert within three miles of Brumegum, October 18.

HIs Majesty having divided his Army into two parts, the one he hath committed to the Command of Prince *Rupert*, E. of *Derby*, *Rivers*, *Lindsey*, and Lord *Grandison*, by which division some advantage ariseth to the Lord Generalls Army, for that Prince *Robert* with His Forces cannot now come upon any occasion to joyn with His Majesty His Excellencie with His Army being gotten between them.

That Prince *Robert* is marched with His Army towards *Warwick*.

It is also informed by divers Letters from *Brumegum*, that the Lord *Willoughby* of *Parham* with about 800. horse and foot in his march towards the Lord Generall, met Prince *Robert* with 8. Troops of horse and about 300. Foot, two or three miles from *Brumegum*, and gave him battle which was very fierce and cruell on either side, but at length the Princes souldiers retreated, and fled, there being slain of the Malignants about 50. and 20. taken prisoners, and of the Lord *Willoughbies* side about 17. The fight being ended, the L. *Willoughbie* with his Forces marched forward to his Excellencie, with whom he hath now joyned himself.

Upon Friday last it was again reported to the E. of *Essex*, that his Maj. would give him battle the next day, but the Extraordinary Rain that fell those two dais prevented the meeting of the Armies.

It is also conceived that His Majesty would not delay the meeting with His Lordship so long, but that he hath about 24. pieces of Ordnance, that he daily expects daily to be brought to His Army from *Ludlow*, *Chester*, *Newcastle*, and some other places, but cannot have them as yet brought, but is in fear they will be stopped and seized on by the Parliament-forces, there being order to that purpose issued out from his Excellency.

His Excellency hath also sent the Lord *Wharton* with 1000. Horse and Foot to clense the County near *Manchester* of the E. of *Derby*, and the L. *Rivers*, who do nothing but plunder and pillage where ever they come.

The said Lords do daily indeavour to march and joyn with His Majesties Army, but are prevented by the said L. *Wharton*, and his Forces, so that it is hoped they must yield, or perish by the sword.

His Excellencie hath also sent Collonell *Cholmly*, Collonell *Berrie*, and Capt. *Boston* with two Regiments of Horse and Foot, and 12. pieces of Great Ordnance to *Wolverhampton*, for the fortifying and securing that town against the Malignants His Majesty with His Army being Retreated, and marched from thence againe to *Shrewsbury*, and is intended to give battle to His Excellency on Monday next, being it is conceived constrained thereto, for that there is no subsistance for His Army any longer, having taken from the Inhabitants of these towns what they can, and cannot march into any other County without fighting.

It was also signified by Letters from His Excellencie to the House of Commons, that His Majesty hath granted a Commission to divers great Papists in the County of *Lancaster* to raise what men they can for His Majesties service of that Faction, and what Money, Plate, or Horse can be by them raised, and to send the same to His Majesty, with power to take perforce and seize upon the goods, mony, horse and Plate of any Persons whatsoever, that shall refuse to contribute the same to relieve his Majesties present necessity, as Enemies to His Majesty, and as disloyall and trayterous Subjects, which many have done according to the said Commission in the further parts of Lancashire, to the great terrour, trouble, and oppression of the Protestants, and well affected persons in those parts of that County.

That His Excellency having information of these proceedings in *Lancashire*, hath sent Captain *Brown* with a Regiment of Horse and Foot, and two pieces of Ordnance to relieve and assist that County, and suppresse the Rebellious and Trayterous Papists and perverse Malignants there Adherents.

This is the true and perfect Relation of all the Proceedings that have hapned since Thursday the 13. of *October*, till the 19. 1642.

The Parliaments Resolution Concerning all those that refuseth to bring in their Mony or Plate.

THat the Bishops in England being the chief Incendiaries of the present great distractions in England, and have imployed their Rents and Profits towards the maintainance of a Civill-Warre *in this Kingdome against the Parliament: The Profits and Revenews belonging to their severall Bishopricks shall be from henceforth sequestred, to be employed for the publike good and safety of the Kingdom.*

That all such as have refused to lend Money, Horse, or Plate, (being able) upon the Propositions, for the service of the King and Parliament, in this time of great extremitie, shall be disarmed; That thereby there may be a timely prevention, that they may not use their Armes to the prejudice of the Parliament, and the whole Kingdome.

FINIS.

CHAPTER VI.

BIRMINGHAM IN TRANSITION.

The Plague in Birmingham—Lord Macaulay's description of Birmingham—"Brummagem Groats"—The "restoration" of St. Martin's—The Gun trade—Birmingham guns supplied to the Government—The Leather trade—Birmingham trades in transition—Birmingham charity—Churches and sects in the seventeenth century.

From the ashes of the fires kindled by Prince Rupert in 1643, Birmingham seems to have steadily risen into prosperity as a manufacturing community whose wares rendered her famous throughout the kingdom.

But in the Black Year 1665, when the Great

Plague visited London and many other parts of the country, Birmingham did not escape the dreadful visitation. The infection is said to have been brought to the town in a box of clothes brought by a carrier, and lodged at an inn called the White Hart. Thereupon followed the usual melancholy scenes which always attended the ravages of this terrible scourge. Houses were desolate; silence reigned in the streets; and on many doors appeared the fatal sign of the presence of the plague,—a large red cross, and the words "Lord have mercy upon this House." The number of victims was so great that the churchyard was insufficient to contain them, and a large pit was dug on Ladywood Green, an acre of waste land near the present church (St. John's), which has since borne the name of "The Pest Ground."

ST. MARTIN'S CHURCH AFTER THE FIRST "RESTORATION."

But still the town grew and flourished. "Birmingham," says Lord Macaulay, "had not been thought of sufficient importance to return a member to Oliver's Parliament. Yet the manufacturers of Birmingham were already a busy and thriving race. They boasted that their hardware was highly esteemed, not indeed as now, at Pekin and Lima, at Bokhara and Timbuctoo, but in London, and even as far off as Ireland. They had acquired a less honourable name as coiners of bad money. In allusion to their spurious groats, some Tory wit had fixed on demagogues, who hypocritically affected zeal against Popery, the nickname of Birminghams. Yet in 1685 the population, which is now [1848] little less than two hundred thousand, did not amount to four thousand. Birmingham buttons were just beginning to be known: of Birmingham guns nobody had yet heard; and the place whence, two generations later, the magnificent editions of Baskerville went forth to astonish all the librarians of Europe, did not contain a single regular shop where a Bible or an almanack could be bought. On market days a bookseller named Michael Johnson, the father of the great Samuel Johnson, came over from Lichfield, and opened a stall for a few hours. This supply was long found equal to the demand."

The unenviable notoriety of Birmingham in the matter of base coinage, together with the part taken by our townsmen in the civil war, caused the town to become the butt of every court wit, and her name the synonym for every species of meanness and villany. Dryden says, in one of his prefaces, "The longest chapter in Deuteronomy has not curses enough for an Anti-Bromingham." In another place we read respecting Shaftesbury's medal, (1682),

"'Twas coined by stealth, *like groats at Birmingham.*"

Tom Brown refers to the same practice in his "Reasons for Mr. Bayes," [*i.e.* Dryden,] changing his Religion: "I coined heroes as fast as *Birmingham groats.*" The affected zeal for the Protestant religion on the part of the country party led to their being nicknamed *Birmingham Protestants.* In fact, the Whigs generally came in for the name of the midland hardware village, and "Whig and Birmingham," "Birminghams royal," "Birmingham pretences," and other uncomplimentary allusions of the same character are to be found scattered through many of the songs and other poetical emanations from Grub Street during the reign of James II.

But in all the base products of our town at that period, surely no worse example of "Brummagem" taste and skill was perpetrated than that of which the fine old church of St. Martin was the victim. We quoted, in our first chapter, a description of this noble fabric as it must have appeared when first completed; of its grace of form and wealth of colour; "a church," as Mr. Bunce truly says, "not unworthy of a town destined to become one of the greatest communities in the kingdom." It would appear, however, according to Hutton, that the stone used in the building of the church was of a soft, friable nature, and, he says, "the rough blasts of nine hundred years [?] had made inroads into the fabric." The churchwardens appear to have had no other idea of preserving the church than by entombing it in a hideous case of brick, which exquisite piece of workmanship was performed in the year 1690, under the direction of Thomas Gisburne and Edward Est, the churchwardens of that year. "They first dressed the church in brick,—tower, nave and chancel; the spire most likely would have been cased likewise, if the bricks could have conveniently been carried up."* "The whole fabric," says the writer just quoted, "was there buried in an ugly tomb, literally bricked up as if like unhappy *Constance* in 'Marmion' it had committed an inexpiable sin, and had received sentence of living death."† This supremely ugly structure remained, a disgrace to the town of which it was the "mother church," until 1872. Hutton's admiration of this piece of

* J. T. BUNCE: History of Old St. Martin's, p. 19.
† ib., p. 18.

work found utterance in a single sentence; "the bricks and the workmanship," he says, "are excellent;"—"commendation," says Mr. Bunce, "not unlike that of an inartistic Church dignitary who, being invited to admire a newly finished piece of sculpture, complimented the carver by saying that it was 'very large.'" The further mutilations which the building underwent previous to its complete demolition in 1872 will be noticed from time to time in their chronological sequence. The first, which we have just described, left the spire uninjured; the porch was also left, and the clerestory might still be seen, above the balustrade with which the nave roof was finished.

While, however, Birmingham gained an unenviable reputation abroad for base coinage, and perpetrated at home an example of base architecture almost unequalled, she still worked in a more honest manner too;—base groats did not form the staple article of manufacture, and the repute in which such goods were held did not altogether obscure the reputation she had earned for skilful workmanship of a more legitimate character. Alexander Missen says in his Travels (in 1690), that he saw at Milan "fine works of Rock Crystal, Swords, Heads for Canes, Snuff Boxes, and other fine works of steel; *but they can be had cheaper and better at Birmingham.*" And if Hutton may be credited, Birmingham enjoyed some little reputation even at Court, in the reign of William the Third. That monarch, he says, was once lamenting "That guns were not manufactured in his dominions, but that he was obliged to procure them from Holland at a great expence, and greater difficulty." One of the members for Warwickshire [Sir Richard Newdigate] being present, told the King "That genius resided in Warwickshire, and that he thought his constituents could answer his majesty's wishes." The king was pleased with the remark, and the member posted to Birmingham. Upon application to a person in Digbeth, whose name I forget, the pattern was executed with precision, which, when presented to the royal board, gave entire satisfaction."* But, from the correspondence on this subject first published in the admirable volume of reports on local products and resources, collected by the Local Industries Committee of the British Association, in 1865, and edited by Mr. Samuel Timmins,† it appears that the local gun trade was not *introduced* under the circumstances described by Hutton, but had existed long before. "The question," says the editor, "was not whether Birmingham should make guns, but whether they could be produced equal to the Government pattern sent down from London, and at a certain price."‡ Mr. Timmins concludes therefore that not only the sword trade but the gun trade also, had been introduced and carried on with much success long before the Revolution fn 1688.

The papers to which we have referred, being the first in which the gun trade of Birmingham is mentioned, will probably interest many of our readers, and we therefore, with the permission of the editor, reprint them here.

The first is a letter addressed by the War Department to Sir Richard Newdigate, and is as follows:—

For their Mats Service
To Sr Richard Newdigate
att Arbury
near
Warwick

These — —

Sr

Pursuant to an order of this Board, Wee have directed the sending to you by the Tamworth Carryer 2 snaphance Musquetts of differing sorts for patternes desireing you will please To cause them to be shewed to ye Birmingham Workemen and upon yor returne of their ability and readiness to undertake the making and ffixing them accordingly. Or the making Barrells or Locks only Together wth the tyme a sufficient Quantity of Barrells can be made in to answer the Trouble and charge of sending an Officer on purpose to prove the same according to the Tower proofe which is the Equall weight of powder to one of the Bullett alsoe sent you And their lowest price either for a compleat Musquett ready fixt or for a Barrell

* W. HUTTON: History of Birmingham, 1781, and later editions.

† The Resources, Products, and Industrial History of Birmingham and the Midland Hardware District: a Series of Reports . . . Edited by Samuel Timmins. 1866.—*Arts.* "The Industrial History of Birmingham," by the Editor, pp. 207-224; and "The Birmingham Gun Trade," by John D Goodman, pp. 381-431.

‡ ib. p. 211.

or a Lock distinct or togeather as they will undertake to make them. We shall thereupon cause further direction to be given as shall be most beneficiall for their Mats service with a thankfull acknowledgmt of yr great favour and trouble afforded us herein. We are

Sr

Office of Ordne — Your most humble Servs
10th of January, — CH. MYDDELTON,
1689.

T. GARDINER, JOS. CHARLTON, WM. BOULTER

(Note by the late Sr Roger Newdegate, Bart—
"Before, all the Guns for the Army were imported from Germany.")

"The term snaphance, used in this letter," says Mr. Goodman, "is thus explained by Grose in his Treatise on Ancient Armour and Weapons. He states that it is derived from the troops who made use of it. These were a set of marauders, whom the Dutch termed 'Snap-hans' or poultry stealers. The use of the match-lock exposed them, when on their marauding expeditions, to this inconvenience, that the light from the burning match pointed out their position. They were unable to provide themselves with wheel-lock guns on account of their expense. In this dilemma they formed the snaphance from a study of the wheel-lock. A flat piece of steel, furrowed in imitation of the wheel, was placed on a steel post, which was screwed beyond the pan, and made moveable. The furrowed piece being brought to stand over it, on pulling the trigger, the flint which was substituted for the pyrites in the cock, struck against it, and the spark was produced. The guns ordered from the Birmingham makers, although retaininng the name, were of course an improvement on the original snaphance, and were no doubt a near approach to the flint lock of modern times."*

A trial order was given, as the result of this example of the skill of Birmingham workmen, in March, 1692, followed by a further order, which we transcribe at full length :—

Contracted and agreed this fifth day of January Anno Dni 1693, and in the fifth year of the Reigne of our Soveraigne Lord and Lady King William and Queene Marye by the Grace of God of England, Scotland, France, and Ireland, Defenders of the faith &c. By virtue of an order of the Right Honble Henry Lord Viscount Sidney Master Genll of their Maties Ordnance and the Board 24th Novem Last Between the Honble the principal Officers of the same on their Maties behalfe of the one part and William Bourne, Tho. Moore, John West, Richd Weston and Jacob Austin of Birmingham in the County of Warwick Gun Smithesof the part as folls, viz.—

Imprimis, The said William Bourne, Tho. Moore, John West, Richd Weston and Jacob Austin do Hereby severally Covenant and agree to and wth the said principall Officers of their Maties Ordnance on their behalfe of themselves and the rest of the Gun-makers of Birmingham that they shall and will make and provide for their Maties Service two hundred Snaphance Musquets every Month for the space of one Yeare from the Expiration of their last Contract Bearing Date the six and twentieth day of March 1692. To be three foot ten inches long, with Wallnutt-tree and Ash Stocks. And that one half of the said Musquets shall have flatt locks engraven, and the other half Round Locks and that all of them shall have brass pipes cast and brass heel plates and all the stocks varnished, and to have six Good thrids in the Breech screws, and that all the said Gun Stocks shall be made well and Substantiall and none of them Glewed.

And also that the said Musquet Barrells shall be Compleatly filed before they are provel and that they shall be proved at Birmingham according to the Tower proofe and a fitt person (who shall be impowered by this Office) shall inspect the same and marke them wth the Office Marke, and (when finished) to survey them. And that powder and bullets shall be provided and sent down at the Charge of this Office for the proofe of the said Armes.

And the said principall officers of their Maties Ordnance (for and on the Maties behalfe) doe agree wth the said William Bourne, Thomas Moore, John West, Richd Weston, and Jacob Austin in behalfe of themselves and the rest of the Gun Makers of Birmingham, that they shall be paid for the said Armes in manner following, viz., for every one hundred severall Armes after the Rate of seaventeene shillings per piece ready money by way of debenture wth in one week after the delivery thereof into their Maties stores in the tower of London or Any other place within this kingdome, as the Board shall order and direct, and also that they shall be paid and allowed three shillings for the carriage of every one hundred weight from Birmingham to the tower and so proportionally to any other place And that the money shall be paid to them without any charge or trouble as they shall direct and Returne the same from time to time to Birmingham.

In Witness whereof the said parties to these prnts Interchangeably have set their hands and seals the day and year first above written

Sealed and delivered — THO : LITTELTON (Sigillum)

in the presence of — JO : CHARLTON (Sigillum)

WILL PHELPS — WM. BOULTER (Sigillum)

* Midland Hardware District, p. 409.

PHOTOGRAPHED BY THRUPP.

BIRMINGHAM: HOUGHTON AND HAMMOND, SCOTLAND PASSAGE.

Among the other early trades for which Birmingham had become noted was that of the manufacture of leather. "It may seem singular to a modern eye," says Hutton, "to view this place in the light of one vast tan-yard. Though there is no appearance of that necessary article among us, yet Birmingham was once a famous market for leather. Digbeth not only abounded with tanners, but large numbers of hides arrived weekly for sale, where the whole country found a supply. When the weather would allow, they were ranged in columns in the High-street, and at other times deposited in the Leather Hall, at the East end of New-street, appropriated for their reception."

STRATFORD HOUSE. (See page 54.)

But at the period at which we have now arrived in our history,—the close of the seventeenth century,—the trade had declined, and early in the next century was almost forgotten, save for the annual election of two officers called "leather-sealers," whose duty it had been in former days to mark the vendible hides, but had then, says our quaint historian, "no duty but that of taking an elegant dinner." When Hutton published his History, in 1781, shops had been erected upon the tan-vats, the Leather-hall had gone to destruction, and the town was reduced, he says, to one solitary tanner.

This was, in fact, the real transition period in our local history. Our trades, as well as the appearance of the town, (to which we shall refer more particularly in our next chapter,) underwent a great change during the closing years of the seventeenth century.

"Though she had before held a considerable degree of eminence," says Hutton, "yet at this period, the curious arts began to take root, and were cultivated by the hand of genius. Building leases, also, began to take effect, extension followed, and numbers of people crowded upon each other, as into a Paradise. . . . But . . . we have only seen her in infancy. Comparatively small in her size, homely in her person, and coarse in her dress. Her ornaments, wholly of iron, from her own forge.

"But now, her growths will be amazing; her expansion rapid, perhaps not to be paralleled in history. We shall see her rise in all the beauty of youth, of grace, of elegance, and attract the notice of the commercial world. She will also add to her iron ornaments, the lustre of every metal that the whole earth can produce, with all their illustrious race of compounds, heightened by fancy, and garnished with jewels. She will draw from the fossil, and the vegetable kingdoms; press the ocean for shell, skin, and coral. She will also tax the animal, for horn, bone, and ivory, and she will decorate the whole with the touches of her pencil."

The change which thus took place in our trades would have a marked effect both upon the town and its inhabitants. From being merely smiths and workers of the coarser kind they became skilled and cunning artificers, with some degree of artistic taste, and this would doubtless have an effect upon the appearance of the town. They would be more careful as to their own houses, and as they would earn considerably higher wages than their fathers who worked in coarser materials, they would be able to bestow more expense in making their homes comfortable. Thus the greater prosperity of the people would be reflected in the improved appearance of the town; and so began the new era, the *modern*, as distinguished from the *ancient* history of Birmingham.

"During the seventeenth and eighteenth centuries," says Mr. Timmins, "the progress of Birmingham manufactures was simply marvellous. Our town seemed to have the power of attracting within its boundaries artisans of every trade and every degree of skill. Although not situated on any of the great highways of the land, it was near enough to be easily accessible. It awarded almost perfect freedom to all who chose to come. Dissenters and Quakers and heretics of all sorts were welcomed and undisturbed, so far as their religious observances were concerned. No trades unions, no trade gilds, no companies existed, and every man was free to come and go, to found or to follow or to leave a trade just as he chose. The system of apprenticeship was only partially known, and Birmingham became emphatically the town of 'free trade,' where practically no restrictions, commercial or municipal, were known. Coal and iron were easily obtainable from the growing mines and iron works of Staffordshire, and every facility was afforded by such proximities, and by the numerous water mills and the central position of the town, for the rapid extension of the hardware trades."

In their prosperity the people of Birmingham do not seem to have been deaf to the cries for help which came to them from their suffering brethren in various parts of the country. From a very curious manuscript book in two volumes, described as "The Town Book," discovered in St. Martin's Church during the process of demolition, Mr. Bunce, in his history of that church, makes a number of exceedingly interesting extracts, and among those of the earliest period (from 1676 to the close of the seventeenth century) are numerous memoranda of various sums collected for charitable and other purposes. Under date June 6, 1679, is an entry of £2. 18s., "collected for a fier at Weedon Northampton Sheer and for Lorgyon in the South of Wilts Sheer;" on the 2nd of May, 1680, £1. 6s. 5d. was collected "for Sufferers by a ffier at Wolston," and on the 30th of the same month a like sum, all but one penny, was collected "for Sufferers by ffyre at Edghll in the county of Salop." Fires would seem to have been pretty numerous at that time, and perhaps the warm hearts which beat within the sturdy frames of the artizans of the hardware village had become widely known, for they do not appear ever to have been appealed to in vain, for during 1682-3 there are entries of sums collected for the relief of "sufferers by ffier" at "Leamington Priors," Snitterfield, Ensham, in Oxfordshire, Stoats by Clure, (Suffolk), "Preston Caudeer in County of Souttanptn," Collumpton, (Devon), Bradneck, (Devon), Channell Row, Westminster, Bassingbourne, and several other towns in which, although fire is not named, this was probably the calamity from which the inhabitants suffered. Again in April, 1684, a collection was made "for poore distressed ffamylys of the Towne of Alrewors who lost ye houses & estates by fire;" and throughout the century other similar entries occur. "A fellow-feeling makes one wondrous kind;" and perhaps the reason for this special commiseration felt by our townsmen for all sufferers by fire may be found in the fact that they had not yet forgotten their own sufferings when Prince Rupert manifested his Burning Love for England, in Birmingham's Flames.

From the charity of our forefathers to their religion is an easy and natural transition, and we may therefore, perhaps, appropriately pause here in our narrative to take a survey of the churches and sects, as they existed in the town during the latter half of the seventeenth century. According to Hutton, the spiritual needs of the worshippers at St. Martin's were ill-provided for during the protectorate of Oliver Cromwell. "One Samuel Slater, a broken-down apothecary, having," he says, "been unsuccessful in curing the body, resolved to attempt curing the soul. He therefore, to repair his misfortunes, assumed the clerical character, and cast an eye on the rectory of St. Martin's; but he had many powerful opponents; among others were Jennens, an ironmaster, possessor of Aston furnace; Smallbroke, another wealthy inhabitant; and Sir Thomas Holte. However, he, with difficulty, triumphed over his enemies, stepped into the pulpit, and held the rectory till the Restoration."*

He seems to have carried his irreverence into the pulpit with him, if Hutton is to be credited,—though the somewhat clumsy pleasantry sounds not a little like Hutton's own,—remarking, in his first sermon that "the Lord had carried him through many troubles; for he had passed like Shedrach, [*sic.*] Meschach, and Abednego, through the *fiery furnace.* And as the Lord had enabled the Children of Israel to pass over the Red Sea, so he had assisted him in passing over the *Small-brooks*, and to overcome the strong *Holts* of sin and Satan."†

"At the restoration," continues Hutton, "suspecting the approach of the proper officers, to expel him from the parsonge house, he crept into a hiding-place, under the stairs; but, being discovered, was drawn out by force, and the place ever after bore the name of *Slater's Hole.*"

In 1665 the living was conferred upon John Riland, Archdeacon of Coventry; of whose character the following description is given by his son:—"He was very constant in his meditations and devotions, both public and private, which he delivered with such plainness and simplicity of speech and deportment, that there was not the least appearance of any unnatural and forced flights and enthusiastic raptures. There was such a strict and universal holiness in his life and conversation, that he is now called in Birmingham 'that holy man.' He was so very affable and humble that he never passed by any one without some particular regard and friendly salutation. He was such a lover of peace that he labored much for it; and when he could not persuade those that were at variance to abate anything of the height of their demands, he many times deposited the money out of his own pocket that he might make one of two contending parties. He was so charitable that he carried about a poor-box with him, and never reckoned himself poor but when that was empty; and it

* Hutton, sixth edition, pp. 253-4. † ib. p. 254.

was not a single charity he gave them, because he not only fed their bodies, but their souls; for when he gave them a dole of bread in the church, he called them together, and then framed a discourse to them, particularly suited to their circumstances. Indeed his exhortations on these occasions were so excellent and edifying, that several of the chief inhabitants came to hear them, and went away, as well satisfied with these, as the poor with the bread." He died at Birmingham in 1672, and was buried in St. Martin's, where a monument was placed to his memory, with a Latin inscription, which is thus translated by Colvile, in his "Worthies of Warwickshire":—

"Sacred to the memory of John Riland (as well as to his dearest wife Cicely, and only daughter, Maria) Archdeacon of Coventry, and minister of the parish, as well as its highest ornament; who corrected unbelief and fanaticism and all the evils of this depraved age, not so much by his writings and sermons, although with spirit in these too, as by the constant and unbending course of an unblameable life. Having in youth, completed an exemplary pupilage at Magdalen College, Oxford, he was speedily elected a Fellow of that Society, and, after a life spent in various places and regions, suffering from the ingratitude of the times, here he settled at last, and here he died in the 53rd year of his age—March 3rd, in the year of our Lord 1672."

"A succeeding rector, William Daggett," says Hutton, "is said to have understood the art of boxing, better than that of preaching: his clerk often felt the weightier argument of his hand. Meeting a Quaker, whose profession, then in infancy, did not stand high in esteem, he offered some insults, which the other resenting, told him, 'If he was not protected by his cloth, he would make him repent the indignity.' Daggett immediately stripped, 'There, now I have thrown off my protection.'—They fought; but the spiritual bruiser proved too hard for the injured Quaker."

From a Terrier of the Rectory, written by this Mr. Daggett, Hutton estimates the value of the living at that time at about £90 per annum.

In 1662, the Act of Uniformity was passed, and, as Birmingham, not being a corporate town, was exempt from the operation of the "Five Mile Act," (which prohibited nonconforming ministers from coming within five miles of any corporate town, or of the place where they had exercised their ministry,) it became a place of refuge for many of those brave men who preferred to sacrifice their livings rather than do violence to the dictates of their conscience, and here they worshipped God, in secret, in the manner which best accorded with their own convictions, from house to house, often in danger of persecution and imprisonment, yet braving all peril and danger for the cause of religious freedom. In 1672, an indulgence was granted, and the first room licensed for public worship, the preacher being an ejected minister of Cheshire, Samuel Fisher, formerly pastor of Thornton-in-the-Moor, in that county. In 1689, the Act of Toleration was passed, which revoked the penalties against attending "conventicles," and for the first time permitted Protestant Dissenters to worship God according to their own conscience, and made it penal for anyone to enter a meeting house for the purpose of molesting the worshippers; and immediately after the passing of this act the Dissenters of Birmingham built for themselves a Meeting House,—the first Dissenting

OLD MEETING HOUSE.

Chapel erected in Birmingham,—on the site of the place of worship which still bears the name of "the Old Meeting House," at the back of Worcester Street, the first minister being the Rev. W. Turton, who had previously officiated in the licensed room since the year 1686. Three years after the building of the first meeting house, the number of nonconformists in the town had so increased that a second society was formed, and another meeting house opened in Digbeth, in 1692, with a Mr. Sillitoe as minister. Of the disturbances of which these two places of worship have been the scene, we shall have to speak in future chapters, as also of the eminent divines who have from time to time ministered therein. Suffice here to say that this second church has enjoyed the ministrations of Joseph Priestley, of John Kentish, and Joshua Toulmin, and of many other eminent, learned, and devoted pastors, of whom we shall make mention hereafter.

Among others who benefited by the Act of Toleration, beside the ejected ministers of 1662, were the members of the newly-formed "Society of Friends," commonly called Quakers. The earliest record of the existence of this society in Birmingham, according to Hutton, is in 1682, but our historian is of opinion that they had existed as a society here for some years previous to that date. They probably met from house to house during the seventeenth and the earlier part of the eighteenth century.

The Roman Catholics had a place of worship near the present church of St. Bartholomew, as still indicated by the name of Masshouse Lane. From the very interesting and trustworthy Guide to Birmingham,* compiled by Mr. William Bates, B.A., we learn that the first stone of this building was laid by Brother Lee, of St. Mary Magdalen, *alias* Randolph, of the Holy Order of St. Francis, on the 23rd of March, 1687; and the church was consecrated on the 4th of September, 1688, by Bishop Giffard of Mandura, a favourite of James II. The church was dedicated to St. Marie Magdalen, and contained three altars: the high altar, in honour of God and St. Marie Magdalen; the north altar, in honour of God and the Blessed Lady; and the south, in honour of God and the Holy Father St. Francis. A convent was also erected adjoining the north-west corner of the church; and the entire cost of the buildings (amounting to £1,281. 2s. 5d.) was raised by subscriptions and donations. James II. gave 125 tons of timber from Needwood Forest; Sir John Gage gave timber valued at £140; Mrs. Ann Gregg gave £250; and the Dowager Queen Catherine gave £10. 15s.

But these costly buildings were not destined to remain long. The storm which burst forth against the King and the Catholics in 1688—the year in which the Birmingham Church and Convent were erected—was felt here as elsewhere, and on the 26th of November, little more than two months after the consecration, the church and part of the convent was defaced, and the interior burnt, to the value of £400, by the orders of Lord Delamere. Seven days later, "the rude hands of irreligion" (as Hutton terms them) finished the work of destruction, ceasing only when they had destroyed the very foundations of the building. Subsequently the Roman Catholics erected a small chapel at Edgbaston, which, after its disuse by that body, still retained the name of the *Mass-house.*

There were, therefore, before the close of the seventeeth century, no less than six "churches" or religious societies in Birmingham, (without counting any of the suburban churches belonging to the Establishment,) viz.: St. Martin's, St. John's Chapel, Deritend, the first Presbyterian Church, on the western side of St. Martin's, and the second on the south-eastern side, the Quakers, and the Roman Catholics.

* A Pictorial Guide to Birmingham: Being a Concise, Historical and Descriptive, Account of the great Midland Metropolis. . . . Birmingham: Josiah Allen and Son, 1849. p. 59.

CHAPTER VII.

APPEARANCE OF THE TOWN—1660-1700.

Birmingham in 1660—Number of streets—The Old Ship Inn—Stratford House—Deritend and Digbeth—St. Martin's Church—The Market Cross—The High Town—New Street—The Beast Market—Bull Street—The Welsh End—The Old Cross—St. Martin's Rectory—The Moat- Alterations and Additions between 1660 and 1700—Early visits of "the strollers."

HUTTON, in his History, quotes from an anonymous author who wrote in 1743, an observation to the effect that "Birmingham, at the Restoration, probably consisted only of three streets." Our historian is, however, of opinion that it consisted probably of fifteen, which he enumerates, and that there were at that time about nine hundred houses. It may be, however, that the earlier writer considered Deritend and Bordesley, Digbeth, Well Street, the Corn Market and Shambles, as one street, High Street and Spicer (Spiceal) Street as the second, and Edgbaston Street, St. Martin's Lane, and Park Street as the third;* regarding the few houses on the various roads out of the town, and the short off-shoots on either side of those three thoroughfares, as not worthy to be designated streets; and if that be the case the two estimates will not differ very widely. Hutton's fifteen streets comprised Digbeth, Moat Lane (called also Court Lane), the Corn Market and Shambles, Spiceal Street, (sometimes called *Mercer* and sometimes *Spicer* Street,) Dudley Street, Bell Street, Philip Street, St. Martin's Lane, Edgbaston Street, Lee's Lane, Park Street, (from Digbeth nearly to Freeman Street,) Moor Street, (as far as Castle Street,) Bull Street, (not so high as the Minories,) High Street, and Deritend and Bordesley. But some of these could scarcely have been worthy of the name of streets so early as 1660.

Probably the first house the traveller reached (entering the town from the same point as Leland did) would be the Old Ship Inn, the traditional head-quarters of Prince Rupert, in 1643. On the rising ground to the left, near to the position taken up by the townsmen in their attack on the Royalist forces, he would see the quaint old half-timbered "Stratford House," from which the fierce struggle on that Easter Monday afternoon might have been watched, not without fear, perhaps, of the "burning love" of the Cavalier Prince. Few other houses would be passed until he reached the "Old Crown." He then enters the "pretty street" called Deritend, passing St. John's Chapel on the left; crosses the river Rea by the old bridge,—with its recesses to enable foot-passengers to take refuge out of the way of any passing vehicle,—and reaches Digbeth,* which then commenced from the Birmingham side of the bridge. Deritend and Digbeth still together form the most picturesque street in the town, with their many windings, and quaint old half-timbered houses,—and we can form no better idea of the appearance of old Birmingham than by passing along this, the real "old town." Our traveller, proceeding up Digbeth, and, after passing these picturesque old houses, would enter Cock Street, or Well Street, as the upper part of Digbeth was then called, (the latter name from the same circumstance as "Digbeth,") from which he would soon reach St. Martin's Church,—not yet desecrated by the ugly brick encasement, but much weatherworn and dilapidated,—and passing the eastern end of it, along the "Corn Cheaping," through the Shambles, (which occupied the place of the present Bull Ring,) and by the old Market Cross, he

* *See* facsimile of Westley's map.

* *Duck's Bath*,—so called from an excellent spring of soft water at the upper end of the street.

would reach the "High Town," the portion of High Street below the end of what was afterwards called New Street, but which was then merely the Stourbridge road, and contained few buildings except the old Free School, of timber, (formerly the Hall of the Gild of the Holy Cross,) and the Leather Hall, both of which were at the High Street end. Beyond that point the thoroughfare (according to Westley's map) was called the Beast Market, and, if Hutton is right in his conjecture, the traveller would find a few houses dotted here and there along Bull Street at the nearest end of the town, although in all probability "Bull Street" was not known by name, being perhaps merely the road out of town to Wolverhampton and Walsall, along which the armed townsmen, under Captain Greaves, were pursued by the Earl of Denbigh, in 1643. There would also be a few houses at the beginning of Dale End, (as we gather from the first of the Civil War tracts,) the upper part of which is called in Westley's map "Broad Street" At the junction of these roads, which had long been called the "Welsh End," the Welsh Cross was afterwards built, and further along the Coleshill road, at the point at which the Stafford road (afterwards called "The Butts," or "Stafford Street,") branched off, was an older cross of the simplest form: a plain stone pillar with short cross-piece, resting on a rude pedestal. We now (accompanying our seventeenth-century traveller on his itinerary through the town) retrace our steps as far as the Market Cross, passing by the *western* end of St. Martin's this time, down Mercer or Spicer

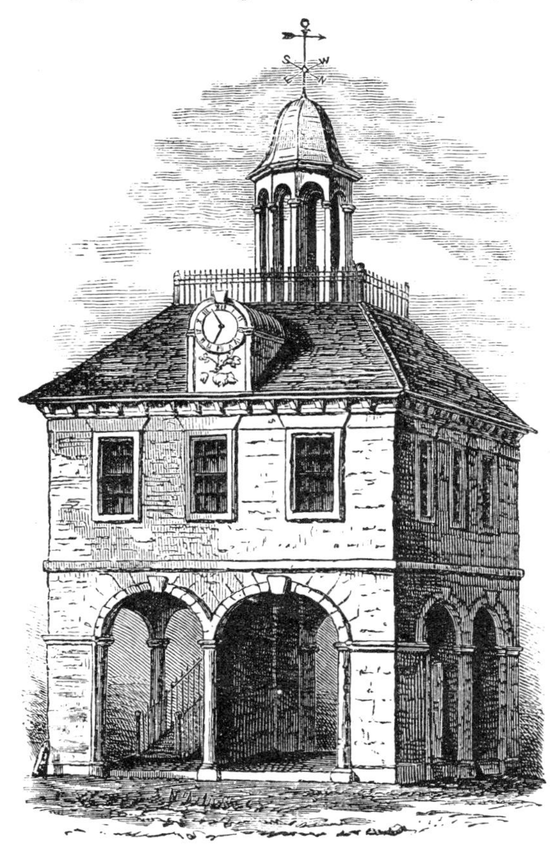

MARKET CROSS.

Street. It was originally called Mercer Street, from the number of mercers' shops; and as the members of that trade dealt also in grocery, it was promiscuously called Spicer Street, which afterwards became corrupted into Spiceal Street. Turning to the right, along Edgbaston Street, our traveller would speedily find himself on the western outskirts of the town, one of the last houses probably being St. Martin's Rectory, an ancient half-timbered house, surrounded by a moat, pleasantly situated opposite the end of the road now called Dudley Street. If our itinerant retraced his steps, and passed down St. Martin's Lane, on the south side of the church, he would, by turning to the right, down Moat or Court Lane, immediately come to the moat surrounding the ancient manorial residence of the Lords of Birmingham, and would thus have completed his survey of the town.

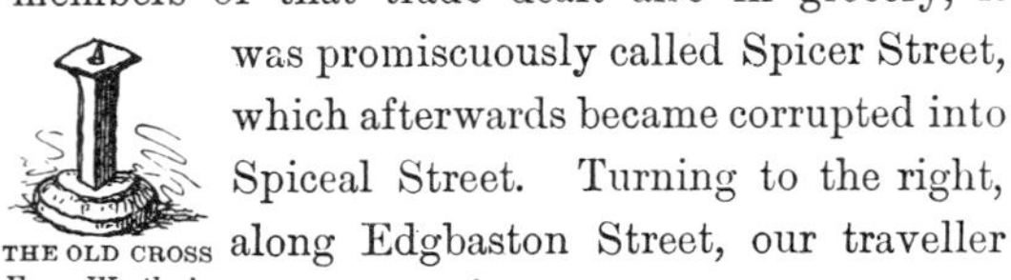
THE OLD CROSS
From Westley's Plan, 1731.

If the traveller, whom we have imagined taking a survey of the town immediately after the restoration, had returned at the close of the century, he would have found considerable changes in its appearance and extent. St. Martin's Church, in its ugly red brick casing, newly finished, would strike him as being anything but an improvement upon the grey crumbling walls of the fine old church of thirty or forty years ago; nor would the two meeting houses of the most unpretending order of architecture which had arisen since his last visit compensate him for the loss of the old church. He would find at least seven new streets, and—if Hutton's calculation is right as to the number of houses at the restoration—nearly three times as many houses. Since he last saw this hive of busy workers, their number had increased threefold; there were, in the year 1700, upwards of fifteen thousand inhabitants. Between High Street, New Street, Edgbaston Street, and Dudley Street, (around the principal Meeting House,) had grown up quite a new town, with several streets intersecting it, among them Old Meeting Street, Colmore Street, and The Froggary. New Street had probably grown at least as far as Peck Lane, and Bull Street as far as the Minories. Going out in the direction of Coleshill, the houses would now extend almost to the Old Cross, while much of the ground between the part of High Street called the Beast Market and Moor Street would be filled up with dwellings. In the town itself, there would be fewer open spaces at the back of the houses which lined the streets, for there were now one hundred courts and alleys. But there were still green fields and pleasant gardens within easy access on every side. The upper end of Moor Street, and all the land below Park Street, was yet under cultivation or used as grazing land. Behind the fringe of houses which shut in High Street from the country on the north-eastern side of the town, fields and gardens stretched out, across which one might look as far as New Hall, which was situated on the crown of the hill now covered by Mount Street and Graham Street. St. Philip's Church was yet unthought of, and the pleasant grassy knoll which was afterwards called Bennett's Hill was far away from the smoke and bustle of the town and the sound of the anvil.

The busy inhabitants had probably by this time begun to taste the pleasures of theatrical entertainments. Occasionally a rude shed of boards in the fields now called Temple Street became the temporary abode of various companies of strolling players. It is not probable that such performers ever attempted anything higher than the "Drolls," of which a number of examples are to be found in a curious book compiled by Francis Kirkman, and published in 1672, called "The Wits, or Sport upon Sport." But among these drolleries were several of the choicest comic scenes from the plays of Shakespeare. "The Humours of Bottom the Weaver," and "The Droll of the Grave makers," (the famous Graveyard Scene from *Hamlet*,) may perhaps have been among those rude performances which delighted our forefathers in the simple shed which did duty for a theatre on that hill-side field which is now in the heart of the great modern city.

CHAPTER VIII.

A PEEP INTO THE OLD TOWN BOOKS.

Sale of reserved sittings in St. Martin's Church—"Utensils and vessells belonging to the Church"—Recasting of the bells—Their several Weights—The Market Cross—The "Royal Touch"—Drums and Colours for Birmingham—Custody of the Fire Engine—Necessity of a Chamber for public meetings—A room built over the Cross—The Welsh Cross—Temple Row.

HAVING glanced in our last chapter at the appearance and extent of the town during the later years of the seventeenth century, it may be interesting now to refer once more to the old Town Books mentioned in our sixth chapter, and by their aid to take a peep at the doings of the inhabitants during the same period.

We begin at Church. In that sacred edifice, even at that early period, the warning of St. James had already begun to be neglected, and the best seats were reserved for those who could afford to pay for them. It is true the sum which entitled the worshipper to one of the favoured seats was not high, the charge being, as appears from these interesting records, fourpence for each sitting. "The Account of those persons that were entered by John Allen and John Walloxall, Churchwardens for the yeare 1676, into Seats in the Church," states that on June 3rd, fourpence was received "of Mr Hurse for his wife's seat," and a like sum from each of the following, during the same year: of Thomas Day "for William Edgleys place," of Richard Bellingsley "for his wifes place being the widow Bakers," "of Mary Cooke for her Mother Alice Graves place," of Richard Lewis "for to reserve his wifes place," of Tobit Manwaring "for his wifes place," and of William Doley, "for his wifes place in the 27 pew in the Middle Aisle." In the next year, 1677, the first receipt is "for Mr. Gregorys place in the new South loft next the pulpitt," the intending new occupant being a Mr. Richard Scott; there are many others during the year, and from the positions in the church being in most cases indicated, they possess more general interest than those of 1676. One of these is for five places (the amount being as usual fourpence for each sitting, without reduction in consideration of the quantity), the sum of one shilling and eightpence being received "of Jonathan Newman and his wife and Benjamin Hawkes and Thomas Townsend and William ———* for 5 places in a seat they have builded it being the hindermost seat between the West Dore and the Staires directly behind William Greaves seat." Later on is a quaint entry of the receipt of the usual amount from John Crumpton "for his Mothers place in the Middle Ile. pew behind the pulpitt by consent of his Mother." The next receipt is from one of the churchwardens named at the commencement of the entries, John Walloxall, "for a place in the New Seats behind the South door at the going up of the Staires that goes up into the west loft for his man to sit in, he being the Churchwarden." His successor, it would appear, built a seat for himself, but honestly debited himself with the usual charge for sittings in the church. The entry is as follows:

> "Nov 7 1678 George Abell and Richard Whyle being then Churchwardens found a vacant place in the Church before the seates where William Greaves did Sitt Richard Whyle at his own cost and charge did build a seat there by consent of his partener joining to the comon Seate for the Churchwardens over against the font, under the old loft for himself and a sonne to set in, and doth accompt to the Towne according to the Custom of the Towne for the grownde . . . . 0 0 8"

* Name undecipherable.

On the 22nd of April, 1682, is recorded the transfer, from the retiring Churchwardens to those newly appointed, of "these utensils and vessells belonging to the Church."

"2 Comunion Cupps with their Covers & Cases
4 Pewter fflagons
2 pewter plats to gather money in
4 trenchors
a Lynnen & a Brancht Carpet for ye Comunion Table
1 Cushon
20 New Leathorne Bucketts
(they will not take charge of Bucketts.)"

THE WELSH CROSS.

The receipt of these articles is duly acknowledged by the new wardens, Samuel Banner and John Rogers, during whose year of office the six bells, then comprising the only peal in Birmingham, were recast, the several weights being entered in the Town Book as follows:

	c.	qs.	l.
"1 Bell wayd	6	3	5
2 Bell	7	1	2
3 Bell	8	3	23
4 Bell	10	0	8
5 Bell	12	1	24
6 Bell	17	3	9
in all	63	1	15"

We have seen, in our former extracts from these books, the willingness of the people of Birmingham to give of their substance to aid those who had suffered from disastrous fires; but while they appear at all times to have gladly responded to appeals of this kind, they were also willing to assist others—and even those of other countries—in distress. On "July ye 17t 1682" was "collected in the Toune of Birmingham by Letters Patent for the persecuted Protestants of ffrance,

£12 15s. 0d." But the inhabitants did not, in their liberality towards others, forget their own town and its necessities. The Market Cross needed to be repaired: a new roof was necessary, and a collection was made for that purpose, the result of which is thus recorded:—

"Recd the 19 June 1683 of the Inhabitants of the Toune the sum of Six pounds fourteen Shillings and Eleven pence towards the Leading of ye Cross.
wetness my hand Wm W. B. Bridgman
wh was pd by our consent
wetness our hands
Geo ffentham
Tho Flentwell
Samuel Tayler
George Abell
William Guest
Ambrose Leay
Thomas Birch"

The next entry recalls an old superstition:

"March 14t 1683 Elizabeth daughter of John and Anne Dickens of Birmingham in the County of Warwick was certefied for in order to obtayne his Majesty's Touch for her cure
Henr Grove Minister
John Birch } Churchwardens"
Heny Porter }

Not many years afterwards, the poor afflicted little son of the Lichfield bookseller, Michael Johnson, (of whose weekly bookstall in Birmingham our readers have already heard) paid his first visit to the metropolis which he afterwards loved so well, for the same purpose. He was 'touched' by Queen Anne, and although only thirty months old at the time, retained throughout his life "a confused, but somehow a sort of solemn recollection of a lady in diamonds, and a long black hood."

In 1692, Birmingham would appear to have become ambitious of martial display. Amongst the disbursements of that year is an entry of one to "Jhon Court, for Drums & Collors" (colours), £3 18s 6d., and in the receipts is one "for Drums and Cullors for Bir." £24 19s. 6d.

Under date May 7th, 1695, is an agreement with a William Burn "to keep the Engine in order and to play it 4 times every year, and the Churchwardens are to give him Twenty Shillings a yeare for the same."

With drums and colours, and a fire engine, still Birmingham was "not happy." The people needed a room in which to hold public meetings, and almost as soon as the eighteenth century had dawned the sum of £47 15s. 3d. was subscribed for the repairing of the Market Cross, and "making a roome over it." In the March of 1703 this room was nearly finished, and the following entry occurs as to the purposes for which it is to be used:

"March ye 22 1703. Wheras there is a Room nearly built over that which is the Butter Cross (the account and charge I have of it is on the other side), itts this day ordered and agreed by vs whose names are vnder written that the key & letting theare of to the best advantage shall be in the power of the Constables ffor the time being, they reserving ffor all publick meetings for the use of the inhabitants, and what advantage is made thereof they shall account for when they give upp there other accounts to the Towne."

In the next year is the first entry of a meeting in the new Chamber:

"Sept. 19 1704. It was then agreed at a meeting at the Chamber over the Cross the Constable Churchwardens and overseers being psent, That for the future noe money shall be spent on the publick account upon any day of Public Rejoycing unless the officer first call a publick meeting at the said Chamber, in order to have the Consent of the Inhabitants unless particular direction shall be given by the Deputy Lieutent Justices of the peace or others in anthority for that purpose."

Where public meetings had previously been held we do not know, but there is an entry in the books of one having been held before the finishing of the Cross Chamber.

"April 7th 1702 Its this day ordered att a Public meeting of the Parishonrs of Birmingham That the Twenty pence that hath used to be paid to the Churchwardens for the Ringing the Bell to any funerall shall not be paid for the future by any person."

The Welsh Cross would appear to have been built in the year 1706, as on the 16th of February in that year "it was ordered that the Constables shall disburse the sum of 18. 12. 0 towards the finishing of the Welch Cross and Chamber over the same." There were therefore now two Chambers in the town in which meetings might be held, but in neither of them was there sufficient accommodation, one would imagine, for anything like a representative town's meeting, even with the comparatively small population of that period.

The next entry of general interest relates to the new Church of St. Philip, a description of which will form the subject of our next chapter.

"1715 Whereas it is thought proper by most of the principal inhabitants of the Town of Birmingham in the County of Warwick that a more Convenient way or passage should be purchased out of Bull Street to the New Church in Birmingham aforesaed Called St. Phillips And whereas at a parech Meeting of the p^{t} [present] principal Inhabitants this day appointed to consult thereupon It appears that a convenient way or place may be purchased, such purchas is ordered."

"This 'passage,'" says Mr. Bunce, "is no doubt the present Temple Row."

We may now leave the Town Books for the present. The few remaining entries of interest in the first book will be referred to in the course of our story, as illustrating the growth of our public buildings, and at a later period we may take a peep at the second book, in the beginning of which for the first time are entered (in addition to those of St. Martin's) the names of the Churchwardens of the Church of St. Philip.

CHAPTER IX.

THE CHURCH IN PROSPERITY, AND "THE CHURCH IN DANGER."

Necessity for a new church—The site of St. Philip's—William Hutton on religious donations—The church built—Description of the building—"The church in danger"—Dr. Sacheverell in Birmingham—His sermon at Sutton Coldfield, and its effects—Riots in Birmingham—Attack on the Meeting Houses.

The rapid growth of the town during the closing years of the seventeenth century and the early part of the eighteenth, rendered it impossible for the single parish church to accommodate the increasing number of the parishioners, and an Act of Parliament was obtained in 1711 (7th Anne) for building a new parish church and parsonage, and making a new parish and a new churchyard in Birmingham, the land being given by Robert Phillips, Esq., an ancestor of the Inge family. It was formerly part of a farm, and bore the name of the Horse Close, afterwards Barley Close. "Thus," says our quaint historian, "a benign spot of earth gave additional spirits to a man while living, and kindly covered him in its bosom when dead." This spot is the summit of the highest eminence in the town, and was stated in a report of the British College of Physicians, published about thirty years ago, to be level with the top of the cross of St. Paul's, London; and is, according to Fullarton's Directory, 475 feet above sea-level.

Some of Hutton's remarks on religious donations (*apropos* of the gift of the land for St. Philip's) are worth quoting here on account of their quaint half-cynical humour. "Sometimes," he says, "we assign our property for religious uses late in the evening of life, when *enjoyment* is over, and almost *possession*. Thus we bequeath to piety what we can keep no longer. We convey our name to posterity at the expense of our successor, and scaffold our way towards heaven up the walls of a steeple. Will charity chalk up one additional score in our favour,

THE NORTH PROSPECT OF ST. PHILIP'S CHURCH, &c., IN BIRMINGHAM.
From the print by W. Westley, 1732.

because we grant a small portion of our land to found a church, which enables us to augment the remainder treble its value, by granting building leases?"

The land given by Robert Phillips for the new Church and Churchyard was at that time quite outside the town, the nearest buildings at that time being those in Bull Street. The building was commenced in 1711, under a Commission, consisting of twenty of the neighbouring gentry appointed, in accordance with the provisions of the Act of Parliament, by the bishop of the diocese; their commission ending twelve months after the erection of the church. The building was not finished until 1719, having occupied eight years in its erection, but was consecrated in 1715, and dedicated to St. Philip, thus, as Hutton puts it, joining the donor's name in partnership with a saint in order to perpetuate his (the donor's) memory, and share with the saintly patron a red letter in the almanack.

"When I first saw St. Philip's, in the year 1741," says our pleasant chatty historian, "at a proper distance, uncrowded with houses, for there were none to the north, New Hall excepted, untarnished with smoke, and illuminated by a western sun, I was delighted with its appearance, and thought it then, what I do now, and what others will in future, *the pride of the place.* If we assemble the beauties of the edifice, which cover a rood of ground; the spacious area of the churchyard, occupying four acres, ornamented with walks in great perfection, shaded with trees in double and treble ranks, and surrounded with buildings in elegant taste; perhaps its equal cannot be found in the British dominions."

The architectural character of this beautiful structure is Italian, consisting of a pedestal line of good height, a range of lofty Doric pilasters, enclosing the large and well-proportioned windows, and a handsome balustrade, which was subsequently surmounted by a row of urns, in the year 1756 (during the wardenship of John Baskerville, the famous printer); but these latter were removed, being in a dangerous condition, a few years before the restoration of the building of which we shall have to speak hereafter. At the western end of the church, between the two entrances, is a square projection above which rises the elegant tower, with Corinthian pilasters, carried upwards by a series of carved figures, within which are enclosed the four dials of the clock. The tower is surmounted by a well-proportioned dome, above which rises a lantern cupola, with a ball and vane. The design for the building was furnished by one of the commissioners, Thomas Archer, Esq.

"This curious piece of architecture," says Hutton, "the steeple of which is erected after the model of St. Paul's, in London, but without its weight, does honour to the age that raised it, and to the place that contains it. Perhaps the eye of the critic cannot point out a fault, which the hand of the artist can mend; perhaps too, the attentive eye cannot survey this pile of building, without communicating to the mind a small degree of pleasure. If the materials are not proof against time, it is rather a misfortune to be lamented, rather than an error to be complained of, the country producing no better."

If we enter the building we shall find its internal appearance fully bear out the expectations raised by the beauty of the exterior. It is said to be capable of holding upwards of 2,000 persons, and consists of a nave and two side aisles, formed by two rows of fluted Doric columns, from which spring arches which support the roof. At the east end is a handsome altar screen; and the ornaments of the building are in every way appropriate. "The organ excels; the paintings, mouldings, and gildings are superb; whether the stranger takes an external or an internal survey, the eye is struck with delight, and he pronounces the whole the work of a master. Its conveniency also can only be equalled by its elegance." *

There is, however, one fault, viz., in the position of the building, which does not range either

* Hutton.

with the boundary lines of the churchyard, or with any of the rows of handsome buildings which surround it. This defect arises from a strict adherence to the canonical regulation for placing the chancel eastward. "It is amazing," says Hutton, "that even weakness itself, by long practice, becomes canonical; it gains credit by its age and its company. Hence, Sternhold and Hopkins, by being long bound up with scripture, acquired a kind of scripture authority." A description of the churchyard and the many interesting memorials of departed Birmingham worthies will be given in our notice of the restoration of the church, a matter which pertains to the New Birmingham rather than the Old.

While the Church in Birmingham was giving unmistakeable signs of prosperity, in the provision made by the erection of St. Philip's, for the increasing number of worshippers, a cry was being raised by various bigots throughout the country, (with Dr. Sacheverell at their head,) of "the Church in danger." "When that flaming luminary, Dr. Sacheverell, set half the kingdom in a blaze, the inhabitants of this region of industry caught the spark of the day, and grew warm for the church. They had always been inured to *fire*, but now we behold them between *two*."* The doctor, according to Hutton, "rode in triumph through the streets of Birmingham," in 1709, where "this flimsy idol of party snuffed up the incense of the populace,"—not of the better sort among them, however; "the more sensible," adds our historian, "withheld their homage." He preached at Sutton Coldfield, where he had family connections, and, we are told, "the people of Birmingham crowded in multitudes round his pulpit." His message to the people in the supposed hour of danger does not seem to have been one of peace and conciliation. "It does not appear," says, Hutton, quaintly, "that he taught his hearers to *build up Zion*, but perhaps to pull her down; for they immediately went and gutted a meeting-house." The fire of hatred towards the dissenters thus wickedly scattered amongst the people of Birmingham, smouldered for about six years, at the end of which period it found vent in serious riots, which broke out on the 16th of July, 1715. On Saturday, July 16, the mob made an attack upon the Lower Meeting House, in Digbeth; but upon the proprietor of the building making a promise that it should be put to other uses, they took out the seats and whatever else they could find belonging to the congregation, and burnt them, leaving the building uninjured. It was afterwards converted into a workshop, but the memory of the early Nonconformists who worshipped on this site is still perpetuated in the name of Meeting House Yard. "The sound of the pulpit," says our quaint historian, "is changed into that of the bellows; instead of an impression upon the heart, it is now stamped upon the button. The visitants used to appear in a variety of colours, but now always in black."

The rioters continued their work of destruction on the next day, (Sunday,) by attacking the Upper, or Old Meeting House, and destroyed nearly the whole of the interior by fire. They also pulled down meeting houses at West Bromwich, Cradley, and Bradley, and burnt one at Oldbury and another at Dudley.

* Hutton, sixth edition, p. 242.

CHAPTER X.

A PICTURE OF BIRMINGHAM, IN 1730-31.

Westley's *Prospect* and *Plan*—New Hall Lane—Whitehall or Steelhouse Lane—"The Butts"—Baptist Meeting House—The New Meeting House—The old Crosses—The Moat—St. Martin's Rectory—Lady Well and the "Cold Bath"—Open Spaces—The Square—The Cherry Orchards—The Inkleys—Rural Walks—Market Places—The Welsh Cross as a Guard House—Growth of the Town, from 1700 to 1731.

We now come to the first elaborate picture of the town,—the first having any pretension to accuracy of detail at all. There had previously existed only the "prospect" in Dugdale's Warwickshire, which was too small and contracted to admit of any attempt at detail. And since the time of Dugdale, as we have seen, the town had not only greatly increased in size, but had been also much adorned and improved. This large "Prospect," drawn by W. Westley, about 1730,* (which is 33 in. by 13½ in. in size, exclusive of margin,) is therefore one of the most interesting documents extant relating to old Birmingham, and, when taken in connection with the "Plan," (also engraved by Westley, in 1731,) will help to give us a better idea of the extent and appearance of the town than we have hitherto obtained.

The three most prominent objects in the "Prospect" are St. Martin's Church, the newly-built Grammar School, (of which an account will be given in our next chapter,) and St. Philip's Church. The latter was, as we have said, on the outskirts of the town. The road on the north-eastern side of it was then called New Hall Lane, and, with the exception of one or two houses at the end now called Monmouth Street, was as yet unbuilt upon. Its appearance at that time may best be seen by referring to Westley's view of St. Philip's, a fac-simile of which is given on page 61.

"New Hall Lane," says a recent writer,* "was a pleasant country road, skirted on one side by the newly laid-out churchyard of St. Philip's, and on the other, from Snow Hill to Paradise Street, by the park and grounds of the Colemore family. The ancient mansion, known as 'New Hall,' stood in lonely grandeur in the midst of this estate, embowered in trees. The roadway of New Hall Street, just on the brow of the hill below Great Charles Street, occupies the site of this house, the approach to which was through a pair of iron gates, which stood immediately opposite the top of the present Bennett's Hill. From these gates to the hall was a broad carriage drive with a fine avenue of lofty elms. The grounds extended from Snow Hill on the right to Paradise Street on the left, and stretched backwards to Warstone Lane and Hall Street. Within this large area the New Hall was the only house, and there was no public road. On the site of the Union Club House there was a deep pool. Where the gold now chinks upon the counter of the District Bank the song of the thrush from the tree-top was then the only music. Where Messrs. Sabin and Stockley now dispense ocarinas and harmoniums in Ann Street the lark nursed her young amongst the cowslips, while her mate warbled to her from the blue sky overhead. The cattle and the sheep that grazed in the pleasant pastures looked clean and white,

* There is no date upon the engraving, but in the sixth edition of Hutton, (Guest's,) it is given as 1720. It could not have been as early as that, however, as the New Meeting House in Moor Street, (which is shown in the engraving,) was not commenced until 1725.

* Mr. Eliezer Edwards, author of the very interesting volume of "Personal Recollections" recently published, and of the many curious and interesting papers on Old Birmingham which have appeared during the past few months in the *Birmingham Daily Mail.*

THE INTERIOR OF ST. PHILIP'S CHURCH.

for in those days steam-engines were not, and the showers of sooty particles that now make everything in the neighbourhood look black and dingy were unknown. The Colmore estate was as rural, as bright, and as fresh as any part of the glorious landscape upon which one looks from the heights of Malvern.

"Nor was the estate wanting in the charm which water gives to a landscape. A small stream came trickling down from the roach pool and entered the estate on the western side. Near where Messrs. Elkington's famous works now stand the stream widened into a pool, and on the site of the flour mills at the foot of Snow Hill was a larger sheet of water called the 'Great Pool.' The stream flowed thence across the 'Wolverhampton Road' on the surface, but a narrow bridge of brickwork stood on each side of the roadway for the convenience of foot passengers. A spectator looking from the north side of the balcony of St. Philip's Church saw open country extending from Sutton and Fazeley eastwards to the noble range of the Clent and Lickey Hills on the west, and in all that broad expanse not a factory chimney smoked, nor was a bit of 'town life' visible. Birmingham lay altogether southwards, and its entire population was only fifteen thousand*—rather less than the present population of Smethwick."

The continuation of New Hall Lane, as will be seen from the Plan, was built upon almost as far as Stafford Street, and was then promiscuously called White Hall or Steel-house Lane, the latter name from "Kettle's Steel Houses," which are shown both on the Plan and the Prospect; in the latter as situated on either side of a continuation of Newton Street. These were the first furnaces in Birmingham for converting iron into steel; and were erected about the beginning of the eighteenth century. The Stafford road had now taken the name of Stafford Street, or "The Butts," as it was sometimes called; "being," says Hutton, "a mark to shoot at, when the bow was the fashionable instrument of war, which the artist of Birmingham knew well how to make and to use." Coleshill Street extended as far as the old Cross, at the end of Stafford Street, (where Dale End now terminates,) and Moor Street (anciently called Mole Street, from the eminence on one side, or the declivity on the other,) was built upon on one side along its entire length. Carr's Lane is called in Westley's *Plan* "Care Lane." Mr. W. Bates, in a MS. note to his interesting *Guide*, gives the following as the origin of the name: "In this locality was the hovel in which was kept the *Cart* used to convey the various sacred matters used in processions to and from the mother Church of St. Martin's; hence *Cart-lane, Car-lane, Carr's-lane.* Mr. James* received this information from Mr. Garbutt, who found it among the records of King Edward's School."

Owing to the "very steep" declivity at the High Street end of this thoroughfare, it was at that time the scene of many accidents, some of which proved fatal. In *Aris's Gazette* (of which journal we shall have more to say hereafter) of the 6th of January, 1745, is the following:

"Birmingham, January 6.—On Wednesday last, [January 1st] a Man who was turning a loaded Waggon from the High Street in this Town, down Car's Lane, a very steep Turning, without Loking the Wheels, by the sudden Motion of the Waggon he was knock'd down by the Shafts, and the Wheels going over him, he received so much Hurt that he died in an Hour afterwards."

Three years afterwards another fatal accident on the same spot is chronicled in that journal, as follows:

"Birmingham, May 2nd, 1748.—On Thursday last, by the sudden Turning of a Cart from the High Street, Carr's Lane, in this Town, the Driver was crushed by the Shafts against the Corner House in such a Manner, that he died in half an hour afterwards."

Park Street (to continue our survey round the *boundaries* of the town) was built upon for more than half its length, and a new meeting house had been erected by one of the sections of the

[* According to the statement at the foot of Westley's "Plan," the population of Birmingham in 1731 (the period of which Mr. Edwards writes) was 23,286. There were 15,032 inhabitants in the year 1700.—R.K.D.]

* The late Rev. John Angell James.

Baptist denomination, in Freeman Street, between Park Street and Moor Street.

Directly behind the Baptist meeting house, in the print, the reader will observe the New Meeting of the Presbyterians, which was commenced about 1725, (after their ejection from the Lower Meeting House in Digbeth, as the result of the Sacheverell riots,) and opened on the 19th of April, 1732. The three gables of the Old Meeting House may be seen behind, and a little to the right of, St. Martin's Church. In the left corner of the picture, is the old Chapel of St. John, from which the line of the street, over the old narrow bridge, which spanned the Rea, may be traced through the town. The old Market Cross is shown in a direct line above the boy on the left side of the globe, and the Welsh Cross a little to the left above the New Meeting. The buildings in the foreground on the right are called in the descriptive key "Cooper's Mills and House." In a direct line above these may be seen "Carlesse's Steel House," and the old cross, at the junction of Coleshill Street and Stafford Street.

Returning again to the left of the "Prospect," the reader will notice the ancient moat, on the site of which, ten years later, a manufactory, with a dwelling house, was erected, and the "moat" itself came at last to the "base use" of turning a thread mill.

A little above it, somewhat to the right, is seen the moated residence of the rectors of St. Martin's, the two moats being connected by a narrow ditch or stream. Close to the rectory is seen the enclosure containing the "Cold Bath" and "The Lady's Well." The latter was "a spring of clear, soft, and pure water," arising "from the exhaustless underground river, by which the numberless pumps of fine water at the lower part of the town [in the neigbourhood of Digbeth, previously referred to in these pages,] are fed; the water here arises to the surface, and appears in the form of a small enclosed pool, of ancient aspect,"* named, in honour of the Virgin, Lady Well.

* [W. BATES :] Pictorial Guide to Birmingham, p. 150.

At the extreme left of the Prospect, in the distance, is seen the old Hall and Church of Edgbaston, to which more particular reference will be made in our notices of the suburbs.

Of open spaces (notwithstanding the surprising number of "courts and alleys" at that period,) there were several in the town. The principal of these was, of course, the Old Square, which is shown on the Plan as having an enclosed garden in the centre. There would appear to have been at least a footway corresponding to the present Union Street and Cherry Street, between High Street and Temple Row. About half way between this foot-way and New Street was situated "Corbet's Bowling Green," the site of which is now crossed by Union Passage. A little higher up, near the point at which Cannon Street now terminates, the old foot-path crossed "Walker's Cherry Orchard." Beyond this, at the end of the path, was the large and pleasant churchyard of St. Philip's, around which was planted a double row of young trees, and across which one might look out upon the open country, having come to the end of the domain of brick and mortar. Temple Street, and the thoroughfare now known as Temple Row West, marked the end of the town on the north-western side. Two meadows occupied the triangular piece of land now bounded by Ann Street, Bennett's Hill, and New Street. The site of the new Corporate Buildings and the Town Hall was also meadowland. "Greenwood's Cherry Orchard" occupied the other triangle formed by New Street, Pinfold Street, and Peck Lane. The Inkleys (spelt on the Plan "Hinklys"—a fact which goes against Hutton's theory of its etymology *) would appear to have been covered with gardens at that time, bounded on the side nearest Edgbaston Street by a pathway called Hinkly Row, running from Dudley Street to "Tunkses Street." To this

* "The tincture of the smoky shops, with all their *black furniture*, for welding gun barrels, which afterwards appeared on the back of Smalbroke Street, might occasion the original name *Inkleys;* ink is well known; leys is of British derivation, and means grazing ground; so that the etymology, perhaps, is *Black Pasture.*" —Hutton, sixth edition, p. 93.

spot the rude theatrical entertainments, which had previously been held on the site of Temple Street, migrated early in the eighteenth century, being driven from their old home by the rapid advance of the more respectable part of the town in that direction. But about 1730, Hutton tells us, "the amusements of the stage rose in a superior style of elegance, and entered something like a stable in Castle Street," one of the narrow lanes which had been found necessary between High Street and Moor Street. "Here," continues our quaint historian, "the comedian strutted in painted rags, ornamented with tinsel. The audience raised a noisy laugh, half real and half forced, at threepence a head."

The continuation of Edgbaston Street, beyond the end of Dudley Street, was now called Smallbrook Street, perhaps after the worthy who opposed Reverend Slater, and is said to have been one of the subjects of his stupid and irreverent punning sermon, referred to in a previous chapter. Hill Street was unknown. It does not appear from the Plan that there existed even a foot-path across the fields and gardens between the thoroughfare now called Paradise Street and "Tunkses Street" aforesaid. At the end of Peck Lane, in Pinfold Street, stood the Pinfold, which gave the name to the street.

Whichever way the weary artizan took after his day's toil, from the centre of the town, he might reach the pleasant green lanes, meadows, and gardens by walking less than half a mile. From the forge or the smithy of Deritend he might take a delightfully rural walk along the lane which skirted the southern side of the moat, to the distant village of Edgbaston, (by way of the Parsonage and Lady Well,) from the steel-houses of White Hall Lane (Steelhouse Lane) and Coleshill Street, across the fields or along the highway to Aston, from Cooper's mills by way of Cary Field toward the Coventry or Stratford Road,—in either direction, within easy distance of his home, the workman might find a pleasant rural walk where the smoke of the town was yet unknown.

Birmingham was still without a market-place where all the articles offered for sale might be concentrated into one point; and the sellers were therefore scattered into various parts of the town. "Corn was sold by sample in the Bull Ring the eatable productions of the garden in the same place. Butchers' stalls occupied Spiceal Street; one would think a narrow street was preferred, that no customer should be suffered to pass by. Flowers, shrubs, &c., at the ends of Philip Street and Moor Street; beds of earthenware lay in the middle of the foot ways; and a double range of insignificant stalls, in the front of the shambles, choke up the passage. The beast market was kept in Dale End; that for pigs, sheep, and horses, in New Street; cheese issued from one of our principal inns, and afterwards from an open yard in Dale End; fruit, fowls, and butter were sold at the Old Cross; nay, it is difficult to mention a place where they were not."*

The Welsh Cross was intended as a Saturday market, as the increasing population required greater accommodation; yet, although it was used to a certain extent for that purpose, "the people," says Hutton, "never heartily adopted the measure."

The upper chamber of this Cross (referred to in the last chapter) was used as a military guard-house. At the end of the first "Town Book" is an entry under date 16th December, 1723, as follows:—

"At a Genrall Meeting of the inhabitants of the Town of Birmingham, it is agreed upon to build a guard house in some convenient place in the Towne aforesaid, as shall be hereafter agreed upon, it appearing to be very ill convenient to the Town and the Inhabitants thereoff that the Guard should be kept at either of the Markett Crosses."

"But this old order," says Hutton, "like some of the new, was never carried into execution. As no complaint lies against the cross in our time, we may suppose it suitable for the pur-

* Hutton, sixth edition, p. 379.

WESTLEY'S EAST PROSPECT OF BIRMINGHAM; PUBLISHED ABOUT 1730.

The following description of the Town is given on the original plate:

BIRMINGHAM, *a Market Town in the County of WARWICK, which by the art and industry of its Inhabitants, has for some years past, been render'd famous all over the World, for the rare choice and invention of all sorts of Wares, and Curiositys, in Iron, Steel, Brass, &c: admir'd as well for their cheapness, as their peculiar beauty of Workmanship.*

pose; *and I know none but its prisoners that pronounced against it.*" In front of this cross were placed those ancient barbarous implements of public torture, the stocks and the whipping-post.

Although some of the old buildings had disappeared which had crowded up the narrow streets of the lower town, the Birmingham proper of earlier times, those streets still retained much of their picturesque disorder. "Could any cunning writer" (says a contributor to the old *Local Notes and Queries*, in the *Journal*,*) "succeed in conveying to us a correct idea of Digbeth and the Bull Ring in those days, he would interest his readers in no small degree. A narrow, winding, gradually rising thoroughfare, pressed close on each side, with the picturesque, overhanging and pointed, gabled, half-timbered erections of the Tudor period; . . . the swinging signs, trade emblems, tavern posts, and shop wares obtruding conspicuously upon the thoroughfare; the broad, badly-kept gutters, frequently flushed from numerous wells; the foot-paths in bad repair, bound up with staves and timber; the streets teeming with large round stones, laid in with gravel; scavengers unknown; constables few; heaps of rubbish plentiful; millers' carts, rumbling teams, and noisy stages everywhere, would be the scene through which the traveller of old would, on his entry into the town, pass on his way to the Church and Market Place, where a far different scene would meet his eye to that presented at the present day. The Old Church, approached by two flights of steps from Digbeth corner; the sexton's house, mid-way up the steps, and miscellaneous shops hemming in the Church on all sides,† (their back premises being in the churchyard itself); Mercers, Drapers, Ironmongers, Saddlers, Grocers, and Outfitters, interspersed here and there with a well or pump; the Bull Ring built up with shops and stalls approaching to mere shambles as the Market Cross is gained; in fact, the whole space occupied with these stalls or standings, 'stall ground,' 'stallages,' 'shambles,' or any other names such erections were worth—and the ground partially covered with crocks, the wares of the dealers, and the spare goods of shopkeepers around, who held the stall rights."

We may here add a few notes as to various improvements made in certain of the public buildings of the town about this period.

A new clock had been recently placed in the Market Cross, as appears by an entry at the beginning of the *second* Town Book, as follows:—

"14t day of July 1727 a note that the neighbours to the Markett Cross have bought a new Clock at their own expense & that it be fixed & kept in good order at the expense of the Town."

Further on in the same book is the following:—

"Sept 2d 1729 To Jonathan Taylor for Painting and Gilding the Deall Board at the Old Cross, 4. 13. 0."

At the mother Church the hands of improvers were still busy, sometimes for good, but more frequently otherwise. A new organ, placed in the church at the cost of the parishioners, (the amount of £300 being raised for that purpose by voluntary subscriptions,) was among the more commendable of the 'improvements' effected at this period. If the church had hitherto used an organ built by that "Bromicham organ-maker" who had re-pealed the organs at Halesowen in 1498, it was certainly none too soon to provide a new one in 1726.

The tasteless restoration of the building in 1690 was probably left untouched until 1733, when another "improvement" was effected; it being "agreed" at a Vestry meeting held on Friday, August 3rd, in that year, "after having consulted at ye time aforesaid the proper workmen, and considered their calculation of the expense, to take off the roof of the Middle Chancell & to raise the walls thereof about Eight or Nine feet at most, & to put therein on each side a convenient number of windows, & to lay the sayd roof on again, in ye same manner it then lay,

* In an interesting article on "The Old Inns of Birmingham," signed "H."

[† Much in the same way as those on the New Street side of Christ Church at the present time.—R. K. D.]

& to finish all ye sayd work at ye Parish charge in a Substantial way."

In the new Church of St. Philip it was ordered, June 13, 1727, "that a fframe of good Timber be erected & fix'd in the Steeple . . . for Hanging of Eight Bells, & that the two Bells already made be hung there with all convenient speed." The first of these bells had already been the subject of a resolution, in the preceding April, to the effect that one Joseph Smith should "receeive the Mettle from Mr. Bradburn" in order to cast the said bell. Only six bells appear, however, at that time to have been provided, it being perhaps thought that the peal of the new church ought not to excel that of the old, which then consisted of the same number.

The increase of the town from 1700 to 1731 may be best seen from the following statement, which we have tabulated from the notice at the foot of Westley's Plan:—

No. of	*1700.*	*1731.*	*Increase.*
Streets	30	55	25
Courts and alleys	100	150	50
Houses	2,504	3,719	1,215
Inhabitants	15,032	23,286	8,254

These figures will enable our readers to complete for themselves the present picture of the town, and we may proceed, in the succeeding chapter, to trace out the history of some of the newer institutions of that period, which were gradually changing the general appearance of the town.

CHAPTER XI.

THE FREE SCHOOLS AND CHARITIES OF BIRMINGHAM,

In the seventeenth century.

The Free Grammar School—The Blue Coat School—Maintenance of the Poor—Erection of a Workhouse—Lench's Trust—Other charities.

If the reader will turn back for a moment to the first chapter of this history, he will find a brief reference to the Gild of the Holy Cross, out of which arose our Free Grammar School. At the time of the dissolution of the religious houses in the reign of Henry VIII., the possessions of this gild were valued at £31 2s. 10d. Certain of these possessions were, in the fifth year of the reign of Edward VI. (at the humble suit of the townsmen), granted by that monarch to the bailiffs and nineteen other inhabitants of Birmingham, and their successors, for the support and maintenance of a Free Grammar School, with one head and one under master. "The grantees and their successors were created a body corporate and politic of themselves, in perpetuity, by the name of the *Governors*, &c.—to have a common seal, and to plead and to be impleaded by their corporate name, in all actions and suits touching the premises, to have the appointment of the two masters, and, with the advice of the bishop of the diocese, to make fit and wholesome statutes and ordinances concerning the government of the school, &c."* The lands thus given back to the people were then valued at £21, the choice being offered to Birmingham and the village of King's Norton, between that amount in money, and the crown lands of that value. King's Norton, with an eye to present good, chose the money, which remains the same annual income to the present day; whilst Birmingham, with perhaps a dim prevision of its future growth and consequent increase in the value of land, made choice of the latter, which has increased in value with the growth of the town, until it is now an enormous

* [W. Bates :] *Pictorial Guide*, etc. p. 106.

revenue, and is likely to increase still further in the future until this institution becomes one of the most richly endowed of any in the country. "There is scarcely a principal street that more or less of this property does not lie in: New Street, High Street, Union Street, Bull Street, Dale End, Moor Street, Edgbaston Street, Spiceall Street, Bull Ring, Digbeth, Park Street, Chapel Street, Coleshill Street, Broad Street, Summer Lane, Pinfold Street, and other minor, but improving, situations." *

The ancient hall of the gild, which then stood at some distance from the town, in the Hales Owen and Stourbridge Road, (now called New Street,) was first used as a school room. It was built of wood and plaster, like most of the buildings of that period. In one of the windows was blazoned the figure of Edmund Lord Ferrers,

(who had married the heiress of the house of Bermingham, and appears to have been a benefactor to the gild,) with his arms empaling *Belknap*, and those of *Perrot* empaling *Byron*, of *Stafford* of *Grafton*, and of *Bermingham*.

In 1707 this building had become worn-out, having stood about three hundred and twenty years, and was taken down to make way for a more pretending edifice. The style of the new building, which occupied three sides of a quadrangle, was somewhat heavy, on account of the wings being brought too near to the street. In the centre of the building was a tower ornamented with what Hutton calls a "sleeping figure" of Edward the Sixth, and containing a clock and bell. On the balustrade was placed, in 1756, a row of vases, at the same time that St. Philip's Church was similarly ornamented. In front of the building were erected "half a dozen dreadful pillars . . . which, like so many overgrown giants, marshalled in battalia, guarded the entrance that the boys wished to shun; and which, being sufficiently tarnished with Birmingham smoke, might have become dangerous to pregnancy."* These "frightful monstrosities" were afterwards removed, whether from such fears as Hutton suggests, we cannot tell.

In the latter part of the reign of Charles II, certain differences occurred among the governors, and a party of them surrendered the charter of the school into the hands of the king, and a new one was granted by James II, on the twentieth of February, 1685. The remainder of the governers thus ejected, commenced proceedings in Chancery for the recovery of the *original* charter, and, six years after, obtained a decree reinstating them in their functions, annulling the new charter, and restoring and confirming the older one. In 1723 the Lord Chancellor issued a commission to inspect the conduct of the governors; and, as the latter disputed the validity of the commission, the matter was heard in Hilary Term, 1725, when the Court decided against the governors. The original seal was, about this time, discarded, and that of the *abrogated* charter adopted. The old one was lost but has since been discovered in the possession of a Mr. Beale of Leicester, and was purchased by order of the bailiff, July 4th, 1801, for the sum of two guineas.

In 1682 the eminent William Wollaston, author of an able work entitled "The Religion of Nature Delineated" (published in 1722), held the office of Usher in this school. He was born March 26th, 1659, and died October 29th, 1724.

"Amongst the old customs of the school, mention may be made of the 'orations' which

* Hutton, sixth edition, pp. 347-8.

* Hutton.

"OLD AND NEW BIRMINGHAM" PORTRAIT GALLERY.—No. 4.

REV. CANON WILKINSON.

PHOTOGRAPHED BY THRUPP.

BIRMINGHAM: HOUGHTON AND HAMMOND, SCOTLAND PASSAGE.

THE FREE GRAMMAR SCHOOL.

were formerly delivered every 5th November, at the 'Old Cross,' as late as the year 1700. The custom of 'barring out' also prevailed in the School, till a riot of a serious nature occurred in 1667, when the building was besieged and fiercely defended; this led to the abandonment of the practice, though remnants of it remained for many years."*

The further history of this institution will be told in a future chapter, at a later period in the history of the town, as we are anxious to avoid anticipating the story of the growth of *New* Birmingham. And we may here observe, that we have endeavoured in the present work, to allow the history of the town to unfold itself gradually, in the course of a consecutive narrative, rather than (as is usual in local history and topography) to break it up into a series of disjointed chapters and descriptions of the various institutions of the town.

In the year 1724 was erected, on the eastern side of the pleasant churchyard surrounding St. Philip's, the Blue Coat Charity School. The object of this excellent institution was to afford orphans, and the children of the poor, clothing, maintenance, a good elementary education, and religious instruction according to the principles of the Church of England. When first erected, as will be seen from Westley's Prospect of St. Philip's, it was but a small, plain and unpretending building, compared with that of the present day. It was greatly enlarged and improved in 1794, (at an expense of £2,800), when the present stone front was added, but the northern angle did not receive its present stone facing until a later date. Although not pretending to any great degree of beauty, the building, says Mr. Bates, "is remarkable for chasteness of style and propriety of arrangement;" and when seen from the churchyard, with an intervening screen of foliage, it is by no means out of harmony with its present surroundings. The only ornaments are two stone figures placed over the main entrance, of a boy and girl, "habited in the quaint costume of the school." These figures were executed in 1770 by Mr. Edward Grubb, (at that time a resident of this town*), the cost being defrayed by a voluntary subscription. Of these works of a local sculptor, Hutton says "they are executed with a degree of excellence that a Roman statuary would not have blushed to own."

"This artificial family," says our historian, "consists of about two hundred scholars of both sexes, over which preside a governor and governess, both single. Behind the apartments is a large area, appropriate for the amusement of the infant race, necessary as their food. Great decorum is preserved in this little society, who are supported by annual contribution, and by collections made after sermons twice a year.

"At fourteen, the children are removed into the commercial world, and often acquire an affluence that enables them to support that foundation which formerly supported them." †

The children, (as indicated by the name of the institution), are clothed uniformly in blue; the dress of the boys recalling the prevailing costume of a century ago; their swallow-tailed coats, muffin caps, knee-breeches, and blue stockings, presenting an exceedingly quaint, old-world figure in the thronged streets of modern Birmingham. About twenty of the children are supported by a bequest made in 1690, by George Fentham, a mercer of the town. These are distinguished from the rest by being clothed in *green* instead of blue. The present annual income is about £5,000.

"It is worthy of remark," says Hutton, "that those institutions which are immediately upheld by the temporary hand of the giver flourish in continual spring, and become real benefits to society; while those which enjoy a perpetual income, are often tinctured with supineness and dwindle into obscurity. The first usually answers the purpose of the living, the last seldom that of the dead."

* MS. Note by Mr. W. Bates.

* He died at Stratford-on-Avon, April, 1816.

† Hutton, sixth edition, p 355.

From a survey of our two free schools, we may perhaps with propriety glance next at the provision made in byegone days for the support and maintenance of our poor.

Previous to the dissolution of the monasteries, the burden of maintaining the poor chiefly lay upon the religious houses. The greater part of the riches of the country were in the hands of the monk, and, although it is certain that the nobility dispensed hospitality to the poor more liberally than in later times, yet, in consequence of the sparseness with which their establishments were scattered, and the smallness of their revenues in comparison with those of the ecclesiastic, it was to the latter, rather than to the former, that the poor looked for relief and support.

"When the religious houses, and all their property, in 1536, fell a sacrifice to the vindictive wrath of Henry VIII.," Hutton tells us, "the poor lost their dependence, and as want knows no law, robbery became frequent, justice called loudly for punishment, and the hungry for bread; which gave rise, in the reign of Queen Elizabeth, to that most excellent institution, of erecting every parish into a distinct fraternity, and obliging them to support their own members." With this admirable system of parochial relief, the necessity for the afflicted poor to wander away from their homes to seek pity and relief elsewhere, no longer existed; "therefore it is difficult to assign a reason," adds Hutton dryly, "why the blind should go abroad to *see* fresh countries, or the man *without feet to travel*."

But although the parochial law was instituted in the sixteenth century, *workhouses* did not become general until the second decade of the eighteenth; and that of Birmingham was not erected until 1733. It was a plain substantial building, situated at the lower end of Lichfield Street, (between that street and Steelhouse Lane), and was erected at a cost of £1,173 3s. 5d. At a later period two wings were added; the *left*, in 1766, at a cost of £400, as an infirmary; and the *right*, in 1779, at a cost of £700, as a place for labour.

Our illustration shows the building with both these wings added, as given in the first edition of Hutton's History, at which period, says that historian, "the stranger would rather suppose [it] was the residence of a gentleman than of six hundred paupers."

On Westley's Plan, the reader will see marked, at the lower end of Steelhouse Lane, an Almshouse. This was one of the first of the valuable institutions of this kind endowed out of the funds provided by the Charity known as *Lench's Trust*.

The Charities of Lench and others, commonly called Lench's Trust, "stand first among the Birmingham charities, being both the most ancient, and at the present time the most actively useful. William Lench, by a deed dated the 11th of March, in the 17th year of the reign of Henry VIII. (*i.e.*, in 1526), placed various properties in Birmingham and the immediate neighbourhood, in the hands of a certain number of feoffees, and ordered that the rents and profits of the premises should be applied 'for the repairing the ruinous ways and bridges in and about the said town of Birmingham, where it should want, and for default of such uses should bestow the rents and profits of the premises to the poor living within the said town, where there should be most need, according to the appointment and disposition of the said feoffees for the time being, or to the major part of them, or to other pious uses, according to the like discretion and appointment.'"

In a very interesting account of this Charity,* Mr. Toulmin Smith points out that it is in reality a *Gild*, that the objects for which it was originally endowed were the same as those sought to be accomplished by the Gilds, and that the disguise under which it was concealed, or, in other words, the fact of its not being *called* a gild, saved it from sharing the fate of the Gilds and other more important religious endowments.

* Toulmin Smith: "Birmingham Men and Names."

Early in the reign of Elizabeth, (Lench's Charity having then been established about forty years,) William Colmore gave an annuity or yearly rent-charge of 10*s.*, derived from a messuage in Corn Cheaping, near to the upper corner of Moor Street *alias* Mole Street, to the feoffees of Lench's land, and willed that the same annuity should be disposed of "as the lands and tenements called Lench's land; and that 5*s.* of the said 10*s.* should be given for the relief of the poor of Birmingham, yearly, on Good Friday."

In the latter half of the 16th century William Wrixam, formerly rector of the parish church, gave a tenement in Spicer's or Mercer's Street, the rents and profits of which were to be distributed among the poor of the parish, according to the discretion of the feoffees.

In the third year of the reign of Charles I., an inquisition was taken at Birmingham under a commission of charitable uses; and the Commisioners having found that some of the leases in Lench's trust had been improvidently granted, decreed that they should be void, and that they should be surrendered within a certain time, and that new leases should be made for terms not exceeding 21 years. They further decreed that the number of feoffees should in future be not less than 14, "and those of the most honest and sufficient inhabitants of the said town."

Out of these funds an almshouse was built in Digbeth, probably at about the same period as that of Sir Thomas Holte, at Aston. This was the *first* of Lench's Almshouses, and stood until 1765, at which date the premises were let on a building lease. In 1691, the almshouse, together with the lands belonging to the Trust,—a croft called the Bellrope Croft, (lying between the Binges and the way between New Street and the Five Ways); a messuage or croft in Moor Street; and another croft near Walmer Lane, (afterwards called Lancaster Street,)—were conveyed to the new trustees. The trusts of the Bellrope Croft were stated to be "to pay or to permit the churchwardens of St. Martin's Church to receive all the rents and profits thereof, to be employed and disposed by them for buying bell-ropes for the said church, and keeping the same in order from time to time."

The *second* block of Almshouse was probably erected immediately after this transfer, on the "croft near Walmer Lane," then pleasantly situated on the outskirts of the town. From their doors or windows the inmates could enjoy one of the fairest prospects of which our delightful county could boast, even in those early days, when black, smoking chimneys were fewer, and the limits of the domain of brick and mortar much more confined than nowadays. Away on the left could be seen in the distance the gently rising eminence of Barr-beacon, and the pleasant hill on which Oscott College now stands. Nearer, and rather more to the right, would be seen the minaret-crowned towers of Aston Hall, and the tall, graceful spire of the pretty village church, rising from the midst of a grove of trees; still further to the right, (almost in the middle of the prospect,) the village of Erdington, crowning the little eminence called Gravelly Hill, and behind it the well-wooded park of Sutton Coldfield; and away to the right might then be seen the beautiful spire of Coleshill Church. This almshouse was indeed a pleasant harbour of refuge for the aged poor, weary and worn with the battle of life, where they might end their days in peaceful retirement, away from the busy hive in which they had toiled during their earlier years.

But the town grew, and ere long surrounded the little group of almshouses; the furnaces of Kettle's steel-houses sent forth smoke to cloud the prospect, and, by and by, rows of houses sprang up in Walmer Lane to block it out altogether.

The later history of this important charity will be given in a future chapter.

In 1690 (by a will dated 24th of April in that year) George Fentham devised a considerable portion of his property, out of the proceeds of which ten poor widows were to be clothed, and a certain number of poor children were to be taught to "know their letters, spell, and read English."

"The seventeenth century," says a writer on the local charites, "seems to have been most prolific of charitable foundations; and as a proof that, up to that time, and for a good while after, the charities of Birmingham, at any rate, were judiciously managed, and that they not only in general answered the end the donors had in view, but also stimulated others to like deeds of benevolence, it may be mentioned that most of those who founded charities at that time were concerned in one way or other in the management of the charities previously existing." In 1697 George Jackson, (who had previously held the position of trustee of Kylcuppe's Gift,) died, and by his will, provided "for the setting and putting forth Apprentice yeareley two or more of the male children of such of the poorest sort of the housekeepers and inhabitants liveing within the Towne parish and Lordship of Birmingham . . . as doe not receive collecion of or from the said Towne or parish."

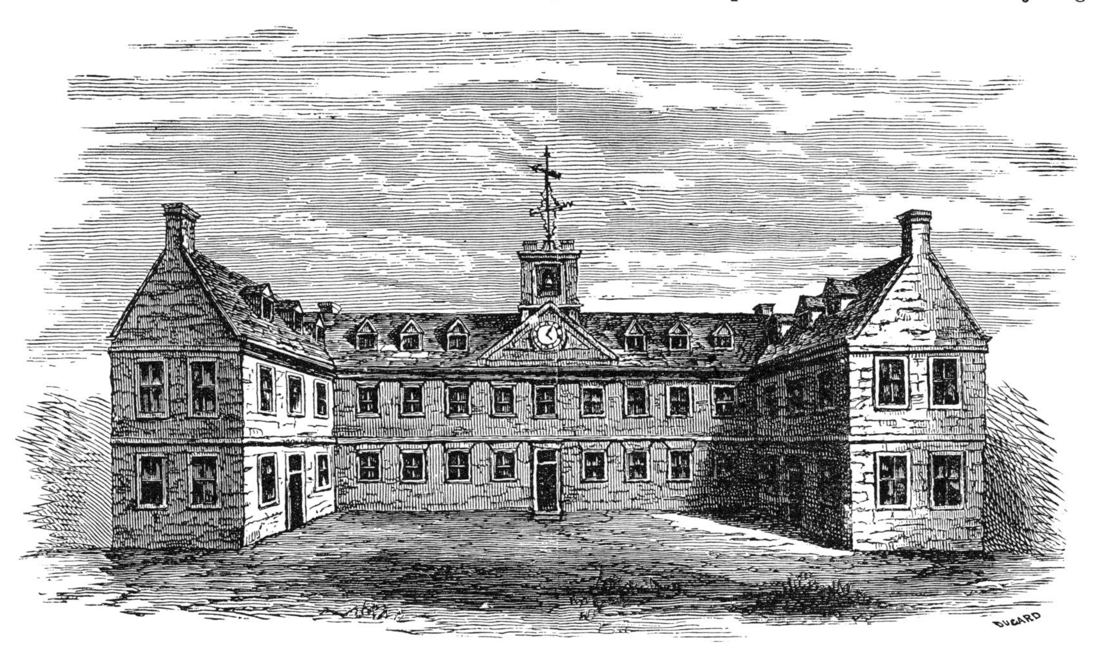

THE OLD WORKHOUSE.

The founder of this valuable charity was a woollen draper of this town; living and keeping his shop (for those were not the days of country residences for tradesmen) in a passage leading from Corn Cheaping to Spiceal Street. These buildings have long since been cleared away, and have given place to the fine open space called the Bull Ring. In religion, he was a Unitarian, or, to speak more correctly, a Presbyterian; and took an active part on the side of the non-juring ministers who were ejected in the reign of Charles II. He was one of the original trustees of the Old Meeting House (the services at which he regularly attended), and his remains were interred in the burial-ground attached to that place of worship.

The following extract from his will explains the object of the charity :—

ITEM I give and devise All my houses tenemts and hereditamts with the apptunces scituate in Deritend in the parish of Aston juxta Birmingham in the said Countye of Warwick with all the outhouses edifices buildings yards gardens hereditamts and apptunces thereunto belonging unto Richard Scott the elder of Birmingham

Linnen Draper Ambrose Foxall of Birmingham aforesaid Cutler William Guest of Birmingham aforesaid Maltster William Collins of Birmingham aforesaid Mercer John Rogers of Birmingham aforesaid Mercer George Wills of Birmingham aforesaid Sadler John Baker of Birmingham aforesaid Tallowe Chandler John Foxall of Birmingham aforesaid Ironmonger Thomas Warren of Birmingham aforesayd Sadler James Lewis of Birmingham aforesaid Boddyes Maker John Gisborne of Birmingham aforesaid Mercer Richard Scott the younger of Birmingham aforesaid Linnen Draper and Abraham Foxall of Birmingham aforesaid Ironmonger and unto their heirs and assignes for ever NEVERTHELESSE upon special Trust and confidence in them resposed that they the said Richard Scott the elder Ambrose Foxall, William Guest William Collins, John Rogers George Wills, John Baker, John Foxall Thomas Warren James Lewis John Gisborne Richard Scott the younger & Abraham Foxall their heires and assignes and every of them shall and will at all times for ever hereafter manage and improve the said houses and pemises to the best advantage they can and receive the rents and proffits as the same shall become due and payable And shall and will yeareyle and every yeare imploy and dispose of the same to such uses and in such manner as is hereafter menconed that is to say that they the said Richard Scott the elder Ambrose Foxall William Guest William Collins John Rogers George Wills John Baker John Foxall Thomas Warren James Lewis John Gisborne Richard Scott the younger and Abraham Foxhall their heires & assignes and every of them shall and will yearelye and every yeare for ever hereafter apply order and dispose of all and every the clear yearelye rents and proffitts of all the said houses or tenemts and pemises with the apptunces (taxes necessarye repairs expenses and other contingent charges in manageing this Trust being first payd and deducted) To and for the setting and putting forth Apprentice yeareley two or more of the male children of such of the poorest sort of the housekeepers and inhabitants liveing within the Towne parish and Lordship of Birmingham aforesaid as doe not receive collection of or from the said Towne or parish of Birmingham aforesaid AND my Will is that for the better continueance of the said tenemts with the apptunces in persons fitt to manage and dispose of the same to and for the intents and purposes aforesaid That whenever it shall happen that the greater number of them the said Richard Scott the elder Ambrose Foxall William Guest Williams Collins John Rogers George Wils John Baker John Foxall Thomas Warren James Lewis John Gisborne Richard Scott the younger and Abraham Foxall dye or depart out of the Towne and Parish of Birmingham aforesayd soe that there shall not be above the number of three at any time liveing That then such three surviveing Trustees shall within three monthes next after they shall be reduced to that number as aforesaid convey setle and assure the said tenements and pemises upon themselves and tenne more substantial and honest Inhabitants in Birmingham aforesaid and soe from time to time for ever hereafter as oft as the case soe happens.

The premises thus devised were originally of the value of £10 2s. per annum, at which they remained until the year 1718, when the property became very dilapidated. From an item in the accounts of this period, of 12s. 2d. "paid labourers for drink," it would appear that the repairs done to them were somewhat extensive, and that the labourers were numerous.

The following items in the year's accounts will probably interest our readers :—

		£	s.	d.
	Pd. Mr. Hooke for copieing the will	0	5	0
	Pd. for a book to keep the accompt	0	3	3
	Pd. for a common seal for ye setting out of boys	0	4	6
	Pd. Patt for repairs	0	1	6
	Pd. at a meeting	0	1	0
18th July.	Pd. to Robert Banner with his apprentise......	2	10	0
,, ,,	Pd. Mr. Hooke for indentures	0	6	0
,, ,,	Expences at binding	0	3	0

Mr. Christopher Hooke, whose name occurs twice in the above entry, was solicitor to the charity from its foundation to 1746. The item of "expences at binding" refers doubtless to that thirst which the formularies attending the binding of apprentices seem always to have engendered, rendering it necessary for that important business to be transacted at the tavern rather than in the lawyer's office. It may be interesting to our readers to know the names of the youths who first benefited by the provisions of the worthy Nonconformist's charity. Some of the trades to which they were apprenticed have disappeared altogether from amongst us. The names and other particulars are given in the accounts of the charity as follows :—

John Hunt, file cutter,	apprenticed to	Richard Price.
Samuel Bentley, whitesmith,	,, ,,	Robert Banner.
Humphrey Wyrley, weaver,	,, ,,	John Haywood.
Benjamin Field, tow dresser	,, ,,	William Sheppard, of King's Norton.
Joseph Warren, knife cutler	,, ,,	Wm. Greaves.
Michael Hope, knife cutler	,, ,,	Wm. Bannister.
George Bagnall, brickmaker	,, ,,	Thomas Knolls.
Thomas Cooper, smith	,, ,,	Wm. Eeeds.
Wm., son of Robert Gilbert, of Derington (the old spelling of Deritend), blaid forger { passer maker and nipper maker }	,,	Wm. Hunt, of Derington.

The nouse at which the "binding" took place in the earlier years of the charity appears from the accounts to have been that kept by Charles Freeth, called "The Bell," in Philip Street, better known, however, to the townspeople as "Freeth's Coffee House." This Charles Freeth was the father of the quaint old verse-maker who styled himself, and was known to others as, "Poet Freeth," of whom we shall have more to say hereafter. "Charles Freeth," says the writer of the articles on the charities referred to above, "never lost an opportunity of summoning the trustees, and the trustees on the other hand never lost an opportunity of repairing to the hostelry of the father of the famous publican poet. They seem to have been merry meetings those at the 'Bell.' We wonder if Baskerville, who at that time taught writing in the Bull Ring close by, and who, as we learn from Hutton, was 'said to have written an excellent hand,' was ever of the party."

But apart from the merry-making aspect of this charity, it would appear to have proved exceedingly useful in the town, and no doubt has, from time to time, been instrumental in teaching an occupation by which they might benefit the town in which they have lived, to many who might otherwise have become a burden to the town, and possibly even worse than a burden—a curse instead of a blessing to their fellow-men.

CHAPTER XII.

SAMUEL JOHNSON IN BIRMINGHAM

Johnson's first visit to Edmund Hector—Carlyle on Johnson—Johnson's earliest essays—His translation of Lobo's *Voyage to Abyssinia*—Hector's assistance—Traces of "Johnsonese" in the Preface—Johnson's second visit to Birmingham.

In the year 1733, Samuel Johnson, having found the drudgery of an ushership at Market Bosworth too irksome for him to bear, accepted an invitation from his friend, Edmund Hector, a surgeon, "to pass some time with him at Birmingham, as his guest, at the house of Mr. Warren, with whom Mr. Hector lodged and boarded."* Whether Johnson had ever visited Birmingham previously we do not know. It is probable, however—judging from the Uttoxeter episode, related by Johnson to Henry White†—that he had occasionally accompanied his father on his journeys to Birmingham market. A portrait of him at this period is thus given by Carlyle :—"Boyhood is now past; the ferula of pedagogue waves harmless, in the distance : Samuel has struggled up to uncouth bulk and youthhood, wrestling with Disease and Poverty all the way; which two continue still his companions. . . . A rugged wild man of the desert, awakened to the feeling of himself; proud as the proudest, poor as the poorest; stoically shut up, silently enduring the incurable : what a world of blackest gloom, with sun-gleams and pale, tearful moongleams, and flickerings of a celestial and an infernal splendour, was this that now opened for him! But the weather is wintry; and the toes of the man are looking through his shoes. His muddy features grow of a purple and sea-green colour; a flood of black indignation mantling beneath. A truculent, raw-boned figure! Meat he has probably little; hope he has less : his feet, as we said, have come into brotherhood with the cold mire."*

Mr. Warren, Edmund Hector's landlord, was the first established bookseller in Birmingham, and finding under the rough exterior of the ex-usher such literary culture and true genius as promised to be of great use to him (Warren being

* Boswell : Life of Johnson.
† Ib.

*Carlyle : Critical and Miscellaneous Essays [Popular Edition]. Vol. 4, 1872. Essay on *Boswell's Life of Johnson*, pp. 94-5.

at that time, according to Boswell, the proprietor of a newspaper), became very attentive to Johnson. Mr. Warren's newspaper would be the first ever published in Birmingham (some years in advance of *Aris's Gazette*), and was the old *Birmingham Journal*, of which a copy of one number is still preserved at the office of the *Daily Post*. In the pages of this little *Journal* appeared the periodical essays of Samuel Johnson; the predecessors of the *Rambler and Idler* essays, which have, perhaps, taken the most distinguished place in literature of all his writings. Having but slender means of subsistence, and at present scarcely any settled plan of life, Johnson determined to stay in Birmingham for some considerable time, and, after six months' sojourn with Mr. Hector, he hired lodgings in another part of the town, at the house of a person named Jarvis—probably a relation of Mrs. Porter, whom he afterwards married. Here he became acquainted with Mr. Porter, a mercer (husband of the Mrs. Porter, above referred to), and with Mr. Taylor, of whose inventions and later life we shall have to speak hereafter. There can be little doubt, however, that the chief attraction which Birmingham had for him was, as Boswell suggests, that of being the home of Mr. Hector, his old schoolfellow and his dearest friend. The interest which Mr. Warren, the bookseller, took in Johnson, led him to join with Mr. Hector in urging upon the young scholar and essayist the desirability of undertaking the translation and abridgment of a "Voyage to Abyssinia," written by Lobo, a Portuguese Jesuit, which Johnson mentioned as having read in the French with pleasure while at Pembroke College. He agreed to commence the work, and as no copy of the work could be procured in Birmingham, he was compelled to borrow from the College Library the copy from which he had first read the narrative. For a while all went on well, and a portion of the work was soon in type, being printed by one Osborn, who was Warren's printer, but "his constitutional indolence soon prevailed," says Boswell, and the work flagged. Mr. Hector, anxious for his friend's credit in the world of letters, urged him to proceed with the work, and, knowing his gentle nature whenever the well-being of a fellow-creature was in question, represented to him that the printer could have no other employment until this book was finished, and that the poor man and his family were suffering. This plea had its desired effect, and Johnson, although feeble and relaxed in body, exerted the powers of his mind in the task of completing the work. He lay in bed with the heavy quarto before him, and dictated the translation to Hector, while the latter wrote it down. The picture of the busy surgeon sitting patiently writing at Johnson's bedside, in the intervals of his professional duties, is one of the most touching in all the records of human friendship.

With the kind assistance of Hector, the book was soon completed, and was published in 1735; but in those days a book bearing a provincial imprint stood but a slender chance of being favourably received, it bore on the title page no evidence whatever of its Birmingham origin, but went forth with a London imprint, a device very common in those days. This was the first literary work of the author who afterwards became the chief figure in the literary history of the eighteenth century. Boswell did not discover in this work any traces of the style which, he says "marks his subsequent writings with such peculiar excellence; with so happy an union of force, vivacity, and perspicuity." But in the preface we detect, here and there, the familiar roll of the Johnsonian dialect, and though, observes his biographer "use had not yet taught his wing a permanent and equable flight, there are parts of it which exhibit his best manner in full vigour." Years afterwards, Boswell tells us, Edmund Burke expressed to him the great delight with which he first read several passages in this first example of the art of writing noble prefaces, of which Johnson was so great a master. It is more than probable that the recollection of this work of translating Lobo's narrative first suggested to Johnson the scene of the charming story of Rasselas.

Early in 1734, Johnson returned to Lichfield, but he appears (from a letter addressed by him to Mr. Edward Cave, the publisher of the now venerable *Gentleman's Magazine)* to have again visited Birmingham in the autumn of the same year. He requests Cave to direct his reply "to S. Smith, to be left at the Castle, in Birmingham, Warwickshire." It was during this second visit that the acquaintance with Mrs. Porter ripened into affection. Miss Porter told Boswell that, when Johnson was first introduced to her mother, "his appearance was very forbidding." He was "lean and lank, so that his immense structure of bones was hideously striking to the eye, and the scars of the scrofula were deeply visible. He also wore his hair, which was straight and stiff, and separated behind; and he often had, seemingly, convulsive starts and odd gesticulations, which tended to excite at once surprise and ridicule." But with all these natural defects and external disadvantages, he possessed many rare qualities which weighed in his favour where personal appearance would have counted as nothing. Mrs. Porter appears to have been a woman of considerable sensibility, possessing, says Boswell, "a superiority of understanding and talents;" and the charm of Johnson's conversational powers, combined with his real goodness of heart, won her esteem and affection. According to Garrick, she herself possessed few personal attractions, but his judgment was probably a superficial one; certainly she must have had considerable intellectual endowments, and these were as great attractions for the scholarly suitor as his own were for her. A story is told concerning his courtship which well exhibits his disregard for mere sentimental objections. The lady, it is said,

THE BLUE COAT SCHOOL.

refused all his offers of marriage for a while, at the same time declining to give any reason for so doing. At last, yielding to his urgent request to tell him why she still refused, she said "an uncle of hers had been hung, and she did not wish to bring disgrace on him." "Is that all," said Johnson; "Why, though I have never had an uncle *hung*, I have two or three uncles who *deserved* it,—so let's get married, and say no more about that."

Her objections having been removed, and she having signified her willingness to accept of his hand, he went to Lichfield to obtain his mother's consent to the marriage, which, says Boswell, he could not but be conscious was a very imprudent scheme, both on account of their disparity of years,* and her want of fortune. But, adds his biographer, Mrs. Johnson knew too well the ardour of her son's temper, and was too tender a parent to oppose his inclinations. "Sir," said the doctor, years afterwards, to Topham Beauclerc, "it was a love marriage on both sides."

DR. JOHNSON.

On the ninth of July, 1735, the couple set out on horseback for Derby, at which place they were to be married. Although they were, according to Johnson's own statement, *lovers* in the truest sense of the word, their conduct towards each other, during this ante-nuptial ride, must have appeared, to the casual observer, anything but affectionate. "Sir," said Johnson to Boswell in speaking of this ride many years afterwards, "she had read the old romances, and had got into her head the fantastical notion that a woman of spirit should use her lover like a dog. So, sir, at first she told me that I rode too fast, and she could not keep up with me: and when I rode a little slower, she passed me, and complained that I lagged behind. I was not to be made the slave of caprice; and I resolved to begin as I meant to end. I therefore pushed on briskly, till I was fairly out of her sight. The road lay between two hedges, so I was sure she could not miss it; and I contrived that she should soon come up with me. When she did, I observed her to be in tears."

We must agree with Boswell that this was "a singular beginning of connubial felicity," but the

* At the time of his marriage Johnson was twenty-seven years of age; Mrs. Porter had just completed her forty-eighth year.

sequel proved that it is not always the compliant lover who becomes the most affectionate husband, and it may be supposed that Mrs. Johnson found in the manly resolute bridegroom a faithful and loving partner, and, in the distinguished position which her husband afterwards achieved, met with that rich reward which her wise choice so well merited.

Of Johnson's future career it is not necessary that we should speak here. Boswell's inimitable biography is now within the reach of the humblest lover of our literature; and if the reader would know more of the struggling young scholar who became the greatest literary celebrity of the eighteenth century, he cannot do better than make the early acquaintance of that enchanting book, which will enable him to enter the circle of Johnson's most intimate friends, to listen to his matchless conversations, and to join the innumerable host of ardent admirers of the great lexicographer, critic, essayist, poet, and conversationalist, of whom it may as truly be said, as he himself said of Oliver Goldsmith, "he left scarcely any style of writing untouched, and touched nothing that he did not adorn."

Johnson visited Birmingham again, after he had became famous, but of that visit we shall have more to say in its proper chronological place in our narrative.

CHAPTER XIII.

"ARIS'S BIRMINGHAM GAZETTE," AND THE APPEARANCE OF THE TOWN, 1741-1750.

The *Gazette* and its rival—Incorporation of the two journals—Expenses of journalism in 1743—Appearance of the Town, from 1741 to 1750—Loyal Celebrations—Amusements of the People—Cock-fighting at Duddeston Hall—Theatrical Entertainments—Mechanical and other Exhibitions.

At the commencement of the fifth decade of the seventeenth century, Birmingham appears to have been without a newspaper. Warren's *Birmingham Journal* had ceased to exist; and no new adventure had, as yet, taken its place. In the month of May, 1741, Mr. Thomas Aris, of London, came to Birmingham in order to settle in the town as a printer, and to establish a weekly journal; and for that purpose took a house in High Street, but, as it was then inhabited, and he could not conveniently enter until Michaelmas, he returned to London. During the interval between his first visit and his settlement in the town, a Mr. Walker, having obtained information of Mr. Aris's intention, anticipated the publication of the *Gazette*, as will be seen by the following address, printed by Mr. Aris in the first number of his new journal: he says,

"That the public may not look on me as an opposer to Mr. Walker, as by the insinuation in his paper he would have me supposed, I will beg leave to state the case.

"In the month of May last, I came to Birmingham in order to settle there as a Printer and Bookseller, and, with the advice of my friends, took the house I now live in, but it being then inhabited, I could not conveniently enter till Michaelmas last, so went back again to London; during which time Mr. Walker, having got information of my intention, came here and printed a Newspaper before I left London; therefore, I appeal to the public, to whom he has made his address in all the papers he has yet published, to determine who is the opposer. And those gentlemen who are pleased to encourage me, may be assured that no pains shall be spared to make the paper agreeable, having settled the best correspondent I possibly could in London for that purpose. T. Aris.'

The first number of Aris's new venture was

published on the 16th of November, 1741, under the title of *The Birmingham Gazette, or the General Correspondent*, at the price of three-halfpence, and bearing a government stamp of one half-penny. Like Cowper's favourite evening companion, it was a "folio of four pages," very small pages indeed, the whole sheet being no larger than a single page of the Birmingham newspapers of to-day. There was very little of local news in it, its four pages being filled chiefly with the paragraphs of the London correspondent referred to in the proprietor's address, and advertisements.

The two papers, Walker's and Aris's, were carried on in opposition for nearly two years, until July, 1743, when, as will be seen from the subjoined address, a compromise took place between the rival publishers; Walker's journal was incorporated with its more successful rival, which appeared at that date for the first time under the distinctive title of *Aris's Birmingham Gazette*, and was raised in price to two-pence; the increase being explained by the proprietor in an address "*To the Readers of this Paper*," as follows:

"Gentlemen,—I am very sensible that to raise the price of any commodity is always both unpopular and hazardous; and even was it not so, the obligation you have laid me under, by your generous encouragement of this paper, would be sufficient to deter me from any attempt to advance the price of it, was it in my power, consistent with my own preservation, to act otherwise.

"But when I assure you it is not so, and that I have already lost a considerable sum by selling it at three half-pence, I flatter myself that no gentleman would take it amiss if I can't continue it at a price which, instead of serving, can only injure me.

"That a great deal of money may be sunk in a very little time by a publication of this nature cannot seem strange to any one who considers that out of every paper one half-penny goes to the stamp office, and another to the person who sells it; that the paper it is printed on costs a farthing; and that consequently no more than a farthing remains to defray the charges of composing, printing, London newspapers, and meeting, as far as Daventry, the Post, which last article is very expensive, not to mention the expence of our London correspondence. The truth is, I had no design originally of attempting the printing a Newspaper for three half-pence; but another paper being published at that price by Mr. Walker, obliged me to submit to the same terms, though now we are both sufficiently convinced that we were in the wrong, and think it high time to drop the opposition, and unite both papers in one. Therefore, for the future, there will be but this paper printed, which will be in conjunction; and as the above is a true state of the case, I hope that those gentlemen who have hitherto honoured me with their favours, for which I take this opportunity of returning my thanks, will not think the advance of one half-penny unreasonable. But in order to make some amends for the additional half-penny, I shall, for the future, enlarge the pages in such a manner as to contain a greater quantity of news than at present; and the public may depend that no pains or expence shall be spared to render this paper as useful and entertaining as possible."

The Gazette continued in the hands of its originator until his death, which occurred in 1761, and remained in the possession of various members of his family until 1789, when it became the property of Mr. Thomas Pearson. The further history of this journal remains to be told at a later period in the history of our local literature.

A complete file of this venerable newspaper, from 1741, the year of its birth, to the present time, is preserved at the publishing office, and thus, for nearly a century and a half, we have as complete a record as can be obtained from the columns of a newspaper of the growth and appearance of the town, and of the life and doings of the people. From this remarkable file, of which few parallels exist in the country, our able townsman, Dr. J. A. Langford (who for some years occupied the position of local editor of that journal), has brought together such a collection of curious and interesting extracts respecting the habits, customs, amusements, and life of our ancestors, and the changes which the town has undergone during the long period of the *Gazette's* existence, as cannot fail to be of the utmost value to the student of our local history, and will enable us in these pages to give a much fuller picture of the town and its people in the eighteenth century than would have been possible without the assistance of these invaluable records.

From the extracts given by Dr. Langford from the first ten years' issues of the *Gazette* we will endeavour to obtain a glimpse at the doings of our ancestors at the date of the commencement of the paper; and perhaps it will be well to look first at the houses they lived in, and their surroundings.

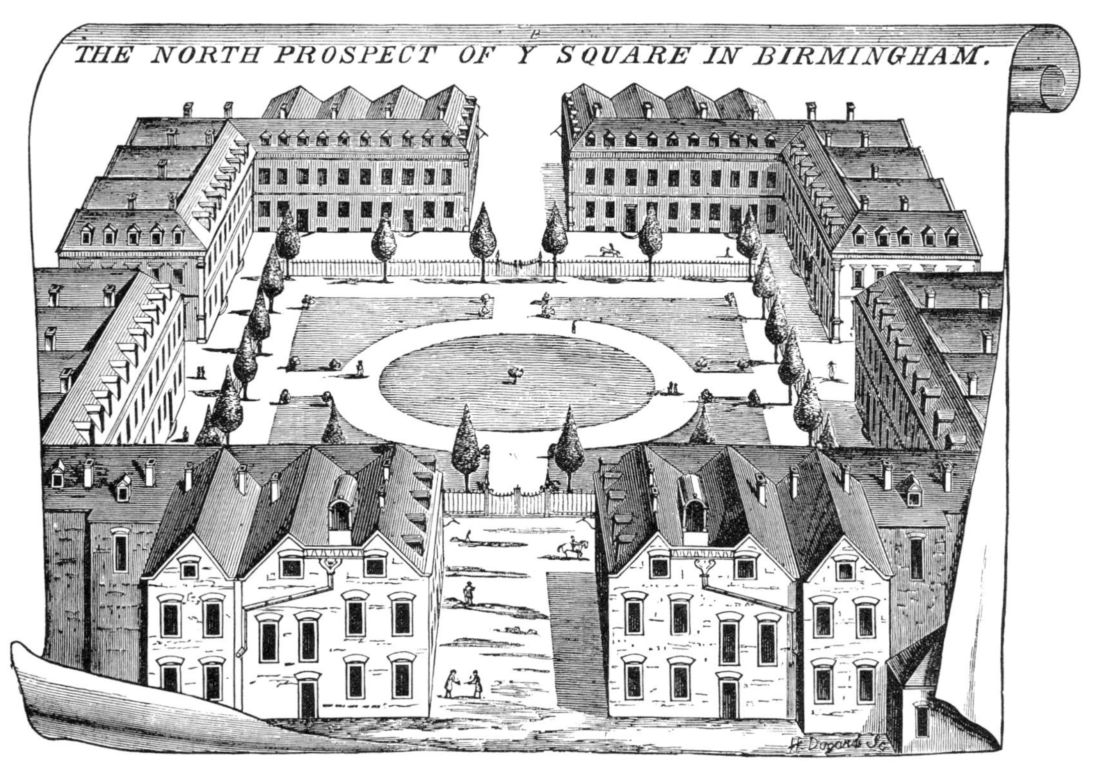

THE OLD SQUARE. *(From the print by W. Westley, 1732.)*

Temple Street, as we have seen in our last survey of the town, was already built upon; but there were still houses in it which might be considered as pleasantly rural. The following might at any rate be envied nowadays, even by the dwellers in our most picturesque suburbs. The date of the advertisement is December 5, 1743:

"To be Sold and entered upon at Lady-day next, a Large Messuage or Dwelling House, situate in Temple-Street, Birmingham, in the Possession of Mr. Charles Magenis, containing twelve Yards in the Front, four Rooms on a Floor, sashed and fronted both to the street and Garden, good Cellaring and Vaults, Brew-house and Stable with an entire Garden walled, and the walls covered with Fruit Trees, the Garden 12 Yards wide, and 50 Yards long from the Front of the House, and extending 22 Yards wide for 26 Yards further, together with a pleasant Terrace Walk, and Summer-House with Sash'd Windows and Sash'd Doors, adjoining to the open Fields, and commanding a Prospect of four Miles Distance, and all necessary conveniences. Likewise another House in the same Street in the tenure of Mr. George Orton, with large Shops,

Gardens, and Summer-House, pleasantly situated, commanding a good Prospect; and set at nine Pounds and ten shillings per annum.

"Enquire of Charles Megenis in Temple-Street aforesaid."

The late Mr. Toulmin Smith (to whose valuable researches respecting the early history of the town we have previously referred) says : "I myself remember Temple Street in much this state. My grandfather (Edward Smith) lived in a house there, the description of which precisely corresponds as to house and garden with this advertisement. I well remember the 'Terrace Walk.'"*

From another advertisement, in the *Gazette* of December 14, 1741, we learn that even in a comparatively old thoroughfare like High Street there was an inn (the original Hen and Chickens) with "a very good Bowling Green joining to it." Such an appendage to a house so situated proves that notwithstanding the number of courts and alleys mentioned in the statement at the foot of Westley's Map, there was as yet little of the overcrowding from which Birmingham, in common with all other large towns, suffers at the present day.

The next extract refers to a house in Lichfield Street, a spot in the very heart of the squalid district from which it is now proposed to clear all the present buildings. Yet, at that time, as Dr. Langford observes, "the houses for the most part had gardens, and were the dwelling-places of people whose descendants have now to seek at Edgbaston, Handsworth, or Erdington, for 'the sweet place of flowers,' as a poet calls a garden."

"To be Sold, the Reversion of a Freehold Messuage, with Shops, Backside, and Garden, in Lichfield Street, near the Square, Birmingham, the Tenant for Life being near ninety years old."

Even Deritend and Edgbaston Street, although in the older part of the town, could, in 1746, boast of houses with gardens. On the 20th of October in that year, the local newspaper contained an advertisement of "a large House with a Brew-house, Shop, and a Pent-house for Shoeing Horses under, *and a large Garden*," situated in the upper part of Deritend; and in the same year was offered "a Good House in Edgbaston Street," with a good stable, garden, and other conveniences; candidates for the occupation of this desirable residence being referred to "Mrs. Sarah Lloyd, at the Slitting Mill," which the reader will find, on looking at Westley's Map, was situated at the back of Digbeth, between the Upper and Lower Mill Lanes.

New Street was at that time quite rural, and, as Dr. Langford observes, "abounded in gardens." The present writer knew a gentleman, only recently deceased, who in his youth had gleaned in a cornfield adjoining the upper part of it, and the editor of the "Century of Birmingham Life" tells of another gentleman, then living, who had gathered blackberries in this part of the town. It would not, therefore, appear so strange to either of those gentlemen as to the majority of Birmingham men and women now living, to read in the *Gazette* of May 18, 1747, of a house to let in that street, "with proper Out-building, Gardening, and other conveniences thereto belonging."

The banks of the Rea, near Deritend Bridge, would seem to have been at that time a pleasant retreat. One is inclined to envy the possessor of so delightful a town residence as was advertised to be let on the 16th of November, 1747. It is described as "a very good new-built House, four Rooms on a Floor, with a Brew-house and Stable, and other conveniences, *a very good Garden, walled in, and a Fish Pond in it, situate very pleasant by the Water Side, near the Bridge*, in Birmingham."

Returning into the upper part of the town, we come to the Old Square, which at that time was known simply as *the* Square. This was the site of the ancient Priory of St. Thomas the Apostle, of the foundations of which some small remains were still visible in the cellars on the south-eastern side of the Square, even as late as 1780, when Hutton wrote his history of the town. From

* A Century of Birmingham Life. [First Edition.] 1868. Vol 1, p. 3.

this pleasantly situated spot might at that time be discerned the Rowley Hills, the villages of Oldbury, Smethwick, Handsworth, Sutton Coldfield, Erdington, and Saltley, as well as most of the suburbs on the southern side of the town. From the little print by Westley, engraved on the corner of the "St. Philip's" plate, it appears that a uniform range of houses had been built on the four sides of the square, the centre being enclosed and adorned with trees and shrubs. Many of these houses still remain, although for the most part altered and modernized. Some have been plastered and painted over, others have an additional storey, others have merely been new-roofed with slates. The following advertisement will give us some idea as to the appearance of these houses in 1748:

To be Sold, two handsome Messuages, with a School Room, Warehouse, and other Back-buildings, in good Repair, with good Gardens, and a large Piece of Land lying behind the said Messuages, situated in the Square in Birmingham, in the Holding of Mr. Sawyer and Mr. Baddeley. — Enquire of Mr. Fisher, Attorney, in Birmingham; or of Mr. Calcutt, Attorney, in Daventry.

Other advertisements might be quoted if space would permit, to show how many pleasantly situated houses might at that time be found in the very heart of the town; as, for instance, one with a *garden wall'd round and other conveniences* in Moor Street; another, *with Brew-house, Gardens, Stables, and all other Conveniences for a Family*, in High Street; an Inn in Lichfield Street, *with a spot of Ground near adjoining for a Bowling-Green;* and many others of a like character might be mentioned, if necessary, to show the pleasantly rural situation of the town at that time. Perhaps the best idea of its appearance, with gardens and outhouses adjoining many of the houses in the principal streets, may be obtained by a journey through one of the smaller towns in the neighbourhood, such as Coventry, Tamworth, and Evesham, where houses similarly situated may be found at the present day.

As to the local events chronicled in the old numbers of the *Gazette*, they are but few and far between, and we are compelled to believe, with Dr. Langford, that there were scarcely any events of a public nature worth recording. "No police reports, no public meetings, no charitable appeals, no literature, no popular educational institutions, no popular lectures, no libraries, no news rooms, no penny readings, no Board of Guardians, no Town Council, no debates of local senates, no orations of local senators to read, no leading articles, for there were no local events about which to write. All seems to have been a dull, dead level of monotonous existence, varied by occasional cock-fights and other brutal sports."

The only item of local news contained in the first number (Nov. 16, 1741) relates to the celebration of the birth-day of Admiral Vernon in Birmingham, November 14, "with all the Tokens of Regard due to that worthy Man." The morning, we are told, was ushered in with the Clamming of the Bells,* and the day concluded with bonfires and drinking success to his Majesty's Arms.

Loyal celebrations seem to have been the principal events in our public life. The 11th of June, 1742, (the first June after the establishment of the *Gazette*,) the anniversary of the Accession of George II. to the throne was "observ'd with the Ringing of Bells, and other Demonstrations of Joy," and the evening was concluded with "Bonfires, and drinking to the Healths of his Majesty and Royal Family, Success to his Majesty's Arms, and to the Healths of those Gentlemen who have appeared conspicuous in the Interest of their country."

Our townsmen, as befitted the makers of implements of warfare, seem to have manifested great interest in all events pertaining to our armies and their movements. The success of the allied forces against the French at Dettingen, in 1743, was celebrated in Birmingham with every token of jubilation; "the Bells of both our Churches," says the *Gazette* of that date, "were set to Ringing, at Noon there were several Discharges of Fire

* *i.e.*, ringing the whole peal simultaneously.

from the Soldiers, and the Evening was concluded with Bonfires, Illumination of Windows, and drinking Success to his Majesty's Arms." The retreat of the Pretender Charles Edward Stuart, and his forces, before the Duke of Cumberland, in 1745, (after they had taken Carlisle, and were marching on towards the heart of England) was also duly celebrated in a similar manner in Birmingham, the evening on which the news arrived being "spent with the highest Demonstrations of Joy, as Bonfires, Illumination of Windows, giving Ale to the Populace, &c." On the 16th of April, 1746, the famous battle of Culloden was fought, and the rebellion finally crushed. On receiving the news, we read, "in every Face here appear'd the greatest joy and loyalty, which were demonstrated by the Ringing of Bells, several Firing from the Companies of the Right Hon. the Lord Gower's Regiment, and in the Evening by Bonfires, Fireworks, giving great Quantities of Ale to the Populace, and an Illumination of Windows throughout the whole Town. The ninth of October, in the same year, was appointed as a day of general thanksgiving, "for the suppression of the late unnatural Rebellion by the Defeat of the Rebels by His Royal Highness the Duke of Cumberland, at the Battle of Culloden," and was kept in Birmingham with a similar effusion of loyalty; the morning being "usher'd in by the Ringing of Bells, which was continued till the Time of Divine Service;" in the evening the illumination of windows is said to have "far exceeded what was ever known here before, the Windows of those Houses in the most remote Parts of the Town being filled with Candle;" and the night was "concluded with Bonfires (at several of which great Quantities of Ale were given to the Populace), Fireworks, and all other Demonstration of Joy."

The day of thanksgiving on account of the Peace of 1749 (April 25,) was observed here with more outward tokens of joy than had characterized any previous celebration of the kind. The usual bell-ringing, illuminations, and bonfires were supplemented by displays, at two different places, of "the grandest Fireworks ever seen here, consisting of a great number of Lime and common Rockets, Wheels, Stars, Suns, &c., and at the Conclusion of those at one of the Places, was an Explosion of near 200 Rockets at the same Time;" and there was "an elegant Entertainment provided, at which were present a great number of Gentlemen. The reporter adds, that "during the whole Time of the Fireworks, we don't hear of any Misfortune that happen'd."

From the advertisement pages of the early numbers of the *Gazette* we may gather also a few notes as to the *amusements* of our ancestors. This subject cannot, however, be contemplated nowadays without a feeling of loathing and disgust at the cruelty and brutality which seems to have pervaded most of the popular sports of that period. This aspect of the national pastimes does not seem to have troubled either the authorities or the leaders of public opinion in the least. No wrathful "leaders" commenting on the cruelty of cock-fighting, bull-baiting, and dog-fighting are to be found in the columns of these old newspapers,—no letters from correspondents burning with righteous indignation,—such events were as regularly advertised as other amusements, and as calmly reported as we now report a cricket or football match. A few of these advertisements will suffice. It will be noticed that the place most famous for these brutal exhibitions in this locality was Duddeston Hall. The date of the first advertisement is June, 1746.

This is to give Notice,—That there will be a Main of Cocks fought at Duddeston Hall, near Birmingham, betwixt the Gentlemen of Warwickshire and Worcestershire, for Four Guineas a Battle, and Forty Guineas the Main. To weigh on Monday, the 9th of June, and fight the two following Days.

Birmingham Cock Match, 1747.—On Whitsun Monday, the 8th of June, will be shewn at Duddeston Hall, near Birmingham, in Warwickshire, Forty-one Cocks on each Side, for a Match to be fought the three following Days, betwixt the Gentlemen of Warwickshire, Worcestershire, and Shropshire, for Ten Guineas a Battle, and Two Hundred the Odd Battle; and also Twenty-one Cocks on each Side for bye Battles, which Bye Battles are to be fought for Two Guineas each Battle.

The next announcement appears nearly two months in advance of the event, viz., on February 29, 1748.

On Monday, the 11th of April, 1748, being Easter Monday, will be a Match of Cocks weigh'd to fight the three following Days at Duddeston Hall, near Birmingham, each Party to weigh Forty-one Cocks, for ten Guineas a Battle, and two Hundred the Main; and each Party to weigh Twenty Cocks for Bye Battles, for Five Guineas a Battle, each Cock to give and take Half an Ounce. The Gentlemen of Worcester and Herefordshire against the Gentlemen of Warwickshire and Staffordshire.

This match is thus reported in the *Gazette* of April 18:

On Tuesday, Wednesday, and Thursday last was fought at Duddeston Hall, near this Town, between the Gentlemen of Worcestershire and Warwickshire, a match of Cocks for ten Guineas a Battle, and two Hundred the Main, and the Bye Battles at Five Guineas each. The Battles won on the Main were equal on each side, and the Odds in the Bye Battles were two in favour of the Gentlemen of Warwickshire.

Many other advertisements and notices of a similar character appear throughout the earlier years of the *Gazette's* existence.

It is far more pleasant, however, to turn from the contemplation of pastimes of this character to the more elevating and refining pleasures of the drama. Our last notice of the stage in Birmingham brought us to Castle Street, where theatrical performances were wont to be given in a stable, at the low charge of threepence for admission. In 1740, however, a theatre was erected in Moor Street, which gave a more respectable appearance to dramatic entertainments, although, if Hutton's account of the mode of advertising them be correct, the theatre was still far below those of other towns in importance and social status. "In the day-time,' says our veracious historian, "the comedian beat up for

ST. JOHN'S CHAPEL, DERITEND, AS REBUILT IN 1735.

volunteers for the night, delivered his bills of fare, and roared out an encomium on the excellence of the entertainment, which had not always the desired effect."

Theatrical amusements would seem, however, to have become more popular during the ten years which intervened between the above date and the period to which this chapter more particularly refers. "We read," says Dr. Langford, "of no less than three places at which plays were acted. There was a theatre in New Street, a new theatre in Smallbrook Street, and another new theatre in Moor Street. The two latter, however, were not licensed for dramatic performances, and their managers resorted to the practice of the man in the streets who sells you a straw and gives you a book. A concert was performed, for admission to which a charge was made, and then the play and afterpiece were given gratis."

The earliest notice relating to the New Street theatre appeared in the *Gazette* of January 31, 1743, announcing a performance for the benefit of Mr. Miller and his wife, the former being, it appears, a member of the "Antient Society of Free and Accepted Masons," for the entertainment of which ancient society was spoken a Prologue and Epilogue made in Honour of them; several "Brotherly Songs" were also announced to be sung on the occasion. The piece performed was Congreve's "Mourning Bride."

During the period which had elapsed since the performances in the Castle Street stable, the tastes and requirements of the play-going public of Birmingham had advanced; and the "rags and tinsel" of those days no longer satisfied them. As all who are familiar with the history of the stage know, David Garrick had by this time begun to effect great reforms in the matter of costume, and although the *period* of the drama was not sufficiently taken into account, the *nationality* of the *dramatis personæ* was, and foreign characters were no longer impersonated in English dresses, at any rate in the principal theatres. So that we are not surprised to hear that a company of players who had regard to accuracy of costume occasionally favoured Birmingham with their presence. On the 18th of May, 1747, the following editorial notice appeared:

We are inform'd from Wisbech, that Mr. Herbert's Company of Comedians will be here, and open the Theatre in Moor Street, on Monday the First of June, with a Tragedy, call'd the Siege of Damascus, with proper Dresses to every Character, and Scenes and Decorations proper to the Play.

On the day of the arrival of Mr. Herbert's company, a more detailed announcement of the piece appeared in the *Gazette*, in which it is said to have been "*wrote by Mr. John Hughes, who died for Joy on its success after the first Night's Performance.*" It is probable that the anxiety for the fate of the piece, which was the author's first attempt, *accelerated* his death, as he was, at the period of its production, in a state of utter prostration, from that most fatal malady, consumption. He had been the beloved and trusted friend of Joseph Addison and Richard Steele, both of whom professed great admiration for his dramatic abilities. The "Siege of Damascus" is printed in the tenth volume of Mrs. Inchbald's British Theatre. "He chose this Story," continues the writer of the *Gazette* notice, "to convince Mankind (as he often declar'd) that amongst Turks the Principles of Honour and Morality were not unknown, and by the character of Phocyas, that he, the invincible else, was to be subdued by Love." The notice further states that "This play has been constantly honour'd in London by the most Brilliant Audiences. 'Tis therefore to be hop'd what has been encourag'd there, will at least be look'd at here by all Lovers of Learning and Taste. *All the Characters in this Play will be dressed in the proper Habits, as the Turks and Greeks there appeared.*"

The same number of the *Gazette* contained a report of a performance at the New Theatre in Smallbrook Street on the previous Friday, of "the Play of 'The Earl of Essex,' and the celebrated Entertainment of 'Harlequin's Vagarics, or the Burgomaster Trick'd' . . . to a crowded Audience, with universal Applause," and states that "by particular Desire, the same Entertainment, with the Comedy of Love for Love, written by Mr. Congreve, (and several Entertainments of Singing and Dancing between the Acts) are to be performed There this Evening."

In order to show the manner in which the unlicensed players announced their performances, Dr. Langford quotes the following, from the *Gazette* of August 4, 1746:

At the New Theatre, in Moor Street, This present Evening, will be perform'd A Concert of Vocal and Instrumental Musick. Boxes, 2*s.* 6*d.* Pit, 2*s.* First Gal., 1*s.* Upper Gal., 6*d.* Between the two Parts of the Concert will be presented (Gratis) a Comedy, called "THE MISER." The Part of Lovegold the Miser by Mr. Breeze, Frederick by Mr. Smith, Clerimont by Mr. Slaiter, Ramilie by Mr. Wignell, James by Mr. Whitaker, Decoy by Mr. Child, Lift the Taylor by Mr. Waher, Mariana by Mrs. Slaiter, Harriet by Mrs. Wignell, Mrs. Wisely by Mrs. Child, Wheedle by Mrs. Smith, and the Part of Lappet by Mrs. Whitaker. To which will be added an Opera, call'd "The Mock Doctor; or the Dumb Lady Cur'd." The part of the Doctor by Mr. Whitaker, Dorcas by Mr. Slaiter, Leander by Mr. Child, Sir Jasper by Mr. Breeze, Dumb Lady by Mrs. Whitaker. To begin exactly at Seven O'clock.

But it must not be supposed from the preceding announcements that Shakespeare was ignored in Birmingham. On the 15th July, 1747, "*A Tragedy called 'Hamlet Prince of Denmark'*" was performed at the Moor Street Theatre, and on the same evening was produced, at the rival house in Smallbrook Street, "A Celebrated Tragedy, call'd Othello, the Moor of Venice, written by the famous Shakespeare."

When theatrical entertainments palled, the seeker after amusement might turn to other exhibitions of various kinds, among which mention may be made of a "curious and unparallel'd Musical Clock, made by David Lockwood," which was exhibited at the sign of the Wheat Sheaf in the Bull Ring, "for the entertaining amusement of the Quality, Gentry, and others." This curious piece of mechanism is described in a lengthy advertisement, in which it is stated to be "a Machine, incomparable in its Kind, as well for the Beauty of its Structure as the Nicety and Perfection of its Performance. Its compositions are admirable, and far more elegant than any yet extant, being the choicest airs taken out of the best Operas, with graces ingeniously intermix'd. Together with French Horn Pieces upon the Organ, German and Common Flute, Flagolett, &c., to the great satisfaction of the most eminent Masters and Judges, as Sonatas, Concertos, Marches, Minuets, Jigs and Scotch Airs, compos'd by Corelli, Alberoni, Mr. Handel, Dr. Bradley, and other eminent Masters." The note subjoined by the advertiser has an eye to the disposal of this curious piece of Mechanism. We wonder if it found a purchaser in the "world's toyshop."

NOTE.—The above Clock plays a Piece of Music every Four Hours of itself, and of Pleasure; is wound up once in Eight Days, and is now to be sold by Edmund Rising, the Owner. This Piece was never here before, nor the like seen. Any Persons that are curious, and desire to see the inside Work, shall be welcome. Our stay in this town will be very short.

From "Fleet Street, near Temple Bar," came one of the predecessors of good Madame Tussaud and Artemus Ward, with a collection of "wax works," which were exhibited in the Chamber over the Old Cross in June, 1746, comprising figures "representing the Royal Family of Great Britain, richly dress'd, and in full Proportion, as they appear on the King's Birthday Day, the late Queen Caroline being dress'd in a Suit of her own Cloaths." They are said to have been "esteem'd by all who have seen them, the most beautiful work that has ever been seen in the Kingdom, being valued at Five Hundred Pounds, and have been shewn to most of the Nobility of the Kingdom with great satisfaction." Visitors were entertained with "a variety of Music, Vocal and Instrumental; the latter perform'd on a Chamber Organ, with two Sets of Keys; the full Organ, with the Stops as follow: Stop Diapason, the Trumpet Stop, the Principal Stop, the Coroned and Fifteenth, the Chair Organ and Flute Stops."

Following the wax works, came an exhibition

similar to that of the clock previously described, with the addition of various feats of legerdemain and other marvels, in May, 1749, thus described by the exhibitor :

This is to acquaint the Curious, that at the Black Boy in Edgbaston Street, Birmingham, this and every Evening during his Stay in Town, Mr. Yeates, from London, will exhibit a Grand, Curious and Splendid Representation of the Temple of Apollo, at Delphos, in Greece. Being the Temple to which Alexander the Great went to inquire who was his Father; whether he had reveng'd his Death on all his Enemies; and where the Heathens of Old repair'd in Times of private Distress, or public danger. This admirable Piece of Art is adorn'd with every Thing that can render it pleasing to the Spectator, having curious Pillars of Lapis Lazuli, and embellish'd with Painting in an elegant Manner. Phaeton is represented petitioning Apollo to let him drive the Chariot of the Sun, which being granted occasions the Fall of Phaeton, who wanting judgment to conduct the Chariot of the Sun thro' the Mid Air, had like, thro' this Misconduct, to have the World on Fire; but was destroy'd by a Thunderbolt from Jupiter, and thrown headlong into the River Padus in Italy, otherwise called Eridanus. Likewise the Triumphs of the Bacchus and Ariadne, represented in a grand and magnificent manner, and adorned with all the Ornaments and Decorations which can fill the Mind with pleasing Ideas, and charm a judicious and curious Spectator. Likewise a curious Organ, which performs several select Pieces of Musick, composed by the best Masters.

N.B. The Machine is in Height twelve Feet, in Breadth nine, and in Depth seven, and not seen through any Glass. In order to afford the Vertuosi an agreeable Amusement, Mr. Yeates will perform his inimitable Dexterity of Hands; Who, for his Cards, and the clean conveyance of his Outlandish Birds, that Talk very agreeably at the Word of command, together with his sudden and surprising production of an Apple-Tree, which he causes to Grow, Blossom, and bear Ripe Fruit fit for any Person to Eat of it in less than three Minutes' Time; and several other surprising Tricks, is allowed, by the curious, to excel all other Performers. Pit 1*s.* Upper Seats 6*d.* The Doors to be open at Six o'Clock, and begin at Seven. Gentlemen or Ladies may have a private Performance, giving two Hours' Notice.

The village of Aston even at that date had pleasure gardens, which would seem to have been almost as attractive as those which at the present day draw their thousands of pleasure-seekers from all parts of the midland counties.

In an early number of the *Gazette* is announced the postponement, on account of the inclemency of the weather, of a "Performance of Music and Fire-Works, at Bridgman's Gardens, at the Apollo, at Aston, near Birmingham. In connection with this fête was announced the performance by Mr. Bridgman and others of "a grand Trio of Mr. Handell's out of Acis and Galatea, and that favourite Duet of Mr. Arne's called Damon and Chloe."

With this notice of an old Aston fête we conclude our notes from the first decade of *Aris's Birmingham Gazette.*

CHAPTER XIV.

THE STORY OF A RUNAWAY APPRENTICE.

The Early Life of William Hutton—An idle week and its consequences—Hutton in disgrace—Determines to run away—Arrival at Derby—A night in the open air—Lichfield—Further misfortunes—A weary tramp to Walsall—First impressions of Birmingham and its People—Good Samaritans at the Old Cross—Journey through the Stocking District—The return home, and end of an eventful week.

THE year 1741—the birth-year of *Aris's Gazette*—is interesting also as the one in which William Hutton first visited Birmingham.

He was born at Derby, on the 30th of September, 1723. In 1738, after having endured many hardships, he entered the service of an uncle, at Nottingham, as an apprentice to the trade of stocking-weaving. Here he appears to have been pretty comfortable, until an unfortunate circumstance, which occurred during the week of Nottingham races, in the month of June, 1741.

"The week of the races," he says, "is an idle one among the stockingers at Nottingham. It was so with me. Five days had elapsed, and I had done little more than the work of four.

"My uncle, who always judged from the present moment, supposed I should never return to industry—though I had lately purchased a suit of clothes with my over-work—was angry at my neglect, and observed, on Saturday morning, that if I did not perform my task that day, he would thrash me at night."

The threat thus held over the young stockinger did not deter him from finishing the week in something like the idle manner which had thus far characterized it. "Idleness," he says, "that had hovered over me five days, did not choose to leave me the sixth." Not that he entirely wasted the day; from his own account it seems he wanted but one hour's work to complete the task which had been set him. He fondly hoped, however, that his uniformly good conduct during the past three years would atone for present delinquencies, and did not suppose his uncle would carry out his harsh threat. But his hopes were doomed to disappointment. Night came, and his uncle found the task unfinished.

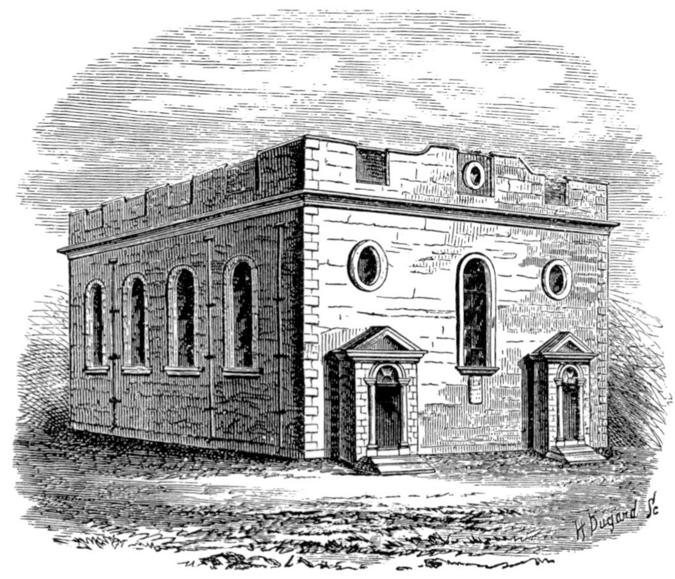

THE NEW MEETING HOUSE.

"You have not done the task I ordered!" he exclaimed.

Hutton was silent.

"Was it in your power to have done it?"

No reply.

"Could you have done it?" he repeated again.

William Hutton was of too noble a nature to take refuge in deceit. "As I ever detested lying," he says, "I could not think of covering myself, even from a rising storm, by so mean a subterfuge; for we both knew I had done near twice as much. I therefore answered in a low meek voice, '*I could.*' This fatal word, innocent in itself, and founded upon truth, proved my destruction. 'Then,' says he, 'I'll make you.' He immediately brought a birch-beesom-steal* of white hazel, and, holding it by the small end, repeated his blows till I thought he would have broken me to pieces. The windows were open, the evening calm, the sky serene, and everything mild but my uncle. The sound of the roar and of the stick penetrated the air to a great distance."

Smarting as he was with bodily pain, he felt even more deeply the wound his pride had received by this semi-public chastisement.

"I was drawing near eighteen," he says, "held some rank among my acquaintance, and made a

* All Midlanders know the common besom, or broom, made of heath, with its "steal" or "stale," (the handle,) usually made of hazel.

small figure in dress; therefore, though I was greatly hurt in body, I was much more hurt in mind by this flogging. The next day, July 12, 1741, I went to meeting in the morning as usual. My uncle seemed sorry for what had passed, and inclined to make matters up. At noon he sent me for some fruit, and asked me to partake of it. I thanked him with a sullen 'No.' My wounds were too deep to be healed with cherries."

The same day a female acquaintance finished the work of humiliation by jeering him about the beating he had received the night before. This stung him to the quick. "I would rather," he said, "she had broken my head."

The idea of running away had been suggested to him on former occasions by an ill-doing fellow-apprentice named Roper; and the humiliation and disgrace he had now undergone led him to adopt this course. He felt that he could not again show himself among his friends and acquaintances without becoming the object of their ridicule and scorn, and resolved to leave the town that very day.

Putting on his hat, as if going to Meeting, he privately slipped up-stairs, early in the afternoon, until the family had departed. As soon as he was alone, he began to pack up his few possessions, clothes, and a little food. He found ten shillings belonging to his uncle, but his scrupulous integrity would not permit him to take more than the actual necessities of his journey required. He, therefore, kept but two shillings, and left the other eight.

The next difficulty was how to escape from the house. There was but one door, and that was locked, and they had taken the key. Contriving, however, to get his encumbrances to the top of a wall about eight feet high, in a back yard, he next climbed up himself, dropped them on the other side, and jumped down after them. Escaping unobserved, save by an acquaintance easily enjoined to secrecy, he started on his journey.

"Figure to yourself," he says, "a lad of seventeen, not elegantly dressed, nearly five feet high, rather Dutch build, with a long narrow bag of brown leather, that would hold about a strike, in which was neatly packed up a new suit of clothes, also a white linen bag which would hold about half as much, containing a sixpenny loaf of blencon * bread, a bit of butter wrapped in the leaves of an old copy-book, a new Bible value three shillings, one shirt, a pair of stockings, a sun-dial, my best wig, carefully folded and laid at top, that, by lying in the hollow of the bag, it might not be crushed. The ends of the two bags being tied together, I slung them over my left shoulder, rather in the style of a cockfighter. My best hat, not being properly calculated for a bag, I hung to the button of my coat. I had only two shillings in my pocket; a spacious world before me, and no plan of operations."

Such was the quaint figure cut by the runaway apprentice as he left Nottingham, casting "many a melancholy look" behind him as "every step set him at a greater distance" from home and friends; and took as he thought an everlasting farewell of all that was so dear to him. "I carried," he says, "neither a light heart nor a light load; nay, there was nothing light about me except the sun in the heavens and the money in my pocket." He did not reach Derby until ten o'clock at night, where the inhabitants, retiring to bed, seemed, to the weary outcast, to be retreating from his society.

He made his way to his father's house, (supposing the inmates had by this time retired to rest,) in order that he might take a fond look at the only homely object which his weary tramp would afford him; but as he came near he perceived the door open, and heard his father's foot not three yards from him, and retreated precipitately. "How ill calculated are we to judge of events," he adds; "I was running from the last hand that could have saved me!"

He took up his abode for the night on the

* Blencon, or Blencorn—*i.e.*, blend-corn, bread made of mixed corn, rye and wheat.—JEWITT.

damp grass, in a close outside the town called Abbey Barns, with the sky overhead and his bags by his side. But there was little repose for him, in his agitated mental condition, and the place was full of cattle, their heavy breathing, together with the clanking of the chains at the feet of the horses, were of themselves sufficient to keep him awake. He rose at four, starved, sore, and stiff; left his bags under a tree, first covering them with leaves, and waited on St. Werburgh's Bridge for his brother Sam, whom he knew would pass that way to the silk-mill at five o'clock.

"I told him," says Hutton, "I had differed with my uncle, had left him; intended for Ireland; that he must remember me to my father, whom I should probably see no more. I had all the discourse to myself, for he did not speak one word."

He then proceeded on his journey, and arrived at Burton-on-Trent the same morning, having travelled twenty-eight miles, without spending a penny. "I was an economist from my birth," he says, "and the character never forsook me."

Continuing his narrative, he says:

"I ever had an inclination to examine towns and places. Leaving my bags at a public house, I took a view of the place, and, breaking into my first shilling, spent one penny as a recompense for their care.

"Arriving the same evening within the precincts of Lichfield, I approached a barn where I intended to lodge; but, finding the door shut, opened my parcels in the field, dressed, hid my bags under a hedge, and took a view of the city for about two hours, though very foot-sore.

"Returning to the spot about nine, I undressed, bagged up my things in decent order, and prepared for rest; but alas! I had a bed to seek. About a stone's cast from the place stood another barn, which, perhaps, might furnish me with lodging. I thought it needless to take the bags (while I examined the place) as my stay would be very short.

"The second barn yielding no relief, I returned in about ten minutes. But what was my surprise when I perceived the bags were gone! Terror seized me. I roared after the rascal, but might as well have been silent, for thieves seldom come at a call. Running, raving, and lamenting, about the fields and roads, employed some time. I was too much immersed in distress to find relief in tears. They refused to flow. I described the bags, and told the affair to all I met. I found pity, or seeming pity, from all, but redress from none. I saw my hearers dwindle with the twilight; and, by eleven o'clock found myself left in the open street, to tell my mournful tale to the silent night.

"It is not easy to place a human being in a more distressed situation. My finances were nothing. A stranger to the world, and the world to me. No employ, nor likely to procure any. No food to eat, or place to rest. All the little property I had upon earth taken from me: nay, even *hope*, that last and constant friend of the unfortunate, forsook me. I was in a more wretched condition than he who has nothing to lose. An eye may roll over these lines when the hand that writes them shall be still. May that eye move without a tear! I sought repose in the street, upon a butcher's block."

He arose early the next morning from his hard couch, and renewed his enquiries after his missing bags, but all to no purpose. Among others he accosted "a gentleman in a wrought nightcap, plaid gown, and morocco slippers," and told him his tale of distress. This gentleman appears to have been one of that class of philanthropists still very common in the world, who feel for the sorrows of humanity, everywhere — except in their pockets. He was touched with compassion at the young wanderer's pitiful tale. "I found," says Hutton, "it was easy to penetrate his heart, but not his pocket."

"It is market-day at Walsall," said the would be philanthropist. "Yonder people are going there; your attention on them may be successful." He acted upon this advice, and joined the little company, who were on their way to that place, the one party with a waggon-load of carrots, and the other with a horse-load of cherries. They continued together until the end of the journey; "but," says he, "I think neither pity nor success were of our party."

His feet were blistered, being unused to travelling; but when he arrived at Walsall he begged a little common beef-fat from a good-natured butcher in that town, and with this he rubbed his feet, and found instant relief. He then cast about him to find employment, but, on application to a man who sold stockings in the market, he learned that there were no frames in Walsall, but many in Birmingham, in which place the stocking-vendor had an acquaintance in the trade, to whom he kindly gave the young stockinger a recommendation.

After resting awhile, therefore, he resumed his journey in the direction of Birmingham, and, on his way thither, saw what to him was a curious sight; the female nail-makers of the Black Country.

"I wondered," he says, "in my way from Walsall to Birmingham, to see so many blacksmiths' shops; in many of them one, and in some two, *ladies* at work; all with smutty faces, thundering at the anvil. Struck with the novelty, I asked if the ladies in this country shod horses? but was answered, 'They are nailers.'"

Arriving on Handsworth Heath he saw, for the first time, the great town which was to become his future home, and which should, to use his own phrase, draw not only his person, but his esteem from the place of his nativity, and fix it upon herself. The first object to attract his attention was St. Philip's Church, which was then "uncrowded with houses (for there were none to the North except New Hall), untarnished with smoke, and illuminated with a western sun." "I was charmed," he says, "with its beauty, and thought it then, as I do now, the credit of the place."

In his *History of Birmingham*, he records his first impressions of the town and its people as follows:

"The environs of all I had seen were composed of wretched dwellings, replete with dirt and poverty; but the buildings in the exterior of Birmingham rose in a style of elegance. Thatch, so plentiful in other towns, was not to be met with in this. I was much surprised at the place, but more at the people. They were a species I had never seen; they possessed a vivacity I had never beheld: I had been among dreamers, but now I saw men awake: their very step along the street shewed alacrity. I had been taught to consider the whole twenty-four hours as appropriated for sleep, but I found a people satisfied with only half that number." He tells us, in his History, of one Obrian, a pavier, who was journeying from London to Dublin, and had intended to stay in Birmingham but one night, on his way; but instead of pursuing his journey the next morning, he determined to stay in the town, and had continued a resident here thirty-five years; "and though," adds Hutton quaintly, "fortune had never elevated him above the pebbles of the street, he had never repented his stay."

"My intended stay," says our hero, "like Obrian's, was one night; but, struck with the place, I was unwilling to leave it. I could not avoid remarking, that if the people of Birmingham did not suffer themselves to *sleep in the streets*, they did not suffer others to sleep in their beds; for I was, each morning by three o'clock, saluted with a circle of hammers. Every man seemed to know and prosecute his own affairs: the town was large, and full of inhabitants, and those inhabitants full of industry. I had seen faces elsewhere tinctured with an idle gloom void of meaning, but here, with a pleasing alertness. Their appearance was strongly marked with the modes of civil life: I mixed with a variety of company, chiefly of the lower ranks, and rather as a silent spectator. I was treated with an easy freedom by all, and with marks of

"OLD AND NEW BIRMINGHAM" PORTRAIT GALLERY.—No. 5.

HENRY HAWKES,

Borough Coroner.

PHOTOGRAPHED BY THRUPP.

BIRMINGHAM: HOUGHTON AND HAMMOND, SCOTLAND PASSAGE.

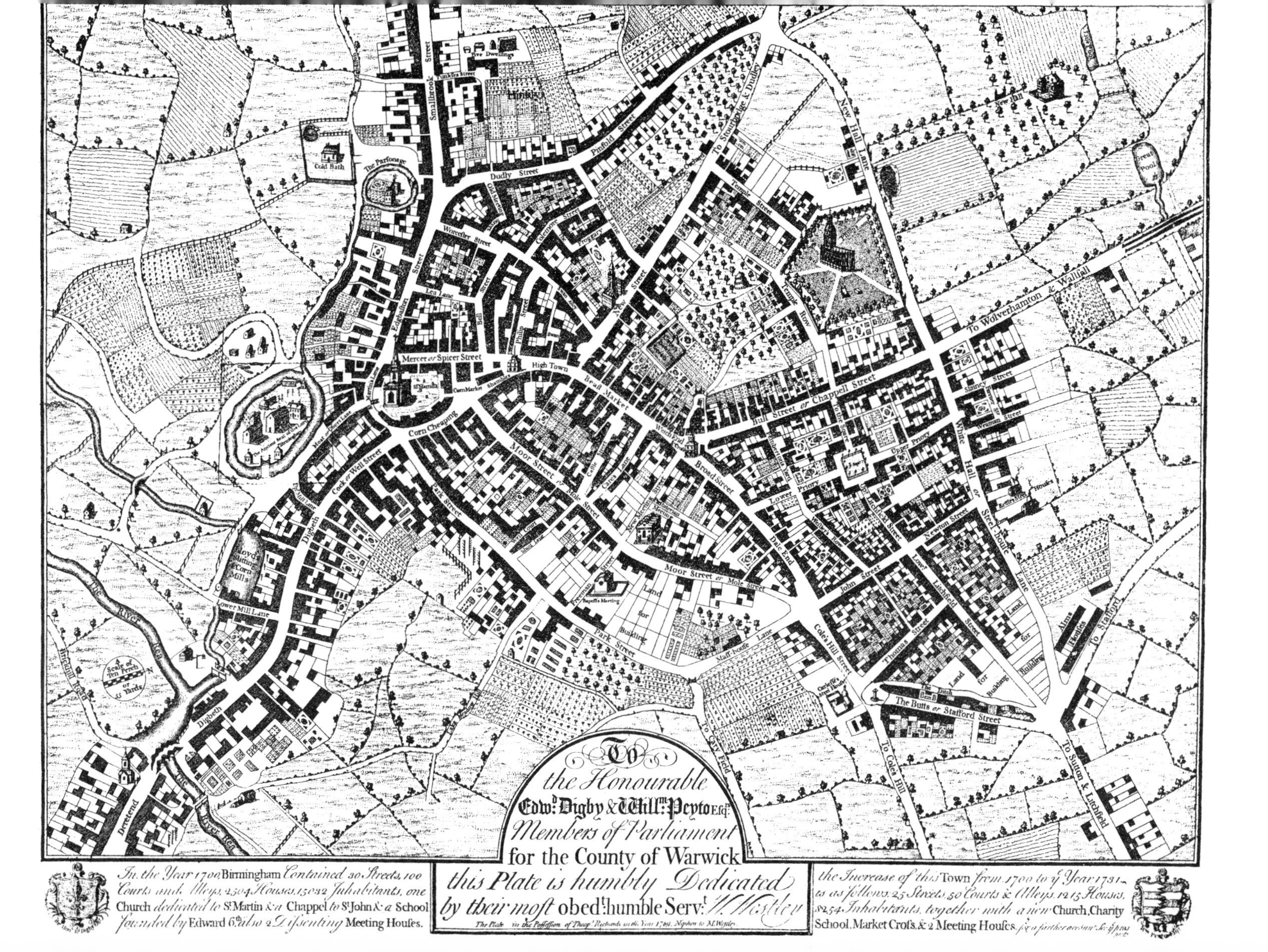
To
the Honourable
Edwd. Digby & Willm. Peyto Esqrs.
Members of Parliament
for the County of Warwick
this Plate is humbly Dedicated
by their most obedt. humble Servt. W. Westley
The Plate in the Possession of Thos. Richards in the Year 1789, Nephew to M. Westley
In the Year 1700 Birmingham Contained 30 Streets, 100
Courts and Alleys, 2504 Houses, 15032 Inhabitants, one
Church dedicated to St. Martin & a Chappel to St. John & a School
founded by Edward 6th. also 2 Dissenting Meeting Houses.
the Increase of this Town from 1700 to ye Year 1731
is as follows: 25 Streets, 50 Courts & Alleys, 1215 Houses,
8254 Inhabitants, together with a new Church, Charity
School, Market Cross, & 2 Meeting Houses.
Smallbrook Street
Dudly Street
Pinfold Street
To Stourbridge & Dudley
New Hall Lane
New Hall
Temple Street
Temple Row
To Wolverhampton & Wallsall
Worcester Street
Edgbaston Street
Lea Lane
Bell Street
Philip Street
Mercer or Spicer Street
High Town
Corn Market
Shambles
Bull Street or Chappell Street
Corn Cheaping
Cock or Well Street
Digbeth
Moor Street or Mole Street
Park Street
Broad Street
Dale End
White Hall or Steel-house Lane
John Street
Lower Litchfield Street
Newton Street
Thomas Street
Cole's Hill Street
The Butts or Stafford Street
Land for Building
Alms Houses
To Stafford
To Sutton & Litchfield
To Coles Hill
To Cary Field
Lower Mill Lane
Cold Bath
The Parsonage
Five Dwellings
Great Pool
Deretend
River Rea
Scale of Ten Perch or Yards

favour by some. Hospitality seemed to claim this happy people for her own."

The weather was exceedingly fine during his brief stay in the town, and this, he says, gave a lustre to the whole. "The people," he says, "seemed happy, and I, the only animal out of use."

Impressed by the example of the busy people of Birmingham, he immediately cast about to find employment. There appeared to be three stocking-weavers in Birmingham; Evans, a Quaker, Holmes, in Dale End, and Francis Grace, at the Gate-way in New Street, the latter being a native of Derby. Hutton went first to Evans, who was the oldest and principal member of the trade in the town, and asked him for employment.

"You are a 'prentice."

"Sir," said Hutton, "I am not, but am come with the recommendation of your friend Mr. Such-a-one, of Walsall."

"Go about your business, I tell you, you are a runaway 'prentice," said Evans angrily.

Thus repulsed, the young stockinger retreated, "sincerely wishing," he adds, "I had business to go about."

He next called upon Holmes, but he was at that moment engaged in waiting upon a customer, and gave the weary seeker after employment a penny to be rid of him.

He then turned towards New Street, to seek Mr. Grace, who had known the Hutton family, being, as already stated, a native of the same town.

"Fourteen years after," says Hutton, "he procured for me a valuable wife, his niece! and sixteen years after, he died, leaving me in possession of his premises and fortune, paying some legacies.

"I moved the same question to him I had done to others, and with the same effect. He asked after his brother at Derby. I answered readily, as if I knew. One lie often produces a second. He examined me closely; and, though a man of no shining talents, quickly set me fast. I was obliged to tell three or four lies to patch up a lame tale, which I plainly saw would hardly pass.

"I appeared a trembling stranger in that house, over which, sixteen years after, I should preside, and that for nineteen more. I stood, as a culprit, by that counter, upon which, thirty-eight years after, I should record the memory. I thought, though his name was Grace, his heart was stony; and I left the shop with this severe reflection, that I had told several lies, and that without the least advantage. I am sorry to digress, but must beg leave to break the thread of my narrative while I make two short remarks.

"I acquired a high character for honesty, by stealing two shillings! Not altogether because I took two out of ten, but because I left the other eight. A thief is seldom known to leave *part* of his booty if he has power over the whole. If I had had money, I should not have taken any; and if I had found none, I should not have run away. The reader will also think with me that two shillings was a very modest sum to carry me to Ireland.

"The other is whether lying is not laudable? If I could have consented to tell one lie to my uncle, I should not only have saved my back, my character, and my property, but also prevented about ten lies which I was obliged to tell in the course of the following week. But that Vast Intelligence who directs immensity, whether he judges with an angry eye, according to some Christians, or with a benign one, according to others, will ever distinguish between an act of necessity and an act of choice."

Turning slowly away, his last opportunity of finding employment gone, he walked in the direction of the Bull Ring. It was about seven o'clock in the evening of Tuesday, the third day of his wanderings. "I sat to rest," he says, "on the north side of the Old Cross, near Philip Street; the poorest of all the poor belonging to that great parish, of which, twenty-seven years after, I should be overseer. I sat under that roof, a silent, depressed object, where thirty-one years after, I should sit as a judge. When property should be in my decision, I should have the pleasure of terminating differences between man and man, and the good fortune to leave, even the loser, satisfied. Why did not some kind agent comfort me with the distant prospect?

"About ten yards from me, near the corner of Philip Street, I perceived two men in aprons eye me with some attention. They approached near. 'You seem,' says one, 'by your melancholy situation, and dusty shoes, a forlorn traveller, without money and without friends.' I assured him it was exactly my case. 'If you choose to accept a pint, it is at your service. I know what it is myself to be distressed.' 'I shall receive any favour,' says I, 'with thankfulness.'

"They took me to the Bell in Philip Street, and gave me what drink and bread and cheese I chose. They also procured a lodging in the neighbourhood, where I slept for three half-pence.

"I did not meet with this treatment in 1770 [twenty-nine years after] at Market Bosworth, though I appeared in the style of a gentleman. The inhabitants set their dogs at me merely because I was a stranger. Surrounded by impassable roads, no intercourse with man to humanize the mind, no commerce to smooth their rugged manners, they are the boors of nature. We are taught to wish good for evil. May the grass grow in their streets!"

The kind treatment which he received from the "good Samaritans" of Birmingham made it difficult to him to leave that "seat of civility," as he styled the town, and he determined to endeavour, for one day, to forget grim care in the gratification of his previously expressed inclination to "examine towns and places,"—a pleasure for which he had already had to pay dearly at Lichfield,—and so on the morning of the following day (Wednesday) made a more minute survey of the town. It may interest the reader to know the extreme boundary of the town as perambulated by Hutton at that date. From his History we learn that, commencing at the top of Snow Hill, along Bull Lane (the New Hall Lane of 1731), the town was still confined to the *left* of the traveller, the land on the right being still unbuilt upon. Through Bull Lane he would proceed to Temple Street; thence, down Peck Lane, to the top of Pinfold Street. Along Dudley Street, across the Old Inkleys, to the top of Smallbrook Street; and back, through Edgbaston Street and Digbeth to the upper end of Deritend. Returning to the top of Digbeth, he would pass along Park Street, up Mass-house Lane, passing the northern end of Dale End, along Stafford Street, and up Steelhouse Lane, to the place from whence he started. We see from this survey that the town had not as yet extended greatly beyond the lines of 1731, but many of the streets then formed were now much better filled up with houses.

On Thursday,—the 16th of July,—he left Birmingham for Coventry and arrived at that city early in the day. Still, however, he saw no opportunity of employment, and again gratified his desire for seeing strange places. But the venerable city does not appear to have impressed him favourably. "The streets," he says, "seemed narrow, ill-paved, and the place populous." The Cross he pronounces "a beautiful little piece of architecture, but composed of wretched materials." The quaint old houses, with their projecting upper stories, seemed to him to wear a gloomy aspect; he humorously conjectures that the idea of the architect in designing the upper projection was "that of shooting off the wet, and shaking hands out of the garret windows." He slept that night at the Star Inn in that city, "not" he adds, "as a chamber guest but as a hay-chamber one."

The next day he walked to Nuneaton, and found that he "had again entered the dominions of sleep." The inhabitants seemed to him to creep along as if afraid their streets should be seen empty. "However," he says, "they had sense enough to ring the word '*'prentice*' in my ears, which I not only denied, but used every figure in rhetoric I was master of to establish my argument; yet was not able to persuade them out of their penetration." His great crime was that he seemed to be only a *boy*. "I thought it hard," he says, "to perish because I could not convince people I was a man." He left the town early in the day, "without a smile, and without a dinner," and reached Hinckley about four o'clock in the afternoon. Here, a native of Derby, named Millward, found him some little employment, at which, during the two hours which were still left of the day, he earned *twopence*. After work, Millward put the usual questions, and charged him with being a runaway apprentice, and this time, utterly broken down, the poor wanderer admitted with tears the truth of the indictment, and told the story of his uncle's harshness and his subsequent adventures. The story of his wanderings aroused Millward's suspicions, and led him to enquire if he (Hutton) had any money. "Enough," he replied, to carry me home;" adding that he might rest satisfied as to his honesty, as he had brought two shillings from home with him.

This only confirmed Millward's suspicions. Two shillings, to carry a lad through a whole week of wandering, in which he had travelled near upon a hundred miles! The thing was absurd to a man accustomed to take things easily, to whom abstinence was probably unknown. "My reader will ask," says Hutton, "how I lived? I answer, as he could not. A turnip-field has supplied the place of a cook's shop; a spring, that of a public-house; and, while at Birmingham, I knew by repeated experience, that cherries were a half-penny a pound." He stayed with Millward until the next morning, and then started off, after thanking him for his kindness; "receiving," he says, "nothing for my work, nor he for his civility."

He passed through Ashby-de-la-Zouch at noon, and arrived at Derby at nine o'clock in the evening, his week of wandering ended, and he once more found himself under his father's welcome roof, where he was gladly received, with tears for his misfortunes, and an opportunity of reconciliation with his uncle, who willingly agreed to make up half the loss the wanderer had sustained at Lichfield, his father consenting to make up the other.

"But I am sorry to observe," adds Hutton, "that it was thought of no more. I thought it peculiarly hard that the promise to punish me was remembered, and the promise to reward me forgot."

Thus ended this eventful episode in the early life of the first historian of Birmingham, whom we must now leave, until the period at which he again visited Birmingham to take his place as one of her worthiest citizens.

CHAPTER XV.

THE CHURCHES AND SECTS OF BIRMINGHAM, 1720-1760.

Rebuilding of St. John's Chapel, Deritend—St. Martin's—Increase of the Peals of Bells at St. Martin's and St. Philip's—St. Bartholomew's Church—The New Meeting House—Erection of a Baptist Meeting-house in Cannon Street—Controversy between Samuel Bourn and Dr. Gill—Carr's Lane Chapel—Methodism in Birmingham—Visits of John Wesley—The Protestant Dissenting Charity School.

We have, in previous chapters, brought down the history of the Churches and sects of Birmingham as far as the year 1720, or thereabouts. Up to that period, as we have seen, there were three Churches in the town belonging to the Establishment, viz.: the Mother Church of St. Martin's, St. Philip's, and the old Chapel of St. John the Baptist, Deritend. In the year 1735 the latter, which had stood more than three hundred and fifty years, had fallen into a state of complete dilapidation, and was taken down, and the present chapel, of brick, with stone casings to the doors and windows, was erected. In 1762 the tower was added, thus completing one of the most unlovely examples of ecclesiastical architecture ever perpetrated. The rigorous adherence of the architect to the custom of placing the chancel due east has thrust that end of the church beyond the line of the street, thus adding to the irregular appearance of this—the oldest and most crooked street in the town. In 1777 eight very musical bells and a clock were placed in the tower. The church is said by Hutton to be capable of accommodating about seven hundred persons.

During the period covered by the present chapter, from 1720 or thereabouts to 1760, the alterations at the two larger churches were not considerable. The work of disfigurement continued unchecked at St. Martin's. Windows were blocked up here, and new and ugly ones opened there, large unsightly pews were erected "where no *pew* should be," and so the building increased in ugliness, and no voice was heard to protest against the sins against taste which were thus committed, chiefly by churchwardens. In 1761 the peal of bells at St. Philip's were increased from six to ten, and as St. Martin's at that time had only eight, and "could not bear to be out-numbered by a junior though of superior excellence,*" the older peal was increased to twelve, "but," says Hutton, "as room was insufficient for the admission of bells by the dozen, means were found to hoist them tier over tier." The probable reason for the increase to twelve was that there might be sufficient to afford scope for the chiming of various airs thereon; for, as Hutton remarks, "only a few tunes can be played on the octave, whilst the dozen will compass nearly all."

An Industrial School was established in connection with St. Philip's Church, and erected in the churchyard in 1724. During the present century (in 1846) the school was removed to more commodious premises in Lichfield Street, capable of accommodating 170 children, boys and girls.

* Hutton.

The increasing population of the town called for additional church accommodation. The town was rapidly extending eastward, and it was necessary that some provision should be made for the inhabitants in the neighbourhood of Stafford Street, Dale End, and the eastern end of Park Street and Moor Street. To supply this need, land was given for the erection of a church in this locality, by John Jennings, Esq.; and his lady contributed £1,000 towards the building fund. In 1749, therefore, Birmingham was provided with a fourth Church, dedicated to St. Bartholomew, which is one of the few local churches provided with a large burial-ground. The building is of brick, very unpretending in its appearance, and is surmounted by what Hutton terms an "infant steeple,—very small but beautiful." The architect very wisely rejected the superstition as to the eastward position, and so enabled the building to range with the lines of the surrounding streets. "Whether the projector committed an error," says Hutton, "I leave to the critics. It was the general practice of the Pagan church to fix their altar, upon which they sacrificed, in the east, towards the rising sun, the object of worship. The Christian church, in the time of the Romans, immediately succeeded the Pagan, and scrupulously adopted the same method; which has been strictly adhered to. By what obligation the Christian is bound to follow the Pagan, or wherein a church would be injured by being directed to any of the thirty-two points of the compass, is doubtful. Certain it is, if the chancel of St. Bartholomew's had tended due east, the eye would have been considerably hurt, and the builder would have raised an object of ridicule for ages. The ground will admit of no situation but that in which the church now stands. But the inconsiderate architect of Deritend Chapel, anxious to catch the eastern point, lost the line of the street; we may, therefore, justly pronounce, "*he sacrificed to the east.*"*

* History of Birmingham, sixth edition, p. 265.

A handsome altar-piece, with fine carvings, was placed in the church by the munificence of Basil, Earl of Denbigh, and the communion plate, consisting of one hundred and eighty-two ounces, was given by Mary Careless. The living, a perpetual curacy, is in the patronage of the rector of St. Martin's.

During this period of prosperity in the various congregations of the Established Church in the town, Dissent also grew and flourished. As we have already stated, in our survey of the town from Westley's Map and Prospect, 1730-31, the congregation of the New Meeting, ousted from their original abode in Digbeth, erected a large and commodious meeting house in Moor Street, about the year 1725, which was completed and opened for worship, April 19, 1732.

JOHN WESLEY.

The Baptists—or a certain section of them — had also erected a small meeting house in Freeman Street, but the first abode of the parent society in Birmingham was a room opposite the place where Nelson's Monument now stands, on the site of the present Market Hall. Increasing in number and influence, they "removed their apparatus and themselves" to a room at the back of No. 38, High Street; and, in 1738, were enabled to build for themselves a meeting house in Cannon Street, on part of the site of Guest's cherry-orchard. To this prosperous little church the older community of Freeman Street joined themselves, and abandoned their original home, in the year 1752.

On the opening of the Cannon Street Meeting House, a pamphlet was published by the Rev. Samuel Bourn, minister of the New Meeting, entitled "A Dialogue between a Baptist and a Churchman, occasioned by the Baptists opening a new Meeting House for reviving old Calvinistical doctrines, and spreading Antinomianism and other errors, at Birmingham, in *Warwickshire*. Part I. By a consistent Christian." This pamphlet called forth a crushing reply from the celebrated Dr. Gill, one of the most eminent and learned divines of the Baptist community. A second part subsequently appeared, which met with a similar fate at the hands of that divine.

The early part of the eighteenth century has ever stood forth in the religious history of this country as an age of indifference and unbelief. The clergy of the Established Church, and the descendants of the puritan Nonconformists who had suffered for their religious opinions in the seventeenth century, joined in throwing over as useless all the dogmatic theology for which their fathers had struggled. In this period of loose creeds the doctrine of Arianism gained ground, and the few among the nonconformists who held fast by the theology of their fathers, seceded from the various congregations and formed themselves into Independent churches. In Birmingham the seceders built a meeting-house in Carr's Lane, which was commenced in 1747 and opened in 1748. It was capable of holding about 450 persons, and this remained the only accommodation for the Independent or Congregational Church in Birmingham until the end of the eighteenth century. It has since been twice re-built and several times enlarged, but of these changes we shall have more to say hereafter.

While the "faithful few" of nonconformity thus protested against the errors which had crept into their churches, there was not wanting in the Established Church of the realm a little handful of her ministers ready, as our great satirist has finely said, "to quit the insulted temple to pray on the hill-side."* Among the first to stand forth and protest against the indifference and corruption of the time were the founders of Methodism, John and Charles Wesley, and George Whitefield. It is not necessary that we should, in these pages, enlarge upon the persecution which these men endured throughout the country during the earlier years of their labours. In Birmingham, whither John Wesley came in 1743, "the stones flew on every side;" and throughout the district known as the Black Country he suffered similar—and often worse—persecution. "I look with reverence," says Thackeray, "on these men at that time. Which is the sublimer spectacle—the good John Wesley, surrounded by his congregation of miners at the pit's mouth, or the Queen's chaplains mumbling through their morning office in their ante-room, under the picture of the great Venus, with the door opening into the adjoining chamber where the Queen is dressing, talking scandal to Lord Hervey, or uttering sneers at Lady Suffolk, who is kneeling with the basin at her mistress's side."†

"The artillery of vengeance," says Hutton, "was pointed at Methodism for thirty years; but, fixed as a rock, it could never be beaten down, and its professors now enjoy their sentiments in quiet." For some considerable time after the planting of the sect in Birmingham its adherents were "covered by the heavens, equally exposed to the rain and the rabble." ‡ Afterwards they held their various meetings in a room in Steelhouse Lane, in the occupation of a Mr.

* W. M. THACKERAY: Lectures on the four Georges.—[Works, popular edition, vol. x, p. 316.]
† ib. p. 316. ‡ Hutton.

Walker, and subsequently they obtained the use of the old play-house, in Moor Street, at the opening of which John Wesley himself preached, on the 21st of March, 1764. William Hutton very aptly sums up the career of this eminent and devoted Christian, "whose extensive knowledge and unblemished manners," he says, "give us a tolerable picture of apostolic purity, who *believed*, as if he were to be saved by faith, and who *laboured* as if he were to be saved by works."

The original meeting-house in Birmingham of the Society of Friends, commonly called Quakers, is said to have been in Monmouth Street, where there existed, before the making of the Great Western Railway, indications of an old burial-ground. Between 1702 and 1705, a meeting-house was erected in Bull Street, which, although very much altered, and twice enlarged, is still in existence, and remains the only abode of the society in Birmingham.

Such were the Churches and Sects of Birmingham during the first half of the eighteenth century. As yet the Roman Catholics had failed to make any progress in the town since the destruction of the Church of St. Marie Magdalen, in 1688. The little chapel at Edgbaston was still the only place of worship belonging to that community in this neighbourhood. If we except the Unitarians we may consider Dissent as yet only in its infancy in the town; but these little churches, which we have seen arising in the weakness of infancy, were destined in the future to bear no unimportant part in the work of enlightening the people around them, in dispelling the clouds of ignorance and immorality, in co-operating in deeds of love and mercy, in endeavouring to make the world better and the lot of suffering humanity easier—to prove a blessing to thousands of the toiling sons of Birmingham yet unborn.

About the year 1760 the Unitarians of Birmingham established a Free School on nearly the same plan as the Blue Coat School; the foundation being intended to support and educate about eighteen boys and eight girls, who were to be employed in various kinds of work during a portion of their time, in such a manner as would best fit them for future usefulness. In 1791 a building was purchased by the society in Park Street, and about £1,200 expended on its improvement. In this the number of boys was increased to 36 and girls to 18, but in later years the benefits of this excellent institution have been confined exclusively to girls. The newer building, in Graham Street, will be described in our notices of Birmingham in the nineteenth century.

CHAPTER XVI.

HOW OUR ANCESTORS TRAVELLED.

Introduction of Stage Coaches into England—Coach *versus* Horseback—Opposition encountered by the early Coaches—A Birmingham Stage Coach in 1679—Influence of travelling on the Progress of the Town—The Old Inns of Birmingham—Rothwell's Coach, 1731.

It may be interesting to our readers to pause for a few minutes in the history of our town, in order to take a glimpse at our ancestors of the eighteenth century on their travels; and to make a few notes as to the old Birmingham coaches.

Although the introduction of stage coaches into England took place as early as the middle of the seventeenth century, they did not become popular for many years; and those who could afford to do so performed their journeys on horseback; as did Samuel Johnson and his bride on their wedding journey to Derby; and many others, looking back on the pleasures of riding through shady country lanes, or along the hard firm roads during frosty weather, regarded the innovation for many years with disfavour. The writer of one of the tracts reprinted in the Harleian Miscellany* pronounces "these coaches and caravans" to be "one of the greatest mischiefs that have happened of late years to the kingdom, mischievous to the public, destructive to trade, and prejudicial to lands." He charges them first with "destroying the breed of good horses, the strength of the nation, and making men careless of attending to good horsemanship;" secondly, with "hindering the breed of watermen, who are the nursery for seamen;" and thirdly with "lessening his majesty's revenue." But notwithstanding the opposition, with which every innovation has to contend, the stage coach held its own, and became the recognised mode of travelling for more than two hundred years, in various forms, and the new convenience was not long in finding its way into the Midlands. In Sir William Dugdale's Diary we learn that, as early as 1679 there was a Birmingham Coach to London. Under date July 16, 1679, he says "I came out of London by the stage coach of *Bermicham* to Banbury." Who was the enterprising originator of this old "Bermicham Coach." we cannot now ascertain.

The facilities thus early offered for Birmingham people to travel, doubtless exercised an influence on the town, as regards local improvements, as well as in enabling the workmen occasionally to visit the metropolis, and to pick up new ideas. "Home-keeping youth," says our great dramatist, "have ever homely wits," and it would appear almost impossible, without the means of intercourse with other great centres of industry and civilization, for a community isolated as Birmingham was from other large towns to have made such rapid pro-

THE OLD PRISON, PECK LANE.

* "The Grand Concern of England."

HUTTON'S FIRST VISIT TO BIRMINGHAM. (*See page 98.*)

"About ten yards from me, near the corner of Philip Street, I perceived two men in aprons eye me with some attention. They approached near. 'You seem,' says one, 'by your melancholy situation, and dusty shoes, a forlorn traveller, without money and without friends.' I assured him it was exactly my case 'If you choose to accept a pint, it is at your service.'

Early Coaching Bill.

(Reduced in facsimile from the original, in the possession of John Suffield, Esq.)

BIRMINGHAM STAGE-COACH,

In Two *Days* and a half; begins *May* the 24th, 1731.

SETS out from the *Swan-Inn* in *Birmingham*, every *Monday* at ſix a Clock in the Morning, through *Warwick*, *Banbury* and *Alesbury*, to the *Red Lion Inn* in *Alderſgate ſtreet*, *London*, every *Wedneſday* Morning: And returns from the ſaid *Red Lion Inn* every *Thurſday* Morning at five a Clock the ſame Way to the *Swan-Inn* in *Birmingham* every *Saturday*, at 21 Shillings each Paſſenger, and 18 Shillings from *Warwick*, who has liberty to carry 14 Pounds in Weight, and all above to *pay One Penny a Pound*.

Perform'd (if God permit)

By Nicholas Rothwell.

The Weekly Waggon ſets out every *Tueſday from the Nagg's-Head in* Birmingham, *to the* Red Lion Inn *aforeſaid*, every *Saturday*; *and returns from the ſaid Inn* every *Monday*, *to the Nagg's-Head in Birmingham* every *Thurſday*.

Note. *By the ſaid* Nicholas Rothwell *at* Warwick, *all Perſons may be furniſhed with a By-Coach, Chariot, Chaiſe, or Hearſe, with a Mourning Coach and able Horſes, to any Part of Great Britain, at reaſonable Rates: And alſo Saddle Horſes to be had.*

gress in the industrial arts, and in other ways, as the history of the town, from the middle to the end of the seventeenth century, gives evidence of.

The next Birmingham Coach of which we have any record is that of Nathaniel Rothwell, running between Birmingham and London, the journey being "perform'd (if God permit) in two days and a half."

The contrast both in appearance and convenience between these old coaches of the first half of the eighteenth century and the coaches of the period which immediately preceded the introduction of railways, is well depicted in a scarce little collection of *Tales of an Antiquary*, published about fifty years ago.

"In my own young days," says the writer of these *Tales*, "they [the stage-coaches] were not formed of that glossy material which now reflects the ever-changing scenes as they whirl lightly and rapidly along, but were constructed principally of a dull black leather, thickly studded, by way of ornament, with black broad-headed nails tracing out the panels; in the upper tier of which were four oval windows, with heavy red wooden frames, and green stuff or leather curtains. Upon the doors, also, there appeared but little of that gay blazonry which shines upon the *quadringæ* of the present time; but there were displayed in large characters the names of the places whence the coach started, and whither it went, stated in quaint and antique language. The vehicles themselves varied in shape. Sometimes they were like a distiller's vat, somewhat flattened, and hung equally balanced between the immense front and back springs; in other instances they resembled a violincello-case, which was past all comparison the most fashionable form; and then they hung in a more genteel posture, namely, inclining on to the back springs, and giving to those who sat within the appearance of a stiff Guy Fau., uneasily seated. . . . The coachman, and the guard, who always held his carabine ready bent, or as we now say, cocked, upon his knee, then sat together; not as at present, upon a close, compact, varnished seat, but over a very long and narrow boot, which passed under a large spreading hammer cloth, hanging down on all sides, and finished with a flowing and most luxuriant fringe. Behind the coach was the immense basket, stretching far and wide beyond the body, to which it was attached by long iron bars or supports passing beneath it; though even these seemed scarcely equal to the enormous weight with which they were frequently loaded. . . . . The wheels of these old carriages were large, massive, ill-formed, and usually of a red colour; and the three horses that were affixed to the whole machine—the foremost of which was helped onward by carrying a huge long-legged elf of a postillion, dressed in a cocked hat, with a large green and gold riding coat—were all so far parted from it by the great length of their traces, that it was with no little difficulty that the poor animals dragged their unwieldly burthen along the road. It groaned, and creaked, and lumbered, at every fresh tug which they gave it, as a ship, rocking or beating up through a heavy sea, strains all her timbers with a low moaning sound, as she drives over the contending waves."

Of such a coach the reader will see a rough delineation in the facsimile of the rude woodcut at the head of Rothwell's handbill, which we give on another page. In later years, the Birmingham coaches, at any rate, presented a somewhat different, and less sombre exterior, which Thomas De Quincey has very graphically described. "Once," he says, "I remember being on the box of the Holyhead Mail, between Shrewsbury and Oswestry, when a tawdry thing from Birmingham, some 'Tallyho' or 'High-flyer,' all flaunting with green and gold, came up alongside of us. What a contrast to our royal simplicity of form and colour in this plebeian wretch! The single ornament on our dark ground of chocolate colour was the mighty shield of the imperial arms, but emblazoned in proportions as modest as a signet ring bears to a seal of office.

Even this was displayed only on a single pannel, whispering, rather than proclaiming, our relations to the mighty state; whilst the beast from Birmingham, our green-and-gold friend from false, fleeting, perjured Brummagem, had as much writing and painting on its sprawling flanks as would have puzzled a decipherer from the tombs of Luxor."*

The slow rate at which these lumbering old coaches travelled,—about three miles an hour,—grew in time to be a source of great dissatisfaction, and to none more so than to the busy, restless people of Birmingham. Discontent has ever been the precurser of improvement, and it was not long before a considerable improvement was effected in the speed of the Birmingham coaches. The first "Flying Coach" in England of which any record can be found was that running between Birmingham and London. It is announced in Walker's Birmingham Paper, of April 12th, 1742, (No 26), as follows:—"The Litchfield and Birmingham Stage Coach sets out this morning (Monday) from the 'Rose Inn' at Holbourn Bridge, London, and will be at the House of Mr. Francis Cox, *the Angel and Hen and Chickens, in the High Town, Birmingham*, on Wednesday next to dinner, and goes the same afternoon to Litchfield, and returns to Birmingham on Thursday morning to breakfast, and gets to London on Saturday night, and so will continue every week regularly with a

ST. BARTHOLOMEW'S CHURCH.

* THOMAS DE QUINCEY: The English Mail Coach [Works: vol. iv., p. 299.]

good coach and able horses." To perform the journey from London to Birmingham in two days and a half does not sound at all like "flying" to modern ears, accustomed to travelling the same distance in a few hours; but to the people of 1742, it was a startling innovation, they never having conceived of a greater speed than three or four miles an hour.

The merchants of Manchester and Liverpool were far behind Birmingham in the matter of travelling. It was not until 1754 that the former started a "Flying Coach," of which it was an-announced that "incredible as it may appear, this coach will actually (barring accidents) arrive in London in four days and a half after leaving Manchester." Three years later Liverpool eclipsed her rival by running a coach (called *a "flying machine on steel springs,"*) which occupied only three days in the journey between that city and the metropolis.

Still Birmingham seemed determined to lead the van in improvements in this as in other matters. The *Annual Register* for the year 1758 describes an improved Birmingham coach, which is represented as going without using coomb, or any oily, unctuous, or other liquid matter whatever to the wheels or axles; its construction being such as to render all such helps useless. The inventor had engraved, on the boxes of the wheels, the words "*Friction Annihilated*, and it was asserted that the carriage would go as long and as easy, if not longer and easier, without greasing, than any of the ordinary stage carriages will do with greasing. "If this answers in common practice," adds the writer in the *Annual Register*, "it is perhaps the most useful invention in mechanics that this age has produced." Whether the invention realised the expectations of its originator or not we cannot say; but as we do not hear of it in connection with modern coach building, it is probable that the "friction annihilator" has passed into the limbo of ingenious, but impracticable inventions, of which the vast library of patent specifications could afford thousands of examples.

The discomfort of the jolting, rolling, lumbering coach was not the only drawback to the traveller's enjoyment. The wretched condition of the roads, and the difficulty of proceeding at anything like a good speed, afforded great facilities for the successors of those "minions of the moon" who plied their calling so successfully at Gad's Hill. It was by no means an infrequent occurrence for the passengers to alight at their destination *minus* money and all other valuables they had incautiously carried with them; unable to pay for the accommodation of the inn, or even for a necessary supply of food. The early numbers of the *Gazette* bear frequent testimony to the dangers of the road, and the wisdom of that custom at which we of the nineteenth century are prone to smile, viz., of the traveller making his will before proceeding on his journey. The earliest notice in that journal of an adventure of this sort refers not to the traveller by stage-coach, but to one who preferred the older and pleasanter mode of travelling—on horseback. "An eminent tea merchant, in Cornhill," one Frederick Bull, was journeying from Wolverhampton to London, in October, 1742, and "was overtaken on the road by a single Man on Horseback, *whom he took for a Gentleman;* but after they had rode three or four miles together, he then ordered him to deliver, *which Mr. Bull took to be in Jest; but he told him that he was in Earnest,* and accordingly robb'd him of about four Guineas and his Watch, and afterwards rode with him three miles, till they came near a Town, when the Highwayman rode off."

A few months later the *Gazette* chronicled an attack on the Coach. On the 18th May, we read, "the Birmingham Stage Coach was robb'd about two Miles from Banbury, and about an hour after the Robbery was committed, the noted Sansbury and his Accomplice, who have infested these Roads, were taken, being drunk, and asleep among the Standing Corn." The "noted Sansbury" was executed shortly afterwards.

The highwayman of that period, as we are

continually reminded in romances of the "Rookwood" and "Paul Clifford" school, was often a chivalrous and high-minded gentleman, of whom the famous Claude Duval was a notable example. They were favoured occasionally with a visit from one of these high-minded gentry in the neighbourhood of Birmingham. On October 1st, 1750, the *Gazette* reported an incident of the kind so frequently referred to by the admirers of the old "knights of the road." On the previous Wednesday Mr. Henry Hunt, of this town, "was stopp'd on Sutton Coldfield, in the Chester Road, by two Highwaymen, who robb'd him of his Watch and Money; *but on Mr. Hunt asking him to give him back some silver, the Highwaymen return'd him six shillings,* and immediately rode across the Coldfield, and robb'd another gentleman in sight of him, and then rode quite off."

There is, however, one other adventure on the road chronicled which eclipses this of Sutton Coldfield, both for cool impudence and gentlemanly bearing on the part of the "Collector." On Tuesday April 30th, 1751, the "Shrewsbury Carravan," we are told, was stopped between the Four Crosses and the Welch Harp by a single Highwayman, "who behaved very civilly to the Passengers, told them that he was a Tradesman in Distress, and hoped that they would contribute to his assistance." The hat thus unceremoniously passed round, was liberally received, for we are told "each Passenger gave him something," so that the whole contribution amounted to about four pounds, "with which he was mighty well satisfied." But although a "tradesman in distress," he had evidently —unlike his brother tradesmen—a soul above coppers; for we read that he "*return'd some Halfpence to one of them, saying he never took Copper.*" He then told them "there were two other *Collectors* on the Road, but he would see them out of Danger, which he accordingly did." This gentlemanly thief may have heard at the theatre, or read in the play itself, of the scruples of Ancient Pistoll on the score of the uglier words "rob" and "steal," but his ingenuity provided him with even a better name than "conveyancer." He evidently felt, however, that the officers of justice had foolish prejudices against even the innocent pursuits of a "collector," for as he left the company whom he had so generously escorted out of danger, we read, he "begged that they would not at their next Inn mention the Robbery nor appear against him if he should be taken up hereafter."

Before leaving the subject of travelling for the present, we may glance for a moment at the old inns of Birmingham. A writer on the Birmingham inns of the 16th century,* enumerates nine taverns at that period; *The Cock* and *The Redd Lyon* in Digbeth; *The Talbot* and *The Dogg* in Spiceal Street; *The Dolphin,* in Corn Cheaping; *The Horse Shoe,* in St. Martin's Lane, (said to have taken its name from the arms of the Ferrers family); *The Swan; The Garland;* and *The Starr,* in the High Town. Later, the *White Hart* (where the fatal basket of clothes arrived, carrying the dreaded plague with them) was established; also, the *Fleur-de-Lis,* in Moor Street. It was at *The Dog* that John Cooper lived, about the year 1500, who gave a croft near Steelhouse Lane to make "Love-days" for the people of Birmingham; from whence the unlovely street which now crosses the said croft takes its name. The donor of this first recreation ground to the town was permitted to bait a bull in the Bull Ring once a year.

The most interesting of the inns named above is the *Swan,* which, during the earlier days of coaching, was *the* Hostelry and Coaching House of Birmingham. It was from this house that Rothwell's coaches ran, and to which they returned, as will be seen from his handbill; and throughout the coaching era *The Swan* figures prominently in many of the *Gazette* advertisements of Coaches to and from Birmingham and various parts of the country.

Besides the *Swan,* an inn in Bull Street, called *The Saracen's Hea,* and *The Castle* (in High

* Quoted on page of 70 this work.

Street) were also well-known Coaching Houses. *The Angel and Hen and Chickens* in High Street, (or "the High Town," as it was then called,) was also rapidly rising into prominence as a Coaching House. It was from this house, as we have seen, that the first "flying coach" started; and from the date of the commencement of *Aris's Gazette* to the end of the coaching days this remained one of the principal houses "on the road." In the earliest notice of the house (quoted in our chapter on *Aris's Gazette,* *) it is simply styled "The Hen and Chickens." The names of the occupiers, previous to 1770, were unknown to the recent historian of the house, but from the announcement of the "flying coach" in 1742, it appears to have been at that time in the occupation of Mr. Francis Cox; as it seems also to have been in the next year, from an advertisement which appeared in the *Gazette* of December 12, 1743, announcing the sale,—"to the best Bidder, on Monday, the 19th of December instant, at the Dwelling-House of Francis Cox, *the Angel and Hen and Chickens,*"—of "a messuage now known by the sign of the Red Lion," in Bordesley. The addition to the sign of "the Angel" was probably made by the new occupier of the house, who entered upon it at or after Christmas, 1741,—in all probability Mr. Francis Cox himself. To this inn, or rather to its successor the New Street "hotel," in later years, came many of the most eminent men of their time, of whose visits—as also of the later history of this celebrated hotel itself—we shall have to speak in future chapters.

To whichever of these old inns the traveller repaired, it is to be hoped that like Shenstone he "found the warmest welcome," different indeed from the cold and formal reception accorded to the traveller by rail at the huge hotel of the present day. How different in these old days, at the *Swan* or the *Hen and Chickens* (the modern hotels have risen above the vulgarity of a "sign") or other of the cosy old hostelries to be found in every town through which a coach passed.

"What cosy old parlours in those days," says De Quincey, "low-roofed, glowing with ample fires, and fenced from the blast of the doors by screens, whose folding doors were, or seemed to be, infinite! What motherly landladies! won, how readily, to kindness the most lavish, by the mere attractions of simplicity and youthful innocence, and finding so much interest in the bare circumstance of being a traveller at a childish age! Then what blooming young handmaidens; how different from the knowing and worldly demireps of modern high roads! And sometimes grey-headed faithful waiters, how sincere and how attentive by comparison with their flippant successors, the eternal 'Coming, sir, coming,' of our improved generation."

CHAPTER XVII.

THE OLD PRISON OF BIRMINGHAM.

Unfrequency of Crime in Birmingham—Idleness and ill-doing—The Prison-house of earlier times—"Bridewell House"—Enlargement of the Prison.

From the records of the old coaching days, with their pleasant associations of shady roads lined with blossoming hedgerows, of breezy commons, and of snug country hostelries, to the history of damp and mouldy prison-houses and their inmates, is a sorry change indeed; but it becomes the duty of a faithful historian to show the gloomy side of the picture as well as the bright, and, however unwelcome the interruption may be, it is a necessary part of our story.

"It is easy," says Hutton, "to point out some places only one-third the magnitude of Birming-

* See page 86.

ham, whose frequent breaches of the law, and quarrels among themselves, find employment for half-a-dozen magistrates, and four times that number of constables; whilst the business of this was for many years conducted by a single justice." He ascribes this law-abiding characteristic of the people of Birmingham to the industry of the people; the hand employed in business having, he says, "less time, and less temptation, to be employed in mischief." To the absence of "idle hands" in the town, therefore, may be attributed the smallness of the gaol accommodation necessary previous to the year 1733.

In earlier times the lord of the manor held a tribunal on his own premises, and probably, as was usual in such cases, a rude prison in some sort would be annexed thereto, with such implements for punishing as were then in use; as, the stocks and the whipping-post, which, as we have seen, were afterwards removed to the Welsh Cross. After the fall of the Bermingham family, one of the lower rooms of the Leather Hall in New Street was used as a prison; "but," says Hutton, "about the year 1728, *while men slept an enemy came,* a private agent to the lord of the manor, and erased the Leather Hall and the Dungeon, erected three houses on the spot, and received their rents till 1776, when the town purchased them for £500, to open the way." Up to this time the only entrance to New Street from the High Town had been through a narrow passage, similar to that at the entrance to Castle Street. In the days of the Leather Hall it acquired (from the use to which the basement had been put) the name of the *Dungeon Entry,* and this name remained for many years after the building of the houses in place of the old hall.

From 1728 to 1733, the town had no other place of detention for offenders, except a dry cellar, belonging to a house opposite the site of the demolished Leather Hall. On the 9th of September in the latter year, however, a meeting of the inhabitants was held in the chamber over the Cross, at which it was "unanimously agreed upon that a Dungeon be forthwith erected at the Publick expense of the said Parish, at the place commonly called Bridewell House, near Pinfold Street;" This was, according to Hutton, "of all bad places the worst; . . . dark, narrow, and unwholesome within; crowded with dwellings, filth, and distress without, the circulation of air is prevented." Its gloomy, forbidding aspect without is well depicted in the engraving on page 104, which is taken from the lithographic print by Mr. Underwood, contained in his series of views of "The Buildings of Birmingham, Past and Present," a work which is now becoming scarce.

This old "Bridewell" was like most of the provincial town gaols of that period; and what they were the reader may learn, if he can endure the recital of the sickening details, from the journals of visits paid to these wretched dens in 1773-5, by that noble-minded philanthropist, John Howard.

Whether the exemplary morality attributed by Hutton to the people of Birmingham suffered a relapse after the building of the new dungeon, we cannot tell; but it would certainly appear that the gaol soon became too small to accommodate its numerous prisoners; for, in 1757, it was found necessary "to take down the Three Houses fronting Peck Lane, in order to enlarge the Prison;" which proceeding was decided upon at a meeting held on the thirteenth of September in that year. This building remained the only local prison until the erection of the building in Moor Street, in 1795; and was not destroyed until 1806, when the building materials were sold for £250. It "has been immortalised in a sarcastic triplet relating to one of the latest wakes and 'bull baitings,' when the authorities of the day

——'Spoiled the wake,
And stole the stake,
And took the bull to the Dungeon.'"

CHAPTER XVIII.

LOCAL MANUFACTURES IN THE EIGHTEENTH CENTURY.

A Second Survey of Local Trades and Manufactures—Experiments in Cotton Spinning—John Wyatt—The Weighing Machine—Seizure of Swords in 1744—The Gun Trade—Buckles—Buttons—"Toys."

We may now take a second glance at the Trades of Birmingham. It will be remembered that our last survey brought us to the close of the seventeenth century, at which period the "transition" was completed, and Birmingham had ceased to be known merely for her works in iron, and had become famous for those innumerable manufactures, both useful and beautiful, by which she earned the title of "the toy shop of the world."

It will be a matter of surprise to those who are unacquainted with Mr. Timmins's interesting volume, referred to in our first notice, to learn that the trade which is now centred in the south of Lancashire, and, indeed, has become the staple trade of that district, was born in Birmingham.

"Long before Richard Arkwright had commenced the Career which ended in a colossal fortune," says Mr. Timmins, "the process of 'spinning by rollers' was first tried in Birmingham." The first thread of cotton spun by machinery, "without the aid of human fingers," was produced in the year 1700, at Sutton Coldfield, by John Wyatt, by an arrangement of rollers in a small model, "without a single witness to the work, the inventor (to use his own words) being 'all the time in a pleasing but trembling suspense.'" The invention was put into practical operation in Birmingham, an engine being fixed in "a large warehouse near The Well, in the Upper Priory," and "turned by two asses walking round an axis." The process was continued on these premises (called the "Cotton Spinning Mill") for some time, the inventor, Wyatt, being joined by Lewis Paul, to whom the invention has sometimes erroneously been attributed—and, at a later period, by Thomas Warren, the bookseller, who published Johnson's translation of Lobo's *Abyssinia*, and with whom, as we have seen, Edmund Hector had lodged during the earlier years of his professional career in Birmingham. The three cotton-spinners, however, were unsuccessful; Warren had sunk a thousand pounds in the speculation, and in February, 1740, became a bankrupt. Misfortune followed the experiment throughout its career, the mill and machinery being offered for sale several times, and eventually the little trade died out. Still the fact remains, that "the first trials of the process of 'spinning by rollers'—the key-stone of the great cotton trade of England—were made in our own town long before Arkwright had studied and perfected the machinery on which his fortune was based;"* and it is more than probable, that, had a Matthew Boulton been at the back of the inventor, to do for Wyatt and his cotton-spinning machinery what he did for Watt and the steam engine, Birmingham might have become the centre of that great industry, and the sound of the loom and the shuttle might never have been heard in the great cities of the north.

John Wyatt may be said also to be the inventor of the weighing machine for carriages, carts, and wagons, which has undergone scarcely any alteration since he originated it. But even this invention was not put into practical operation until 1767, after Wyatt's death, which occurred in 1766. He was followed to the grave by Matthew Boulton and John Baskerville, the latter having, says Mr. Timmins, "arrayed himself on the occasion, in a rich suit, decorated with gold lace."

The Jacobite rebellion of 1745, and the alarm excited by it, gave considerable stimulus to the local trade in implements of warfare, especially swords. It will be remembered that during the Civil War the Birmingham sword-blade manufacturer, Richard Porter, refused to supply a single

* S. Timmins.

weapon to the Royalists, although they offered to pay him liberally if he would do so; but the sword-makers of the eighteenth century would appear either to have become better affected toward the House of Stuart, or else to have possessed fewer scruples on the score of political morality; for they willingly executed large orders for the army of "bonnie Prince Charlie."

Occasionally these consignments of arms for the rebels were intercepted by the Government. In 1744 a large chest of basket-hilted swords, sent from Birmingham to the Belle Sauvage, on Ludgate Hill, London, was seized and taken to the Tower; and in October of the same year a seizure was made of two thousand Birmingham cutlasses, which had been sent to the Saracen's Head. No swords were ordered from Birmingham by the Government, so far as is known, until nearly the end of the eighteenth century.

The gun trade—which had been introduced, or at any rate greatly stimulated, under the circumstances detailed in our former chapter on the local trades, would probably be influenced by the rebellion to even a greater extent than sword-making. After the peace of 1714, when the demand for military guns had in all probability ceased, the manufacturers would be in a position to turn the new trade to account in the production of fowling-pieces and other guns required for the trade. The Jacobite rebellion, however, could serve to stimulate the manufacture of guns to be used in warfare, and the too frequent necessity for new supplies of these instruments of death, during the latter half of the century, effectually prevented this branch of the trade from falling into decay.

One of the principal fancy trades which had arisen in Birmingham during the "transition period" was that of manufacturing Buckle. William Hutton observes that the "Revolution was remarkable for the introduction of William, Liberty, and the Buckle;" but this statement is incorrect as far as the buckle is concerned. They had been worn as early as the fifteenth century, but had fallen into disuse, and had been only *revived* at the period of the Revolution; and the resucitated fashion reigned for nearly a century. They were first made at Bilston, but the facilities for making them at Birmingham gradually drew the trade entirely away from the former place. They were generally made from a metal called Tutania, a name said to have been derived from that of its inventor, one Tutin; but many inferior materials were also used, —pinchbeck, "silver-plate," and an inferior kind of white metal called by the workmen "soft tommy." A story was told by the late Matthew Davenport Hill, Recorder of Birmingham, in an address delivered before the members of the Birmingham and Midland Institute, of a workman, who, while engaged in making buckles of this latter material, was overheard by his master cursing the wearer most vehemently. "Why do you curse the wearer?" asked the astonished master." "Because," replied the buckle-maker, "I know when he wears these buckles he will curse the maker, and I thought I would be before-hand with him?"

Buckles were made in various forms and sizes, from the small buckle on the band of the hat or the knee to the huge shoe-buckle which nearly covered the foot; and were sold at from one shilling to five and even ten guineas a pair. When the fashion was at its height it was almost universal, and Birmingham supplied the greater number of these articles for America and the whole Continent. Alas, however, for the mutability of human fashions! In 1790 the buckle was dethroned, and the "effeminate shoe-string" took its place. In vain did the unfortunate buckle-makers endeavour to arrest the changing fashion; it was "void of feeling, and deaf to argument," as their petition truly expressed it. They appealed to the Prince of Wales in 1791, to assist in giving employment to "more than 20,000 persons" who, in consequence of "the prevalence of shoe-strings and slippers" were in great distress; and both he and the Duke of

York ordered their gentlemen and servants to discard shoe-strings and return to the buckles. It was, however, all in vain. Another petition was forwarded the next year to the Duke and Duchess of York; but the fashion was dead, and no attempt to galvanize it into life again could hope to succeed, and so one of the great staple trades of Birmingham died out before the close of the eighteenth century.

Another of the trades dependent upon the fickle goddess Fashion was that of Button-making. During the latter part of the seventeenth and the first half of the eighteenth century, the buttons worn were for the most part made with the needle, and this branch of industry was encouraged and protected by various Acts of Parliament in the reign of William and Mary, to prevent the importation of all foreign buttons made with hair, as well as to prevent the manufacture of *covered* buttons, leaving a hard substance underneath the hair or silk exterior. Prints of that period exhibit the costumes as being covered with buttons to an extravagant and ridiculous extent, wherever a button could possibly be affixed to the garment; a fashion which is thus satirized in one of the comedies of the period:

"Next, then, the slouching sleeve, and our large buttons,
"And now our coats, flank broad, like shoulder-mutton;
"Faced with fine colours—scarlet, green, and sky,
"With sleeves so large, they'll give us wings to fly.
"Next year I hope they'll cover nails and all,
"And every button like a tennis ball."

But about the middle of the eighteenth century, the fashion in buttons changed, and those of mohair and satin gave place to others of metal, mostly gilt. This was a department of trade in which Birmingham could excel, and button making speedily became one of the staple trades of the town. Gilt buttons were soon in great demand. According to contemporary prints and descriptions, the large cloth coats were loaded with them, almost as extravagantly as those of their fathers had been with buttons of other materials. A writer in the *St. James's Chronicle* of 1763, referring to the display of tradesmen aping their betters, speaks of "the myriads of gold buttons" which they wore, and makes special mention of a smith with whom he had come in contact, wearing "a coat loaded with innumerable gilt buttons." The much-admired buttons increased in favour rather than diminished, and were adopted by many ladies in preference to woven ones, and so the button makers flourished. It was truly, as it has been happily described, the Augustan age of button making in Birmingham.

And while buckles, and buttons, and weapons of warfare were in steady demand, there was also a large miscellaneous trade growing up in the light steel toys which were then coming into use. "Toys" has too often been a misused and misunderstood term, as regards the products of Birmingham. Our town has never, like Holland, taken "pleasure in making what the children of England take pleasure in breaking;" children's toys have never been a part of the manufactures of Birmingham. A century ago, before the discovery of gold and silver in large quantities in the far west of North America, and before the gold of Australia had been dreamt of, those precious metals were of course very much scarcer and dearer, and the steel toy trade of that period corresponded to a great extent with the jewellery trade of modern times. Brooches, studs, bracelets, watch-chains, châtelaines, sword-hilts, and scores of other light ornaments and trifles of various kinds, were then made of steel and were very fashionable; and it was in the manufacture of these that Birmingham earned the title given by Edmund Burke, which has remained to the present day, of "the Toy shop of the World."

In the manufacture of nearly all these lighter articles, great excellence was shown by Matthew Boulton, but the story of his great enterprise is one which will require a chapter of itself; we therefore leave the survey of our local trades for the present with the simple mention of his name.

CHAPTER XIX.

JOHN BASKERVILLE.

Early Birmingham Printers—Baskerville's early life—His residence at Easy Hill—"The pattern-card of his trade"—Productions of his press—Sale of his plant—His will, etc.

THE history of the art of Printing, as practised in Birmingham, does not carry us very far back into antiquity. The earliest book which has yet been discovered with a local imprint is dated 1717, and bears the following lengthy title :

A Loyal Oration, giving a short Account of several Plots, some purely Popish, others mixt; the former contriv'd and carry'd on by Papists, the latter both by Papists and also Protestants of the High-Church Party, united together against our Church and State : As also of the many Deliverances which Almighty God has vouch-saf'd to us since the Reformation. Composed by James Parkinson, formerly Fellow of Lincoln College, in Oxford, now Chief Master of the Free School of Birmingham, in Warwickshire, and spoke by his Son, on the 10th day of December, 1716. And now Publish'd at the Request of Captain Thetford, Captain Shugborough, and several other Officers of the Prince's Own Royal Regiment of Welsh Fusileers, and other Loyal Gentlemen. To which is annex'd by way of Postcript, the Author's Letter to the Reverend Mr. Higgs, Rector of St. Philip's Church, in Birmingham, who upon hearing this Loyal Speech, was so displeas'd and nettl'd with it, and particularly with that Passage in it that relates to bidding Prayers which he constantly uses, that on the Sunday following he could not forbear reviling the Author in his Sermon, calling the Speech a scurrilous Discourse, and the Composer thereof a Slanderer and Calumniator. Birmingham : Printed and Sold by Matthew Unwins, near St. Martin's Church. 1717.

In all probability, therefore, Matthew Unwins was the first printer established in the town; and that he had not long introduced the enlightening art into Birmingham at the date of the "Loyal Oration" may be assumed from the fact that the author of that tract had published another, two years previously, which he had been obliged to have printed in London. It is just possible, however, that another printer may have preceded Unwins by a year or so, as there exists (in the possession of Charles H. Bayley, Esq., of West Bromwich) a unique copy of a little duo-decimo of sixty-four pages entitled "A Help against Sin, in our ordinary discourse. . . . Published by the author R. H. [Amersley], Chyrurgeon in Walsall, Staffordshire, 1719. *Birmingham, Printed by H. B., in New Street.*" In this work the author refers to "a little book called 'Advice to Sunday Barbers,'" which "some years past" he had "put out," of which, he says, there were but few printed. If, therefore, this "Advice" was printed in Birmingham, it would be earlier than the "Loyal Oration," although the fact of the earlier tract by the author of the latter being printed in London goes against the supposition that "H. B." was the first Birmingham Printer, or that Matthew Unwins printed the "Advice to Sunday Barbers."

But the earlier productions of the local press were, like those of most other provincial towns, very poorly printed, the paper, ink, and letter-cutting being of the commonest possible quality. Beauty was a thing not to be thought of, so long as the printing served its primary purpose of being legible. The wretchedness of the work-manship in these early books and pamphlets, and the desirability of producing books which should be beautiful as well as useful, appears to have been impressed upon the mind of John Basker-ville, a young writing-master, who taught a school in the Bull Ring in 1737. He was a native of Wolverley, in Worcestershire, but, like many other young men of genius or ability, was attracted early in life to the busy and rapidly-increasing town which had arisen on the borders of his native county. Here he started in life as a cutter of "grave-stones in any of the hands," at his house in Moor Street—"his window slate," says Mr. Timmins, "being still in existence, and showing, in a marvellous manner, the form and style of the 'letter' he afterwards delighted to produce."

As a teacher of writing, the beauty of his pen-manship was celebrated; he possessed "an exquisite taste for ornament and proportion generally,"* and this caused him to excel in all his various pursuits. From stone cutting and penmanship, he turned his attention, in 1740, to japanning. Being fond of painting, "he either introduced, or effected an entire revolution in, the manufacture of japanned articles,"† and rendered all his productions in this department admirable as works of art. In 1745 he took, on a building lease, a pleasant little estate of eight acres, (on the site of which Broad Street and Easy Row now stand,) to which he gave the name of Easy Hill, and erected for himself a house in the centre of the grounds, out of the din and bustle of the busy town, and yet within easy access of it; "but the town," says Hutton, "as if conscious of his merit, followed his retreat and surrounded it with buildings."

In the advertisement of the sale of the house and its surroundings, in 1788, the estate is said to consist of "about seven Acres of rich Pasture Land in high condition, Part of which is laid out in Shady Walks, adorned with Shrubberies, Fish Ponds, and Grotto; the whole in a Ring-Fence, great part of it enclosed by a Brick-Wall."

Here he continued his business as a japanner, and, with the eccentricity of which we have already given an example in the case of John Wyatt's funeral, set up a carriage, every panel of which was a distinct picture, accurately and beautifully painted,—which Hutton aptly describes as "*the pattern-card of his trade*,"—which was drawn by a handsome pair of cream-coloured horses. But while thus busily engaged in making a fortune out of the trade of japanning—"supplying the common and material wants of mankind"—"the love of art, and the aspiration for something higher," says Mr. Timmins, "found full expression, and produced unparalleled results." John Baskerville's love of letters, and his dissatisfaction with the existing state of typography, led him, in 1750, to turn his attention toward the subject of producing such examples of the art of printing, as should do honour to the noblest

JOHN BASKERVILLE.

* HAWKES SMITH : Birmingham and its vicinity, part 3, p. 19.
† ib.

works of the ancient classics and of the most eminent authors of our own country. Several years were spent in experiments, and upwards of six hundred pounds were sunk before he could produce a single letter to please his fastidious taste, "and some thousands," adds Hutton, "before the shallow stream of profit began to flow." In 1757 he published his first work, a magnificent edition of Virgil, sold at one guinea, for which Matthew Boulton was one of the first subscribers; and this was followed in 1758, by a handsome octavo edition in two volumes, of the Poems of John Milton, and a quarto, entitled, "Avon, a Poem," written by the Rev. John Huckell. In 1761 followed a quarto edition, in four volumes, of the works of Joseph Addison, and an octavo, in three volumes, of the Dramatic Works of Congreve. The same year saw the issue of the second volume of his splendid quarto series of the classics, Juvenal and Persius, which was followed, at intervals, by Horace, Lucretius, Catullus, Tibullus, and Propertius, Sallust and Florus, and Terence. In 1763 he issued the magnificent Cambridge Edition of the Bible, an immense folio which has been pronounced to be the finest example of typography ever produced; another (smaller) folio Bible bears his imprint, but this is said to be spurious. Besides these greater works he also published an edition of the Book of Common Prayer, a quarto edition of Barclay's famous "Apology" for the Quakers, an edition in four volumes of Ariosto, a Greek Testament, a duodecimo series of the classics, and several contemporay works of inferior importance, among which was one, a mere quarto tract of a few pages, which from some cause or other is the rarest of all his famous productions, —"An Ode to the *Yatch* [*sic*] which conveyed the Princess Charlotte to England." Possibly the curious misprint in the title-page may have something to do with its rarity.

These works, which, as Macaulay says, "went forth to astonish all the librarians of Europe," are still highly prized for the excellence of form, elegance, and sharpness of the letters, the brilliancy of the ink, and the beautiful whiteness of the paper, as compared with that of other books of the period, and have become famous not merely among the librarians and literati of Europe, but throughout the world, among book-lovers everywhere, by all who can appreciate beautiful typography, whether as professors of the art or as lovers of literature generally. "Wherever the art of printing is admired, and its choicest works are collected, there the Birmingham printed works of John Baskerville find a high and honourable place. Not only did he design and cast his unrivalled type, but he made his own paper, prepared his own ink, worked his own presses, and probably bound some of his own books.*

In 1765 he made advances, through his friend Benjamin Franklin, then in Paris, to the literati of France, with a view to the disposal of his types in that capital, but the French were at that time so reduced by the war of 1756 that "so far from pursuing schemes of taste, . . . they were unable to repair their public buildings, but suffered the scaffolding to rot before them." †

Being unable to effect a sale of his printing business, he continued to make use of the valuable materials for producing beautiful and readable editions of various standard works until his death, which occurred on the 8th of January, 1775. He died childless, and the splendid appliances for the art of printing, which had cost him years of labour and many thousands of pounds, failed to find a purchaser in this country, and to our lasting disgrace, were allowed, after lying a dead weight four years, to go out of the country which prides itself on its noble literature, and were purchased by a literary society of Paris for £3,700, and used to print a splendid edition of the works of Voltaire.

"Invention," says Hutton, "seldom pays the inventor. If you ask, what fortune Baskerville ought to have been rewarded with? 'The *most* which can be comprised in five figures.' If you

* S. Timmins. † Hutton.

further ask, what he possessed? 'The *least;* but none of it squeezed from the press.' What will the shade of this great man think, if capable of thinking, that he has spent a fortune of opulence, and a life of genius, in carrying to perfection the greatest of all human inventions; and his productions, slighted by his country, were hawked over Europe in quest of a bidder?"

His character and appearance are well described by Hutton, who knew him during the latter part of his life; he says: "In private life he was a humourist; idle in the extreme; but his invention was of the true Birmingham model, active. He could well design, but procured others to execute; wherever he found merit, he caressed it. He was remarkably polite to the stranger, fond of show; a figure rather of the smaller size, and delighted to adorn that figure with gold lace. During the twenty-five years I knew him, though in the decline of life, he retained the singular traces of a handsome man. If he exhibited a peevish temper, we may consider, good nature and intense thinking are not always found together. Taste accompanied him through the different walks of agriculture, architecture, and the finer arts. Whatever passed through his fingers bore the lively marks of John Baskerville." His aversion to Christianity, in which he expressed a disbelief, in his will, led him to prepare for himself a mausoleum in his own garden, that he might not lie among Christians, and directed, in the same document, that his remains should be placed therein. This interesting but somewhat painful document—painful in its abnegation of that faith which alone can lighten the gloom of the grave—runs as follows:

"Memorandum, That I, John Baskerville, of Birmingham, in the county of Warwick, on the 6th day of January, 1773, do make this my last Will and Testament, as follows:—First, I give, bequeathe, and devise unto my executors hereafter named, the sum of £2000 in trust, to discharge a settlement made before my marriage to my wife Sarah. I also give to my executors the lease of my house and land held under the late John Ruston, in trust, for the sole use and benefit of Sarah my wife, during the term of her natural life, and after her decease to the uses mentioned below. And my further Will is, that the sum of £2000 shall be raised and paid to my wife out of my book debts, stock in trade, and household furniture, plate, and china. (N. B. The use of my furniture, plate, and china, I have already given by deed to my wife for the term of her natural life, but this will makes it entirely her own.) I appoint and desire my executors to make an inventory and appraisement of all my effects whatsoever, within six weeks after my decease. I also give to my executors hereinafter named, the sum of £100 in trust, to the sole use and benefit of my nephew John Townsend, to whom I also give my gold watch, as a keepsake. I further give to my executors, in like trust, the sum of £100, for the sole use and benefit of my niece Rebecca, the wife of Thomas Westley, as an acknowledgement of relationship. I have heretofore given by will, to each of the last named relations, a more considerable sum: but as I have observed, with pleasure, that providence has blessed their endeavours with success, in acquiring a greater fortune than they ever will expend the income of; and as they have no child or chick to inherit what they leave behind them, I have stayed my hand, and have thereby reserved a power to assist any branch of my family that may stand in need of it. I have the greatest esteem and respect for each of the above parties. I also give to my executors, in like trust, the sum of £150, for the use of my nephew, Richard Townsend, butcher. I further give to my executors the sum of £300, to be disposed of as follows:—To Joseph, Thomas, and Jacob, sons of Thomas Marston, by his wife Sarah, my niece, £100 each, as they shall severally attain the age of 21 years. But should any of them die before they come to that age, then such hundred pound shall be divided, share and share alike, among the survivors. I also give to Isaac, the son of Thomas Marston, the sum of ten pounds for pocket money; and my reason is, being patronized by his worthy uncle, Mr. Thomas Westley, who, if he behaves well, will put him in the way to acquire an easy fortune. But I must not forget my little favourite; I, therefore, give to my executors, in trust, the sum of £500, for the sole use and benefit of Sarah, the daughter of Ferdinand and Sarah De Mierre (my wife's daughter) to be paid her when she attains the age of 21 years; but should she happen to die before that age, my pleasure is, that my wife shall have the disposal of the said £500 at her pleasure, signified in her last Will. I also give to my executors the further sum of £1400, in trust, to the following uses, viz.:—to Rebecca Westley, John Townsend, Richard Townsend, and to the four sons of Thomas Marston, by his wife Sarah, my niece, the sum of £200 each, to become due and payable (only) on the day of my wife's future marriage, which, if she chuses, I wish her happy equal to her merit; but if she continues a widow, the last mentioned legacies are entirely void. I further give to my executors, in trust, all my goods and chattels, household furniture, plate, and china, not disposed of as above, to the following uses: first, for the payment of my several legacies and debts (if any) and all the residue and remainder (except the sale of my lease as below) to the sole use and benefit of my wife Sarah. I further give to my executors, in trust, the reversion of the lease of my house and land, held under my good friend the late Jonathan Ruston, together with fixtures in the house (particularly the fire place, including the grate, fender, &c., together with three leaden figures) all plantations of trees and shrubs of every kind, including my grotto, and whatever contributes to beautify the place: That the whole shall be sold by public auction, after being properly advertised in some of the London and neighbouring county papers. The money arising from such sale, I give to the following uses; (viz.) first, £500 to the committee, for the time being, of the Protestant Dissenting Charity School of Birmingham, in trust, towards erecting a commodious building for the use of the said charity; £700 more, arising from the said sale, I give and bequeath as follows: £400 to be shared equally between the sons of Thomas Marston, by his wife Sarah; to Jonathan, John, and Richard Townsend, my nephews, £100 each; to Rebecca Westley, my neice, £100, and my will is, that this and the above-mentioned sum of £100 shall be entirely at her own disposal, and not subject to the controul and intermeddling of her husband. And yet her receipt alone shall be a sufficient discharge to my executors: £800 more arising from the said sale, I give to the three sons of Jonathan Ruston, in even and equal shares, viz.:—John, Daniel, and Josiah Ruston. What further sum of money may arise from the sale of the above lease, I give to the sole disposal of my wife Sarah, by her last will. As I doubt not the children of my late worthy friend will endeavour to traduce my memory, as they have already done my character, in having my lease on too easy terms, I therefore think proper to declare, that at the time I took the aforesaid lease, I paid the full value of it, and have laid out little less than £6000 upon the premises. But as the increase of the town has since enhanced its value, I have made an acknowledgment as above, which I always proposed to the sons of my most valued friend, and which would have been much more considerable if they had refrained from injuriously abusing me. I had even given, by will, the reversion of my leases to Martha Ryland, upon the death of my wife's eldest son, and my intended successor, but her unprovoked petulant malice, and spleen, and abusive treatment of me without cause, convinced me of her rancour of heart, and determined me as above. My farther will and pleasure is, and I do hereby declare, that the devise of my goods and chattels, as above, is upon this express condition, that my wife, in concert with my executors, do cause my body to be buried in a conical building in my own premises, heretofore used as a mill, which I have lately raised higher and painted, and in a vault which I have prepared for it. This, doubtless, to many, will appear a whim; perhaps it is so, but it is a whim for many years resolved upon, as I have a hearty contempt for all superstition. . . .

THE GENERAL HOSPITAL: AS IT ORIGINALLY APPEARED.
From the engraving in the first edition of Hutton, 1781.

I expect some shrewd remarks will be made on this my

"OLD AND NEW BIRMINGHAM" PORTRAIT GALLERY.—No. 6.

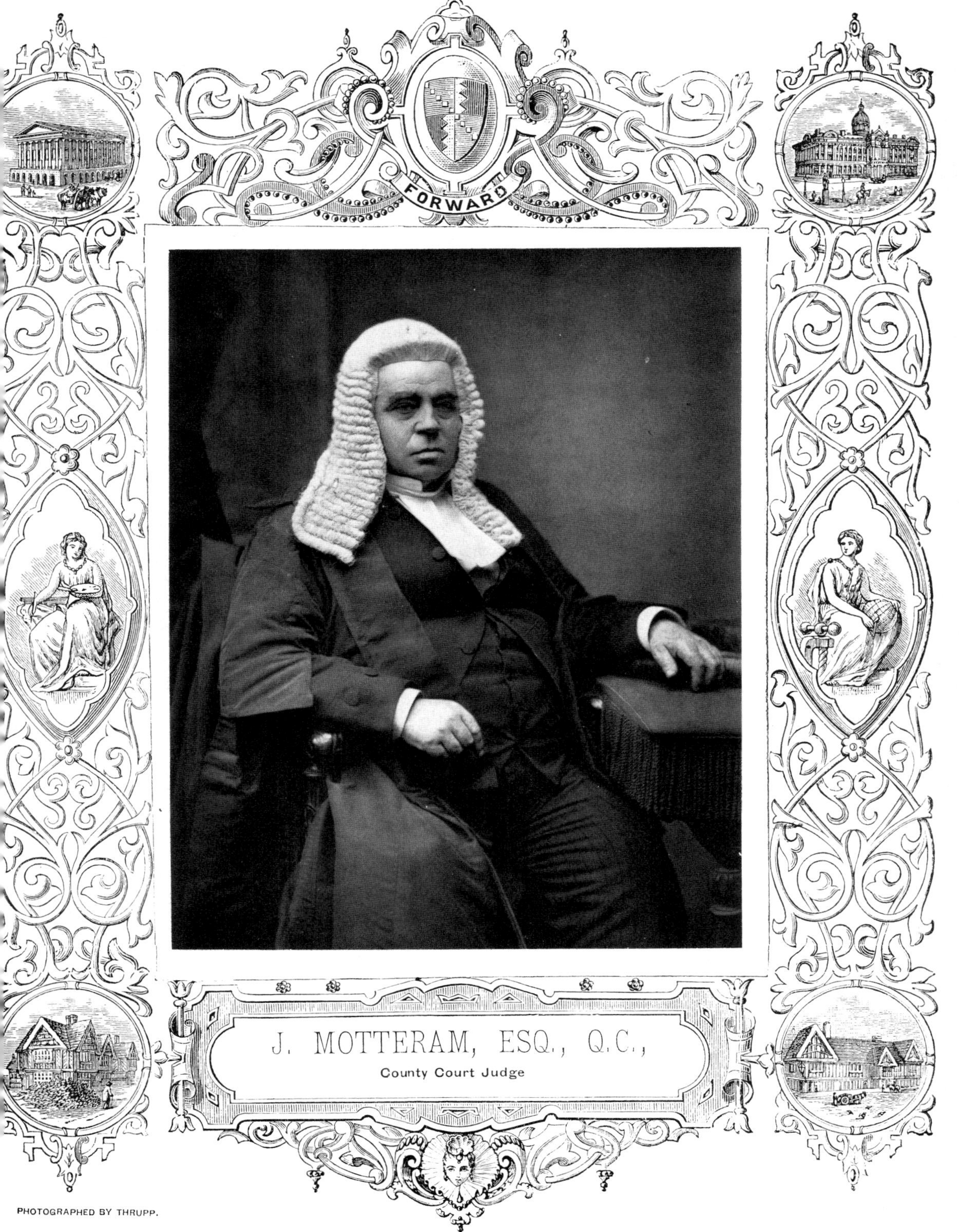

J. MOTTERAM, ESQ., Q.C.,

County Court Judge

PHOTOGRAPHED BY THRUPP.

BIRMINGHAM: HOUGHTON AND HAMMOND, SCOTLAND PASSAGE.

declaration, by the ignorant and the bigoted, who cannot distinguish between religion and superstition, and are taught to believe that morality (by which, I understand, all the duties a man owes to God and his fellow creatures) is not sufficient to entitle him to divine favour.* . . .

This morality alone I profess to be my religion, and the rule of my actions, to which I appeal how far my professions and practice has been consistent. Lastly, I do hereby appoint my worthy friends, Mr. Edward Palmer, and Josiah Ruston, my wife's brother, joint executors of this my will, in most perfect confidence (as I know the integrity of their hearts) that they will, jointly and cordially, execute this my most important trust, committed to them with integrity and candour, to each of whom I leave six guineas, to buy a ring, which I hope they will consider as a keepsake."

In witness, &c., Sarah Stuart, Joseph Bridgewater, John Webster.

Baskerville's house, which became the property of Mr. Ryland, was partially destroyed in the Riots of 1791, of which we shall have to speak hereafter, but much of the façade of the house may still be seen amid the huddled mass of buildings at the lower end of Broad Street; it being now used as a manufactory. When the land was laid out for wharves, in 1821, the coffin was taken up, and was found, together with the contents, to be in perfect condition, and was finally re-interred in one of the catacombs under Christ Church.

"Great as the triumphs of the art of printing have been, and numerous as are the laurels which Birmingham has won, there are few nobler chapters in our local story than those which record how, a century ago, in a material and commercial age, John Baskerville made our town famous throughout the civilised world for the production of the best and greatest works of man, in a style which has rarely been equalled, and even now, has never been surpassed." *

* In the above copy of Baskerville's will we have followed the usual custom, in omitting those portions which refer to Christianity.

* S. Timmins.

CHAPTER XX.

BIRMINGHAM IN 1760.

Colmore Row and Ann Street—"Conygree Stile Close"—"Perrot's Folly"—Gosta Green—Growth of the town in the direction of St. Mary's—Old Vauxhall—Matthew Boulton on Snow Hill—"The Salutation"—Footpath through New Hall grounds—Poetical Descriptions of Birmingham.

Our last general survey of the town was taken from the interesting prints by W. Westley in 1730-31. We have since taken note of the growth and appearance of Birmingham only in occasional details, and with reference to particular localities. It will assist us in gathering together the separate threads of our narrative if we now, taking our stand in the gallery above the dome of St. Philip's, in the year 1760, once more survey the town as a whole, and take note of the extended boundary, and the new objects of interest in the picture.

Looking first to the north, at our feet, we notice a few houses arising in what we have hitherto known only as New Hall Lane, but is henceforth, (as a building lease dating from 1745 states,) to be called Colmore Row, thereby perpetuating the name of the owner of the New Hall Estate; as the continuation of the lane, "called Bull Lane, but then speedily to be made into a street, and to be called Ann Street," was to keep in memory the christian name of the granter of the lease, Ann Colmore. Congreve Street was a mere footpath through a piece of land called Conygree Stile Close, probably from its having been a rabbit-warren; hence came the name Coney-grove Street, which in time became corrupted to Congreve Street.

New Hall is still standing, with a portion of the surrounding grounds, but the town has advanced somewhat towards it. On the western side of the town th^ buildings are beginning to surround the pleasantly-situated little estate of John Baskerville, called Easy Hill. Rising in the distance, beyond Easy Hill, may be discerned a tall tower, which forms an entirely new feature in the prospect, having been built only about two years previous to the date of our present survey,—in 1758—by John Perrot. This tower, which is seven stories high, was probably originally intended for an observatory, although it has been said—on what authority we cannot tell—that its builder, being a keen lover of the sport of coursing,—erected it in order to enable him, when old age prevented him from taking part in such sports, to watch others engaged in it, from the upper stories of the tower. It has been called "Perrot's Folly," but is now more generally known as "The Monument," and from this name is derived that of Monument Lane, or, as it is now called, Monument Road.*

New Street, we notice, is filling up more closely. The are not now so many fields and gardens as before, and between St. Philip's and that street many new buildings have arisen. The Baptist Meeting-house now stands on part of Guest's Cherry Orchard; Temple Street is built upon along its entire length. Beyond New Street the dismal-looking prison may be discerned, at the junction of Peck Lane and Pinfold Street, opposite the end of Dudley Street.

The Leather Hall has disappeared from the end of New Street, as already stated, and in its place the end of that thoroughfare is blocked (with the exception of a narrow gateway,) by a row of houses. The beast market is still held in High Street, but it is not destined to remain there long; an act being passed in 1769 to remove it to Dale End, and the sheep and pig market to New Street, (the pudding-bag end), between Worcester Street and Peck Lane, exactly opposite the Grammar School, where the bleating, grunting, and squealing of the animals exposed for sale would not conduce very much to the scholastic quiet generally supposed to reign in such quarters.

Turning towards St. Martin's we find scaffolding erected at the east end of the building. The churchwardens have ordered "the plan drawn by Mr. Hyrons, for building a vestry" to be carried into execution; and that ugly excresence on the south side of the chancel is in course of erection. Looking out along the crooked line of "the street called Dirtey" we notice the new chapel of St. John the Baptist, which has taken the place of the worn-out building of the fourteenth century; but as yet the square tower is not completed. Along the whole of this street, beyond the chapel and "The Old Crown," houses have been built, as far as Camp Hill; but nearly all have gardens, and those near the river have private walks down to the banks of what is yet a bright rippling stream, from which the disciples of Izaak Walton may enjoy the gentle sport with pleasure and profit; and at the upper end of the street portions of the old deer park still remain.

Turning towards the south-east the object which first attracts our attention is the new church of St. Bartholomew, surrounded by a pleasant churchyard. "Wherever a chapel is erected," observes Hutton, "the houses immediately, as if touched by the wand of magic, spring into existence." This is the case around St. Bartholomew's, and the churchyard is rapidly becoming the only green spot in the vicinity. Coleshill Street and Stafford Street are built upon, as is also the road to Aston as far as Gosta (or Gosty) Green, which does not yet entirely belie its name. About the origin of the word "Gosta" a good deal of speculation has been indulged in. Hutton fancifully conjectures it to have been *Goose Stead*, "once a track of commons, circumscribed by the Stafford Road;"

* In a recently published work the view from this tower, when first built, is represented as including the tower and dome of St. Philip's Church, *in an unfinished state*, surrounded by scaffolding, looking "like an huge net of wickerwork." This is, however, entirely incorrect, as it would have been possible, from the *finished* tower and dome of St. Philip's, to have seen, from the distance, the scaffold surrounding Perrot's Folly, or even to to have watched the *commencement* of the building of that tower.

others have supposed it to be a corruption of "gusty,"—from its exposed situation; it is, however, far more probable that the name is derived from the prevalence of *gorse* and ling in that locality, as the phrase "gosty land" is still occasionally used to denote land on which gorse grows too profusely.

The growth of the town in this direction has not yet effaced the country altogether. There are at least five acres of pasture land still remaining in Walmer Lane, as Lancaster Street is called, which were, in 1759, "let to the highest bidder," at Charles Freeth's Coffee House. The same year is remarkable for the impetus given to the building trade, from what cause it is now difficult to say—so that, according to the *Gazette*, "there are now more new buildings carrying on in this Town than have been for many years past, and more are contracted for, that only wait for hands to execute, which at this time are very much wanted." This rapid extension of building probably showed itself in the district to which we have now turned; *viz.*, Steelhouse Lane and Lichfield Street, and the land lying between the first-named thoroughfare and the site of the General Hospital, the building of which had not as yet, however, commenced. The increased number of houses in this locality is evidenced by the necessity for a new church, (St. Mary's,) which was built a few years after the date of our present survey.

Between Gosta Green and the place from which we take our survey of the town lies the workhouse, situated at the lower end of Lichfield Street, at present without either of the wings depicted in our engraving on page 77. At our feet, on the eastern side of St. Philip's church-yard, is the Blue Coat School; not as it appears in the nineteenth century, but in its original form, as shown in Westley's Prospect. In the distance we catch a glimpse of Duddeston Hall, which has now become the "Vauxhall" of Birmingham, "a large genteel pleasure-garden, neatly laid out and planted, with a large Bowling-Green," a place "greatly resorted to by the Inhabitants of Birmingham, as well as from other places."* As our readers are already aware it was too frequently the scene of the brutal exhibition of cock-fighting. Just beyond Bull Street we notice the trimly-kept Square, and the Friends' Meeting House; and turning north-eastward we reach the end of our survey at Snow Hill, where Matthew Boulton is steadily working his way as a manufacturer of Birmingham "toys," producing such sterling work as should overthrow the vulgar prejudice—which even thus early insisted on the local wares being stamped "London made," †—and convince the world that such contempt for the productions of "Brummagem" was undeserved. Little does he think, as he toils in his Snow Hill factory, that in a few years' time he will be engaged in selling "what all the world desires to have,—*Power*," at the great manufactory which is to make the name of Soho famous all over the world; himself being—as Boswell happily terms him—"an *iron chieftain*, a father to his tribe."

At the bottom of Snow Hill is an inn of the old-fashioned, comfortable sort, called "The Salutation," having good gardens, and two bowling greens, where the tired tradesman and artisan may, after the business of the day is over, enjoy the pleasures of the country within easy reach of the town, never dreaming of the time when the green sward shall have become a grimy coal wharf, and the air, which is now so sweet and refreshing, shall be laden with poisonous smoke and odours by no means enjoyable.

Glancing again at the still charming grounds surrounding New Hall, we notice a foot-way running through the same, and envy the people who have such a delightful walk almost within the very town itself. But it is not destined to remain long for the public benefit. By one of those selfish acts which are in the nineteenth century depriving the public of so many charm-

* *Aris's Gazette*, May 23, 1763.

† "This is to give Notice That at the Pin Warehouse in Corbett's Alley, in the High Street, Birmingham, are to be sold, *Joseph Allen's best London Pins, as good as are procured by any of the trade, and as cheap as in London*, by John Allen, Peruke Maker."
—*Aris's Gazette*, 1752.

ing by-path walks, the owner of the estate, Charles Colmore, Esq., attempted in 1764 to close the gate of the New Hall walk against the people of Birmingham, with the exception of a few "gentlemen and ladies who may wish to have keys for their convenience,"—which keys Mr. Holloway, the steward, "has orders to deliver for their service." But the people were unwilling to lose so pleasant a walk without a struggle. The matter was brought to a trial at Warwick Assizes, in 1764, between George Holloway and the inhabitants of Birmingham, and a verdict was given for the former, who, on the 19th of May in that year erected a gate to obstruct passing over the road in question, but, we are informed by the *Gazette*, the said gate "was broke down by a great number of rude people." It was not, however, by brute force that the inhabitants who had tried the question at law wished to retain the privilege, and accordingly, on the Monday after this petty riot, they offered, in the columns of the *Gazette*, "a reward of five guineas to any one who should discover the person or persons that encouraged and promoted the breaking the said gate in so riotous a manner, being determined to suppress any such illegal proceedings"; and furthermore wrote and sent a letter to Mr. Holloway, as follows:

"Birmingham, May 19th, 1764.

"Mr. George Holloway,

"Sir,—We are very much concerned at the riotous Proceedings of this Day; and have such an Abhorrence to Practices of this kind, that we will gladly join you in discovering and punishing the Offenders in this or any future illegal Outrage that concerns the Road in Question."

As we muse over the struggle for this old right of way, we are brought back from our imaginary survey in 1760, to the time in which we live, when the old footpath is gone, and the grounds are gone also, as well as the people who obstructed and those who resisted the obstruction—all have passed away, and no one questions the "right of way" now over the New Hall estate,—and now that pleasant foot-path has become a noisy street, which does not invite the rambler in search of natural beauty and peaceful retirement, for none pass along it unless called thither by business or other necessity.

We cannot do better than conclude this chapter with two *poetical* descriptions of the town, which appeared in the *Gazette* in the year 1751. The first is wrttten in the manner of Spenser, and bears evidence of thought and refinement on the part of the writer. The Mr. B—— to whom the poem is inscribed was the famous printer of whom we have recently spoken, John Baskerville:—

INDUSTRY AND GENIUS;

OR, THE

ORIGIN OF BIRMINGHAM.

A FABLE

Attempted in the Manner of Spencer.
Inscribed to Mr. B—

1.

O B—— ! in whom, tho' rare, unite
The Spirit of Industrie and eke the Ray
Of bright inventive Genius; while I write
Do Thou with Candour listen to the Lay
Which to fair Birmingham the Muse shall pay,
Marking, beneath a Fable's thin Disguise,
The Virtues its Inhabitants display;
Those Virtues, whence their Fame, Their Riches rise,
Their nice mechanic Arts, their various Merchandise.

2.

On Avon's winding Bank, with Flowers besprent,
Whilom y-dwelt a thrifty, sober Swaine,
On Care and Labour aye was he intent,
And lowing Herds, and Flocks upon the Plaine,
And plenteous Crops, rewarded well his Pain:
Cheap his Attire, and frugal were his Meals;
His Bags were swell'd with no dishonest Gain,
A hard rough Hand the Source of Wealth reveals,
Ne idle Hour he knows, ne Weariness he feels.

3.

High Industrie was he, of Parents poor,
But soon by Labour, he removen had
Their Poverty; and from his well-got store
Their aged Limbs with Decency y-clad;
But now, alas! their Bosoms waxen sad,
That he, their only Child, ne Wife essays,
Ne little Grandlings brought their Hearts to glad
With idle Parlance, and with childish Plays
To cheer, and lengthen out the Evening of their
Days.

4.

But near at Hand, in Bower of Jessamy
And Roses, mixt with rare and curious Ar
A Maiden dwelt, so fair, that only she

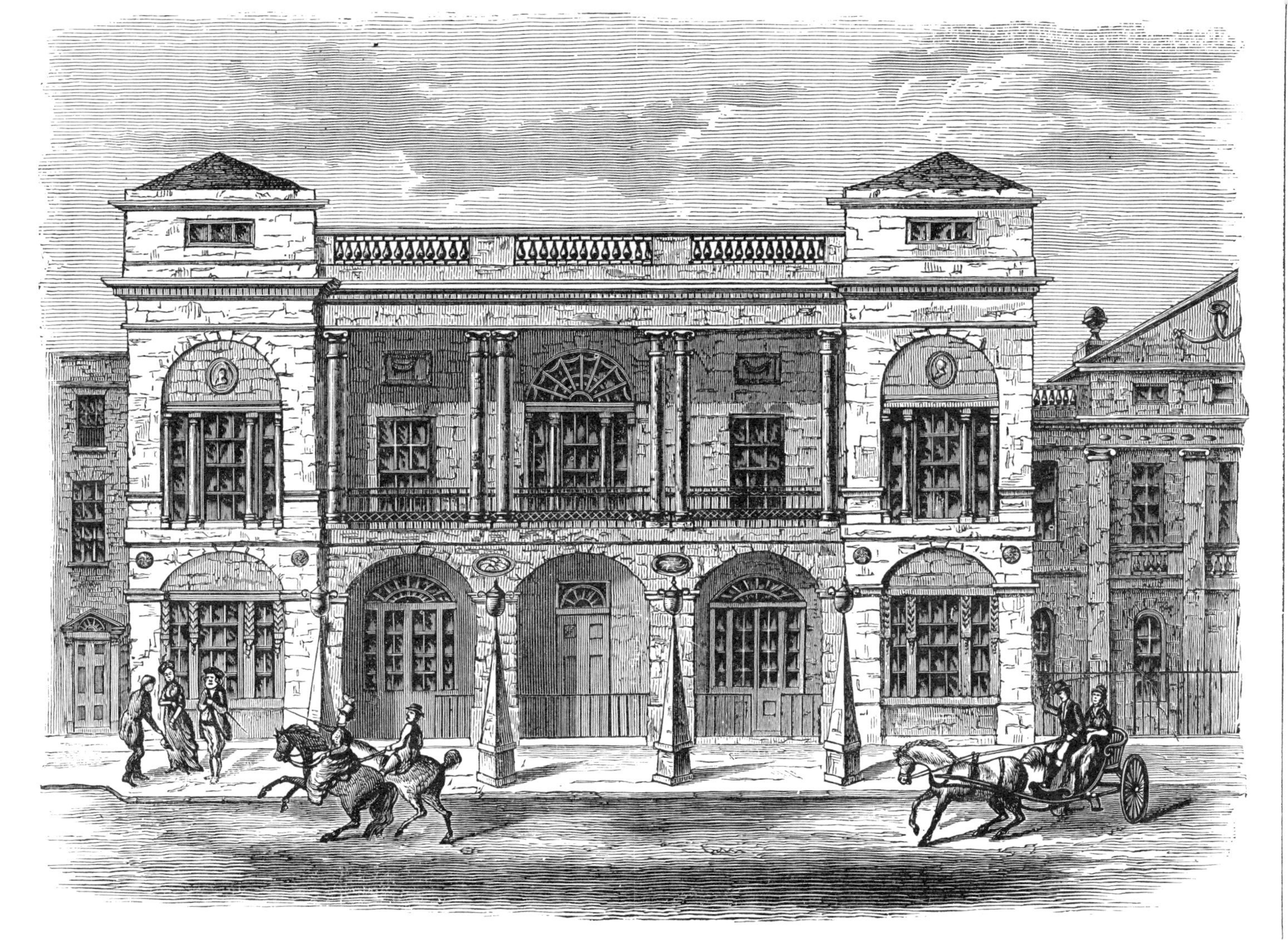

THEATRE ROYAL, NEW STREET.
(*From an old Print.*)

Was Theme of every Tongue and every Heart,
Yet few to claim her Love might boast Desert.
Sith to her Beauty joined, was clearly seen
A Wit so bright, a Mind with every Part
Of Science so adorned, that well I ween
Her meed in antient Greece had been the Muses Queen.

5.

All in the clear Conception of her Mind,
The fairest Forms of Things depainted were,
And the least Shade of Difference she would find
'Twixt every object brought into compare,
Grace still distinguish'd her Productions rare
From those of common Artists : Her nice Hand
Obedient was to execute, with Care
And Elegance, her Fancy's least Command :
Geniæ y-clep'd she was, admired by all the Land.

6.

It chanc'd as on a Day the careful Wight
On Hill and Dale, in Field and Meadow sought
A wandering Ewe, stray'd from his Flock by Night,
That Fortune to her Bower his Footsteps brought;
He gaz'd, admir'd, and soon her Beauty wrought
His Heart to Love. He woo'd the peerless Maid,
And long with humble Zeal her smile besought;
The Blush of yielding Modesty betray'd
At length her vanquish'd Heart and mutual Love display'd.

7.

This happy Union soon produc'd a Race
Of docile Sons, in whom the Mother's Mind
Her Ingenuity and matchless Grace
Shone with the Father's Perseverance join'd,
And now to social Amity inclined
A Town they builden straight, high Birmingham,
Where still their numerous Offspring dwell combin'd,
Whose useful Thewes, and curious Arts proclaim
To all th' admiring World, from what rare Stock they came.

This very ingenious performance was published in the *Gazette* of January 28, in the above-named year. The following, purporting to be a letter from a Birmingham Mechanic to a friend at Warwick, had been written as early 1733, but the modesty of the author had kept him from printing it, until the appearance of the Spenserian Fable suggested its publication in the local journal :—

A Letter from a Mechanick in the busy Town of Birmingham, to Mr. Stayner, a Carver, Statuary, and Architect, in the sleepy Corporation of Warwick.

Dear Friend

If you can leave your Borough, still and fair,
To breathe awhile in more sulphureous Air ;
Can leave the Place where Heroes first drew breath,
And, worn with toils, return'd and courted death ;
The Place for Cradles, or for Tombs so fit,
Where Morpheus, undisturb'd, can nodding sit
With ease and silent slumbers bear the sway,
And influence you all both Night and Day ;
Then raise your Head, and rub each heavy Eye,
And to your Nostrils Hellebore apply :
When broad awake, for Vulcan's Province steer
Each Cyclop will rejoice, to see famed Stayner here,
Nor fancy Semnos' Caves with Forges found,
Or ponderous Hammers there on Anvils bound.
If full North West, twice seven miles you go
You'll see the cloud above, the thund'ring Town. below,
Boldly advance, nor Salamanders fear,
You'll be convinc'd that Vulcan's Forge is here ;
That Æneas' Shield divine was made,
Achilles' Armour, Hector's dreadful Blade ;
Here Guns and Swords Cyclopean Hands divide,
And here with glittering Arms the World is still supply'd.
Here Implements and Toys for distant Parts,
Of various Metals, by mechanic Arts,
Are finely wrought, and by the Artists sold,
Whose touch turns every Metal into Gold ;
But 'tis in vain, alas ! we boast our Skill ;
Wanting thy Arts, we are deficient still.
Oh ! come and join us, teach us to excel
In Casting, Carving, and in Building well ;
Yet here delightful Fabricks* you'll behold
Of Iron, Brass, and artificial Gold ;
In these great Mulciber's chief Factors dwell
Whilst he retir'd to his awful Cell ;
Beneath Old Wedgb-ry's† burning Banks it lies,
Where Thousands of his Slaves, with glaring Eyes,
Around him wait, or near him do reside
In Suberterraneous Caverns, deep and wide ;
Where, by their Chief's Command they sap like Moles,
Supplying every Smithy Hearth with Coals ;
There let them delve, whilst in the growing Town
In jolly Bacchanals our Cares we drown.
Come, Stayner, come, then shall the circling glass
From Friend to Friend, in sparkling Brimmers pass ;
To Arts and Science every Bowl shall flow,
'Till we as great as the old Grecians grow,
'Till then farewell, thou Son of famous Angelo.

Nor were these the only effusions of local poets in praise of their native town. In the last month of the preceding year—a few weeks before the publication of the above—Mr. Brodin delivered a prologue at the Theatre, as follows :

A Prologue (spoke at the Theatre in Birminghan, in praise of the town, by Mr. Brodin) :—

Athens, in Days of Yore, for Arts was fam'd,
And Rome's immortal Glory stands proclaim'd.

* The Money that built them was got by these metals.
†Wednesbury, famous for Coal Mines, and subterraneous Fires.

A Theme of no less Honour claims our Praise,
Too great, too copious, for my scanty Phrase,
A Town which Virgil's self might nobly own;
In its Description he atchiev'd Renown.
Here Clink of Hammers, and repeating Blows
Of warlike Sledges, terrify its Foes.
To you from Norway, Sweden, and from Spain
Incessant sails do plough the boistrous Main.
From different Climes they steer each well-fraught Keel
Of plated Iron, or unpolish'd Steel,
Which wrought and burnished by the Artist's File,
They won'dring gaze, nor know their Native Soil.
To trace the various Branches of each Art,
Transcends my Skill, altho' how fain my Heart.
Some Bard endow'd with more poetic Fire
Must finish that to which I can't aspire.
A nobler Subject Poet never chose,
A Maze wherein his Fancy he may lose.
Here Raphael or Da Vinci may divide
With Brother Artists too the Pencil's Pride.
No more let Semnos boast, her Artist God
In Birmingham has fix'd his best Abode;
Venus attends him with a Look serene,
And Paphos mourns to lose her Cyprian Queen.
Thus blest with every Grace the Powers can give,
May Birmingham long flourish and e'er live.

With this prayer, which every man and woman of Birmingham should echo to-day, we close the present survey of the town.

CHAPTER XXI.

THE GENERAL HOSPITAL.

Necessity for a Hospital—An Objection answered—The building decided upon—First Subscribers—Music and Charity—Names of the Founders—Site of the building—Delays—Hospital *v.* Theatre—The building completed—Early History of the Institution.

WHEN the year 1765 was drawing to a close, and the first touch of the coming winter led men to think of the poor, and especially of the *sick* poor, by whom the icy hand of winter is always most keenly felt, an advertisement appeared in *Aris's Birmingham Gazette*, Nov. 4, 1765, as follows:—

"A GENERAL HOSPITAL, for the Relief of the Sick and Lame, situated near the Town of Birmingham, is presumed would be greatly beneficial to the populous Country about it, as well as that place. A Meeting therefore of the Nobility and Gentry of the Neighbouring Country, and of the Inhabitants of this Town, is requested on Thursday the 21st Instant, at the Swan Inn, at Eleven in the Forenoon, to consider of proper Steps to render effectual so useful an undertaking."

This advertisement was drawn up by Dr. John Ash, an eminent physician of this town, who practised during a considerable portion of the last century, and resided in the neighbourhood of Duddeston, now called (after the doctor himself) *Ashted.*

The rapid increase of the population of Birmingham, and the danger attached to many of the occupations which they followed, rendered it necessary that some provision should be made to supply, in case of sickness and bodily injuries, competent medical assitsance, which the majority were too poor to provide for themselves. There were those, however, as there always have been, whenever any useful measure is projected, ready to cast a wet blanket on the enthusiasm of the projectors of the hospital, and—like their prototype, Ebenezer Scrooge—reminded the philanthropic doctor that there existed a *workhouse*, to which was also attached an *infirmary*, and what more could the sick poor need? To this Dr. Ash replied in the following announcement, which appeared in the *Gazette* of November 18:—

"It having been objected, to the Usefulness of the above-mentioned design, that the present Infirmary established at the Workhouse, will answer all the Purposes of it, it may be necessary here to observe that more than half the Manufacturers in the Town of Birmingham are not Parishioners of it, and cannot be entitled to any Relief from the present Infirmary: Many of them are Foreigners, but the greatest Part belong to the Parishes of the neighbouring Country."

At the meeting called by Dr. Ash, which was held on the date announced, and was well attended, it was resolved that "a Building for the reception of proper objects, be erected within a measured mile of the Town of Birmingham, with all convenient speed, and that the Society for the conduct and support of this Hospital be known and distinguished by the name of "the Trustees of the General Hospital at Birmingham, in the County of Warwick, for the relief of the Sick and lame." Furthermore, a provisional set of rules for the government of the proposed Hospital was adopted, and a subscription commenced which, in a few days, amounted to a thousand pounds, besides upwards of two hundred pounds annual subscriptions which were promised at the same time. Amongst the principal donors were the Earl of Aylesford, (£50); the Countess of Aylesford, (£10 10s.); the Earl and Countess of Dartmouth, (£31 10s. and £21 respectively); Lord Willoughby de Broke, (£31 10s.); Sir Lister Holte, Bart., of Aston Hall, (£21); Lady Holte, (£10 10s.); Sir Charles Mordaunt, (£31 10s.); Sir Henry Bridgman, Bart., the ancestor of the present Earl of Bradford, (£21); Lady Bridgman, (£10 10s.); Sir Roger Newdigate, (£31 10s.); Sir Henry Gough, Bart., (£21); Lady Gough, (£10 10s.); Charles Adderley, Esq., of Hams Hall, ancestor of the present Lord Norton, (£52 10s.); Charles Jennens, Esq., who is known as the editor of several of the plays of Shakespeare, (£50); William Dilke, Esq., of Packwood, (£15 15s.); Mrs. Dilke, (£10 10s.); and many of the principal inhabitants of Birmingham, including Dr. Ash, the promoter of the scheme, Messrs. Boulton and Fothergill, (*Matthew Boulton*, of Soho), Mr. John Taylor, Messrs. Sampson Lloyd and Sampson Lloyd, junr. (founders of the Bank of Taylor and Lloyds, still in existence as Lloyds' Banking Company, Limited), John Baskerville, and many families still well known in Birmingham. Among other donations is one of ten guineas from "the Musical Society of Sambroke's, in Bull Street," who also became annual subscribers of two guineas; and thus was commenced that alliance between Music and Charity which has ever marked the history of this noble institution, and which has reflected as much honour on the disciples of that refining and ennobling art as it has conferred benefit upon the institution itself; and, as Mr. Bunce observes, "from the humble association above named we may possibly trace the germ of those great Festivals from which the Hospital has derived such essential assistance."*

From £1,000 the donations to this great undertaking soon swelled to £2,000, and the annual subscriptions to £600, and the promoters, feeling themselves justified in commencing active operations, held another meeting on Christmas eve, when the provisional rules were confirmed, and a committee appointed. The names of this first committee, the founders of one of the noblest institutions of which Birmingham can boast, were as follows:—

THE EARL OF DARTMOUTH
THE EARL OF AYLESFORD
SIR CHARLES MORDAUNT, BART.
SIR LISTER HOLTE, BART.
SIR ROGER NEWDIGATE, BART.
SIR HENRY BRIDGMAN, BART.
SIR HENRY GOUGH, BART.
WILLIAM BROMLEY, ESQ.
SIMON LUTTRELL, ESQ.
CHARLES COLMORE, ESQ.
JERVOISE CLARKE, ESQ.
BENJAMIN, PALMER, ESQ.
RICHARD GEAST, ESQ.
WILLIAM DILKE, ESQ.
ABRAHAM SPOONER, ESQ.
JOHN TAYLOR, ESQ.
HENRY CARVER, ESQ.
SAMUEL GARBETT, ESQ.
DR. JOHN ASH
DR. WILLIAM SMALL
MR. JOHN KETTLE
MR. MATTHEW BOULTON
MR. SAMPSON LLOYD
MR. JOSEPH SMITH
MR. SAMUEL GALTON
MR. JOHN TURNER
MR. THOMAS ABNEY
MR. JOSEPH CARLES, ATTORNEY
MR. FRANCIS PARROTT, SURGEON
MR. WILLIAM JOHN BANNER

* "History of the Birmingham General Hospital and the Musical Festivals," p. 8, to which we are indebted for the above list and other interesting details respecting the early history of the hospital.

The next business was to select a site for the proposed building, and this important duty was entrusted to the projector of the scheme, Dr. Ash, who selected the land in Summer Lane on which the Hospital now stands, then in the possession of Mrs. Dolphin, from whom the committee purchased, at £120 per acre, "all those four closes, pieces, or parcels of Land, Meadow, or Pasture Ground, situate, lying, and being together near a place called the Salutation, in Birmingham aforesaid, containing, by estimation, eight Acres or thereabouts, be the same more or less, adjoining at the upper end or part thereof into a Lane there called Summer Lane, and at the lower end or part thereof unto a lane called Walmore Lane."* Upon this site—which Hutton characterizes as "very unsuitable," being "in a narrow dirty lane, with an aspect directing up the hill, which should ever be avoided,"—the building was speedily commenced, a plan having been obtained from a Mr. Vyse. It was designed to accommodate one hundred patients, and estimated to cost about three thousand pounds. The Committee conducted the work of erection themselves, engaging Messrs. B. and W. Wyatt to act as superintendents or clerks of the works, at a remuneration of £150. Matters went on well

THE HOUSE IN THE OLD SQUARE,
"In which Edmuud Hector was the host and Samuel Johnson the guest."

* Walmer Lane; afterwards called Lancaster Street.

during the year 1766, until November, when, the funds being almost exhausted, it was considered expedient to suspend operations for the winter. In the following May, (1767), an attempt was made to revive the interest of the inhabitants of the town and neighbourhood in the progress of the hospital, by appealing again for subscriptions; but it was all in vain. All the interest of the wealthier inhabitants was just then centred in the proposed Birmingham Canal, which promised to prove a profitable speculation; and so, while the funds of the hospital languished, it was necessary to limit the number of shares which a single person should be permitted to take in the canal speculation, so great was the anxiety to subscribe towards an object which promised golden returns.

Until February, 1768, no further note of progress appears since the last recorded meeting of of the Board, and the finances were in a worse condition, if possible, than before,—inasmuch that the secretary's salary, only £10 a year, had not been paid. Another appeal for help was made in April, stating that the building was covered in, and that the rooms for patients were being fitted up. At a meeting held on the 3rd of May, the Board resolved that "a Musical Entertainment should be established," and appointed a committee to conduct the undertaking, consisting of the following gentlemen:—Mr. John Taylor, Mr. Isaac Spooner, Mr. John Taylor, jun., Dr. Ash, Dr. Small, Mr. Henry Carver, jun., and Mr. Brooke Smith.

This first "musical festival"—the forerunner of the famous series of triennial festivals which commenced ten years afterwards—is thus announced in the *Gazette*:—

"On Wednesday, Thursday, and Friday, the 7th, 8th, and 9th of September, the Oratorios of L'ALLEGRO, &c., ALEXANDER'S FEAST, and the MESSIAH will be performed here.

"L'ALLEGRO ED IL PENSEROSO,

"Will be at the Theatre in King-Street, on Wednesday Evening, the 7th inst.

"And ALEXANDER'S FEAST

"On Thursday Evening, the 8th,

'Between the several parts of which Mr. PINTO will play a Solo; and Concertos will be introduced by the other Performers, on their several Instruments.

"On Thursday Morning will be performed in St. Philip's Church, at Ten o'Clock, Mr. Handel's Grand TE DEUM and JUBILATE, with an Anthem of Dr. Boyce's, suitable to the Occasion, and Mr. Handel's celebrated CORONATION ANTHEM;

"And the MESSIAH, or SACRED ORATORIO,

"At the same Place, on Friday Morning, the 9th.

"On the Wednesday and Thursday Evenings, after the Oratorios, will be a Ball, at Mrs. Sawyer's in the Square

"The principal Vocal Parts will be performed by Mrs. PINTO, Mr. NORRIS, Mr. MATTHEWS, Mr. PRICE, &c. Instrumental by Messrs. PINTO, MILLAR, ADCOCK, JENKINS, PARKE, LATES, HOBBS, CLARK, CHEW, &c., &c.

"The Oratorios will be conducted by Mr. CAPEL BOND, of Coventry.

"The Music at the Church on Thursday Morning is to be opened with a TRUMPET CONCERTO by Mr. BOND."

The historian of the Festivals informs us that Mr. Pinto, the principal instrumentalist in the above concerts, was a famous violinist, and was for several years leader of the band at Drury Lane Theatre; his wife, who was the principal vocalist, was well-known under her maiden name (Brent) as a singer, and a favourite pupil of Dr. Arne, who wrote expressly for her the part of Mandane, in "Artaxerxes." Mr. Norris was a Bachelor of Music, settled at Oxford, and well-known both there and in the metropolis.

The performances were attended with considerable success, being attended by "brilliant and crowded audiences," and on Thursday morning the Countesses of Dartmouth and Aylesford "very obligingly stood to receive at the Church door."

The gross receipts at these entertainments amounted to £800, of which the committee were enabled to pay over £299 7s. 4d. to the funds of the hospital. "It is gratifying to observe," says Mr. Bunce, "that from the first the Festivals have been marked by the selection of music of the highest class. Notwithstanding that even at the remote period of which we are writing Birmingham was decidedly a musical town, it still must have been a bold experiment to have offered to the public a series of performances including the 'Messiah' and other works then scarcely appreciated even by persons of cultivated taste, and certainly distasteful to many, if not to most, of the amateurs who had acquired a relish for inferior and frivolous music, against the popularity of which Handel found it so difficult to contend."

Notwithstanding the success of these entertainments, the interest in the progress of the valuable institution for whose benefit they were undertaken, still flagged, and that to so great a degree that in May, 1769, it was necessary, in annonncing a meeting, to intimate that dinner would be provided, in order to ensure a sufficient attendance. The funds had fallen to such an extent that the building could not be completed; and it was, therefore, resolved that the remaining (unused) building materials should be sold and the unfinished structure insured, all further efforts being deferred until more hopeful times. From this period until 1776 there is but one reference to the existence of the institution—a notice in the *Gazette* of May 8, 1769, (the month which saw the temporary abandonment of the hospital) threatening to punish certain "disorderly persons" who had "done considerable damage" to the neglected building, by "frequenting there to play ball, &c."

The listlessness with which the inhabitants saw this noble institution—to which doubtless many a poor sufferer had looked hopefully, but in vain, —lying in an unfinished state, and probably falling somewhat into decay, contrasted with the eagerness with which they took up the scheme of re-building the theatre, immediately after its destruction by fire, in 1774, roused the indignation of a young clerk in a mercantile house in the town, who was also a member of the Baptist Church in Cannon Street, named Mark Wilks,—afterwards a famous minister of Lady Huntingdon's Chapel at Norwich. Determined to arrest the attention of the public to the disgraceful contrast, he published the following poetical dialogue:

"POETICAL DREAM,

Being a Dialogue between the Hospital and New Playhouse, at Birmingham.

At close of day, within a rural bower,
I sat me down, to muse away an hour;
But nightly silence, so profoundly deep,
Soon lull'd me into calm and quiet sleep;
And as I slept, I thought I heard a noise,
Then look'd around, and to my great surprise,
I saw the Hospital and Playhouse near,
Both in profound discourse, which you shall hear:

Hospital.

Hail, Playhouse, hail! thee I congratulate,
Whilst I bemoan mine own bewildered state;
Near seven years were my foundations laid,
Ere thine were dug, or ought about thee said,
Yet I've been long abandon'd human thought,
Whilst thou, in haste, are to perfection brought.

Playhouse.

Cease, Hospital, why should'st thou thus repine?
Though thou art neglected, 'tis no fault of mine;
Thy use is hospitality, I know,
Or thou'dst been finished many years ago:
My use thou know'st is different from thine:
In me the rich and opulent shall shine;
But halt, and lame, and blind must be thy guest,
And such as are by sickness sore oppress'd.

Hospital.

'Tis true mine is an hospitable door,
And should stand open to receive the poor:
The rich from me can no advantage gain,
Which causes me in sackcloth to remain.

Playhouse.

Well, stop awhile, I'll now demand of thee,
Show me the man who e'er got ought by me;
No good or profit can in me be found,
My entertainments with expense abound.

Hospital.

Oh, epicureans value not expense,
When buying trifles to amuse their sense;
But though I loudly their assistance crave,
Yet I, alas! can no assistance have.

Playhouse.

It must be wrong, I do in conscience own,
That such unkindness should to thee be shown,
That thou by Christians thus should slighted be,
Whilst I'm caressed, and crown'd with dignity.

Hospital.

Oh, Theatre, it is indeed a shame,
That they should e'er be honour'd with the name;
Could Christians in a Playhouse take such pride,
Whilst I in dormancy so long abide?

Playhouse.

Yes, Christians can; pray do not go so far;
I hope you do not think they heathen are.

Hospital.

Indeed, they are no better in my view,
Or else they never could delight in you.

Playhouse.

Ah, that is certainly a grand mistake;
The best of Christians should their pleasure take.

Hospital.

And so they do, but thou hast none to give;
Their pleasure is the needy to relieve.

Playhouse.

If that's the case, then Christians are but few.

Hospital.

Indeed, Theatre, that I think is true,
Sure I this gloomy aspect should not wear,
If all were Christians who the name now bear.

Playhouse.

Well, be it so; I will no more pretend
To take their part—let this contention end;
Each pious mind our gentry justly blame.

So I awoke, and lo, it was a dream."

But this dialogue did not succeed at once in arousing the public to finish the hospital. It was not until the close of 1776 that any further steps were taken to obtain pecuniary assistance to enable the committee to complete the work. On the 16th of August in that year a meeting was held, and a report on the condition of the building and of the funds was laid before them. It was ultimately decided to call a public meeting of the inhabitants of the town and neighbourhood, and the following notice was issued :—

"Many Gentlemen of this Town and Neighbourhood, having taken into Consideration the improper State in which the Building of the General Hospital at present stands, and being very desirous to see it answer the laudable Intention for which it was begun, do hereby Request a General Meeting of the Nobility and Gentry, as well as of the Inhabitants of the Town, at the Hotel, in Birmingham, on Friday the 20th of this instant at Ten o'clock in the Forenoon, to concert the most effectual Measures to Prosecute the Undertaking, and speedily to render this charitable Design useful to the Public."

The meeting was held, as announced, on the 20th of September, at the "Birmingham Hotel"—afterwards called the "Royal," which was then a new institution, having been erected by subscription in the year 1772, in Temple Row,—and in the next week's issue of the *Gazette* an announcement was published, stating :

	£	s.	d.
"That the Money expended on the Building, contingent Expences, &c., (including the purchase of Land, £942, and interest paid thereon to Christmas last, £359 3s. 8d.), amounted to	6,853	13	1
"That the Money already received for Benefactions, Subscriptions, &c., amounted to	3,970	10	4
"So that a Debt has been incurred of	£2,883	2	9

"This does not include any Charge for Interest, except that for the Land as above, and one Year's Interest on £200. Messrs. Taylor, Lloyd, and Co., who are the principal Creditors, will be content with 3 per Cent. per Ann. for what they paid in advance.

"The Building is well executed on a large extensive Plan, and capable of receiving upwards of 100 Patients in the most commodious Manner.—The Estimates of three different Builders were laid before the Meeting, by which it appeared that it would cost between £1,000 and £1,100 to compleat the Building, exclusive of the Furniture."

The sum of £740 was subscribed at the meeting, and a canvass of the principal residents in the town and neighbourhood decided upon; but this resolution was not put into practice until February, 1777. As a result of this appeal, a number of the friends of the institution increased their subscriptions.

The prospects of the hospital began now to revive, and the building progressed favourably and in June, 1778, another Musical Performance was resolved upon, to take place in the following September. This was the first of the triennial festivals, which have been regularly held, (with two exceptions,) up to the present time; but as we purpose devoting several chapters to the history of this institution, it will not be necessary to make further reference here to the Festival of 1778 except to state that it produced nearly £800, of which £170 went to the funds of the Hospital, the profits being shared between that institution and the fund for the erection of St. Paul's Chapel, of which we shall have to speak in a future chapter.

By the end of July, 1779, the arrangements were completed for the reception of patients, and on the 4th of August a meeting was held, at which Lord Craven was appointed president, and the Members of the County (Sir Charles Holt, Bart., and Sir T. G. Skipwith, Bart.,) vice-presidents. It was reported that the physicians of the town had offered their services as medical officers gratuitously, and surgeons who were desirous of connection with the institution were requested to send in applications. On the 13th of September the medical staff of the institution was elected, the first physicians being Dr. Ash, Dr. Smith, Dr. Withering, and Dr. Edward Johnstone; and the first surgeons Messrs. Robert Ward, George Kennedy, John Freer, jun., and Jeremiah Vaux.

The Hospital was formally opened on the 20th of the same month,—nearly fourteen years after the first meeting which had been held on its behalf. There were at the opening of the institution only forty beds,—less than half the number originally proposed. During the first week ten in-patients were admitted, and four nurses were appointed, at four guineas per annum, with a promise of an additional guinea "if they behave well;" a barber was also appointed to shave the patients twice a week, at a salary of 10s. 6d. per quarter.

ST. MARY'S CHURCH.

Having now reached the period at which the hospital was opened,—from which we shall be obliged to retrace our steps in the ensuing chapters,—we may leave the history of this noble institution for the present, until we have brought theother portions our story down to the date at which we close the present chapter.

CHAPTER XXII.

WILLIAM HUTTON IN BIRMINGHAM.

His second visit to the town—Settles as a bookseller in Bull Street— Removes to High Street—His courtship and marriage—Speculations—The Transit of Venus—Local honours—The Court of Requests, etc.

In the February of 1750, William Hutton paid his second visit to Birmingham,—*this* time with a view to a permanent settlement in the town. Since his memorable week's journey in 1741, he had seen many changes. In 1746 his uncle had died, and the young journeyman, finding the stocking trade distasteful, had turned his attention to bookbinding. He had attempted to establish a connection as a bookseller and bookbinder at Southwell, in Nottinghamshire, which he characterises as being "as despicable as the road to it." At the date above mentioned, he turned his thoughts toward the town which had so favourably impressed him ten years before, and journeyed here "to pass a judgment on the probability of future success." Here he found "three eminent booksellers for mental improvement, Aris, Warren, and Woollaston." Considering, however, that "the town was large, and crowded with inhabitants," and that he might, perhaps, "mingle in that crowd unnoticed by the three great men"—for, he quaintly adds, "an ant is not worth destroying,"—he determined to try his fortune as a bookseller here. On the 10th of April, in the same year, therefore, he entered Birmingham for the third time, and, after traversing the town a whole day in order to find a suitable shop, agreed with a Miss Dix for the lesser half of hers, at No. 6. Bull Street, for one shilling a week. It will interest those who are in the habit of noticing coincidences, to know that the same year which saw William Hutton's first serious attempt as a bookseller, (for the Southwell venture was scarcely worth mentioning), was that in which Baskerville made his first attempt at printing. He entered upon his new establishment on the 25th of May, and, for the first year—a year of hardship and of the most rigid frugality—he lived almost alone, without making a single acquaintance. He "had entered a new world, in which he lived a melancholy life; a life of silence and tears." In 1751 he found two friends in Mr. Dowler, a surgeon, who lived opposite to him in Bull Street, and Mr. Grace, a hosier, (upon whom, as the reader will doubtless remember, he called, when seeking employment in 1741), who occupied one of the houses which blocked up the High Street end of New Street. "Great consequences," he observes, "often arise from little things. The house adjoining that of Mr. Grace's, in the High Street, was to be let. Both [Mr. Grace and Mr. Dowler] urged me to take it. I was frightened at eight pounds rent. However, both persuaded; one drew and the other pushed till they placed me there." Here he pursued his business "in a more elevated style, and with more success."

He soon had "a smiling trade," and in addition to *selling* and *binding* books, he also commenced lending them; and so may be said to have established the first circulating library in the town. In his amusing autobiography, he relates his several experiences when in search of a wife at this period. He had been very much troubled in the management of his household affairs. One housekeeper, in his absence, sold his books for what they would bring, left the shop, and got drunk with the money. Another came well recommended by a Nonconformist Minister, who assured him that she would not cheat him as she feared the Lord. "He might be right," adds Hutton, "but she cheated my dumplings one Sunday by setting them to boil without water. When we returned from Meeting they were burned to a cinder." It was therefore necessary that he should find a housekeeper who should also be a "partner for life." His sister had visited him in 1751, bringing with her an intended wife. The latter, he tells us, was "tolerably handsome, and appeared agreeable." But love, as he quaintly remarks, "is a delicate and shy bird, not always caught at first sight; besides, everything formal operates against it." The pre-arranged match fell through; "we behaved," he says, "with civility, but neither of us taking fire, the matter died away."

In his new occupation of librarian he encountered many of the gentler sex, and some of them he found "so obliging as to show an inclination to share with him the troubles of the world;" but the inclination would appear to have been all on one side, and he still remained alone. In the November of 1753, however, he met for the first time the lady who was destined to become his wife,—a niece of Mr. Grace, Miss Sarah Cock, (or as it is spelt in the register of the marriage, *Cox*), of Aston-on-Trent, near Derby, whom that gentleman had taken as his housekeeper. Hutton dined with Mr. Grace, as he had at that time no housekeeper; and so the acquaintance with Miss Cock ripened into affection. On the 23rd of June, 1755, they were married at St. Philip's Church, in the presence of Mr. Grace and Mr. William Ryland, who had become one of Hutton's firmest friends. Many years afterwards, when the partnership had been dissolved by death, he wrote concerning his wife as follows: "I found in her more than ever I expected in woman. Just in proportion as I loved her, I must lament her loss. If my father, with whom I lived only fourteen years, who loved me less and has been gone forty, never is one day out of my thoughts, what must be those thoughts towards her who loved me as herself, and with whom I resided an age?"

The next year (1756) saw the birth of his daughter Catherine, who became the constant, affectionate, and solicitous companion of her father to the day of his death, and remained unmarried during a life of upwards of ninety years' duration.

During the same year he was induced by his intimate friend, Robert Bage, to embark in the stationery enterprise, purchasing of him two hundred pounds' worth of paper, and hung out a sign, *The Paper Warehouse*, the first in Birmingham. This department of his business he subsequently developed by manufacturing the paper himself, erecting a mill for that purpose on Handsworth Heath; but this speculation proved disastrous, as he knew but little of the process of paper-making, and was consequently obliged to trust almost entirely to his men.

In 1761 he writes, "I still pursued the mill scheme, till lost in a labyrinth. The workmen saw my ignorance, and bit me at pleasure. 'Let us fleece Hutton; he has money.' I discharged them all, let the work stand, and left myself at rest." But the millwrights would not suffer him to rest while the property lasted. One of them endeavoured to persuade him "at what a small expense it might be converted into a corn mill, and what amazing profit would attend it;" and into this trap he fell an easy prey. But in the next year he makes an entry in his autobiography: "I found, as a miller, I was cheated on all sides, which induced me again to discharge the people, and suffer the mill again to stand, with a determination never to move it again. I also sold my horse for four guineas, resolving to keep no more." He ultimately sold the mill for eighty guineas, to a Mr. Honeyborn, to be used in polishing brass nails; and, on examining his accounts, and taking into consideration the hindrance to his ordinary business, resulting from his paper-making and corn-grinding experiments, he estimated that he had lost, in these two schemes, nearly a thousand pounds.

In the year 1761 he makes an entry concerning the transit of Venus, which occurred in that year, which will interest our readers at the present time:—

"I saw the transit of Venus over the sun's disk. She appeared a small black spot moving over the face of the sun, the size of a large fly or bee. I think it was the fifth of June."

In 1763 he again refers to the prosperous state of his business, and the absence of rivals in the trade; remarking, that he began to doubt whether the mill had been any loss, for, he adds, the disappointment had raised that commercial spirit, which would not have been raised without it.

"When life glides smoothly along," he writes, in 1765, "incident is not to be expected. The man who sleeps in peace, has no tale to tell." This was the case with himself for many years after the above date, and his history is simply that of increased prosperity, occasional journeys into Derbyshire and Nottinghamshire, and municipal —or rather parochial—honours at home. His Birmingham life, in fact, became principally devoted to the service of his fellow townsmen. His first step towards public life was that of being summoned upon the Low Bailiff's Jury, in 1765; in 1768 he was chosen Overseer of the Poor, and "thought himself elevated beyond his ancestors; for none, within the reach of tradition, had equalled it." He *näively* adds: "Perhaps I was the first overseer in Birmingham that ever rejoiced at the office. When, in the evening, I met my five new brethren at the Castle, they were all affected; some provoked, and some cast down, while I kept up the joke, and brought them to a smile. Some of them afterwards acknowledged I did them a service." His opposition, in this capacity, to the Lamp Act—the "improvement scheme" of 1768—will be referred to more particularly in our next chapter.

The next year he purchased half an acre of land at Bennett's Hill, Saltley, near Washwood Heath, and built a house for himself, where he resided until his death.

In 1772 he was chosen a Commissioner of the Court of Requests, which was instituted by Act of Parliament, in the year 1752, for the more easy and speedy recovery of debts, under 40s., within the town of Birmingham and the hamlet of Deritend. The court was originally held in the chamber over the Old Cross,—on the steps of which Hutton sat to rest, a silent, depressed object, dusty and travel-stained, without money and without friends, on that memorable fourteenth of July, 1741, on which he made his first appearance in the town of which he was destined to become so distinguished a citizen.

The court was subsequently removed to a house in a recess at the back of High Street, nearly opposite New Street, which had been known formerly as *Mansell's Tea Warehouse*, and is at the present time, we believe, called "*the Old Court Tea Warehouse.*"

The cases which Hutton decided as Commissioner of this court formed the basis of one of the most remarkable of all his works, which bears as its title the name of the court. The humour and shrewd common sense which characterises all his writings is, perhaps, better exemplified in many of these decisions, than in any other of his numerous volumes. As the subject is one of local interest, we cannot refrain from quoting a few examples.

The following is a graphic description of the beadle of the Court as he existed in Hutton's time:—

"When I first sat in this Court the clerks and the beadle were under a private contract; the beadle was chargeable with every expense, was to pay the clerks an annual stipend, and appropriate the residue of the profits to himself. This genius of the Court was William Bridgens Barton, nominated Gentleman in all deeds of lease and release, who, though possessed of about ten thousand pounds, was seldom master of a shilling, but frequently borrowed a trifle of his own servants to pay his reckoning or to satisfy a kind nymph. Notwithstanding this barrenness of cash, a stranger would think he was fond of money, for his littleness of temper would at any time suffer him to run of an errand for twopence. He was equally averse to receive and pay money. If he accidentally met a person in his debt he shunned him by running away or hiding himself in obscurity. If one came to pay, 'Let it be,' was the word. Those who dunned him always found him in haste, received ample promises forgotten in a moment, but his good nature, of which he had a large portion, always warded off the blow. Though he daily gave and took credit, he kept no private books of account his counting-house was his memory, which was very retentive, but when he died it was locked up, with its contents, for ever. He was landlord to a farm near twenty years without ever receiving a shilling rent. Always in a hurry without making progress, he despatched nothing quick, but the tankard. Expedition never discovered itself but in getting drunk, in which he became so expert by daily practice that he could accomplish it in ten minutes; I have known him drive a post-chaise to Warwick for as much liquor as he could turn into his vessel. It was indifferent to him whether he slept in a bed, upon the hearth of an alehouse, or under a manger, or whether he staggered thither or was carried. He wrote an excellent hand, was master of figures, and well understood the business of an attorney's office. His fondness for employment induced him to work without profit, and yet from his random conduct his employment became loser. His shoes received their last tincture of black from the currier. It was of no consequence to him whether he wore a shirt a week or a month, whether his neckcloth was tied under his chin or over his ear, or whether the top or the bottom of his wig was uppermost. His beard and his linen were equal strangers to the suds.

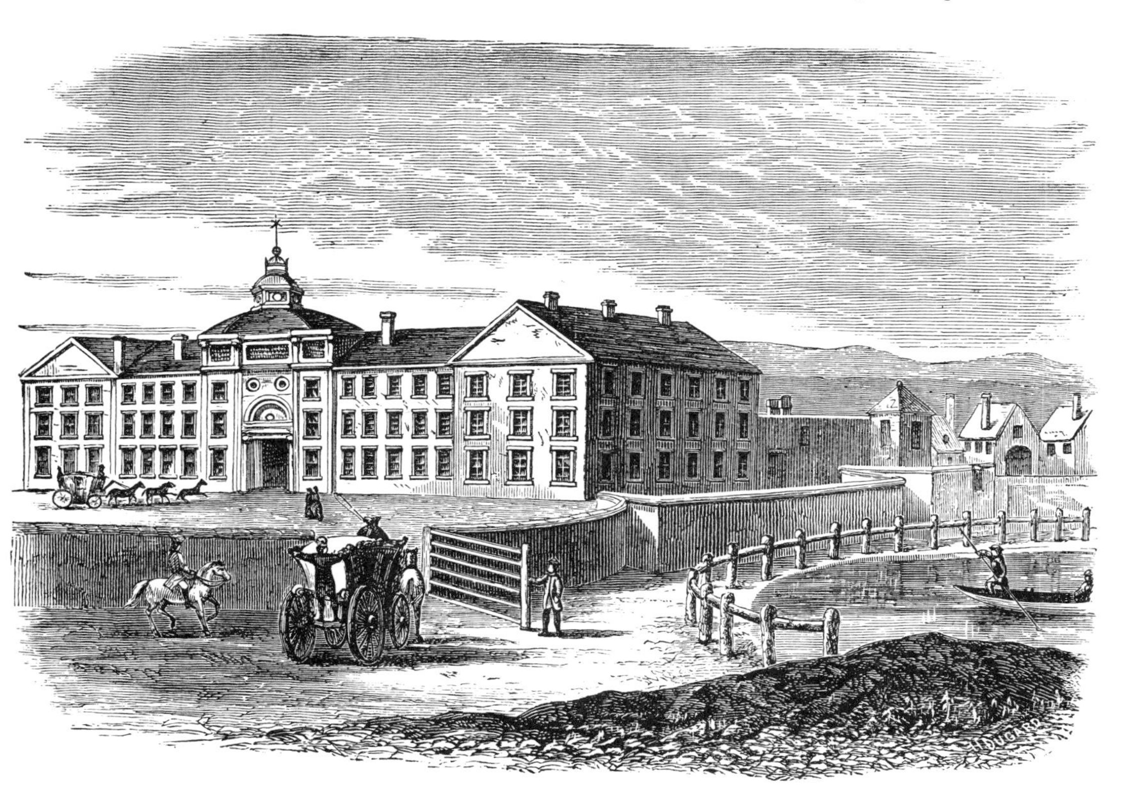

THE SOHO MANUFACTORY.

"The money belonging to the suitors must of course pass through the hands of this good-natured sloven, or rather pass into them, for it seldom came out. The result was the Court dwindled, the suitors complained, the Bench remonstrated, he promised, the evil grew, and the clerks were obliged to take their department into their own hands, since which time it has been conducted with prudence.

"All sides were pleased and the current of property was now to run in its right channel. Still by the laws of his office the money arising from executions must submit to the touch of his fingers, and we were again obstructed. 'Of what use is the Court,' says the suitor, 'if we cannot have justice. We had better lose our money by the debtors than be defrauded at another expense by the beadle.'

"The Commissioners entertained serious thoughts of discharging him; and perhaps three months would have finished their purpose, if in the interim the strength and quantity of his liquor had not sent him into another world. There he could not conduct matters much worse than he had done in this."

A very just decision is recorded with respect to the propriety of each individual bearing his share of the expense of any public improvement from which he derives benefit; which the author quaintly entitles

"THE PUMP.

"*Defendant.*—I have never paid anything, neither have I a right to pay. I gave no orders to have it done. I never promised payment, neither has any man a right to lay out my money.

"*Commissioner.*—Should you think it fair if all the neighbours went free and the whole expense was saddled upon you?

"*Defendant.*— No.

"*Commissioner.*—Then what reason is there that you should go free and your neighbours bear the whole? Had they been all of your mind, they would have been deprived of one of the greatest blessings we know, or rather, like you, would wish to enjoy it at the expense of another. If you have never paid to former repairs, they have granted you a favour you do not deserve. As they have all an equal right to the pump, they have all an equal right to pay. If you gave no orders it was not because orders were not necessary or the water not wanted, but that another, more spirited than yourself, might step forward and furnish you with a pretext. If you had promised payment you would have stood in a more honourable light. He lays out his money himself who pays for a necessary article which cannot be had without; but if you take that article at the expense of your neighbour, you do him an injustice, so shall we if we do not order payment."

In another decision he enforces the oft-forgotten rule that the finding of lost property does not give the finder the right to keep it.

"A PICTURE OF A MAN FROM THE LIFE.

"A woman lost her needle-book, containing 5s. 6d., all she had in the world, in consequence of which her children were starving for bread. The man who had found it refused to return it, and boldly supported his claim to the property. He had fairly found it, and everything a man finds is his own.

"*Court.*—And so you apprehend the street gives a title to whatever lies upon it. You forget that property cannot change its owner without an act of that owner. You can inherit no title but from her, and she has given you none. If you accidentally find a person's title-deeds, will it give you a right to the estate? Should a man take up your watch, should you think he had a right to keep it? or rather would not you hold forth in a different style, and proclaim that power of right which obliged him to restore it? It may be generous to reward the finder, but he can demand nothing; neither has the person who wishes to conceal, or refuses to return what he finds, a right to expect a gratuity. We are sorry that half this is your case. A gentleman some years back was travelling in Nottinghamshire with a servant who carried a portmanteau in which was £2,000 to pay for an estate. By some accident it slipped unperceived off the horse. When the loss was discovered the servant posted back. An old woman, with the portmanteau on her head, whom they had lately passed, exclaimed, "I know what you are galloping after; here is the treasure you lost; take it and welcome." She was afterwards introduced to the master, who gave her five guineas. Both parties were pleased, and whenever his affairs led him to Nottingham, he sent for the old woman, and always gave her a kiss and a guinea; each had a different relish, but both were very acceptable. We shall allow you what you do not deserve—one shilling; make an order against you for the rest, and leave you to reflect how you stand with the world and how you might have stood. Had you sought out the loser, freely returned the property without a fee, for she wanted and you did not, you would have stood upon honourable ground. You may farther reflect that your honesty will never be called in question, for of this you have publicly made shipwreck; your capacity may, for as every loser of a cause pays the fees, you have for twelve paltry pence bartered away seventeen and a character."

Many others might be quoted from among the numerous cases recorded in this most interesting volume, showing how mother-wit, joined to sound common-sense, enabled Hutton to adjudicate wisely, even in the most involved and difficult cases, and gave to Birmingham one of the most equitable of judges, who has made her Court of Requests famous throughout the country. "Hutton," says his biographer, Llewellyn Jewitt, "abhorred chicanery, and held in utter detestation all attempts at cheating, extortion, lying, deceit, and oppression, and his judgments never failed to carry with them a sting to those who were guilty of any of these practices."

The Lamp Act, which he had opposed so strenuously, was obtained in 1769, and an amendment of the Act for lighting and cleaning the streets, removing obstructions, etc., was passed in 1773; and in the latter year Hutton was chosen a Commisioner for the carrying out of the provisions of these Acts. How necessary these reforms were may be gathered from his *History of Birmingham.* The builders of the houses on the various streets had each proceeded according to his own interest or fancy, without regard to the public convenience. "There is," says our worthy Commissioner, "no man to preserve order, or prescribe bounds; hence arise evils without a cure: such as a narrowness, which scarcely admits light, cleanliness, pleasure, health, or use; unnecessary hills, like that in Bull Street; sudden falls, owing to the floor of one house being laid three feet lower than the next, as in Coleshill Street; one side of a street like the deck of a ship, gunnel to, several feet higher than the other, as in Snow Hill, New Street, Friday Street, Paradise Row, [afterwards called Paradise Street,] Lionel Street, Suffolk Street, Brick Kiln Lane, and Great Charles Street. Hence also that crowd of enormous bulk sashes; steps, projecting from the houses and the cellars; buildings which, like men at a dog-fight, seem rudely to crowd before each other; pent-houses, rails, palisades, &c., which have long called for redress."*

Previous to the passing of the Lamp Act, in 1769, the only persons who had power to reform these abuses were the Lord of the Manor and the freeholders. These, so far from interfering, were among the worst offenders, especially the former. "Others," says Hutton, "trespassed like little rogues, but he like a lord. In 1728, he seized a public building, called the Leather Hall, and converted it to his private use. George Davis, the constable, summoned the inhabitants to vindicate their right; but none appearing, the Lord smiled at their supineness, and kept the property. In about 1745, he took possession of the Bull Ring, their little market-place, and began to build it up; but although the people did not bring their action, they did not sleep as before, for they undid in the night what he did in the day. In 1758, when the houses at No. 3 were erected, in that extreme narrow part of Bull Street, near the Welch Cross, the proprietor, emboldened by repeated neglects, chose to project half a yard beyond his bounds. But a private inhabitant, who was an attorney, a bully, and a freeholder, with his own hands, and a few hearty curses, demolished the building, and reduced the builder to order. But though the freeholders have power over all encroachments within memory, yet this is the only instance upon record of the exertion of that power."

All these encroachments gave Hutton, as one of the Commissioners, "a fine opening to reduce things to order." His plan, he tells us in his autobiography, was to execute the Act with firmness and mildness, obliging all to conform. But the conscientious determination of the one was over-ruled by the voice of the many. "There were," he says, "clashing interests among the Commissioners. Some would retain their own encroachments, or serve their friends; then how could they vote down others? A rich man met with more favour than a poor one. The blame of some removals fell upon me, being strenuous, a speaker, and not backed by the Board. I lost some friends; as they did not act in a body, nor consistent, I declined attendance."

The story of Hutton's life from this period to the riots of 1791 is somewhat uneventful, and, as we shall have to refer particularly to his experiences in our narrative of that disgraceful episode in the history of our town, we will for the present take our leave of him.

* History of Birmingham, sixth edition, p. 91.

CHAPTER XXIII.

THE STORY OF SOHO.

The Snow Hill Manufactory—Character of Matthew Boulton—His removal to Soho—Joined by Mr. Fothergill—Assay Office—Savery's steam engine—James Watt's improvements—His character—Soho in 1774—The Soho Mint—Boulton's coinage—Eginton's process for copying oil-paintings—The Copying Press.

A HISTORY of local enterprise, from which the story of the famous Soho factory was omitted, would bear some resemblance to the oft-quoted performance of the tragedy of *Hamlet*, with the part of the melancholy Dane left out. That story, as Mr. Timmins well says, "is not only one of the brightest chapters in the annals of our town, but is one of the greatest incidents in the industrial history of our land."

Matthew Boulton—who was a native of Birmingham, having been born here on the 3rd of September, 1728—had, as already stated in our chapter on "Birmingham in 1760," previous to 1762, established himself on Snow Hill as a manufacturer of "toys,"—buckles, clasps, chains, and other trinkets,—which exhibited good workmanship joined to artistic design, worked out by the best men he could procure. It has been said of him that he "would buy any man's brains," and in this lay his great secret of success. "He did not expect perfection. He patiently trained them to their work if they were inexperienced before. He was a keen judge of character, a clear-headed, catholic-minded man—a very 'chieftain of labour,' who knew how to put every man in his proper place, and to make the most of all. His pleasant manners, his genial temper, his unflinching justice, made him honoured, loved, and feared. While he was generous, he was just; and in the difficult art of managing men he has never been surpassed. He exacted the best of everything—the best of material—the best of work—the best powers of men—and he reaped his reward." *

* S. Timmins: Birmingham and Midland Hardware District, p. 218.

In the beginning of the year 1757, Handsworth Heath was precisely what it was when William Hutton first passed over it, in 1741, a barren heath, occupied only as a rabbit-warren, the only house being that of the warrener. But in that year, John Wyrley, Lord of the Manor of Handsworth, granted a lease for ninety-nine years, to Messrs. Ruston and Evans, with liberty to divert Hockley Brook and to form a pool for the requirements of a water-mill for rolling metal. In 1762, the lease was purchased by Matthew Boulton, who rebuilt and enlarged the mill, and transplanted thither his Snow Hill "plant." This was, however, very soon found to be insufficient to enable him to carry out his great projects; and, in 1764, the foundations were laid of the great factory which became the scene of so many noble triumphs. The new building was completed in 1765, and consisted of four squares, with connecting ranges of workshops, capable of accommodating a thousand workmen, the cost being about £9,000.

He was now joined by a Mr. Fothergill—the reader will remember the joint names of the firm in the first list of subscribers to the General Hospital—and the two men instituted a correspondence in all the chief cities of Europe, seeking for talented workmen, in order to establish a school of artists for designing and modelling; the result was that such a degree of perfection was attained, in the design and manufacture of metal ornaments, in imitation of *ormolu*,—vases, candelabra, tripods, etc., as had not hitherto been known in England. The manufacture of silver and plated wares was also introduced, and became so important a branch of trade that it became necessary, in 1733, to establish an Assay Office in Birmingham.

Matthew Boulton's many projects—all of which had proved successful—led him to seek for additional power to carry them into execution, the water power being wholly insufficient to meet the requirements of the manufactory, and in 1767 he erected a steam engine, on the plan of Savery. This was unsatisfactory, and the enquiries which its failure elicited, led to an acquaintance with James Watt, then a mechanic in Glasgow, who had already perfected certain valuable improvements in the steam engine. Watt shortly afterwards obtained a patent for these improvements, (Jan., 1769), and subsequently, in the same year, came to Soho, where he erected one of his improved engines, and after demonstrating its practicability and utility, obtained, in 1775, an extension of the term of his patent for twenty-five years. "Great as the genius and invaluable as the inventions of James Watt were," remarks Mr. Timmins, "they would have been wasted but for the indomitable energy, the untiring hopefulness, and the commercial genius of Matthew Boulton. Where the timid and invalid inventor would have failed, and have left his great discoveries to be revived when he had long departed, Matthew Boulton gave exactly the element of commercial success. His refined taste, his unbounded energy, his almost reckless profusion, had made Soho famous even for its minor manufactures, but when the steam engine was added, its success was complete. After endless troubles, wearying delays, disasters of all kinds, perseverance had its reward, and Boulton and Watt have a united and immortal name. While Watt was a quiet, patient, plodding inventor, retiring in manners, and nervously anxious, Boulton was a

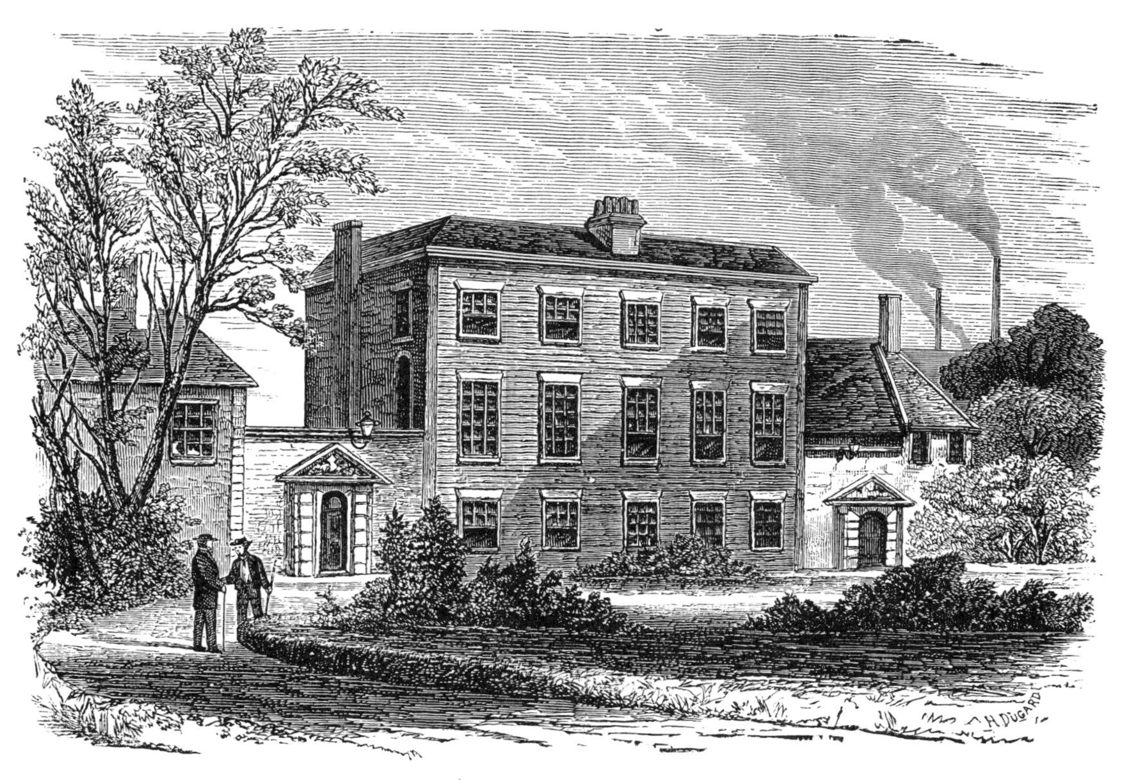

WATT'S HOUSE, HARPER'S HILL.

man of the world, ready in resource, sanguine in temperament, never disheartened by the most threatening disasters, and never 'bating one jot of heart or hope.'"

A contemporary account of the great Soho factory, from a very rare little Birmingham Directory, (Swinney's), published in 1774, a copy of which is in the possession of Mr. Timmins,—as indeed what that relates to old Birmingham is not?—may interest our readers :—

"This place is situated in the Parish of Handsworth, in the County of Stafford, two Miles distant from Birmingham. The building consists of four Squares, with Shops, Warehouses, &c., for a Thonsand Workmen, who, in a great variety of Branches, excel in their several Departments; not only in the fabrication of Buttons, Buckles, Boxes, Trinkets, &c., in Gold, Silver, and a variety of Compositions; but in many other Arts, long predominant in France, which lose their Reputation on a Comparison with the product of this Place: And it is by the Natives hereof, or of the parts adjacent, (whose emulation and taste the Proprietors have spared no Care or Expense to exeite and improve), that it is brought to its present flourishing State. The number of ingenious mechanical Contrivances they avail themselves of, by the means of Water Mills, much facilitates their Work, and saves a great portion of Time and Labour. The Plated-Work has an appearance of solid Silver, more especially when compared with that of any other Manufactory. Their excellent ornamental Pieces, in Or-Moulu, have been admired by the Nobility and Gentry, not only of this Kingdom, but of all Europe; and are allowed to surpass anything of the kind made abroad; And some Articles lately executed in Silver-Plate, shew that Taste and Elegance of Design prevail here in a superior Degree, and are, with Mechanism and Chymystry, happily united. The environs of this Building was Seven Years ago, a barren, uncultivated Heath; tho' it now contains many Houses, and wears the appearance of a populous Country: And notwithstanding the number of People in that Parish is double what they were a few Years since, yet the Poor's Rates are diminished, which is a very striking instance of the good effects of Industry."

Among the many manufactures to which the steam engine was found applicable was that of *coining*, for which purpose a mill was erected, in 1778, at which, by the aid of a few boys, eight machines were worked, each capable of striking from seventy to eighty-four pieces a minute. The process of manufacture was thus described by one of Boulton's intimate friends, Dr. Erasmus Darwin, author of the *Botanic Garden*, and other poetry of a like mechanical order :—

"Now his hard hands on Mona's rifted crest,
Bosom'd in rocks, her azure robes arrest;
With iron lips his rapid rollers seize,
The lengthen'd bars in their expansive squeeze;
Descending screws with ponderous fly-wheels wound
The tawny plates, the new medallions round;
Hard dies of steel the cupreous circles cramp,
And with quick fall his massy hammers stamp.
The harp, the lily, and the lion join,
And George and Britain guard the splendid coin."

Boulton's mint machinery, as finally improved by himself, was so perfect that it has been used, with very few alterations, up to the present time. His design was to produce a coin which should be "inimitable," but in this he did not succeed, as his splendid coinage was imitated by lead pennies, faced with copper, almost as soon as it appeared. What Boulton did, however, in that direction, served as a simple and useful test of the genuineness of the copper money of that period. He made his twopenny pieces of exactly 2oz. weight, and eight of them measured a foot; the pennies weighed 1oz., and seventeen measured two feet; the half-pennies weighed ½oz., and ten measured a foot; and of the farthings (¼oz.) twelve measured a foot. Of the genuine pence, sixteen weighed a pound, while the counterfeits were often eighty-four to the pound. Twenty tons of copper, making 716,800 pennies, were struck every week, for many months. In addition to copper money, silver was also coined, for some of the colonies; and many fine and valuable medals were also struck from time to time at the Soho mint.

In 1779 an invention of a very different character from anything which had previously seen the light at Soho astonished the art world of that day. Francis Eginton,—of whom we shall have more to say in a future chapter,—practised at this great home of the arts, an ingenious process for copying oil-paintings—the productions being very much like the modern "oleographs." It has been conjectured by some that in this process the art of photography was called into use, but of this there is no evidence. Whatever the exact "process" was cannot now be ascertained, the production having been suppressed, in the interests of art. Two large pictures, apparently by Loutherbourg, have been preserved in Birmingham, which have been mistaken for original oil-paintings, but have proved, on examination, to have been produced by mechanical means,—probably by the means invented by Francis Eginton.

But of the many other ingenious and artistic productions of the great Soho factory, during the *earlier* period of its existence,—and they included, among other, now common articles of daily, use the "copying-press," which Boulton himself perfected, to the terror of certain M.P.'s, who feared that it would produce forged bank notes—we have not space at our command to tell; and as the *later* history of this establishment,—beginning with the manufacture of steam-engines, would take us farther on into the history of our town than we have yet reached in the other parts of our narrative, we must postpone the remainder of the story until we have brought other portions of the history of Birmingham down to the same date, when we will once more take up the thread of "the Story of Soho."

CHAPTER XXIV.

PUBLIC LIFE AND EVENTS, 1750-1775.

"His Majesty's Servants"—The King Street Theatre—Pulpit *v.* Stage—"As You Like It"—"King John"—Mrs. Ward and Master Kennedy—The Shakespeare Jubilee 1769—The Theatre Royal New Street—Bradford's Plan—"The Canal Frenzy"—Samuel Johnson in Birmingham again—Dr. Ash and Ashted.

It will be remembered that in the chapter on the establishment of *Aris's Birmingham Gazette*, we took the opportunity to illustrate from the pages of that journal, (assisted by the volumes of Dr. Langford's "Century of Birmingham Life"), the public life of our town during the first decade of the *Gazette's* existence. We now purpose taking up the thread of the narrative at the year 1750, and to inflict upon our readers another miscellaneous chapter—not altogether from the *Gazette*, however, this time,—as the events we have to record, during the period indicated at the head of this chapter, are too numerous, and at the same time of scarcely sufficient importance, to occupy separate chapters of themselves.

We take up first the history of the stage. At the point at which we last took notice of it, the town boasted three temples dedicated to Thespis, but only one of them of any importance, viz., that in Moor Street, erected in 1740. The New Street and Smallbrook Street houses would appear to have died out as quietly as they came into existence. In 1751, Hutton tells us, a company arrived who announced themselves "His Majesty's Servants, from the Theatres Royal, in London; and hoped the public would excuse the ceremony of the drum, as beneath the dignity of a London company." This novel announcement, he says, "had a surprising effect; the performers had merit, the house was continually crowded, the general conversation turned upon theatrical exhibition, and the town was converted into one vast theatre."

The growth of the public appetite for the drama led to the erection, in 1752, of a second permanent theatre, in King Street, and two London companies delighted the town. "The pulpits took the alarm," says Hutton, "and in turn roared after their customers; but the pious teachers forgot it was only the fervour of a day, which would cool of itself; that the fiercer the fire burns, the sooner it will burn out. This declaration of war fortunately happening at the latter end of the summer, the campaign was over, and the company retired into winter quarters without hostilities." When the appetite for the drama had again declined it became evident that two theatres could not find support in the town as yet, and the Moor Street house was very soon closed, and subsequently let to the Methodists, as a meeting house.

It may be interesting to the lovers of the drama to know something of the kind of plays selected for representation in the town, afer the establishment of the more legitimate theatres. A poetical critique in the *Gazette*, July, 1761, gives the names of two well-known pieces :

"When Salop's Sons from Labour rest
And Phœbus journeys down the West,
Theatric-Bills invite :
I go, with many hundreds more,
And drop two-Shillings at the Door,
To see 'em every Night.

I went to see the Jealous Wife,
And what cou'd more resemble Life,
Or touch the human Heart ?
O — CUTTER with his Comic-Song,
Delighted the attentive Throng,
And each one topp'd their Part.

What need I then exhibit Names,
Since purest Critics sound Acclaims ?
And say—'their Rival Queens
'Had those who acted here before
Been present at—they'd Play no more,
'But sell their Cloaths and Scenes.'"

In 1764, the local journal informed its readers, on July, 25th, that "the English opera of *Love in a Village* will certainly be perform'd at the Theatre in King Street on Friday next : And that the Masque of *Conus*, written by Milton, is now in Rehearsal, and will be speedily perform'd at the same Theatre, with new Dresses and Decorations." The same year Shakespeare's "As You Like it" was presented at the King Street theatre,—the only one then remaining, as the reader will remember,—and the framer of the announcement ventured upon a bit of dramatic criticism which will amuse our readers. After announcing the performance of the comedy, by particular desire, for the benefit of Miss Ward, he says :

"This Comedy, tho' one of the first Productions of that immortal Genius, has been allowed by all the Dramatic Writers to be at least equal, if not excel, any other of his Performances. The established Reputation it ever has and still continues to hold, with all Judges of Literature, and Frequenters of the Theatre, both for Variety of Character and Incident, True Humour, and Usefulness of Morals, speaks louder in its Favour than all that can be said in Praise of its Merit."

Shakespeare held his own on the local stage. During the next year "King John" was produced; with the performance of which one spectator was so delighted that he rushed into print with a gushing piece of criticism, which, as local dramatic criticism was at that time an uncommon article, we quote entire :

To the Printers of the Birmingham Gazette.

I have in the course of this Summer, when the Weather could permit, attended the Play-House in this Town, and have been sometimes pleased with the Performance; particularly with the Maid of the Mill, King John, &c. ; and now I mention King John, I must take notice of the very excellent Performance of two characters played by Mrs. Ward and Master Kennedy ; there was not a dry eye in the House ; Mrs. Ward's great Feeling and masterly manner of conveying her Grief, made each Person present feel as much as if they were in the Circumstances : and the Pleadings by Master Kennedy to Hubert, where he is about to lose his eyes, astonished the Audience, that a Boy so young could be so Natural, and yet so forcible as to omit nothing that the oldest Actor on the Stage would have made Use of to gain the Applause of the Audience. I think 'tis Pity that Merit is not more encouraged here. Master Kennedy, I am told, played the character of Prince Arthur twice before his Majesty, and that the Duke of York, and the present Princess of Brunswick, took great Notice of him, and paid him many Compliments when the Play was over.—I hope he will meet with Encouragement, as I hear he is to have Part of a Benefit ; and as he cannot be supposed to have Acquaintance, being too young to Keep Company, 'tis hoped the Encouragers of Merit, particularly the Ladies, will make a Point of sending for his Tickets, and let the Town see it is not always owing to keeping a deal of Company, or an Overgrown Interest, that always makes a great Benefit. I am your Constant Reader,

BENEVOLIUS.

In September 1769, David Garrick designed and carried out a Jubilee at Stratford-on-Avon in honour of Shakespeare,—and of David Garrick. It will not be necessary to describe in these pages the doings at Stratford, the dinners, balls, pageants, fireworks, illuminations, and other

"OLD AND NEW BIRMINGHAM" PORTRAIT GALLERY.—No. 7.

J. THACKRAY BUNCE,

Editor "Daily Post."

PHOTOGRAPHED BY THRUPP.

BIRMINGHAM: HOUGHTON AND HAMMOND, SCOTLAND PASSAGE.

JOHN ASH, M.D., FOUNDER OF THE GENERAL HOSPITAL.
(From the Portrait by Sir Joshua Reynolds.)

festivities,*—in which, probably, many of the inhabitants of Birmingham took part,—but it may interest good Shakespeareans who remember the noble manner in which Birmingham commemorated the tercentenary of the poet's birth, in 1864,—by establishing a Shakespeare Memorial Library,—to know that the Jubilee of 1769 was not allowed to pass unrecognised in the town. An edition of the great dramatist's writings had been printed by Robert Martin, with Baskerville's types, at the suggestion of Garrick, and was sold at Stratford during the Jubilee. A few days before the celebration the following advertisement appeared in the *Gazette*:

On Monday next [Aug. 30] will be published,—A Medal of the inimitable Shakespeare, struck either in Silver or Copper, done from that intended to be worn by Mr. Garrick, at the approaching Jubilee, which is an improved Likeness of that Great Man. Ladies and Gentlemen may have them either in Cases for the Pocket, or with Pendants for the Bosom, at Mr. Westwood's, Engraver, in Newhall-Walk; or at the Toy-Shops, in Birmingham; they may likewise be had at Mr. Payton's, at the White-Lion, in Stratford, and the Toy-Shops there.

*** Ladies and Gentlemen may have them struck in Gold on the shortest Notice.

On the 25th of September the same journal announced a musical performance, which was to take place on Thursday, October 5th, at the Theatre in King Street, consisting of "all the Songs, Glees, Catches, and Roundelays lately performed at the Stratford Jubilee," the vocal music being assigned to "Mr. Parsons and others," and the instrumental parts contributed by "the best Performers of this town, and from Gloucester, Worcester, and Lichfield, &c." Garrick's famous Ode was also "humbly attempted by a Gentleman of this Town;" "a New Occasional Prologue" is also announced, being, in all probability, "humbly attempted" by the reciter of the Ode.

While on the subject of music, we quote for our readers' amusement, a curious addendum to an announcement in the local journal of an exhibition of a collection of sculptures on view "at the Seven Stars, in the High-Street," to the effect that "*a sober honest Man, that can blow a French Horn or Trumpet well, may hear of Encouragement.*" The old show-man who penned the above must have been an ancestor of Artemus Ward; we cannot help being reminded of poor Artemus's "experienced moonist of good parentage," whom he was so anxious to meet with.

The year 1774 was one of activity in matters theatrical in Birmingham. In that year the King Street theatre was enlarged and beautified, and many improvements were effected to minister to the comfort of visitors; so that, according to Hutton, "it had few equals." In the same year a new theatre was erected in New Street, probably on or near the site of the miserable structure which had done duty as a theatre some years previously,—referred to in our last notice of the stage. It was the proposed building of this new house which prompted Mark Wilks to write the "Poetical Dream," quoted in Chapter XXI; but the publication of that poem, while it may have aroused public feeling in favour of completing the Hospital, did not prevent the erection of the Theatre. The cost of the latter, which was on "an extensive plan, and richly ornamented [with] paintings and scenery," was £5,660. In 1780 a handsome portico was added, (said to have been designed by Harrison, of Chester,) consisting of a massive piazza, surmounted by a light and graceful balcony, supported by two pairs of Ionic columns, with wings at either end, on the front of which, in the upper compartments, are two medallion busts, of excellent workmanship, representing respectively, Shakespeare and Garrick. This handsome addition to the building caused our old historian to pronounce it "one of the first theatres in Europe." It was, during its

* Foote sarcastically described it, in his "*Devil on Two Sticks,*" as follows: "A jubilee, as it hath lately appeared, is a public invitation, circulated and urged by puffing, to go post without horses, to an obscure borough without representatives, governed by a mayor and aldermen who are no magistrates, to celebrate a Great Poet, whose own works have made him immortal, by an ode without poetry, music without melody, dinners without victuals, and lodgings without beds; a masquerade where half the people appeared bare-faced, a horse-race up to the knees in water, fireworks extinguished as soon as they were lighted, and a gingerbread amphitheatre, which, like a house of cards, tumbled to pieces as soon as it was finished."

earlier years, under the management of Mr. Yates, the celebrated comedian.

Before leaving for the present the history of the local theatres, we may quote, for our readers' amusement, Poet Freeth's verses on the conversion of the Moor Street Theatre into a meeting house for the Wesleyans:

On a PLAY-HOUSE being turned into a METHODIST MEETING HOUSE.

I sing not of battles, nor sing of the state,
But a strange metamorphose that happen'd of late,
Which if the comedians of London should hear,
Who knows—it may put the whole body in fear.
Derry down, &c.

Where dancing and tumbling have many times been,
And plays of all kinds by large audiences seen;
These wicked diversions are not to be more,
Poor Shakespeare is buffetted out of the door.

The story is true, the tale it is strange,
And people might well be alarm'd at the change;
Instead of a Dryden, a Johnson, or Lee,
You nothing but purest devotion can see.

Behold, where the sons of good humour appear'd,
The scenes are thrown down, and a pulpit is rear'd;
The boxes on each side converted to pews,
And the pit all around nought but gravity shews.

The music's sweet sound, which enliven'd the mind,
Is turn'd into that of a different kind;
No comic burletta or French rigadoon,
But all join together, and chant a psalm tune.

When told that fam'd W—l—y* appear'd on the stage,
The grave ones began to reflect on the age;
But those in the secret approv'd of the case,
For 'twas done to drive Satan away from the place.

If through the land this example should take,
A strange reformation it surely would make;
All writings dramatic would certainly cease,
If COVENT' and DRURY should catch the disease.
Derry down, &c.

In the year 1750, Samuel Bradford made a survey of the town, with a view to the publication of a new plan, none having appeared, so far as we know, since that of Westley, in 1731.

It would seem, from the following advertisement, which appeared in the *Gazette*, August 6, 1750, that considerable delay occurred in its publication.

"To the subscribers for the Plans of Birmingham, &c. The proprietor having been greatly retarded by the illness of his principal assistants, in engraving the plan of Birmingham and map of the county, and by that means is rendered incapable of publishing according to his promise; he assures them that the work is now continued in great forwardness, and will be ready to deliver to the subscribers some time in October; and that subscriptions are taken in as usual by Mr. Bradford; Mr. Jefferys, in Digbeth; Mr. Jackson, printseller, in Birmingham; and by the booksellers of Birmingham, Coventry, and towns adjacent."

Notwithstanding this promise, the year 1750 ended without the plan having appeared, and nearly four months of the new year had elapsed before the long-expected print was published. In the month of April, 1751, an advertisement appeared, however, in the *Gazette*, announcing "that the Plan of Birmingham (if desired) is to be delivered to the Subscribers next Week." On the 29th of the same month the plan was issued; being, as stated on the imprint, "Published according to the Act of Parliament, by Thos. Jeffreys, at the corner of St. Martin's Lane, Charing Cross, London, April 29, 1751." Some years ago Mr. John Rabone threw out the suggestion in the "Local Notes and Queries" of the *Birmingham Journal*, that the "Thos. Jefferys, of St. Martin's Lane, London," the engraver and publisher of the plan, and the Mr. Jefferys, in Digbeth, "by whom, as set forth in the advertisement quoted above, subscriptions for the plan were received, were one and the same person; adding, that if this fact could be proved, it would "add another name to the roll of Birmingham worthies, who, whatever their hands found to do, did it well and thoroughly, and thus laid down an ever-speaking protest against the 'well enough' methods so much in vogue in the present day."

As the plan is rare, it will interest our readers to see the descriptive letter-press which is engraved thereon, which is as follows:

"Birmingham is a Market Town, situated in the North West part of the County of Warwick, 52°.33 North Latitude, distant from London 88 computed & 116 measured Miles: the present number of Houses are 4170, and Inhabitants 23688.

"This Town has been suppos'd to derive its name from one Birming, whose dwelling-house formerly stood here, ye termination Ham in ye Saxon Language signifies home or dwelling place. In ye reign of Edwd. the Confessor it

* John Wesley; *see ante*, p. 1C3

was the Freehold of one Vluuine, and in that of William the Conqueror was in possession of William Fits Ausculf, who then resided at Dudley Castle. Hen. III. by a Grant allow'd them to hold a Market every Thursday in ye Year. In ye 35th of Hen. III. a Charter was given for two Fairs to be kept annually, one to begin on ye Eve of Holy Thursday, and the other on the Eve of St. John the Baptist.

"K. Edwd. VI., in the 5th Year of his reign, erected a Free Grammar School for Boys, which is little inferior to any School in England as to its Revenues.

St. Philip's Church was erected in the Reign of King George I., who gave £600 towards the finishing of it. St. Bartholomew's Chappel was lately built and consecrated in the Year 1750. This Town, tho' very large and populous, has only two Churches and two Chappels, viz., St. Martin's and St. Philip's Churches. St. Bartholomew's Chappel, which belongs to St. Martin's Parish, and St. John's Chappel in Deritend, belonging to the Parish of Aston, but there are several Meeting Houses for Dissenters of almost all denominations, a Charity School for Boys and Girls and a large handsome Workhouse.

"This Place has been for a long series of years increasing in its buildings, and is superior to most Towns in ye Kingdom for its elegance and regularity, as well as Number and Wealth of the Inhabitants; its prosperity is owing greatly to ye Industry of ye People, who have for many Years carried on an extensive Trade in Iron and other Wares, especially in the Toy Business, which has gain'd the Place a name and a great esteem all over Europe."

There is also an "Alphabetical List of the Streets and Lanes, with the Numbers of Houses and Inhabitants in each," which is also worth quoting here:

	House.	Inhab.
Aston Street and Upper Gosty Green	54	294
Bell Street	39	179
Bewdley Street	14	53
Bordesley	83	405
Buckle Row	5	19
Bull Street	140	819
Bull Lane	14	80
Button Alley	4	18
Butts Lane	1	3
Cannon St. and Needless Alley	64	568
Carr's Lane	36	207
Castle Street	25	162
Chapel Row	7	33
Chapel Street	43	205
Charles Street	8	31
Cherry Street and Crooked Lane	28	190
Church Street	2	9
Coleshill Street	37	199
Colmore Row	36	268
Colmore Street	58	359
Cooper's Mill Lane	7	25
Corbett's Alley	4	19
Corn Cheaping	29	162
Cross Street	1	4
Dale End	181	932
Deritend	198	1,096
Digbeth	303	1,646
Dock Alley	13	51
Duddeston Street	—	—
Dudley Street	104	602
Edgbaston Street	151	879
Farmer Street	7	27
Freeman Street	16	137
Froggery	25	147
St. Bartholomew Street	—	—
Hands's Square	26	140
Harlow Street	—	—
High Town	247	1,565
Hill Street	3	16
Hinkleys	37	275
Jenning Street	1	5
John Street	59	348
King Street	36	217
Leek Street	—	—
Lease Lane	23	148
Lichfield Street	104	841
Livery Street	—	—
Lower Minories	11	58
Lower Priory	17	90
St. Martin's Lane	11	49
Masshouse Lane	16	77
Mill Lane	16	114
Moor Street	195	1,076
Moat Lane	43	252
New Street	105	649
New Meeting St.	21	149
Newport Street	1	—
Newton Street	54	312
Old Meeting St.	34	231
Park Street	156	944
Peck Lane	35	187
Philip Street	38	213
Pinfold Street	97	532
Pitt Street	—	—
Porter Street	—	...
Queen's Alley	10	45
Shut Lane and Well Court	7	55
Sand Street	1	4
Slaney Street	60	302
Smallbrook St.	101	795
Snow Hill	84	471
Spicer Street	41	249
Square	16	129
Stafford Street and Ditch	85	408
Steelhouse Lane	122	645
Swinford Street	5	19
Temple Alley	3	19
Temple Row	17	129
Temple Street	53	316
Thomas Street	52	316
Tonks Street	13	57
Upper Minories	4	4
Upper Priory	23	155
Walmor Lane	2	9
Weaman Street	78	486
Westley Street	68	402
Wood Street	35	204
Worcester Street	66	349
Houses Inhabited	4,058	23,688
Not Inhabited	112	—
Total	4,170	23,688

It will be interesting, with the assistance of the fac-simile, to compare this plan of the town in 1750, with the survey made by Westley, in 1731. The reader will, of course, notice, in the first place, the great difference in the area covered by the town; and in looking at the two plans side by side, it will be necessary for him to consider the top of Westley's to be that of the *upper edge of the book*, (*i.e.*, the *left* side of the engraving as originally issued,)—to look at the two plans, in fact, in the same position in relation to the letter-press,—as he will then see them as nearly as possible from the same point of view as regards the position of the various streets.

Beginning at the north-western corner of the map, we notice that Snow Hill is now built upon, (on the opposite side from the New Hall estate) beyond the stream which runs between that thoroughfare and the Great Pool; the last house marked being the Salutation Inn, with its Bowling Green. Behind Snow Hill, parallel with Steelhouse Lane, the buildings appear to extend, for a short distance, as far as Slaney Street; but as we get further down Steelhouse

Lane, the buildings on the north-western side become fewer, until, after passing Newton Street, the thoroughfare is on that side open to the country.

The first Methodist Meeting House (referred to in chapter XV.) will be found on Bradford's plan in the place occupied by Kettle's Steelhouses on Westley's. Further along, between Steelhouse Lane and Lichfield Street, will be seen the Workhouse.

On the eastern side of Stafford Street, the old name of that thoroughfare will be found commemorated in "Butts Lane," (now called Tanter Street,) and from that point to the corner of Aston Street the land is marked "for building." Lower down, the reader will notice several new features in Bradford's plan, "St. Bartholomew's Chappell," and the block of houses eastward beyond Moor Street. The "land for building" shown on Westley's plan between that street and Park Street is entirely built upon; a portion of it being occupied with the "play-house," in which "the famed Wesley appear'd on the stage;" standing back from the street, being approached by means of a narrow passage between two houses. In Deritend, the New St. John's Chapel is shown, without the tower, which was not added until 1762. Heath Mill Lane is called "Cooper's Mill Lane"—leading to the mill which forms so prominent a feature of Westley's Prospect—and Floodgate Street bears the name of "Water Street," although, as shown on the plan, the Flood-gates were then in existence. Another interesting feature of this rare plan is that it has all the principal inns marked; the *Castle and Falcon* and the *White Hart*, in Digbeth, the former nearly opposite Mill Lane, and the latter, on the same side, a little below Park Street; the *Dolphin* in the Corn Cheaping, (Bull Ring,) and the *Anchor*, almost opposite, in Spicer or Spiceal Street; the *Swan*, in High Street, below New Street; the *Hen and Chickens*, on the other side of the same street, on the site now occupied by Scotland Passage; the *Bull's Head*, near he Welsh Cross; and the *Salutation*, at the bottom of Snow Hill. The various meeting-houses are marked, including those which had arisen since the publication of Westley's plan, but it is curious to notice that while that in Carr's Lane is called "*Presbiterian*," that belonging to the Baptists', in Cannon Street, is styled an "*Independent Meeting House.*" Other local institutions of the period are also shown on the plan: the various markets, as described in a previous chapter; the Moat, which still existed, although a manufactory now occupied the site of the ancient castle of the lords of the manor;* the moated Parsonage, the two Crosses, (the old cross at the end of Stafford Street having apparently been removed;) the Post Office, opposite the Grammar School, in New Street; the Blue Coat School; the Pound, at the end of Pinfold Street and Peck Lane; the weighing machine, at the top of Bull Street and Snow Hill; the houses surrounding St. Martin's Church are also shown.

Turning to the pleasant park surrounding New Hall, we find the upper end, nearest Colmore Row, cut up into streets, and partly built upon. Livery Street and Church Street appear, the former extending beyond the great Pool, the latter to the point at which it is now intersected by Bread Street,—which did not then, however, exist. Little Charles Street, (which in 1870 became a part of New Edmund Street,) bears two names, on Bradford's plan; from Newhall Street (called on the plan "Newport Street,") to Church Street it is "Charles Street," and from thence into Livery Street it bears the name of "Hill Street,"—the present street of that name being unknown at that

* An advertisement in the *Gazette* of Jan. 4th, 1768, thus describes it :—

"To be Let, and entered on at Lady-Day next, for the Term of 21 Years, or longer if required, All that Messuage or Tenement, commonly called the Moat House, containing four Rooms on a Floor, and being three Stories high, with a large back Kitchen thereto adjoining, and convenient Warehouses, Shopping, and other Buildings contiguous thereto, situate in the Moat-Yard, in Birmingham, and late in the Occupation of Mr. Thomas Abney. The Premises are moated, all round, and are very fit and convenient for carrying on a large Manufactory, there being Buildings which, at a small Expence, may be converted into Work-Shops capable of employing 300 Workmen. For particulars enquire of Mr. Joseph Webster, in Digbeth, Birmingham."

date, and its site covered by a grove of trees and several meadows. Our local authorities appear to have been anticipated by their ancestors, in their idea of beautifying our public thoroughfares by planting trees therein, as the plan before us shows a line of trees on either side of New Street, on the western side of Temple Street, along Colmore Row, and in the Old Square. Among the streets shown on the plan which have since changed their names, may be mentioned Bewdley Street, (Ann Street,) Bull Lane, (Monmouth Street,) Harlow Street, (Edmund Street,) Swinford Street, (the upper portion of New Street,) Corbett's Alley, (Union Street,) and Swan Alley, (the upper portion of Worcester Street,) as well as those already referred to on the Colmore Estate.

With these few notes on the special features of this very rare and interesting old plan, we leave the facsimile of the print itself in the reader's hands, trusting that he may find some amusement in tracing out other particulars of the old town, as surveyed by Samuel Bradford, in 1750.

The seventh decade of the eighteenth century is memorable in the history of Birmingham, as having seen the introduction of canal navigation into this locality. The inland situation of the town, and the difficulty of transplanting the heavy goods manufactured here, caused the movement to be taken up with energy, offering, as it did, a cheaper and more expeditious mode of transit, and one far more suited to the requirements of the local trade.

The first English canal (which was made by deepening and widening the ancient Roman "Foss Dyke," from Lincoln to the River Trent,) was undertaken by Henry I., in 1121; but for more than five hundred years no further progress was made in inland navigation until 1608, when the New River Canal was begun. But the first modern canal, (*i.e.*, of the *eighteenth* century,) was the Sankey Brook Canal, in Lancashire, which was begun in 1755, and which proved exceedingly prosperous and useful to the district, and remains a valuable property to the present time; and from that date the "canal frenzy," as Hutton in his autobiography terms it, grew with a rapidity only equalled by that which characterised the railway projects in the nineteenth century. The "silent highways," as the canals have been termed, were as great a change to the people of the eighteenth century, accustomed as they had been to the clumsy, tedious, and uncertain waggons, and the slow and equally uncertain pack-horses, on the old, ill-kept roads, as the railways were to the people of the first half of the nineteenth century.

Birmingham was not slow to avail herself of the new mode of transit. On the 26th of January, 1767, an advertisement appeared in the *Gazette*, calling a meeting to take into consideration a scheme for cutting a canal through the South Staffordshire coal-field, to join the Wolverhampton Canal. The meeting was held on Wednesday, January 28, at the "Swan Inn," at which "a great number of the inhabitants of the Town" were present, and it was unanimously agreed to have the line of the proposed canal surveyed; the celebrated engineer, Brindley, being applied to for that purpose. On the 8th of June, the *Gazette* contained the following report of a meeting at which Brindley submitted his plans:

BIRMINGHAM NAVIGATION.

Swan Inn, June 4th, 1767.—At a numerous Meeting held this day, Mr. Brindley produced a Plan and Estimate of making a navigable Canal from the Town to the Staffordshire and Worcestershire Canal, through the principal Coal Works, by two different Tracts, and gave it as his Opinion that the best was from near New-Hall, over Birmingham Heath, to or near the following Places, viz., Smethwick, Oldbury, Tipton Green, Bilston, and from thence to the Staffordshire and Worcestershire Canal, with Branches to different Coal Works between the respective place.

As the Undertaking seems of great Importance, it is agreed that there be a Meeting appointed at this place, on Friday next the 12th Inst., at Four o'Clock in the Afternoon of the same Day, in order to open a Subscription to raise a Fund for the Expence of obtaing a Law, and completing the Work, which it is supposed will not exceed the Sum of £30,000 including all Expences. In the mean time Mr. Brindley's Plan, Estimate, and Opinion, and some Calculations of the Coal likely to pass, may be seen at Mr. Meredith's, Attorney at Law.

It is expected that a Committee for the Conduct of this Undertaking will be chuse at the said Meeting.

We read further, in the *Gazette* of July 15th, that—

Birmingham Navigation, July 10th, 1766.—Whereas several numerous public Meetings have been held at the Swan Inn, to consider of a Plan for making a navigable Canal through the principal Coal Fields in this Neighbourhood by Smethwick, Oldbury, Tipton Green, and Bilston, in the Counties of Salop and Stafford, to join the Canal now making between the Trent and Severn, at Addersly, near Wolverhampton, Mr. James Brindley having mads a Survey of it, estimated that the Expence would not exceed the Sum of £50,000 and on the Friday the 12th Day of June last, in Pursuance of an Advertisement for that Purpose, a Subscription was opened to apply to Parliament for Powers to make such Canal, and for compleating the same. There is already £35,000 subscribed; the Subscription Deeds will continue open at Mr. Meredith's, Attorney at Law, Birmingham, until the 26th of July Inst. unless the whole sum of £50,000 be sooner subscribed. At the same Place the proceedings of the Committee appointed for the Conduct of the application may be referred tc. By Order of the Committee.

JOHN MEREDITH, Solicitor.

By this time upwards of £35,000 was already subscribed towards carrying out this project. A bill "for making a Navigable Canal from Birmingham to Wolverhampton" was introduced in Parliament during the next session, (1768,) and received the roayal assent on the 26th of July in that year. On the "agreeable news" reaching Birmingham, "the bells were set to ringing, which were continued the whole day."

The length of the canal was about twenty-two miles, and the expense of making it about £70,000, divided into shares of £140 each, of which no one was allowed to purchase more than ten. From "A List of the Proprietors of the Birmingham Canal Navigation," (issued March 30, 1770,) we find that these shares were five hundred in number, and that the full number of ten were held by the following gentlemen: Thos. Anson, Esq., of Shuckbro'; Ann Colmore; Jer. Clarke, Esq., of Westbromwich; Peter Capper, Redland; Henry Carver, Esq.; the Earl of Dartmouth; James Farquharson; John Franncis; Samuel Galton; John Galton, Bristol; the Earl of Hertford; Sir Lister Holte, Bart., of Aston Hall; John Kettle; John Lane, jun.; Thomas Lee; Henry Venour; Joseph Wilkinson; and William Welsh. John Ash, M.D., (founder of the General Hospital,) held five shares, as also did Richard Rabone, John and Edward Sneyd, (respectively,) Dr. Wm. Small, Thomas Westley, and others whose names are well known and (in many cases,) honourably represented by their descendants in Birmingham to-day. Strange to say, the Father of Soho held only three shares. Among other shareholders may be mentioned, Poet Freeth, (who held one share,) Joseph Guest, Samuel Aris, James Brindley, (the engineer,) Joseph Carles, John Grew, Michael Lakin, Samuel Pemberton, jun., Daniel and Josiah Ruston, etc.

"This grand work," says Hutton, "like other productions of Birmingham birth, was rather hasty; the managers, not being able to find patience to worm round the hill at Smethwick, or cut through it, wisely travelled over it, by the help of twelve locks,—with six they mount the summit, and with six more descend to the former level; forgetting the great waste of water, and the small supply from the rivulets, in climbing this curious ladder, consisting of twelve liquid steps." *

The summit of this watery ladder is said to have been 460 feet above the level of the sea; but the inconvenience of the numerous locks being a source of continued complaint, the company eventually called in the aid of Telford to remove them; hills were cut through to a perpendicular depth of more than seventy feet, and other improvements effected, so that "the aspect of this canal," says Mr. Bates, writing in 1849, "is not surpassed in stupendous magnificence by any similar work in the world."

The first boat-load of coals was brought to Birmingham by this canal Nov. 7th, 1769, the year of the Stratford Jubilee; and the two events were commemorated by the local poet, John Freeth, (of whom we shall have more to say in our next chapter,) in an ode which is printed at the commencement of his *Political Songster*, of which a few stanzas may interest our readers:

* History of Birmingham, sixth edition, p 439.

INLAND NAVIGATION:

AN

ODE.

For ancient deeds let History unfold
The page where wonder's are enroll'd,
And tell how JASON, from the *Colchian* shore,
The golden fleece in triumph bore,
A nobler theme the Mind inspires,
And every skiful Artist fires
With heart-felt joy a work to see
Cut out for grand utility ;
A project form'd, by which, 'tis plain,
That thousands must advantage gain :
And sure that plan must be of noble use,
Which tends in price provision to reduce.
Blest Navigation ! source of golden days
Which Commerce finds, and brightens all its ways.

Sons of *Commerce* haste to pleasure,
For the joy belongs to you ;
May you live to reap the treasure
That must happily ensue.
Treasure, from *Staffordian* plains,
Richer than *Peruvian* mines,
And by what the Artist gains
All his principal designs.

CHORUS.

Not a Son of limping VULCAN
But must truly joyous be ;
ENVY from the banquet skulking,
'Tis the Artist's Jubilee*.
So quick in performing this weighty affair,
So great was the industry, prudence, and care,
Eighteen months have scarce run,
Since the work was begun :
How pleasing the sight !
What a scene of delight !
As the barges come floating along :

Then cease from your toil,
Nor hammer nor file
Be handled to-day,
All care shall away,
Whilst bonfires are blazing,
(What can be more pleasing ?)
All free-cost to gladden the throng.

Could our Forefathers from the shades but trace
The noble plan
Their Sons began,
To what amazement would the work appear !
A train of Vessels floating by the place,
Where sprightly steeds, at trumpet sound,
In contest wing'd along the ground,
And thousands to the pleasures would repair.

But, what were those days,
Compared to these ?
Each day at the *Heath* is a fair ;
To see Bridges and Locks,
And Boats on the Stocks,
Are numbers continually there.

Every breast, elate with joy,
Gladly views the happy day ;
Cease dissension,
Lamp contention,
From these regions haste away,
We alone on Trade depend ;
Be in that our emulation,
'Twill support our Navigation,
And the liquid tract extend.

But for this good care and trouble,
Which has nobly been display'd,
For our Coals, this instant, double
What we give, we must have paid.

Griping souls, that live by fleecing,
And upon their teams depend,
To all ranks of life how pleasing,
That their day is at an end.

Long their tricks were overbearing,
Now the vile oppressors may
Sell their nags and burn their geering,
For the roads 'twill better be.

CHORUS.

Not a Son of limping VULCAN
But shall joyous be to-day ;
ENVY from the banquet skulking,
'Tis the Artist's Jubilee.

* * * * * *

What mortals so happy as *Birmingham* Boys ?
What people fo flush'd with the sweetest of joys ?
All hearts fraught with mirth at the Wharf shall appear,

Their aspects proclaim it the Jubilee year,
And be full as gay in their frolicksome pranks,
As they who were dancing on *Avon's* green banks.

There never in war was for victory won,
A cause that deserv'd such respect from the Town ;
Then revel in gladness, let harmony flow,
From the district of *Bordsley* to *Paradise-Row ;*
For true feeling joy on each breast must be wrought,
When Coals under Five-pence per hundred are bought,

* * * * * *

Birmingham, for arts renown'd
O'er the globe shall foremost stand :
Nor its vast increase be found
To be equall'd in the land.
If the will of fancy ranges
From the *Tagus* to the *Ganges,*
Or from *Lapland* Cliffs extend
To the *Patagonian* Strand,
For mechanic skill and pow'r,
In what kingdom, on what shore,
Lies the place that can supply,
The world with such variety ?

* * * * * *

*The first Boat load of Coals was brought to Town November the 6th, 1769, the Year of the Stratford Jubilee.

Still may our Vessels, o'er the briny deep,
To sundry ports their various courses keep :
May Navigation, Liberty's dear friend,
Her wonted fame to greater lengths extend ;
Open her sluices and through mountain force,
To distant Lands an easy intercourse :
And *Birmingham*, for every curious art
Her Sons invent, be *Europe's* greatest mart ;
In every Kingdom ever stand enroll'd,
The grand Mechanic Warehouse of the World !

The fact which our local poet celebrated in his verse, ("Coals under five pence per hundred are bought,") is thus set forth in a more prosaic manner in the local journal of Nov. 6 :—

"It is with Pleasure we congratulate the Public on the probability of Coal being brought by Water near this Town in a few Days ; and that the Canal Company have not only resolved to sell the same this Winter at their Wharf for Fourpence Half-penny per Hundred, long weight of 120lb., but to fix the Price of their Delivery in every Street thereof : and in order for the better accommodation of the Poor, they have determined to establish Coal-Yards in different Parts of the Town, as soon as possible, where it will be sold in Quantities so small as Half Hundreds, or less ; and, indeed, there is great Reason to believe, that the Price of Coal will come (after the present winter) cheaper than Four-pence Half-penny per Hundred ; and that the Gentlemen who have the conducting of this important Affair, will use all possible Means to prevent Impositions of every kind."

An office for the transaction of the company's business was erected at the western end of Paradise Street, (then called Paradise Row,) which still remains, and from the steps of which, it is said, John Wesley preached during one of his visits to the town. The proprietors of the canal obtained from Sir T. Gooch a *perpetual lease* of six acres of land for the construction of their wharves, on the south side of Broad Street, at a rental of £47 per annum.

THE CANAL OFFICE.

The last year of the period marked out for us in the present chapter—1775—is interesting as having seen Samuel Johnson once more in Birmingham,—not as on the occasion of his first visit, in 1733, a poor scholar, seeking employment and glad to undertake the meanest literary drudgery, —but full of honours, (having recently received his diploma as Doctor of Laws, from the University of Oxford,) having taken his place, as Thackeray afterwards said of Dickens, at the head of the whole tribe of men of letters of his time, as poet, essayist, lexicographer, biographer, and critic,—he would scarcely be recognised as the young translator of Lobo's *Abyssinia*, and writer of the essays for Warren's *Birmingham Journal*. But he has not, in his days of prosperity, forgotten the friend of his youth, and we find him on the 10th of June in the year named, taking a post-chase,—driving was his favourite exercise,—from Oxford to Birmingham, intending to have passed a day or two with Edmund Hector, but he finds his friend's house already occupied with company, and so drives on to Lichfield. A few weeks later (August 27th) he writes, "I have passed one day at Birmingham, with my old friend Hector,—*there's a name!*—and his sister, an old *love*. My mistress is grown much older than my friend." Quoting Horace (Od. iv. 13), he adds, in reference to this lady :—

> "———What of her, of her is left,
> Who, breathing Love's own air,
> Me of myself bereft?"

His love, however, appears, from a conversation with Boswell during his next visit to Birmingham, to have been of a quiet, unromantic character. Unlike many whose early love has been doomed to disappointment, he did not feel that for him the world contained no other woman whom he could make his wife. His loquacious biographer had probed him on this occasion with the question, "Pray, Sir, do you not suppose that there are fifty women in the world, with any one of whom a man may be as happy as with any one woman in particular?" "Ay, Sir," said Johnson, "fifty thousand." "Then, Sir, you are not of opinion with some who imagine that certain men and certain women are made for each other, and that they cannot be happy if they miss their counterparts." "To be sure not, Sir," returned the doctor, "I believe marriages would in general be as happy, and often more so, if they were all made by the Lord Chancellor, upon a due consideration of the character and circumstances, without the parties having any choice in the matter." We hope there are not many to be found to day, who would endorse the worthy doctor's opinion on this subject.

The next year—1776—we find the doctor again in Birmingham, being this time accompanied by his *fidus Achates*, James Boswell. They had travelled from Oxford, calling at Stratford-on-Avon and Henley-in-Arden. From the latter place they set out early on Friday, March 22nd, and arrived in Birmingham about nine o'clock. After breakfast, they called on Edmund Hector, in the Old Square, (for he had also, like his friend, risen to a position of ease and prosperity,) "but," says Boswell, "a very stupid maid, who opened the door, told us that 'her master was gone out; he was gone to the country; she could not tell when he would return.' In short she gave us a very miserable reception." Johnson observed that "she would have behaved no better to people who wanted him in the way of his profession." Addressing the girl again, he said, "My name is Johnson; tell him I called. Will you remember the name?" The poor maid was probably confused at the doctor's rough manner and ponderous style of speech, and replied again, ("with rustic simplicity, in the Warwickshire dialect," Boswell tells us,) "I don't understand you, Sir." "*Blockhead*," said the doctor, "I'll write." He, however, attempted once more to make her understand him, and roared loudly in her ear, "*Johnson*," "and then," says Boswell, "she catched the sound."

The two visitors then left the Square and called on Mr. Lloyd, a quaker, and one of the founders of the bank which still bears the name of one of the most honoured families of Birmingham; but here again they were doomed to disappointment. Mr. Lloyd was not at home, but Mrs. Lloyd was, and received them courteously and invited them to dinner. Johnson remarked to Boswell that "after the uncertainty of all human things at Hector's, this invitation came very well."

They next took a walk through the town, and Johnson expressed his pleasure at its growth. Since his sojourn and courtship in the town it had indeed altered it appearance. When he left it on the morning of that memorable ride to Derby he had reached the open country by the time he passed the house in which Hector now lived. Had he wished to be married in Birmingham, he had choice of but two churches, St. Martin's and St. Philip's, beside the little chapel in Deritend. Now there were four, and the old Chapel of St. John the Baptist had given place to a larger, and—according to the taste of the times—handsomer building, capable of holding more than seven hundred persons. *Then* the only dramatic performances in the town were to be witnessed in the fields near Temple Street, now there were two handsome theatres. When he translated Lobo's *Abyssinia* there was but a single bookseller's shop in the town, and only the rudest appliances for the production of the book; now the booksellers were somewhat numerous, and he might have purchased as fine a library of books, and as good a collection of prints, at the shop of William Hutton, as anywhere in the kingdom; while for printing, John Baskerville had made the town famous throughout the civilized world.

As they walked about they met both of the gentlemen they were in search of; first Mr. Lloyd, and afterwards "*friend Hector*, as Mr. Lloyd called him." Johnson and his friend Hector would appear to have soon forgotten the presence of the other two, in their joy at meeting each other once again; and, says Boswell, "Mr. Lloyd and I left them together, while he obligingly showed me some of the manufactures of this very curious assemblage of artificers." They all met at dinner at Mr. Lloyd's, and were entertained with great hospitality.

The quiet simplicity of manners, as well as the spiritual-mindedness of this quaker family charmed both Boswell and Johnson, insomuch that the latter, tory and churchman that he was, felt bound to admit that "he liked individuals among the quakers, but not the sect." Boswell evidently felt that it would not be safe to introduce, in Johnson's presence, at Mr. Lloyd's, any questions concerning the peculiarities of their faith. His love of books, however, frustrated his good intentions, and, asking to look at Baskerville's fine quarto edition of "Barclay's Apology," it happened to open at the chapter on baptism, and Johnson's controversial spirit was let loose. He entered into an argument on the subject, in a manner which Boswell himself admits was by no means gentle, and, taking up a false position to begin with, he soon became entangled in the meshes of the controversy, and his quiet and gentle quaker opponents had the advantage of him. It was certainly a most ill-timed, as well as unfair attack upon the religious opinions of the people who had received him as a guest in so hospitable a manner, and probably no one regretted it after calm consideration more than the worthy doctor himself.

Mr. Hector accompanied Boswell on a visit to the famous manufactory of Matthew Boulton, at Soho, which, he tells us, the ingenious proprietor showed him himself to the best advantage. "I wished," says Boswell, "Johnson had been with us; for it was a scene which I should have been glad to contemplate by his light. The vastness and the contrivance of some of the machinery would have 'matched his mighty mind.' I shall never forget Mr. Boulton's expression to me, 'I sell here, Sir, what all the world desires to have—POWER. He had about seven hundred people at work. I contemplated him as an *iron chieftain*, and he seemed to be a father to his tribe." The loquacious biographer of Johnson tells further a story of Boulton's relations with his workpeople. "One of them," he says, "came to him complaining greviously of his landlord, for having distrained his goods. 'Your landlord is in the right, Smith, (said Boulton). But I'll tell you what: find you a friend who will lay down one half of your rent, and I'll lay down the other; and you shall have your goods again.'"

Returning from Soho, Boswell found Johnson "sitting placidly at tea, with his *first love*, [Mrs. Careless], who, though now advanced in years, was a genteel woman, very agreeable and well-bred."

Boswell wished to have remained longer in the town, but his companion, (for whom Birmingham does not appear to have had many charms, notwithstanding the number of friends he had in the place,) was anxious to get on to his native city, Lichfield, to which place they journeyed in the dark, and when Johnson saw the lamps of the city, he said, "Now we are getting out of a state of death." To him the quiet seclusion of the 'city of the dead' seemed to possess far more life than the busy bustling town they had left two hours before. And so passes the figure of "the hero as man of letters" from the history of Birmingham for ever.

THE MOAT. (*See p.* 147.)
From a Pen and Ink Sketch (by W. Hamper) in the possession of T. Avery, Esq.

If the reader will turn again for a moment to the *facsimile* of Bradford's Plan, he will see that in 1750 the town ended, in the direction of Coleshill Street, a little beyond Stafford Street. Further on he will notice the land marked "for building," but that for only half the distance along Coleshill Street; beyond that, it is open country, under cultivation. "I well remember," says Hutton, "seventy-one years ago, July 15th, 1741, standing with my face towards the east against Pritchett's timber yard, now the carrier's warehouse, Dale End, when all the lands before me, to the garrison, were meadows, and on my left not a house was erected."

Towards the end of the third quarter of the century, however, a change came over the prospect. Dr. Ash, of whom we have already heard, in connection with the General Hospital, obtained from Sir Lister Holte a lease, for ninety-nine years, of a large plot of land adjoining the Coleshill Road, and there he erected what Hutton calls "a sumptuous house." In addition to his connection with the General Hospital, he had great claims upon the respect and esteem of his fellow-townsmen, both as an eminently skilful physician, and an active and worthy citizen. He was, as we shall see in our next chapter, one of the first commissioners appointed to carry out the provisions of the Lighting and Street Improvement Act, (generally known as the "Lamp Act);" he was one of the shareholders or proprietors of the Birmingham Canal; the originator, as we have seen, of the General Hospital, and one of its first physicians; and in every way seems to have identified himself with the public life and improvement of the town in which he lived. In 1783 he saved Hutton's life, as the historian himself tells us. In our historian's autobiography he gives a more detailed account of his illness. Death from an inflammation was hourly expected. When the first sympton of improvement appeared, the doctor, Hutton tells us, with quaint circumstantiality, "holding the curtain in his hand said, 'You are as safe as a bug in a rug.'" It is impossible to repress a smile—looking at the stately and dignified portrait of the worthy physician, by Sir Joshua Reynolds—when we recall this droll announcement of his patient's recovery from what seemed likely to have proved a fatal illness.

Dr. Ash's practice began to decline, and this, says Hutton, "hurt his spirits, and he told me he had built on ehouse too much." He disposed of the lease in 1789 to Mr. John Brooke, an attorney, left the town, and spent the remainder of his days in London. He was threatened, in his old age, with mental alienation, and devised a curious method of curing it, by sedulously applying himself to the study of botany and mathematics, which he continued until his mental faculties had regained their equilibrium. A magnificent portrait of him by Sir Joshua Reynolds, (already referred to), was placed in the Board-room of the General Hospital, and is generally considered to be one of that great master's finest works. An engraving of it, (from a drawing by Mr. G. H. Bernasconi, of this town,) appears on page 143.

The estate was soon covered by streets, and became one of the most populous outskirts of the town, taking the name of *Ashted*, from its first resident. But the history of the rise and growth of this old suburb, and of the breaking up of the other old estates in the immediate vicinity of the town, must be reserved for a future chapter.

CHAPTER XXV.

THE LAMP ACT.

The preliminary meeting, Feb., 1765—Action postponed—Meeting of the inhabitants in December, 1768—Additional Clauses—Proposed Street improvements—Opposition—William Hutton's reasons for opposing the measure—Opposition meetings and canvas—The case clearly stated—A curious argument—Hutton's defence of the improvements—Epigram by "Poet Freeth"—The Act passed—The first Commissioners—Various clauses—The second Act.

It now becomes our pleasant duty to tell the story of the first Birmingham improvement scheme. We have already referred to this subject in our second notice of William Hutton,* but it will be necessary here to give a more detailed account of that movement by which the town for the first time in her history acquired something like real control over the encroachments of her citizens upon the public ways, and inaugurated that long series of local improvements which have raised her from the position of a vast straggling village to that of a noble city, and have culminated in the great scheme which is now in active operation, for clearing a large area of those wretched dwellings with which our ancestors, in their ignorance or neglect of sanitary laws, and in their anxiety to occupy every available foot of building land, covered the finest situation in the town.

On the 7th of February, 1765, a meeting of the inhabitants was held "at the House of Joseph Cooke, Victualler, in the Cherry Orchard," to consider the desirability of obtaining an Act of Parliament for "repairing, cleansing, and enlightening the Streets of this Town,"—that desirable reform being likely to "tend to the Suppression of many Disorders therein, and to the Preservation of the Persons and Properties of the Inhabitants." The following plan of the intended Bill was submitted to the consideration of the meeting:—

"That every Inhabitant, within the Town, who shall be seized of a real Estate of such Yearly Value, or possessed of a Personal Estate alone, or real and Personal Estate together, to such Amount as shall be then agreed upon, shall be Trustees for putting the said Act into Execution, who, or the major Part of them, being not less in Number than seven, shall have full power to Purchase Lamps, and to appoint Scavengers, Rakers, Lamp-Lighters, and other proper Officers, (with reasonable Salaries,) and to remove them at Pleasure, and to issue out Orders, from Time to Time, for the Repairing, Cleaning, and Lighting the said Streets; and at their annual or other Meetings to appoint Assessors, who shall have Power to Assess upon every Person holding or occupying any Messuage, House, Malthouse, or any other Building, or Garden Ground, within the said Town, (in the same manner as the Rates for the Poor are usually assessed, or as near thereto as can be,) any Sum, not exceeding one Shilling in the Pound, to be collected yearly or oftener, as the Trustees shall direct; with Power to appoint yearly so many Collectors as shall be thought necessary, who are to take upon them the Office under a certain Penalty to be agreed upon, but not to be obliged to serve more than once in seven years, with Proper and necessary Powers in the said Trustees to compel the assessing, collecting, paying, and applying the said Money for the Purposes aforesaid, and for settling and determining any disputes relating to the said Act, or the Execution thereof."

The intended application to Parliament, however, had to be postponed, "on account of the shortness of time allowed by the Hon. House of Commons for receiving Bills," the 16th of February being the last day; and the subject fell into abeyance until the end of 1768.

In the December of that year, however, the matter was revived in earnest. The first note of the revival is to be found in the *Gazette* of December 19, as follows:—

"A Meeting of the Inhabitants is desired at the Chamber over the Cross, on Tuesday next, at Eleven o'Clock in the Forenoon, to consider of a Petition to Parliament for Lighting and Cleaning the Streets of this Town, &c."

At this meeting the inhabitants unanimously agreed to petition Parliament for an Act to light

*pp. 136-7.

and clean the streets, and likewise to insert in the said Act the following clauses :—

"To Purchase and take down the House in the Bull Ring in the Possession of Francis Moles, the upper Round-about House, and the Houses at the end of New-Street, belonging to Sir Thomas Gooch and Henry Carver, Esq. ; to remove Nuisances in the Streets, and for the removal of the Beast-Market to Dale End; the Money for the above Purposes to be raised by a Rate upon the Inhabitants, not to exceed Eight-pence in the Pound per Annum."

The house in the possession of Francis Moles was one of those which, as we have said in a previous chapter, surrounded St. Martin's Church much in the same way as those on the south side of Christ Church, in New Street. Dr. Langford says of Moles' house, "Mrs. Price, my mother-in-law, remembers it quite well. The bed rooms were over the gate and part of the walk by which the people went to church."

Some idea of the choked-up appearance of the church may be obtained from the annexed facsimile of that portion of Bradford's Plan.

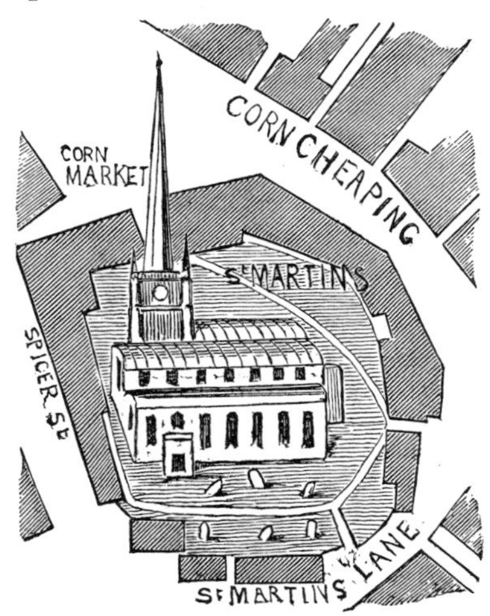

The Upper Round-about House was in the Bull Ring, which was still blocked up with buildings, as shown in both Westley's and Bradford's plans.

We have already* described the appearance and position of the houses which blocked up the end of New Street, but the reader will be better able to understand the wretched appearance of the entrance to what has become the principal street of the town, before the Lamp Act came into operation, from the small section of Bradford's plan given below; showing the end of New Street in which the swine market was then held.

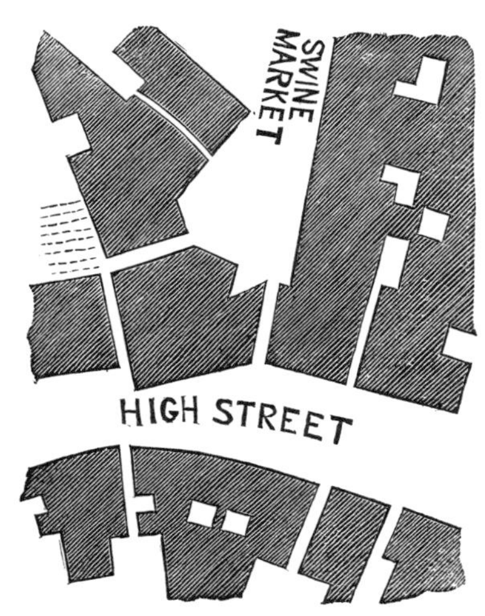

Like all projects, however beneficial, which involve the expenditure of public money, the Lamp Act met with opposition from unreasoning economists, "who seemed to prefer continuing in darkness and mire without tax, to cleanliness, light, and wider streets with eightpence in the pound to pay."* One expressed himself in the local journal in favour of a voluntary subscription, rather than a compulsory rate, (hoping, no doubt, by that means to enjoy the benefits of the local improvements without being called upon to contribute to their cost,) and stated that "a majority appeared greatly dissatisfied with that part of the scheme of enforcing a law to compel, when numbers were ready to subscribe to remove nuisances." But perhaps the greatest opposition was encountered amongst the local governing bodies themselves. William Hutton, who was an overseer of the Poor, admits in his autobiography that the opposition arose "more by his means than any other person's," and adds "an obvious reason." The historian occupied two of the houses which blocked up the end of New Street,

* Page 70.

* JEWITT: Life of William Hutton, *p.* 183.

and, as they suited him, he was disinclined to give them up for the improvement of the street.

"All the terms the opposition could obtain, and which were all I wanted," he says, "after many hundred pounds had been spent, were that the buildings should not come down, nor be included in the Act."

With the new year we find the opposition to the proposed improvements increasing, a meeting of the opponents being held at the "Seven Stars," on the 16th of January, 1769, at which it was determined "that a fair Enquiry should be made of every Inhabitant thro' the six Districts or Quarters of the Town, who pay the Parochial Dues, whether they chuse or disapprove the said Act." The result of this enquiry was that 237 inhabitants declared themselves in favour of the improvements, while the objectors numbered 1,236. In announcing the result of the poll, in the *Gazette*, the opponents of the said Act added that, as "the general Voice of the People is against the Act, it was thought advisable to open a Subscription to prevent such Act passing into a Law, which was accordingly done, and very liberally subscribed to, an Example that 'tis hoped will be followed by all who are inclinable to defeat so oppressive and ill-judged a Scheme."

In the same issue of the local newspaper which contained the announcement of the result of the canvas, appeared a letter signed "T. F.," showing how the votes against the scheme were obtained. "The enquiry," says the writer, "was very unfair, [the inhabitants] being only asked if they were for a perpetual tax of eightpence in the pound, not specifying the Advantages to be received; and a great many names were put down contrary to the inclinations and express orders of the different persons; and at the same time the true state of the case was not known to a great many to whom the above application was made." This correspondent, in continuing his letter, takes the opportunity of setting the case in a clear and concise view, and as his statement embodies, in a few brief sentences, the early history and objects of the movement, it is worth quoting here in full:—

"A Meeting was desired, by public Notice in the Churches upon the 28th of August, to be held upon the Thursday following, when it was the unanimous Voice of the Persons Present, that the Present intended Application should be made; and a further Meeting advertised, and was ordered agreeable to their Desire. A great many Persons met in consequence of the said Notice, and it was their unanimous Opinions that a Subscription should be immediately set forwards, and those present subscribed each a Guinea, to the amount of Fifty, and several Persons went about the Town for a further Subscription, which met with the greatest Encouragement; another Meeting was afterwards appointed, when about four or five Persons appeared against the intended Bill; but so great a Number being for it, a Committee was appointed of the most respectable Persons in Town, to consider what should be applied for, and the intended Application was confined to the undermentioned Particulars; that Power be petitioned for a Rate upon the Inhabitants not to exceed Eight-pence in the Pound per Annum, Two-pence of which is to be appropriated towards the removal of Nuisances, and Sixpence for Lighting the Streets: the above Two-pence will be entirely dropt, when the following Buildings are removed, which will not exceed six Years, and may be very reasonably expected to be purchased in four Years; the Buildings to be removed are the Old House in the Bull-Ring, leading to the Church-Yard, the upper Round-about House, and to open the Way into New-Street.

"To remove the Nuisances that remain in the Street, such as, lately, that before Mr. Luke Bell's Door, which lay Six Months in the principal Street, and entirely obstructed the Foot Way. A small Fine to be levied after Notice upon Continuance.

"To oblige the Drivers of all Water-Carts* and others carrying for Hire, to have a Halter to the Head of the Shaft Horse, by which he shall be led when passing through the Streets of the Town; to have the Houses in each Street Numbered and Painted, upon the Door, or Door Posts; and to have the Beast Market removed from the High-street to Dale-End; these are the Clauses intended to be introduced into the Bill; and though a Power may be obtained, that 6d. in the Pound may be levid, it is expected, that not above Four-pence in the Pound will be wanted, for Lighting the Streets; and no impartial Person can imagine, that any one that rents a House of Eight Pounds a Year, can think it a great Burden to pay Four Shillings per Annum, if the Whole is collected, and if Four-pence in the Pound will be sufficient, no more than Two Shillings and Eight-pence per Annum will be required, and all other Houses in Proportion; and the Public Advantage of having lighted and clean Streets, will more than compensate for the Payment."

Still, notwithstanding this calm and lucid

* Employed in selling water for drinking purposes, obtained from the Digbeth and Lady Wells.

statement of the case, prejudice yet existed, and occasionally shows itself in the *Gazette's* correspondence column in a very droll character; as in the case of the simple individual who argued that the comparatively few robberies and accidents having occurred in the town "may perhaps be in part ascribed to its want of Lamps!" "Opportunity," says this wiseacre, "makes a Thief, so Lamps frequently give a Villain an Opportunity of perpetrating Mischief, which is prevented by Darkness, and his fear of being observed prowling about the Streets with a Light; and this seems to be verified by the City of London, which is watched and lighted at a very great Expence, yet, nevertheless Robbery and Mischief is very frequent there, for the truth of which I appeal to the daily Papers." He also feared that the "lighting the Affluent or Extravagant Home from Taverns and Ale-houses in dark Nights" might lead to an increase of tippling and other vices, and gravely suggested that instead of rating the inhabitants for town improvements, "a *temporary* Duty of 3d in the Pound" should be levied, "to purchase two large Pieces of Ground for burying the Dead, and erecting two stately Edifices, to the Honour and Glory of God, the Ornament of the Town, and the eternal felicity of Thousands unborn."

"POET FREETH."

Ever the same. Fanatical opponents of necessary reforms, and especially sanitary reforms, would have the money cast into the treasury, or "given to the poor," rather than *wasted* in obtaining that virtue which a great religious reformer has placed next to Godliness itself.

It is gratifying to know that Hutton's opposition to the scheme did not extend to the lighting or other improvements in the direction of cleanliness and comfort, but had reference solely to the removal of his premises.

"It was justly observed," he says, "that robbery was a work of darkness, therefore to introduce light would, in some measure, protect property. That in a town like Birmingham, full of commerce and inhabitants, where necessity leads to continual action, no part of the twenty-four hours ought to be dark. That, to avoid darkness, is sometimes to avoid insult; and that by the light of 700 lamps, many unfortunate accidents would be prevented. It was also observed, that in course of time, the buildings in some of the ancient streets had encroached upon the path four or five feet on each side; which caused an irregular line, and made those streets eight or ten feet narrower, that are now used by 70,000 people, than they were when used only by a tenth part of that number; and, that their confined width rendered the passage dangerous to children, women, and feeble age, particularly on the market day and Saturday evening. That if former encroachments could not be recovered, future ought to be prevented: And that necessity pleads for a wider street now than heretofore, not only because the inhabitants, being more numerous, require more room, but the buildings, being more elevated, obstruct the light, the sun, and the air, which obstructions tend to sickness and inconveniency.

"Narrow streets, with modern buildings, are generally dirty, for want of these natural helps; as Digbeth, St. Martin's Lane, Swan Alley,* Carr's-lane, &c. The narrower the street, the less it can be influenced by the sun and wind, consequently the more the dirt will abound; and by experimental observations on stagnate water in the street, it is found extremely prejudicial to health. And also, the larger the number of people, the more the necessity to watch over their interest with a guardian's eye." †

* This, as will be seen from Bradford's Plan, formed the upper portion of Worcester Street, (from New Street to Philip Street,) and was subsequently widened.

† History of Birmingham, third edition, 1795; pp. 157-8.

In March "Poet Freeth" contributed to the discussion an Epigram "On the Bill for depending for removing Public Nuisances."

EPIGRAM.

Wonder not that this Contention,
Feuds and Jealousies create;
Envy, Discord and Dissension,
Are true Copies of the State.

The greatest Nuisances we want
Fairly from the Land to shove,
And worse than any Town Complaint,
And ev'ry Day are seen above.

J. F.

It is pleasant to be able to record that the opposition was unsuccessful. On the 24th of April the *Gazette* announced that the Act had been passed by the House of Commons on the previous Friday (April 21st) with only one vote in the negative, and on the first of May the same journal contained the welcome news that it had received the assent of the upper house on Thursday April 27, and awaited only the Royal Assent to give effect to its provisions. This final stage was reached early in May, and the first act of parliament for the improvement of the town became law, "and thus, after a sharp fight, the foundation was laid of regular local government in Birmingham."* It was entitled:

"An Act for laying open and widening certain ways and passages within the Town of Birmingham, and for cleansing and lighting the streets, ways, lanes, and passages there, and for removing and preventing nuisances and obstructions therein."

The preamble of the Act is as follows:

"Whereas the Town of Birmingham, in the County of Warwick, is a large, populous, and trading Town. And whereas certain ways and passages within the said Town are too narrow for the commodious issuing and repassing of passengers, waggons, and other carriages, to the great danger and inconvenience of the inhabitants of the said Town, and of persons resorting thereto. And whereas it would greatly tend to the convenience of the said Town if a certain ancient building siutate near the Market Place, called the Upper Roundabout House, was taken down, and the ground upon which the same now stands was laid open. And whereas it would add greatly to the safety and advantage of the said Town if the streets, lanes, ways, and passages thereof were kept clean and properly lighted, and kept free from nuisances, obstructions, and annoyances.

* J. T. Bunce: History of the Corporation, i, 75.

Fifty Commissioners were appointed, who, according to the Act, were to be inhabitants of the town, rated to the poor at not less than £15 a year, or possessed of real or personal estate of the value of £100. Our readers will doubtless be interested in learning the names of our first local legislators, who were named in the Act, as follows:

John Ash, M.D.	Michael Lakin
William John Banner	Thomas Lutwyche
John Baskerville	Thomas Lawrence
Samuel Bradbourne	William May
Thomas Bingham	Benjamin Mansell
James Butler	John Moody
Samuel Baker	John Oseland
Henry Carver	Thomas Pemberton
Francis Coales	William Russell
Thomas Careless	John Ryland
John Cope	Thomas Russell
Thomas Falconbridge	Richard Rabone
John Freer	John Rogers
Samuel Freeth	William Small, M.D.
John Ford	Joseph Smith
Samuel Garbett, Esq.	John Taylor, Esq.
Samuel Galton	Joseph Thomas
Richard Goolden	John Turner, sen.
John Gold	John Turner, jun.
Samuel Harvey	Joseph Wilkinson
Gregory Hicks	William Walsingham
James Jackson	William Welch
John Kettle	Elias Wallin
Sampson Lloyd, sen.	Joseph Webster
Sampson Lloyd, jun.	Thomas Westley

It will not be necessary here to repeat in full the provisions of the Act, most of which have already been mentioned in the preliminary discussion and the "statement of facts" on page 158. A few curious notes therefrom, may, however, amuse and interest the reader. The inhabitants, for instance, were (for the convenience of the scavengers) to sweep the streets and ways for a space of twelve feet from the front of their premises, "every Friday, between the hours of six in the morning and two in the afternoon," and were also to "collect and put together the dirt and soil in the said streets, lanes, ways, and passages, with the least obstruction to the way, road, and passage therein respectively that may be, to the end the same may be ready for the scavenger to carry away." The space in front of void houses, dead walls, waste land, "churches, churchyards, chapels, meeting-houses, the school called the Free School, and other public buildings," was to be cleansed by the town scavengers, and the scavengers were to ring a bell to give notice to the inhabitants that they might bring out ashes and other refuse from their houses for removal. Private sweepings might be undertaken by the Commissioners, on an annual payment being made by the householder for that purpose.

The market "for the sale of neat cattle within the said town," which had "usually been held in the principal street and greatest thoroughfare, called the High Street, to the great danger and inconvenience of all persons living and resorting there," is to be removed to "that part of the street called Dale End, which is between the house now in the occupation of Clement Satterthwaite and the end of Chapel Street." The buildings scheduled for purchase are named as follows: (1) "At the entrance into New Street; four Tenements fronting the High Street; two of them in the occupation of W. Hutton, one of Jn. Greaves, and one of Th. Brueton with five tenements *backwards*," or in the rear of those mentioned; "the front towards the High Street (including the present Passage about 12 feet) being about 64 feet; the front towards New-street about 70 feet." (2) "The Upper Round-about House in the occupation of Samuel Willets or his Under Tenants," about twenty-eight feet by nineteen feet. (3) "The house fronting the Corn Market, in the occupation of Francis Moles; [one of those surrounding St. Martin's Church,] the front towards the Corn Market about fifteen feet; on the side towards the Passage leading into St. Martin's Church-Yard, about thirty feet; and the back part thereof, towards the said Church-Yard, about fifteen feet." Hutton's houses, as we shall see, did not come down until an Extension of the Act had been passed, in 1773.

The new Commissioners met for the first time on the 22nd of May, at the Castle Inn, and resolved (1) "That, in order no one may plead Ignorance of the Law, the following Advertisement [an Abstract of the Act] should be inserted." (2) "That the Regulation as to the removal of the cattle market to Dale End be dispensed with 'till Thursday the 25th inst., and that the Town Cryers do publish the same by Bell on the Fair Day, and the two following Thursdays, and that the Beadles do attend in the High Street on the 25th inst., and the 1st of June, to prevent Country People incurring the Penalty through mistake." (3) "That unless Annoyances are removed as the Act of Parliament directs, the Offenders will be immediately proceeded against." (4) "That the Commissioners do meet at the Castle Inn on Tuesday next the 23rd inst. at four o'clock in the afternoon, when they will be ready to receive proposals from any person or persons inclined to fix Names at the ends of the Streets, and Number the Houses."

The second act, for the extension of the Commisioners' powers, as well as of their number, was passed in 1773, and immediately afterwards they announced their intention of proceeding with the negociations for the purchase of the houses at the end of New Street. Our readers will doubtless remember Hutton's ground of opposition to the first Act, in 1768, and it will be interesting to see his reasons for complying with its provisions in 1773. Under date 1772, in his autobiography, he says :—"By an amendment of the Lamp Act, my houses must come down. It happened that the old house where I now reside, [in High Street, opposite the end of New Street,] was upon sale.

ST. PAUL'S CHAPEL,
Previous to the erection of the spire.

I durst not let the opportunity slip, but considered it a tool by which I must carry on trade. I purchased it for eight hundred and thirty-five guineas. It was then under a mortgage for £400. I was obliged to pay the residue; and as the premises would open to New Street were my two houses removed, I now wished them down."

The new Act provided that twenty-nine persons should be added to the fifty Commissioners previously appointed; viz., Richard Anderton, Samuel Aris, Matthew Barker, William Capper, John Francis, Sampson Freeth, *William Hutton,* William Hodgkins, Joseph Jukes, Edmund Wace Patteson, Edward Palmer, Samuel Pemberton, jun., Samuel Ray, William Ryland, Josiah Rogers, Samuel Steward, Timothy Smith, John Taylor, jun., John Ward, Thomas Wight, (grocer,) Daniel Bond, Thomas Colemore, of Edgbaston Street; William Dutton; William Holden, of New Street; John Harris, of Cannon Street; Luke Bell, Walter Oakley, Thomas Gisbourne, and Joseph Thomason.

Of William Hutton's appointment as a Commissioner our readers have already heard,* as well as of his action thereon, and the way in which his zeal for the carrying out of the provisions of the Act was checked by the self-interest of his brother Commissioners; we cannot, however, help remarking here that his indignation at the manner in which they sought to benefit themselves and their friends rather than to carry out the act in its integrity, seems somewhat incongruous by the side of his own action in the matter of the High Street premises.

We shall have to speak of the appearance of the town under the Commissioners in a future chapter.

CHAPTER XXVI.

"POET FREETH" AND THE BIRMINGHAM BOOK CLUB.

Freeth's Coffee House—The Book Club—Poetical invitation cards—"Pudding-time"—"Our good friends at Boston and those at New York"—Bunker's Hill—"J. Free"—Baskerville's Printing—Hard Times—Taxation—Birmingham Streets—Ecclesiastical Navigators—Popular Amusements—End of the World—"Banbury thumps"—Longing for Peace.

In our notice of the old charities of Birmingham* it was mentioned that the meetings in connection with one of those foundations (Jackson's charity) were held at Charles Freeth's Coffee House, in Bell Street. This house became noteworthy, both for the quality of the entertainment, and the genial character of its host. Amongst the lovers of good-fellowship who gathered, after their daily labour was ended, for the evening gossip, around the fireside of this snug old-fashioned hostelry, would be seen the merry, good-humoured face of mine host's promising son; a lad much given to making verses, and fitting them to the popular airs of the day. By-and-by the son took his father's place, and the coffee-house kept by "Poet Freeth" became the favourite resort of all classes.

About the middle of the eighteenth century, a few book-lovers of the town formed themselves into a society for the purpose of purchasing and circulating among themselves such books as they desired to read; and from this little society arose the Birmingham Book Club, which has now flourished for more than a century and a quarter, and "still exists in a green, vigorous, and flourishing old age."† The early meetings of this society were held at the house of "Poet Freeth," who was one of its most active members, by whom the invitations to their annual dinners were sent out, written in verse, as became one who was reputed for his "poetical" talents. These invitation-verses contain many references to passing events, and usually conclude by giving the

* Chapter xi., p. 79.

* Chap. xxii.; page 137.

† J. A. Langford. LL.D.

toast of the evening. From a very complete collection of these tickets, in the possession of W. Franks-Beale, Esq., of Chester Road, Erdington, we are enabled to give our readers a few examples of Freeth's versifying abilities. The earliest is dated Nov. 29, 1770. The host says, in inviting his friends to the annual feast :—

SIR,
In this wrangling fluctuating State-juggling Age,
When we neither have Peace, nor in War dare engage ;
(Tho' they tell us to Day that *Jamaica* is lost,
It may be contradicted the very next Post.)
I beg you'd for once, as 'twill drown Care and Sorrow,
Reverse the old Phrase, and take Thought for to-morrow :
In Mirth giving Sentiment, Story, or Song,
Ne'er fear but the Hours will pass chearful along ;
There's nothing I know of can slacken the Cheer,
For I cannot expect a King's Messenger here ;
And the Talons of Law, Truth, and Reason repels,
For Chief Justice *Mansfield* has lost all his Nails.
So beg you'd attend, and see what's to be done,
'Tis exact Pudding-Time when St. *Martin's* strikes One.

Nov. 29, 1770. J. FREETH.

The phrase "pudding-time," which occurs in several of these earlier invitations, seems to indicate that at Poet Freeth's the old-fashioned custom of "pudding first" was respected.

The annual dinner of 1771 was held on the date of the *invitation* of the previous year, consequently the card of invitation is dated Nov. 28. It is the smallest in the collection, and would seem to indicate that card-board was somewhat scarce, as it is printed on *the half of a playing-card* :—

SIR,
He that would taste of noble Fare,
Let him To-morrow here repair ;
For by PARNASSUS 'tis my Pride,
To have my Table well supply'd.
No Bard good Living e'er refuses,
For Roast Meat never sours the Muses :
And feasting Days in this good Town
Where ne'er I trow more frequent grown.
At Pudding-Time bid Care begone,
Twenty may dine as well as one.

Nov. 28, 1771. J. FREETH.

Our freedom-loving fathers, in their enjoyment (at a very early season of the year) of "young ducks and green peas," did not forget their cousins across the Atlantic, who, in 1775, were fighting for national independence. Accordingly, we find them remembered at the meeting on the 16th of June in that year :—

SIR.
As few when the Season its kindness displays,
But love to partake of young Ducks and green peas,
And as in the Town there is known to be plenty,
To-morrow I purpose to cater for twenty,
Pudding time is at One—to the Custom adhere,
For the summons must please that invites to good Cheer :
In the TOASTS of the Day as a friend to the Land,
And foremost for FREEDOM may EFFINGHAM stand,
Not forgetting Lord GRANBY a SAVILLE and BURKE
Our good friends at BOSTON and those at NEW YORK.

J. FREE.

Birmingham ; June, 15th 1775.

The same sentiment is expressed in the invitation-verses issued Nov. 21st in the same year :—

SIR.
Whilst some to the Throne are ADDRESSES conveying,
For Slaughter and Slavery servilely praying,
And false as their Language is fulsome pretend,
They'll hazard their Lives, and their Fortunes they'll spend ;
Accept from a Lover of peace this PETITION,
To festive enjoyment the Card of admission :
Next FRIDAY I purpose to garnish my Board,
For Feasting I always to fighting preferr'd.
As friends to Conciliat'ry Measures are those,
Who wish well to COMMERCE and FREEDOM espouse,
May those who oppose 'em and more Blood would spill,
Be forc'd into Service, and mount BUNKER's HILL.

J. FREE.

November 21st, 1775.

It will be noticed that in the two preceding invitations the poet adopts the signature of "J. Free," which appears on all the cards from this date to 1786.

In June, 1776, the poet appears to have lacked either inspiration or theme, for he contents himself with the following brief note :—

"Sir,

"FRIDAY next being FEAST DAY, the Favour of your Company is humbly requested to DINE at J. FREE'S, at ONE o'Clock.

"June 12, 1776."

The invitation card of 1778 bears evidence—in the appearance of the type and the general neatness which renders it a contrast to every other in the series—of its having been printed with the types of John Baskerville. The next card of interest is that of June, 1782 :—

SIR.
As a Glass of good Port for the reigning Disease,
Is the only Specific that best seems to please ;

By Way of preventive, in making a Trial,
I trust to a Bottle you'll have no denial;
On Friday my best I intend to uncork,
And to those who can brandish a good Knife and Fork,
I mean as a Relish to throw in their Way,
Young Duck, Ham, and Chicken, but not a green Pea:
(A Bumper to RODNEY, the Subject will bear it,
I'd toast him in Water, but rather in Claret;)
Then please to attend and see what's to be done,
Time of Action commences at Half after One.

BIRMINGHAM,
June 11, 1782. J. FREE.

In the next we find the publican-poet complaining sadly of the times:—

SIR,

On Friday observe, *Beef* and *Pudding's* the Text,
I'll live well this Year, if a Bankrupt the next,
And that, or sing Ballads, will sure be my Lot,
For the Profits on Ale-selling scarce boil the Pot:
Though heavy Complaints in the Land have arose
Respecting the Times—you'll my Freedom excuse,
For those in Distress, recent Actions have shewn,
The *Colliers* have Feelings, but *Maltsters* have none;
And Riots are certain to sadden the Year,
When Six-penny Loaves but Three-pounders appear.
But Murmuring cease, 'tis a Folly to grieve,
Time and Patience will all our Misfortunes relieve,
Let a Bumper go round, since a Peace is at Hand,
To ELIOTT the brave, and his Veteran Band.

BIRMINGHAM, Nov. 27, 82. J. FREE.

Taxation, "the blessed Effects of the American War," has begun to fall heavily upon the much-enduring British public, and the first note of it—a note which is seldom absent again from Freeth's rhymed invitations—appears in 1783:—

STAMP DUTIES.

SIR,

For FRIDAY prepare, the Enjoyment embrace,
Of Feasting before the fresh Duties take Place;
For Tax upon Tax may be carried too far,
The *blessed* Effects of the *American* War;
Which, again to pursue, let *Lord North* have the lead,
And he'll tax every Tooth a Man has in his Head:
The Burthens, tho' hard, we are still to have more,
And TRADE's to be flogg'd, without *hurting* the Poor;
For a Tax on RECEIPTS, amongst other such Jokes,
Is one of CHARLES FOX's *luxurious* Strokes,
That slipt the OLD BUDGET— a *Beauty* not known,
'Till CHARLES and his BLUE-RIBBON'D LORDSHIP made one:
A *general Reform* has been fought for in vain,—
There is but one Method Redress to obtain;
Many Plans may be formed—yet there's nothing so sure,
As the TOWER-HILL STAMP public Evils to cure.

BIRMINGHAM, June 18, 1783. J. FREE.

The card issued 1784, bears the name of Swinney as printer, who succeeded Baskerville in the business of type-founding. In the verses contained thereon Freeth refers to "Birmingham streets,—always needing repair,"—but this was before the days of wood pavement; what would the old poet say if he could see them in 1878?

SOCIETY FEAST.

SIR,

FRIDAY next, if you've nothing material on Hand,
Let the plentiful Board your Attention command;
The Limb of a Goose, on a Plate of Green Peas,
I make not a Doubt, will the Appetite please:
Look sharp for a While, and, if one will not do,
Disdain to be sparing—make certain of two.

As to Matters of State, strange as may be the Rout!
Not much does it matter who's IN or who's OUT:
As GOVERNMENT WHEELS I can only compare
To *Birmingham Streets*——always wanting Repair;
For when LEVIES run high, and are chearfully paid,
Ducks and *Drakes* of the Cash, are too frequently made.

May the Youth at the Helm, whom the People admire,
Inherit those Virtues which dwelt in his Sire!
And a Bumper be given—That Wrangling may cease,
Less TAXES, more TRADE—and with all the World PEACE!

Birmingham, June 9th 1784. J. FREE.

In the next Freeth changes his metre, but increased taxation is still the burden of his song:

SOCIETY FEAST.

SIR,

On the tenth day of June
Should my Voice be in tune,
To sing (though my powers are small),
About those who Trade,
The STATE-PACK-HORSE have made,
I'll endeavour to honour your call.

But over stout Ale,
As a Song or a Tale,
Not the mind altogether will suit;
I therefore to please,
Shall have GEESE and GREEN-PEAS,
With BEEF and PLUMB-PUDDING to boot.

Tho' PITT loses ground,
I hope 'twill be found,
That the YOUTH one good ACTION has done,
By clapping a TAX,
Upon BACHELOR's backs,
And letting the Females alone.

BIRMINGHAM, J. FREE.
June 8, 1785.

In his next year's rhyme, he has a sly hit at the "canal frenzy," to which we have referred in a previous chapter:—

SOCIETY FEAST.

SIR,
My regular Summons I trust you'll obey,
The sixteenth of June is for Feasting the Day ;
And in a short Time though much Work may be done,
I beg you'd be seated by Half after One.
The Seasons are kind, Plenty covers the Ground,
Yet the ROAST BEEF of England brings Six-pence per Pound
'Tis a CATCH as CAN World, some for this, some for that,
The STOCKS still advance, NAVIGATION is flat ;
Many minds in a Contest were lately concern'd,
And the Heads of the Church NAVIGATORS are turn'd !
Providing a War very soon should take Place,
Our Monarch, I hope, will consider the Case ;
Think, think GRACIOUS GEORGE, of the BISHOPS, I pray,
One Half keep at home—let the Rest go to Sea.

J. FREETH.

BIRMINGHAM, June 13, 1786.

Our next card has reference to several popular amusements in the town at that period. The "Dancing Dogs" had made their first appearance here in 1785, from Sadler's Wells Theatre, and were announced to "exhibit their astonishing performances . . . at the New Street Theatre, after the entertainments of rope and wire-dancing, *tumbling*, and other feats of activity *by the famous Little Devil* and the rest of the company from Sadler's Wells." That "the famous Little Devil" was in Birmingham at the date of Freeth's card, (November, 1787) is shown by the following paragraph from the *Gazette* of the 5th of that month :—

"The Little Devil and La Bella Espagñola, who are confessedly unrivall'd in their profession, were near making their exit in a very disagreeable way, on Friday Evening, at the Theatre in this Town. Some evil-minded person in the pit having diabolically cut the tight-rope in several places, which certainly endangered the limbs (if not the lives of the performers). It was, however, happily perceived time enough to prevent any misfortune, though it deprived the audience for that night of some part of the agreeable and wonderful performance. We hope the managers will, in future, appoint some faithful person to detect the perpetrator of such cruelly wanton acts, and spare no expence in punishing them."

It is time now to return to the verses which refer to these performances :

SOCIETY FEAST.

Dinner exactly at Half past One.

SIR,
ON Friday next, St. ANDREW'S Day,
I beg my Summons you'll obey,
For thro'he Kingdom, Reason says,
NOVEMBER'S short and gloomy Days,
Require, from hence dull Care to chace,
With LIQUOR which the Nerves will brace.
The Heart that's sound will Friendship prize,
What's Life without convivial Joys ?
Bad as Trade is, or bad may keep,
TUMBLERS a glorious Harvest reap ;
And DANCING DOGS and DEVILS swarm,
With antick Feats the Town to charm ;
—But when the Appetite is keen,
In choicest FARE—as *Charms* are seen—
Honour the Call, good Cheer you'll find,
And RELAXATION give the mind.

Nov. 28th, 1787. J. FREETH.

The townsfolk seem to have been troubled, in 1788, by a prophecy of the approaching end of the world; and to this, as well as to the trial of Warren Hastings, which had commenced on the 13th of February in that year, reference was made by the local poet in his invitation to the usual Society Feast on the 10th of June :—

SOCIETY FEAST.

SIR,
I have not a doubt but young GEESE and green PEAS,
Next Friday, well cook'd, will the Appetite please ;
Your Attendance I beg—well assur'd that my Board
Will plenty of other good Dishes afford—
Such as CHICKENS and HAM, as the Season may suit,
The finest of BEEF and PLUMB-PUDDING to boot :
Besides, after playing a good KNIFE and FORK,
I've Ale stout and bright—and I mean to uncork,
Of PORT, a few Bottles, by way of fair trial,
And long as it lasts you will have no denial.
All this to accomplish I find myself able,
Better Fare PETER PINDAR had ne'er on his Table
The Promise is handsome—what POET can beat it ?
Nor care I a Button how oft I repeat it—
For if on the Words of a Sage we depend,
The World will *in forty-eight Years have an end* ;
So whether or not WARREN HASTINGS gets by,
There scarce will be Time Sir ELIJAH to try—
Then a Bumper give round, when the Heart is at ease,
"That our Children may make the best Use of their Days."

Birmingham, June 10, 1788. J. FREETH.

It would appear, from the "Society" laureate's verses of November 1789, that pugilism was at that time a favourite pastime in the town. "*Banbury* thumps" doubtless had reference to a hero of 'the ring' of that name :—

SOCIETY FEAST—on FRIDAY next.

Dinner at Half-past One.

SIR,
My CONTEST, which full thirty minutes will hold,
I hope, to attend you will feel yourself bold ;

OLD AND NEW BIRMINGHAM" PORTRAIT GALLERY.—No. 8.

PHOTOGRAPHED BY WHITLOCK.

BIRMINGHAM HOUGHTON AND HAMMOND, SCOTLAND PASSAGE.

BOTTLE-HOLDERS and SECONDS I've always at hand,
To answer whilst combating ev'ry command ;
Yourselves are to watch how the moments go on,
The time is your own—as to UMPIRES I've none ;

WILLIAM HUTTON.

For I trust, when engaging, whate'er may be done,
No *blood* will be spilt, tho' the *claret* may run :
Tho' the fight should be furious, and nothing be spar'd,
No dread will you have when your elbows are squar'd.
On the whole, you may find an agreeable day,
As I have not a doubt but you'll meet with fair play ;
PLUMB-PUDDING, BOIL'D BEEF, and GOOD ALE are the *trumps*,
For the *stomach* much better than BANBURY THUMPS.

Nov. 25, 1789. J. FREETH.

The invitations of succeeding years have but few special features of interest, until we reach 1793, when the poet made the strife and turmoil on the Continent the burden of his verse :—

SOCIETY FEAST.
ON FRIDAY NEXT.
☞ *Dinner at Half-past One o'Clock.*

SIR,

THE World's in an uproar, and when it will cease,
What mortal can tell ? there's no Prospect of Peace,
On tiptoe some Thousands continually are,
To see what the Winds from the Continent bear :
Variety will from Dame Fortune be had,
One Day we have good News, the next brings us bad ;
But tho' we of Conquests are happy to boast,
As "War begets Poverty,"—this is my TOAST :

"May the OLIVE BRANCH gladden the Year NINETY-FOUR,
"FREE TRADE and GOOD FELLOWSHIP all the World o'er."
J. FREETH.
BIRMINGHAM, November 27, 1793.

In 1794 the invitation took the form of a note, from "Smith, Son, & Smith," followed by eight lines of verse in a more hopeful strain than many of that decade :—

SIR,

THE Favour of your Company to *Sup* at *J. Freeth's*, on FRIDAY next, will much oblige,
Yours,
December 2, 1794. *Smith, Son, & Smith.*

A JOCULAR hour, with a good-natur'd Friend,
What mortal can have an objection to spend ?
And since to be happy, united, and free,
The beauty of Life is—as all will agree ;
Good will to promote, and true friendship to nourish.
That ENGLAND—OLD ENGLAND for ever may flourish,
My TOAST is—"To COMMERCE a speedy increase,"
"And all the world over, a PERMANENT PEACE."
J. F.

Green peas were later in the following year, and the feast was perforce lacking in that customary item :—

Society Feast,
ON FRIDAY NEXT,
Dinner exactly at Two o'Clock.

SIR,
THE Stomach, if rightly in tune,
Young GEESE will undoubtedly please ;
But though near the middle of June,
I fear we shall lack of GREEN PEAS.

My Liquor is brilliant and stout,
If short in the eatable Score,
Then make the Deficiency out,
By drinking a Bottle the more.

The Black Feather'd EAGLE of *Prussia*,
Our Ministry nicely cajoles ;
The over-grown SHE-BEAR of *Russia*,
Has shamefully pluck'd the poor POLES.

But now for the Toast of the Day :—
"May PEACE quickly gladden the Shore,
"HUMANITY ev'ry STATE sway,
"And HARMONY all the World o'er."
J. FREETH.
Birmingham, June 10, 1795.

If space would permit, we might continue our quotations from these genial invitations of the mirth-loving host of the "Leicester Arms," but to do this would carry us further into the history of our town than we are prepared at present to advance, and would occupy a greater proportion of this history than their actual importance warrants ; but as we shall have occasion again to refer to the writings of Freeth, at a later date, we may perhaps then find space for a few more of these sprightly missives.

While on the subject of the entertainment provided at an old-fashioned inn, our readers may be interested in knowing something of the cost of good living in those days. An old tavern bill is before us, dated December 28, 1797, for entertainment received at Charles Wilday's, Shakespear Tavern, New Street, as follows :—

	£	s.	d.
Dinners	—	12	0
Tea and Coffee	—	4	0
1 Red Port	—	3	6
2 Sherry	—	9	0
Witness eating	—	1	0
Ale	—	7	0
Rum	—	1	0
Paper	—		6
Porter / Ale	—	2	6
Fruit	—	4	6
	2	5	0
Servant		3	6
Coach Hire		5	0
	2	13	6

CHAPTER XXVII.

THE CHURCHES AND SECTS OF BIRMINGHAM, 1760-1780.

Proposals for building two new churches—The Act passed—Musical Entertainments in aid of the building of St. Mary's—Description of St. Mary's—The building of St. Paul's—The Festival of 1778—The Eginton Window—The New Meeting and Dr. Priestley—Cannon Street Meeting-house—Methodism—Carr's Lane—Scott's Trust, etc.

WE now once more take up the story of the churches and sects in Birmingham, at the date at which our last notice closed, viz., 1760.

As we have already seen, in our survey of the town in 1760, the church accommodation was already becoming inadequate to the needs of the rapidly growing population and greatly extended area covered by the town, especially in the direction of New Hall and the district lying between the General Hospital and Steelhouse Lane. To meet this want an association was formed to raise the necessary funds for building two churches in the localities mentioned, and a statement was laid before the inhabitants, in the columns of *Aris's Gazette*, March 2, 1772, as follows :

The great Want of Public Places of Divine Worship in this Town, having induced Numbers of the Inhabitants to take into Consideration the Expediency of building one or more additional Churches, several public Meetings have been held for that Purpose ; when it has been unanimously resolved that at least two additional Churches were wanted for the Accommodation of the Inhabitants, the present not being capable of containing One Tenth Part of those professing the Doctrine of the Church of England : To take off so great a Reproach from Civil Society, and remove even the Appearance of Contempt for Holy Religion, it was determined, if possible, to obtain so pious and valuable an acquisition, and to that End Application was made to the Several Proprietors of Land contiguous to the Town, requesting Land for so good a Purpose, without Regard to Partiality of Situation, two of whom (viz.), Miss Weaman, and Charles Colemore, Esq., not only consented to give the necessary Land, but Subscribed liberally towards perfecting the Business.

Success having attended the Matter thus far, Subscriptions were set on Foot for Monies to apply to Parliament, and a Petition agreeably thereto has been presented for Leave to bring in a Bill for building two Churches, one of which is intended to be built near to Catherine-Street,* and the other near to New Hall.

The following Plan for which has been adopted :—

1st.—That separate Subscriptions be opened to raise Money for building the Churchet, with Houses for the Residence of the officiating Clergymen ; such Subscriptions to be paid by Four equal instalments, giving six Months' public Notice of the Days of Payment.

2dly.—That the Gentlemen in the Neighbourhood and every Subscriber of Twenty Pounds be appointed Trustees for the Conduct and Direction of the Business.

3dly.—That the Salary to each Officiating Clergyman be fixed by Parliament, at not more than Two Hundred Pounds, nor less than One Hundred and Fifty Pounds, per Annum, to arise from the Kneelings.

4thly.—That the rents of the Kneelings between the two extremes be fixed by the Trustees.

5thly.—That the Surplice Fees be fixed by Parliament.

6thly.—That no Diminution be made in the Fees of the Incumbents of Saint Martin's ; on the contrary, that they receive their full fees for all Offices performed at the new Intended Churches.

7thly.—That certain Districts be marked out for the Officiating Clergymen, to have the Cure of Souls, visit the Sick, and do the necessary Duties ; but that such Districts be not deemed separate Parishes, or be subject to separate Assessments, but the Buildings to be kept in Repair by the General Levy of the Town.

8thly.—That two Wardens be appointed to each of the Churches, who shall take a proportionable Part of the Town in collecting the Levy.

9thly.—That the Pews and Kneelings be disposed of to the Subscribers by Ballot, according to their respective Subscriptions, with such other Clauses and Regulations as are usual, or as Parliament may think proper to adopt.

The Persons who have hitherto prompted this Business will, in a few Days, begin to collect Subscriptions, but thought it necessary, previously thereto, to advertise the Inhabitants of their Intentions, at the same Time to disavow every Degree of Partiality in the Choice of the Spots of Land identified, and to assure the Inhabitants that they have been actuated only by Dispositions to render the Objects in View as extensively useful as might be.

* Now Whittall Street.

Separate Deeds of Subscriptions will be handed about, so that every Individual will make which Church he pleases the object, no Persuasions being intended to be used; but they hope, and have no Doubt, that the Necessity of the Case will plead for itself, and that every Individual will cheerfully contribute his Quota, influenced only by a Desire to promote so pious and necessary a Work.

The appeal for subscriptions was liberally responded to, and before the close of the month "a bill was ordered to be brought into Parliament for one or more Churches in this Town"; the Act was obtained during the same session for building two Chapels, as proposed by the association. On the 29th of July a meeting of the trustees was held, at which it was decided to call upon all those who had promised subscriptions "towards erecting, finishing, and completing one of the said Chapels, upon the land of Mary Weaman, and in the said Act distinguished by the name of the Chapel of St. Mary," to pay into the hands of Mr. John Cottrell, of Walmer Lane, the collector appointed by the trustees, twenty-five per cent. of the amount promised.

In December, an advertisement was inserted in the local newspaper requesting "any Architect or Builder capable of such an Undertaking, to send or deliver in Plans, Elevations, and Estimates, sealed up," to Mr. John Cottrell; and further added a brief description of the intended chapel as follows: "The said Chapel to be built in an Octagon or any other Form as the said Architects shall think proper, and to contain 1,000 sittings. The Breadth of the Seats to be two Feet eleven Inches, the Middle Isle eight Feet, and the outside Isles to be four Feet wide."

A series of musical performances, similar to the festivals of later years, were given in the September of 1774 in aid of the funds for the completion of the chapel. The *Gazette* of September 12th contained the following notice of these performances:

On Wednesday last the Musical Entertainments began here, when Handel's Grand Dettingen Te Deum, Jubilate, and Coronation Anthem, were performed in St. Philip's Church to a crowded and respectable Audience, and in the Evening at the New Theatre, Alexander's Feast was exhibited with great Applause.—On Thursday Morning, at St. Philip's Church, the Oratorio of Judas Maccabæus; and in the Evening, at the Theatre, a Grand Miscellaneous Concert, was performed to a very brilliant and numerous Company, with reiterated Plaudits, in which the Vocal Performers, particularly Miss Davis, and Mrs. Wrighten discovered very capital Powers; and the Instrumental Performance in general gave the highest satisfaction.—And on Friday Morning the Sacred Oratorio of Messiah was performed at the Church.—The Produce of the different Entertainments is supposed to amount to about 800*l.*, which sum is to be applied towards the Completion of St. Mary's Chapel.—The Balls on Wednesday and Thursday Evenings were uncommonly splendid, and were honoured with the Presence of many Persons of the first Rank and Distinction in this Kingdom.

The land for the building was given by Dorothy and Mary Weaman; the latter also gave largely towards the fund for its erection, and in her was vested the right of presentation; her memory being perpetuated in the name of the saint to whom the chapel was dedicated. The building was (as described in the instructions to architects) of an octagonal form, and was built of brick, "not overcharged," says Hutton, "with light or strength," having a neat, but small, stone steeple on the western side, containing one bell, and a clock. The latter, in Hutton's day, "was seldom seen to go right; but," he adds, "the wonder ceases if there are NO WORKS within." The interior is spacious, but somewhat gloomy, from the smallness of the windows; it contains nave, chancel, side aisle, and gallery, and will accommodate nearly 1700 persons.

In the case of the numerous churches of Birmingham it will be difficult to observe our usual rule as to strict chronology, as the events in their history, subsequent to their foundation, are generally too unimportant to form the subject of a second notice. We propose, therefore, to anticipate, in these cases, the general history of the town, by completing the history and description of each church in a single notice.

The Chapel of St. Mary was, in 1841, made a district church, and a population of 8500 souls assigned to it. The living (which was first held by the Rev. John Ryland) was originally worth about £200 per annum, is now about £250.

The large and pleasant churchyard was, about 1830, planted with trees, and contains several interesting memorials, including one of the pious Hester Ann Rogers.

In 1776 the preliminary steps were taken for the erection of the second church authorised by the Act of 1772. On the 18th of March the following announcement appeared in the *Gazette :*

Birmingham, March 14, 1776.—RELIGION.—At a Meeting held this Day, of the Trustees appointed by Act of Parliament, for Building two Chapels in this Town, it was resolved to begin ST. PAULS, as soon as a sufficient Sum shall be subscribed for that Purpose ; and they intend waiting on the Public to solicit their generous Contributions for so necessary an undertaking.

GEORGE HOLLOWAY.

N.B.—Subscription Books are also left with Pearson and Rollason, Printers of this Paper.

The building was not, however, commenced until the next year, the first stone being laid on the 29th of May. A brief account of the ceremony appeared in the local journal of June 2nd, as follows :—

On Thursday last, the first Stone of St. Paul's Chapel was laid by one of the Trustees, and under the stone was placed a Medal, with an Inscription in Commemoration thereof.—As it is intended to execute the Building not only with as much Expedition as possible, but with that Permanency and Taste which may do credit to the Town, it is therefore hoped that every necessary Encouragement will be given to the Undertaking.

The land for the building was given by Charles Colmore, Esq. ; and the design was furnished by Mr. Francis Goodwyn. The *Gazette* announced, in December, that the Chapel would be ready for consecration by the first of March, 1779, but, according to a MS. note, by William Hamper, in a copy of the third edition of Hutton's History of Birmingham,* it was not consecrated until 1780.

It is most substantially built of stone, but was originally exceedingly heavy in appearance, owing to the absence of a spire, having only a low, square tower, (as will be seen from our engraving on page 162) ; the tower, although forming part of the original design, remaining unbuilt for more than forty years.* When added, however, (in 1823,) it relieved, by its light and elegant appearance, the otherwise exceeeding ugliness of the building itself.

In the year 1778, as mentioned in our chapter on the early history of the General Hospital, the second Musical Festival took place. The hospital was not, as yet, opened, and,—like the Chapel in course of erection,—stood greatly in need of an addition to its funds. The Committee which had been formed for the building of the Chapel requested the Hospital Board to unite with them in "giving an Oratorio" for the joint benefit of the Chapel and the Hospital. This suggestion met with the approval of the Hospital Board, and the performances were fixed for the 2nd, 3rd, and 4th of September. The programme was as follows :

On WEDNESDAY Morning next, the 2d of September, at St. PHILIP'S CHURCH, will be performed, in the Course of the Service (which will begin at Half-past Ten precisely) The Overture of ESTHER ; HANDEL'S Grand DETTINGEN TE DEUM and JUBILATE ; an ORGAN CONCERTO by Mr. HARRIS ; Dr. BOYCE'S ANTHEM ; the OLD HUNDREDTH PSALM accompanied ; and, after a SERMON to be preached by the Rev. Mr. YOUNG, HANDEL'S Grand CORONATION ANTHEM. In the Evening, at the THEATRE, in New Street, a GRAND MISCELLANEOUS CONCERT consisting of select Vocal and Instrumental Pieces, by the principal Performers.

On THURSDAY Morning the 3rd, at St. PHILIPS, the ORATORIO of JUDAS MACCABÆUS, and between the Acts an ORGAN CONCERTO by Mr. CLARK. In the Evening at the THEATRE, the Serenata of ACIS and GALATEA ; between the parts of which will be introduced some favourite Pieces, and an ODE to MAY composed by Mr. HARRIS.

On FRIDAY Morning the 4th, at St. PHILIPS, the sacred ORATORIO of MESSIAH. In the Evening at the THEATRE, a GRAND MISCELLANEOUS CONCERT, consisting of several capital Pieces, by the principal Performers.

Principal Vocal Performers, Miss MAHON, Miss SALMON, Messrs. NORRIS, MATTHEWS, PRICE, SALMON, &c., &c.

Principal Instrumental Performers, Mr. CRANMER (First Violin at the Opera House, London), Messrs. CARVETTO, PARK, ASHLEY, STORACCI, JENKINS, MAHON, &c., &c. The other Parts of the Band, which

* In the possession of Mr. Alderman Avery.

*Mr. W. Bates, in a MS. note to his admirable Guide, says, "The following lines will be remembered by many as having been chalked on the walls about the town :—

'A large town, a proud people,
A fine church, and no steeple.'"

will be very full, by the most approved Performers, and the celebrated WOMEN CHORUS SINGERS from Lancashire.

N.B.—There will be a BALL each Evening at the HOTEL.

The gross receipts from these performances amounted nearly to £800, of which £170 fell to the share of the Hospital, and an equal sum to the building fund of St. Paul's Chapel.

In 1791, a beautiful stained glass window, designed by West, was placed over the Communion Table. It was executed by Francis Eginton, (of whom we shall have more to say in our second notice of Soho,) and is divided into three compartments, the central one representing the Conversion of Saint Paul, and those on the sides the Descent of the Holy Ghost, and the Death of Ananias. Nicholls, in his *Anecdotes of the Literature of the Eighteenth Century*, remarks of this window, "that it would be unjust to Mr. Eginton, of Birmingham, not to add that the whole is a most brilliant ornament, and admirably executed."

If they be happy who have no history, then we may assume that the period covered by the present chapter must have been one of continued happiness and prosperity in the two Unitarian Societies of the town. No event of interest has to be chronicled concerning this denomination, until we reach the year 1780,—the last of our present period,—when, "Mr. Hawkes declining the pastoral care" at the New Meeting, "the congregation judiciously turned their thoughts towards the celebrated Doctor Priestley, F.R.S., one of the first philosophers of the age, whose merit seems obvious to every eye but his own."*

Joseph Priestley,—"a man no less distinguished by social and Christian virtues, than scientific and literary attainments,"†—was the son of Jonas Priestley, a cloth-dresser, living at Fieldhead, in the parish of Birstall, near Leeds; and was born March 13, 1733.

The birthplace of the great philosopher has shared the fate of his last home in Birmingham, having been pulled down some years ago. It was "a little house of three small rooms, built of stone and slated with flags." * His mother died when he was only seven years old, and he was taken charge of by an aunt, a Mrs. Keighly, a pious woman, who, he tells us, "knew no other use of wealth, or of talents of any kind, than to do good;" and at her expense he received an education to fit him for the Christian ministry, the efforts of his teachers being greatly aided by the young scholar's intense love of learning.

His aunt encouraged him in his fondness for books, and as her house was the resort of many dissenting ministers—chiefly, it would appear, of the less orthodox type, albeit she herself was of the Calvinistic persuasion,—the young student was brought in contact with men of culture, whose conversation doubtless exercised an influence upon his own religious convictions. As soon as his health would permit, he was sent to the Dissenting Academy at Daventry, which was under the direction of Mr. (afterwards Dr.) Rushworth, successor to the eminently pious and learned Dr. Doddridge. He found here that freedom of opinion in the discussion of religious subjects which was most congenial to him, and, while at the Academy, came to "embrace what is called the heterodox side of every question." His first charge, after leaving Daventry, was at Needham Market, in Surrey; and here the congregation soon began to express their dislike, both of their young pastor's stammering mode of utterance, and of the "uncertain sound" which he "gave forth" concerning the doctrine of the Divinity of Jesus Christ; and they "fell off apace." Finding himself unpopular and almost deserted by his congregation, and consequently reduced in worldly circumstances, he issued proposals to teach classics and mathematics for half-a-guinea a

* Hutton.
† W. Bates, B.A.

* Lecture on "Joseph Priestley: his Life and Chemical Work," by Professor Thorpe. Manchester, 1874.

quarter, and to board pupils for twelve guineas a year. This project, however, was unsuccessful, and he commenced a series of twelve lectures on "The use of the Globes," but the attendance did not even pay for the necessary globes.

From Needham he went, in 1758, to Nantwich, in Cheshire, and there again combined the duties of pastor and schoolmaster. He had now renounced all the doctrines of "orthodoxy," and while at this place he published his first theological work, on "The Scripture Doctrine of Remission," in which he endeavoured to refute the doctrine of the Atonement. In 1761 he was invited to Warrington, to succeed Dr. Aikin as tutor in the languages and *belles lettres*, in the Dissenting Academy of that town; and now his literary life began in earnest. In addition to teaching Latin, Greek, Hebrew, French, and Italian, he delivered courses of lectures on Oratory and Criticism, on Elocution, on Logic, on History and General Policy, and many other subjects. He became acquainted with Benjamin Franklin, too, about this time, and formed a friendship which influenced all his future career, and gave that stimulus which was necessary to induce him to enter in real earnest on the study of natural philosophy. At Franklin's suggestion he undertook to write his "History and Present State of Electric Science," his friend having also furnished him with books for the purpose. In 1765 the University of Edinburgh conferred upon him the honorary title of LL.D. While at Warrington he married the daughter of a wealthy ironmaster of Wales, with whom he lived happily; but as the income from the chair of languages and *belles-lettres* was insufficient for the maintenance of a family, he accepted an invitation to become pastor of the dissenting congregation worshipping at Mill-hill Chapel, Leeds, and removed thither in 1767. He had now sufficient leisure to enable him to devote greater attention to experimental philosophy, and here he "commenced that brilliant series of discoveries by which other hands and other brains than his accomplished the destruction of one of the biggest stumbling blocks to human knowledge of which history has any record."*

In 1773 Lord Shelburne, desiring a librarian and literary companion, applied to Dr. Price for assistance in obtaining a suitable person for the post, and the latter recommended Dr. Priestley, who was at once appointed at a salary of £250 a year and a separate house. He travelled with Lord Shelburne on the continent, and made the acquaintance of the principal men of science in the French capital; and when in England enjoyed sufficient leisure to enable him to continue his scientific researches. He remained with Lord Shelburne seven years, and in 1780, for reasons into which it is unnecessary that we should inquire, he left his lordship's service; and immediately afterwards received the invitation to which we have already referred, to become the pastor of the New Meeting, in Birmingham. Catherine Hutton, the daughter of our first historian, writing to a friend, December 25th, in this year, says: "The celebrated Dr. Priestley has taken up his residence among us for the sake of facilitating his philosophical experiments, and Mr. Hawkes, one of the preachers at the New Meeting, having resigned his place, it has been offered to the Dr., and it is generally believed he will accept it. If he do, you may expect to hear of my becoming a convert to his religion, for I am weary of Calvinistic monotony and nonsense."†

As our present period does not extend beyond the date of Dr. Priestley's arrival in the town, we must leave for a future chapter any reference to his life and labours in Birmingham, and the events which followed his ministry at the New Meeting.

The changes at the New Meeting were not the only events in the history of the Birmingham Nonconformists during the year 1780. In that year, the Baptists, finding their meeting-house in

* Professor Thorpe.

† She had hitherto attended (with her father and mother) the Independent Meeting House in Carr's Lane.

Cannon Street too small to hold the number of worshippers thereat, were "induced to enlarge the place of worship, at the expence of about 800*l.*, in which is observable some beauty, but more conveniency." *

The meeting-house of "the people called, in scorn, Quakers,"—otherwise the Society of Friends, —would appear to have been improved, and perhaps enlarged, during the latter part of the eighteenth century, and is described by Hutton, in 1781, as "a large and convenient place, and notwithstanding the plainness of the profession, rather elegant." It was doubtless at the expense of one or more of the wealthier members of this estimable society that Baskerville printed the handsome quarto edition of Barclay's Apology, in 1765.

ST. JAMES'S CHAPEL, ASHTED.

Of the Methodists we have but little to say in the present chapter. In 1755 the venerable founder of the society had called at Birmingham on his way from Bristol to the North of England, and described it as "a barren, dry, uncomfortable place. Most of the seed," he writes, "which has been sown for so many years, the 'wild boars' have rooted up; the fierce, unclean, brutish, blasphemous antinomians have utterly destroyed it. And the mystic foxes have taken true pains to spoil what remained, with their new gospel." * In 1760 he found here a society of little more than fifty persons; and in the next year, when he

* Hutton

* Tyerman: Life and Times of John Wesley, ii., 195.

preached in the town, the room was far too small for the congregation. In 1764 he preached again in the town, in the old Moor-Street theatre, which the Methodists had obtained, as we have previously stated. After service, the mob gathered, and threw dirt and stones at people going out.

But, as the time of which we now write passed on, the humble sect began to enjoy rest from persecution, and soon became a flourishing society. Writing in 1768, Wesley remarks that the tumults of so many years continuance, were "now wholly suppressed by a resolute magistrate." Here he met "with a venerable monument of antiquity, George Bridgins, in the one hundred and seventh year of his age, still able to walk to preaching, and retaining his senses and understanding tolerably well."

The only events to be recorded, in the period under notice, in the history of the Carr's Lane Meeting, have reference to its financial prosperity. In 1771 the interest of £800 was bequeathed to the society by the will of John England; and in 1779 Joseph Scott assigned "certain messuages and lands in and near Walmer Lane, in Birmingham," producing a rental of £40 18s., "part of the said premises to be appropriated for the interment of Protestant dissenters; part of the profits to be applied to the use of a religious society in Carr's Lane, at the discretion of the trust, and the remainder for the institution of a school to teach the mother tongue."

THE GENERAL HOSPITAL: SHOWING THE TWO WINGS ADDED IN 1790.

Altogether, as regards the less important denominations of Birmingham, this period cannot be said to have been one of prosperity. The Roman Catholics were yet without a place of worship in the town, and had to journey two miles to the nearest chapel, that of Edgbaston. The Jews had a small synagogue in the Froggary, in which they still preserved "the faint semblance of the ancient worship;" but "their whole apparatus" seemed to Hutton "no more than the drooping ensigns of poverty." Several of the newer sects —the disciples of Swedenborg, and the Countess of Huntingdon's Connection, for instance—were not yet represented in the town at all. But in the next period we shall see the various communities of dissenters in great prosperity, growing and increasing on every hand. We shall find newer societies flourishing side by side with those previously established in the town; but it will be our unpleasant duty to close that record of prosperity by a narrative of events in which those who ventured to differ in their religious opinions and form of church government from the Church of the State, were called upon to suffer persecution and peril, as well as great temporal losses, at the hands of the ignorant and the lawless. Therefore, although we must close this chapter without recording great prosperity among the churches of nonconformity, it is satisfactory to be able also to leave it for the present free from the stain which darkens the next period in the history of religion in Birmingham.

CHAPTER XXVIII.

THE BIRMINGHAM TRIENNIAL MUSICAL FESTIVALS:

First Period, from 1768 to 1799.

The early Festivals—Service on behalf of the Hospital, 1781—Commencement of the Triennial Festivals—"Goliah"—Handel Celebrations—Anonymous Donation of £500 to the Hospital—Poem by Freeth thereon—the Festival of 1787—Mr. Yates and the Festival Committee—Mrs. Billington—Repetition of the "Messiah"—The Festival of 1790—Madame Mara—Enlargement of the Hospital—A disastrous year—Postponement of the Festival—The Festival of 1796—Poems on Mrs. Second, by Collins—Buckles *versus* Shoe-strings —The Festival of 1799—Receipts and profits of each meeting.

The history of the Birmingham Musical Festivals is divided by Mr. Bunce into three periods,—the performances given during the last century; those which took place in the period between the commencement of the present century and the opening of the Town Hall in 1834; and those which have been given since that event. We cannot do better, therefore, than adopt the same division; and shall anticipate, by a few years, the general history of the town, in our first chapter on "those great Musical Celebrations which have done so much to make the name of Birmingham famous throughout Europe, as the cultivator and promoter of the musical art in its highest developments."*

The first of these celebrations took place in 1768, and has been already noticed in these pages;* it will be unnecessary, therefore, further to refer to it in the present chapter. Ten years afterwards,—in September 1778,—it was resolved to give another series of musical performances, for the joint benefit of the Hospital and St. Paul's Chapel, and this also has already been recorded in our notice of the chapel.†

The sum of £140 is frequently set down in lists of the Musical Festivals, as the net produce of a musical celebration in the year 1781; but strictly speaking, no musical performance took place in that year. On Monday, the 23rd of July, however, a sermon was preached at St. Philip's, on behalf of the Hospital, by the Bishop of Chester, after which a collection was made, amounting to £128 6s. 1d.; and this sum (with,

* J. T. Bunce: History of the Musical Festivals, p. 63.

* Chap. xxi., p. 128. † Chap. xxvii., p. 171.

perhaps, several donations immediately afterwards, amounting in all to about £140) has usually been set down in the lists as the produce of a Festival, probably in order to connect the *triennial* festivals with that of 1778.

But the triennial series did not properly commence until 1784. In the March of that year, the Hospital Board resolved "That some Musical Performances be thought of, for the benefit of the Charity, to take place after the meeting of the Three Choirs in the Autumn." During that year there were musical gatherings at Salisbury and Liverpool, as well as at Gloucester, and there was consequently some difficulty in selecting a suitable time for the Birmingham meeting; but it was ultimately decided to hold it on the 22nd, 23rd and 24th of September. The steward of that year, Viscount Dudley and Ward, having offered to place at the disposal of the committee a new oratorio entitled "Goliah," by Atterbury, it was decided that it should take the place of the usual Thursday evening concert; and the composer generously devoted to the Hospital the profits arising from the sale of the work.

The famous Handel commemoration at Westminster Abbey, which had been commanded by the King, in the same year—the supposed centenary of Handel's birth,—suggested to the Birmingham committee the idea of making their Festival of 1784 a commemoration of the great master of harmony. The first day's performance, at St. Philip's, comprised the Occasional Overture, Purcell's Te Deum and Jubilate, Handel's Anthem, "O come let us sing," and his Coronation Anthem. On Wednesday evening, at the Theatre, New Street, the concert included "the favourite pieces performed at the Pantheon, by command of his Majesty, in commemoration of Mr. Handel." On Thursday morning, at St. Philip's, the service consisted entirely of a selection from Handel's works, being the same as that performed at the Westminster Abbey celebration on the 3rd of June; and included the Dettingen Te Deum, the Overtures to "Esther" and "Tamerlane," the Dead March in "Saul," several anthems, and the Double Chorus from "Israel in Egypt"—"The Lord shall reign." Thursday evening, as we have already said, was devoted to Mr. Atterbury's "Goliah," and on Friday morning the Handel commemoration was brought to a close with the performance of his divine masterpiece, "The Messiah." In the evening the Festival itself was brought to a conclusion with a miscellaneous concert at the theatre, "consisting of select pieces by the most capital performers." The principal vocalists at this Festival were the Misses Abrams and Master Bartleman; and the chief instrumentalists were Messrs. Wilson, Ashley, Gariboldi, and Clarke. The band was supported by the large double drums used in the celebration at Westminster Abbey; and both band and chorus are described as having been very full. Among the many distinguished visitors who honoured the Festival with their presence on this occasion, were Lord and Lady Plymouth, Lord and Lady Ferrers, Lady Windsor, Sir Robert and Lady Lawley, and Sir Edward Littleton. The gross amount produced by these performances was £1,325, and the profits £703.

Shortly after the Festival in this year, a "lady unknown" gave £500 to the funds of the Hospital; upon which our local poet Freeth wrote the following lines:—

"November 15th, 1784.

"On a Benefaction of Five Hundred Pounds being presented to the General Hospital, by a Lady unknown.

"Of Russell, though much has been said,
And the maidens the flowers have strew'd,
To say, "the curmudgeon is dead,"
The epitaph—who can think rude?
With benevolence known to abound,
The virtue must be that excels;
Where no ostentation is found,
The essence of charity dwells.——F."

From this time, with but two exceptions, the Musical Festivals were held triennially, and rapidly grew in importance. Greater interest was aroused among the clergy of the town, as well as among the nobility of the surrounding neighbourhood. The Rev. Charles Curtis, rector of St. Martin's, the Rev. T. Young, of St. Paul's, and the Rev. J. Darwall, of St. John's, Deritend, were on the committee. At the next celebration, in 1787, the Earl of Aylesford was elected President, and the Earl of Plymouth, Viscount Dudley and Ward, and Sir George Shuckburgh, Bart., acted as stewards. A quarrel, however, between the committee and Mr. Yates, the manager of the Theatre, seemed likely to mar the prospects of the Festival. The latter, considering the remuneration offered him for the use of the theatre to be inadequate, announced a performance for the evening before the commencement of the Festival, notwithstanding that the theatre was indispensably required by the committee for a rehearsal on that evening. In vain the committee remonstrated,—the manager was determined, and probably would not have yielded, had they not threatened to take legal proceedings to close the theatre for the remainder of the season. This, however, brought him to his senses, and he consented to forego the promised performance. But soon afterwards another cause of offence would appear to have arisen, and again the manager announced his intention to play on the day required for rehearsal, Tuesday, August 21st. The committee met on Wednesday, the 16th, (less than one week from the commencement of the Festival,) and appointed a deputation of five persons to wait upon Mr. Yates, and endeavour to persuade him "to give up the idea of playing." This he once more agreed to do, but again his obstinate spirit obtained the mastery, and the deputation had scarcely rejoined their committee when a messenger arrived from Mr. Yates demanding compensation, and threatening that if not liberally dealt with he would play, not only on Tuesday, but on Friday also. Another meeting of the committee was convened for the next morning, and a letter sent to the vacillating manager demanding a final answer. According to the minutes of the committee the only reply vouchsafed by Mr. Yates was "a verbal *messuage*" to the effect that he "would do as he pleased." Upon this, the committee returned word that they would not use his theatre at all, and that they were determined to prevent his theatrical performances immediately. Accordingly they engaged Mr. Swann's amphitheatre, in Livery Street, for the evening concerts; and notice was given to Mr. Yates's actors that they would be prosecuted if they "should attempt to speak on the stage hereafter under Mr. Yates's management;" several persons being hired to attend at the theatre in order to have proofs against such as ventured on playing. The manager now saw that to continue opposition to the wishes of the committee would be to court ruin, and on Sunday, the 19th, he sent a humble apology, offering the use of the theatre for the whole week. This new aspect of affairs rendered it necessary that a meeting of the committee should be held at once, Sunday though it was, and, strange to say, all the clerical members were present; and it was resolved to accept Mr. Yates's offer, but, in order to punish him for his obstinacy, it was also determined that not one farthing should be paid to him for the use of either the theatre or the orchestra. And thus the dispute ended; and now matters looked more promising as to the success of the Festival, which was opened on Wednesday, August 22nd, with a Morning Service at St. Philip's, in the course of which a selection from the works of Handel, Purcell, and Boyce, was given. Miscellaneous Concerts at the Theatre occupied each evening; on Thursday morning the majestic harmonies of "Israel in Egypt" (called by Dr. Macfarren "Handel's mighty masterpiece") were for the first time heard in Birmingham. On Friday Morning the ever-glorious "Messiah" was so enthusiastically received, (partly owing to the "extraordinary ability and the singular gracefulness of style" of the celebrated Mrs. Billington, who, according to a contemporary record, "sang with the most powerful sensibility, and failed not to excite usual admiration,") that a second performance of that oratorio was demanded, and was given, on the Saturday, to an overflowing audience.

The total receipts of the Festival amounted to nearly £2000, the profit accruing to the Hospital being £964.

At the Festival of 1790, which was held August 25th, 26th, and 27th, the only oratorio performed was the "Messiah," the remainder of the music, both at the church and the theatre, being selected from the English and Italian composers, but chiefly from Handel. This year was signalized by the appearance of the celebrated Madame Mara,—her appearance here being owing, says the historian of the Festivals, to Lord Dudley, (by whom she was much esteemed, and whose house at Himley she was visiting) who probably paid the expense of her engagement, as the committee return his lordship a vote of thanks "for his generous offer of the services of Madame Mara and her husband."

The other lady vocalists were Miss Mahon and the Misses Abrams; and among the instrumental performers was Mr. Charles Knyvett, whose brother,—the better known William Knyvett—was in later years the Conductor of the Festivals. The proceeds amounted to £1,965 18s., and the profits £958 14s. 8d.

During this year, the Hospital was enlarged by the addition of two wings: which added considerably to its completeness and convenience, as well as to its external appearance, as represented in our engraving on page 175."

In 1793 the triennial sequence of the Festivals had once more to be broken. The state of trade, and the oppressive taxation, which formed the burden of many of Poet Freeth's verses during these years, (as quoted in a previous chapter,) were, perhaps, worse in 1793 than in any year of that decade, until 1800; and these, added to a local calamity, (the burning of the theatre, August 7, 1792,) which deprived the committee of the only suitable concert-room, together with the fact that "the public mind was directed rather towards the stern alarms of war, than attuned to the cultivation of the harmonic art," rendered it highly undesirable, as well as a most hazardous speculation, to attempt to hold the usual triennial Festival in that year.

It was at first proposed to postpone the Festival for one year only, but it was ultimately decided to allow the three years to pass without the usual musical celebration, and to resume the series in 1796. The next meeting, therefore, was held in the August of that year, the Earl of Aylesford acting as Steward. The "Messiah" was again the only oratorio performed, and the evening concerts are described as comprising "the most favourite airs, duets, trios, overtures, and concertos, by the first masters." The principal vocalists were, Madame Mara, Mrs. Second, the Misses Fletcher, and Messrs. Nield, Kelly, and Bartleman. Among the instrumental performances were Robert, John, and Charles Lindley, and F. Cramer.

The singing of Mrs. Second on this occasion so favourably impressed a local poet, Collins,—the well-known author of "To-Morrow," of whom we shall have more to say in a future chapter,—that he wrote the following impromptu verses:

"On hearing the young & beautiful Mrs. SECOND sing at the Musical Festival, in Birmingham, for the Benefit of the General Hospital there.

"When the great Cognoscenti, full ripe from the Schools,
Like Aristarch, flush'd with dogmatical rules;
Fame's weathercock veering, found ways how to fix it,
And manag'd the vane with a meer *Ipse Dixit;*
They of Mara pronounc'd, and dispute it who durst,
That, of all vocal Prodigies, SHE was the FIRST!
But, as flowers in Autumn will fade and decay,
And leaves shrink and dry till they drop from the spray;
So the Vet'ran in fame, past her heyday and prime,
Must like time-beating Stephen,* be beaten by Time.
And though not convinc'd while with thousands imburs'd,
That 'The First may be Last, and the Last may be First;'
Yet, if Fate seconds Fortune, that doughty old dame,
The next Idol to rear on the topstone of Fame;
Who with thrilling sensations enraptures the throng,

* An allusion to the well-known and oft-quoted epitaph on a musician,
"Stephen and Time are now both even,
Stephen *beat time*, and Time beat Stephen."

While the Loves and the Graces add charms to her song :
Though Mara, 'mong warblers, the First is now reckon'd,
The Time will yet come when the FIRST will be SECOND ! "

When the poet again heard Mrs. Second, her name,—which must have subjected her to persecution from every wretched punster in the land,—once more inspired him to sing her praises in punning verses :

" To Mrs. Second ;
On hearing her sing a second time.
" Blest with those Powr's the FIRST Applause to claim,
How strangely paradoxical thy Name !
FIRST of the vocal Train, by all confess'd,
Yet SECOND call'd, and so by all address'd !
A strange Misnomer, which provokes a Pun,
Since thou, sweet Warbler, Second art to none !
For who points out, or would correct thy Faults,
But must correct himself, on Second Thoughts ?
And yet, could I, with Mimic Force command
A Voice, to echo thine at Second hand,
With such a Gift of Imitation blest,
Of Songsters I should prove the Second best !
But I to Fame shall never take that Flight
I see, without the Gift of Second Sight.
Yet, since thy FIRST-RATE Melody imparts
A FIRST-RATE Charm, to captivate our Hearts,
As all, from First to Last, throughout the Throng,
Second with Plaudits thy enchanting Song ;
And with *One Voice* assert, as they opine,
'A Syren's *Voice* would *Second* be to Thine,'
Second, in Name alone, shall SECOND be,
While, in thy Praise, the World will Second ME ! "

At this Festival, a most ingenious ruse was adopted by the numerous pickpockets who, according to the local newspapers, appear to have come down from London specially for the occasion. Taking advantage of the local feeling against the reaction in favour of shoe-strings *versus* buckles, at that period, the thieves hustled the locally unpopular wearers of shoe-strings, denouncing them as unpatriotic despisers of fine old English customs, and in the tumult which ensued, plied their calling vigourously, and managed to reap a good harvest. The proceeds of the Festival * amounted to £2,043 18s., and the profits £897.

* The prices of admission ranged from half-a-crown to half-a-guinea in the morning, and from three to six shillings in the evening ; and the tickets to the balls, (of which there were three) were charged five shillings and sixpence.

The last Festival of the eighteenth century was held in September, 1799. " Great efforts had been made," says Mr. Bunce, " to enlist the support of the principal residents in the county, as well as those in the town. The Earl of Warwick undertook the post of Director, and the list of patrons was enlarged by the addition of the names of Lords Hertford, Dartmouth, Aylesford, Dudley, Willoughby de Broke, Craven, Middleton, Brooke, and others. The result was that the attendance of country gentlemen was materially increased. By strengthening the band and chorus, as well as by engaging a large number of principal performers, the Committee laid the foundation of the eminence the Festivals have since attained, and thus paved the way for that new and greater epoch which commenced with the advent of the present century."* The "Messiah" was again the chief attraction, and the rest of the programme comprised selections from Handel, Corelli, Geminiani, and other composers. Madame Mara occupied, for the third time, the position of principal vocalist, and was supported by Miss Poole, Messrs. Harrison, William Knyvett, and Bartleman. Again the three famous Lindleys were among the instrumentalists, together with Holmes, Cantelo, Erksine, the Leanders, Cramer, (leader of the band,) Harris, (organist,) and others. As this was the most influential musical gathering held in Birmingham, during the last century, so it appears also to have been the greatest financial success, the receipts being £2,550, and the profits £1,470.

It will be interesting to show at a glance, the growth of this noble institution during the last century, by a tabulated statement of the receipts and profits of each meeting :—

YEAR.	GROSS RECEIPTS.			PROFITS.		
	£	s.	d.	£	s.	d.
1768.	800	0	0	299	7	4
1778.	800	0	0	170	0	0†

* History of the Festivals, pp. 75-6.

† This amount represents only half the profits of the Festival, as they were equally divided between the Hospital and the St. Paul's Chapel Building Fund.

YEAR.	GROSS RECEIPTS.	PROFITS.
1781.	No Festival. Service at St. Philip's, July 23	128 6 1
1784.	1325 0 0	703 0 0
1787.	1980 0 0	964 0 0
1790.	1965 18 0	958 14 8
1793.	No Festival.	
1796.	2043 18 0	897 0 0
1799.	2550 0 0	1470 0 0
Total to 1799	£11,464 16 0	£5,590 8 1

With these facts and figures we close the *first period* of the history of Birmingham Festivals.

CHAPTER XXIX.

THE FIRST HISTORY OF BIRMINGHAM.

The first announcement—The engravings—The price to be raised to non-subscribers—The author's profits—Opinions on the work—Further delays—The author's preface—Description of the volume—The second edition—Growth of the town—Hutton's Juvenile correspondence.

We have now to notice briefly an event which ought to interest every inhabitant of Birmingham—viz.: the publication of the first history of the town—"a history which notwithstanding its shortcomings, its errors of omission and commission, is still a book to which we all turn with delight, and ought to speak of with respect."*

It was first announced as "by a Gentleman, an Inhabitant," in the preliminary advertisement in the *Gazette* of March 5th, 1781, which ran as follows:—

Proposals for publishing by Subscription, In One Volume, Octavo, Price 7s. 6d., The History of Birmingham, From the earliest Accounts down to the present time. Which will be enriched with 24 Copper-Plates, representing the Public Buildings, a view and Plan of the Town, &c., &c., by a Gentleman, an Inhabitant.

The next week's issue of the paper contained the same announcement, but with the addition of the name of William Hutton as the author. On the 29th of October, another advertisement appeared, announcing that in consequence of the delay attending the production of the plates, the principal of which "are engraving by that eminent Artist Mr. Walker of London," the work cannot be finished until the beginning of December; adding, also, that "the great expense incurred by the number of Copper Plates given in the work, will unavoidably oblige the Author to advance the price to non-subscribers." The price to subscribers remained the same; viz.: seven shillings and sixpence; and the volume was to contain "seventeen Copper Plates, some of which will be well worth 2s. 6d. each."

This was Hutton's first literary work, and he had begun to collect materials for it as early as 1775, but in that year, "a circumstance of a private nature occurring," led him to abandon his project. In 1780, however, he once more turned his attention to the history of the town he loved so well; and the first nine months of the year were employed in this labour of love. "Fearing my ability," he says, "I wrote with dread. Rollason, the Printer, was pleased with it, and showed it to Dr. Withering, who pronounced it 'the best topographical history he had ever seen.' I had for it seventy-five copies, the profit upon which amounted to about forty pounds. To venture into the world as an author, without having had a previous education, was a daring attempt. It was setting my knowledge against that of the Public: the balance was very uneven. This was afterwards considered the best book I ever wrote. I considered it in a less favourable light."

Under date 1781 in his autobiography, he writes:

"I supped January 31st, with a large company

* J. A. Langford.

at the Bull and Gate. Rollason, my printer, was there ; spoke highly of the History, and made no doubt but those printed upon large paper would, in twenty years, sell for a guinea."

Although announced for publication in December, and bearing the date of 1781 on its title page, it did not actually appear, according to Hutton's own statement in his autobiography, until March 22, 1782. It was entitled, "An History of Birmingham, to the End of the Year 1780. By W. Hutton. Birmingham: Printed by and for Pearson and Rollason ; and sold by R. Baldwin, Paternoster Row; B. White, Fleet Street; J. Robson, New Bond Street ; S. Hayes, Oxford Street ; and J. and J. Fletcher, Oxford. MDCCLXXXI."

The Preface is so characteristic of the author, in its quaint, witty apology for his unprofessional style, and its odd mixture of modesty and egotism, that notwithstanding its length, we cannot forbear quoting it entire :—

A PREFACE rather induces a man to speak of himself, which is deemed the worst subject upon which he can speak. In a history we become acquainted with things, but in a preface with the author, and, for a man to treat of himself, may be the most difficult task of the two ; for in history, facts are produced ready to the hand of the historian, which give birth to thought, and it is easy to clothe that thought in words. But in a preface, an author is obliged to forge from the brain, where he is sometimes known to forge without fire. In one, he only reduces a substance into form ; but in the other, he must create that substance.

As I am not an author by profession, it is no wonder if I am unacquainted with the modes of authorship ; but I apprehend the usual method of conducting a pen is to polish up a sounding title-page, dignified with scraps of Latin, and then to hammer up a work to fit it, as nearly as genius, or want of genius, will allow.

We next turn over a new leaf, and open upon a pompous Dedication, which answers many laudable purposes ; it becomes a pair of stilts, which advances an author something higher.

As a horse-shoe, nailed upon the threshold of a cottage, prevents the influence of the witch, so a first-rate name, at the head of a Dedication is a total bar against the critic ; but his great name, like a great officer, sometimes unfortunately stands at the head of wretched troops.

When an author is too heavy to swim of himself, it serves as a pair of bladders, to prevent his sinking.

It is farther productive of a solid advantage, that of a present from the patron, more valuable than that from the bookseller, which prevents his sinking under the pressure of famine.

But, being wholly unknown to the great names of literary consequence, I shall not attempt a Dedication, therefore must lose the benefit of the stilt, the bladder, and the horse-shoe.

Were I to enter upon a dedication, I should certainly address myself, "To the Inhabitants of Birmingham ;"

Dear little Jack
I have sent thee a little letter
seal'd with a whole wafer and
I design to come and see thee
soon and bring thee some Shre
-wsbury cakes I will bring a
little horse and thou shalt ride
with me.

Facsimile of a letter written by William Hutton, at the age of seven, to his brother.

for to them I not only owe much, but all, and I think among that congregated mass, there is not one person to whom I wish ill. I have the pleasure of calling many of those inhabitants friends, and some of them share my warm affections equally with myself. Birmingham, like a compassionate nurse, not only draws our persons, but our esteem, from the place of our nativity, and fixes it upon herself: I might add, "I was hungry, and she fed me; thirsty, and she gave me drink; a stranger, and she took me in." I approached her with reluctance, because I did not know her; I shall leave her with reluctance, because I do.

Whether it is perfectly consistent in an author, to solicit the indulgence of the public, though it may stand first in his wishes, admits a doubt; for, if his productions will not bear the light, it may be said, why does he publish? but, if they will, there is no need to ask a favour; the world receives one from him. Will not a piece everlastingly be tried by its merit? Shall we esteem it the higher because it was written at the age of thirteen? because it was the effort of a week? delivered extempore? hatched while the author stood upon one leg? or cobbled while he cobbled a shoe? or will it be a recommendation, that it issues forth in gilt binding? The judicious world will not be deceived by the tinselled purse, but will examine whether the contents are sterling.

Will it augment the value of this history, or cover its blunders, to say, that I have never seen Oxford? That the thick fogs of penury prevented the sun of science from beaming upon the mind? That necessity obliged me to lay down the battledore, before I was master of the letters? And that, instead of handling systems of knowledge, my hands at the early period of seven, became callous with labour.

OLD BUILDING CALLED "HOCKLEY ABBEY."

But, though a whole group of pretences will have no effect with the impartial eye, yet one reason pleads strongly in my favour—no such thing ever appeared as A History of Birmingham. It is remarkable, that one of the most singular places in the universe is without an historian: that she never manufactured an history of herself, who has manufactured almost every thing else. If such a production had ever seen the light, mine most certainly would never have been written. A temporary bridge, therefore, may satisfy the impatient traveller, till a more skilful architect shall accommodate him with a complete production of elegance, of use, and of duration.

Although works of genius ought to come out of the mint doubly refined, yet history admits of a much greater latitude to the author. The best upon the subject, though defective, may meet with regard.

It has long been a complaint, that local history is much wanted. This will appear obvious, if we examine the places we know, with the histories that treat of them. Many an author has become a cripple, by historically travelling through all England, who might have made a tolerable figure had he staid at home. The subject is too copious for one performance, or even the life of one man. The design of history is knowledge, but, if simply to tell a tale be all the duty of an historian, he has no irksome task before him, for there is nothing more easy than to relate a fact, but, perhaps, nothing more difficult than to relate it well.

Having, many years ago entertained an idea of this undertaking, I made some trifling preparations, but, in 1775, a circumstance of a private nature occurring, which engaged my attention for several years, I relinquished the design, destroyed the materials, and meant to give up the thought for ever, but the intention revived in 1780, and the work followed.

I may be accused of quitting the regular trammels of history, and wandering in the fields of dissertation; but, although our habitation justly stands chief in our esteem, in return for rest, content, and protection, does it follow that we should never stray from it? If I happen to veer a moment from the polar point of Birmingham, I shall certainly vibrate again to the centre. Every author has a manner peculiar to himself, nor can he well forsake it. I should be exceedingly hurt to omit a necessary part of intelligence, but more so to offend a reader.

If grandeur should censure me for recording the men of mean life, let me ask, which is preferable,—he who thunders at the anvil, or in the senate?

The man who earnestly wishes the significant letters Esq. spliced to the end of his name, will despise the question; but the philosopher will answer, "They are equal."

Lucrative views have no part in this production; I cannot solicit a kind people to grant what they have already granted; but if another finds that pleasure in reading, which I have done in writing, I am paid.

As no history is extant, to inform me of this famous nursery of the arts, perfection in mine must not be expected. Though I have endeavoured to pursue the road to truth; yet, having no light to guide, or hand to direct me, it is no wonder if I mistake it; but we do not condemn so much as pity, the man for losing his way, who first travels an unbeaten road.

Birmingham, for want of the recording hand, may be said to live but one generation; the transactions of the last age die in this; memory is the sole historian, which, being defective, I embalm the present generation, for the inspection of the future.

It is unnecessary to attempt a general character, for if the attentive reader is himself of Birmingham, he is equally apprized of that character; and, if a stranger, he will find a variety of touches scattered through the piece, which, taken in a collective view, form a picture of that generous people, who merit his esteem, and possess mine.

The volume consisted of two hundred and ninety-two pages (xii., 280), and is a very creditable example of local book-work. The illustrations (of which we have availed ourselves in illustrating the appearance of old Birmingham in this work), were engraved by R. Hancock, a very celebrated engraver at that period, from drawings by Pickering. No plates bearing the name of Walker (the engraver named in the advertisement) appear in the volume. The list of subscribers contains the names of Dr. John Ash, Matthew Boulton, Francis Eginton, Dr. Priestley, Dr. Withering, and many other well known local worthies; also Mark Noble, F.S.A., the biographer of Oliver Cromwell, the celebrated Dr. Disney, F.S.A., Richard Gough, the antiquary, and others.

The second edition of Hutton's History was issued, in numbers, in the beginning of 1783. It was advertised in the *Gazette*, January 27th; and in that advertisement Hutton gives a very graphic account of the rapid growth of the town. "If," he says, "an acquaintance with our Country is necessary, an acquaintance with a principal Part is peculiarly so. BIRMINGHAM in many Points of View may be considered in that Light; her Name is echoed through the Commercial World; there is not a Village without her Manufactures: This Seat of Invention furnishes Ornament and Use. Her astonishing Increase is beyond Example. The Traveller who visits her once in six Months, supposes himself well acquainted with her; but he may chance to find a Street of Houses in the Autumn, where he saw his horse at Grass in the Spring. A pitiful Market Town, in an Inland County, by pure Industry, in a few Years, surpasses most of our Cities. Thus singularly circumstanced, she naturally calls for a History, and invites a Reader."

In this edition appeared several additions, among others the series of notices of surrounding places of interest, the notes for which were gathered during the summer of 1782; in walking excursions to places of antiquity within fifteen miles of his home.

Seven editions of the work have appeared, in all, the latest having been issued in weekly numbers only twelve months ago.

It may perhaps interest our readers to possess a facsimile of a quaint little letter, written by the historian to his brother John,—or, as he calls him, on the superscription, "Jacky"—at the age of seven years. The original of this exceedingly interesting and amusing document is in the possession of W. Franks-Beale, Esq., of Chester Road, Erdington; to whose kindness we are indebted for permission to make the facsimile which appears on page 182.

We cannot close this brief notice of the first history of our town without expressing surprise that, in honouring so many of her worthy citizens in enduring brass and marble and on canvas, Birmingham has utterly forgotten or ignored her first historian, who was also one of the most indefatigable of her citizens, prominent in every movement for the welfare of the town of his adoption; eager to serve her in every public capacity: a judge in her court of conscience, a member of the commission for carrying out the provisions of the Improvement Act, a guardian of the poor,—and last, but not least, one of those who bravely suffered in the cause of civil and religious liberty in the local reign of terror in 1791;—ought not *this* man to have a statue or other memorial in our midst?

CHAPTER XXX.

PUBLIC LIFE AND EVENTS, 1775—1790.

John Howard's Visit to the Birmingham Prison—Proposal to build a new Prison on the site of Christ Church—The old Dungeon in Bordesley—Counterfeit half-pence—Volunteers for the American War—Hanson's Plan of Birmingham—Pitmore and Hammond—The "Canal Frenzy" again—Mails to Birmingham—Commemoration of the American Revolution—Thanksgiving for the King's recovery.

We now take up once more the chronicle of local events.

In the eighth decade of the eighteenth century a country gentleman who had happened to be appointed High Sheriff of the County of Bedford, was led to inquire into the treatment of prisoners, and the condition of the prisons, in his county. One of these latter was the famous "Den" in which was dreamed that glorious "Dream" of the tinker of Elstow; a damp, noisome place, whose foundations were in the slimy bed of the river Ouse. The wretched state of affairs revealed to the High Sheriff during his visitation throughout the county stirred his generous spirit to its very depths, and he resolved to undertake a crusade against these filthy, disgusting dens, and against the cruel treatment to which the prisoners were too often subjected. In order to fit himself for the work he resolved to visit the gaols throughout the whole of England; and soon the name of John Howard, the prison philanthropist, was known and blessed by suffering prisoners all over the country.

The condition in which he found the Birmingham prison will be best told in his own words:

"The gaol for this large, populous town, is called the Dungeon. The court is only about 25 feet square. Keeper's House in front; and under it two cells down seven steps: the straw is on bedsteads. On one side of the court two night-rooms for women, 8 feet by 5 feet 9 inches; and some rooms over them; on the other side is the gaoler's stable, and one small day-room for men and women; no window: above is a free ward for court of conscience debtors, who are cleared in forty days: this is a sizeable room, but has only one window 18 inches square. Over it is another room, or two.

"In this small court, besides the litter from the stable, there was a stagnant puddle near the sink, for the gaoler's ducks. (Gaoler's poultry is a very common nuisance; but in so scanty a court it is intolerable.) The whole prison is very offensive. At some particular times here are great numbers confined. Once in the winter of 1775 there were above 150, who by the care of the magistrates had a supply of proper food, broth, &c.

"License for beer: fees 2s. No table. Neither clauses against spirituous liquors, nor Act for preserving the health of prisoners, are hung up.

"1774, Nov. 10.	Debtors 7.		Offenders 2.	
1776, Sep. 11.	,,	7.	,,	5.
1779, Aug. 23.	,,	0.	,,	8."*

The humane inquirer again visited the gaol in 1788, and gives the following additional particulars:

"The court is *now* paved with broad stones, but dirty with fowls. There is only one day room for both sexes, over the door of which there is *impudently* painted, *Universal Academy.*†

"Neither the Act for preserving the health of prisoners, nor clauses against spirituous liquors, hung up. The gaoler has no salary, but has still a license for beer.

"1788, Feb. 14.—Prisoners, 13."

Of the Debtors' Prison he writes:

"No alteration. Clauses against spirituous liquors not hung up. Court of conscience debtors for sums under 20s. are *now* discharged in 20 days. As liquors are introduced by visitors, and through the windows, which are towards the street, most of these prisoners think their confinement little or no punishment.

"1788, Feb. 13.—Prisoners, 7."*

Writing of this vile dungeon in 1780, Hutton makes the following suggestion, which we are happy to say was not carried into practice, albeit the site is disfigured by as ugly an example of church architecture as ever man designed. He says:

"As a growing taste for public buildings has for some time appeared among us, we might, in the construction of a prison, unite elegance and use; and the west angle of that land between New Street and Mount Pleasant [Ann Street], might be suitable for the purpose; an airy spot in the junction of six streets. The proprietor of the land, from his known attachment to Birmingham, would, I doubt not, be much inclined to grant a favour."

The prison philanthropist also visited the old gaol of the parish of Aston, situated in High Street, Bordesley. Here he found "Two damp dungeons down ten steps, and two rooms over them. Court not secure. No water. Gaoler no salary: he keeps an ale-house."† There were, on the occasion of Howard's visit, five prisoners. An old friend to whom we showed these notices perfectly remembers this old dungeon. "It was," he says, "an old-fashioned public-house with a bulk-window, and, I think, bore the sign of the 'Brown Lion.' Over the window, on the front of the house, was fastened up a set of manacles, such as used to be put upon highwaymen,—there they hung as a terror to evil-doers.

"About the year 1830 the house was kept by Jemima Brownell, and the prison-keeper was W. D. Brownell. The prison was known as 'Brownell's Hole,' and there all prisoners had to be taken for Aston, Deritend, Bordesley, &c.

"The place was far from secure; and I have heard of cases where, while the fun was fast and furious, and the ale was being drunk in the fore part of the house, prisoners have been helped out and smuggled across the fields which then

* John Howard: *State of the Prisons in England and Wales.* 1780. p. 269.

† "There being no proper place for the confinement of idle and dissolute apprentices, either here or in the county Bridewell at Warwick, the punishment for small offences is often omitted till unhappy youths are ruined. Some such young creatures I saw in the county gaol: and some of these boys I again met with on board the hulks."

* *Account of the principal Lazarettos in Europe*, etc., 1789, p. 159.

† Ib. p. 159.

extended from Bordesley over the Garrison Grounds and away to Saltley and Aston."

In this period of his interesting chronicle Dr. Langford quotes several paragraphs from the *Gazette*, relating to the unusual prevalence of counterfeit half-pence. A letter appeared in that journal on the 29th of January, 1776, from "An Enemy to Imposition," directing attention to the scandalous practice of purchasing bad half-pence "at near 20 per cent. cheaper than the Mint coin," and compelling those who require change for gold to take a considerable portion of the amount in copper, much of which was so bad that it could not be circulated elsewhere than in this town of base coinage. "It is too notorious," continues this correspondent, "that Mr. T——, in London, formerly an Inhabitant of this Town, has sold considerable Quantities here and in the Neighbourhood. If all honest Persons would absolutely refuse to take such as are obviously Counterfeits, the Growth of this Evil would be checked, and a few Informations (which I have Reason to believe will soon be laid against both Vendors and Purchasers), would perhaps totally eradicate it." The injustice of this system is very sensibly pointed out by the writer: "An industrious Nailor, for instance, who labours hard all the week for four or five Shillings, receives a part even of this small pittance in such base, unlawful coin, which he takes with him into the country, and offers for the necessaries of life; but there the tradesman refuses them: they then either remain on the poor man's hands, or are more injuriously employed at the ale-house, to the manifest destruction of his health, and perhaps the ruin of his family." These being, as he says,

OLD WINDMILL IN HOLLOWAY HEAD.

no mere suppositions, but facts, which occurred every day, "the necessity of putting a stop to this evil cannot but be obvious to every man;" and it is not to be wondered at that, after so lucid a statement of the facts of the case, a public meeting of the principal inhabitants of the town was held three weeks later, in "the Chamber over the Old Cross," "at which it was resolved to offer a Reward of Twenty Pounds, to such Persons whose Evidence shall convict any Offenders herein." To the announcement of this decision, in the *Gazette*, was appended the statement that "the real Value of 2s. 6d. worth of Counterfeit Half-pence is not more than 3d." Intending subscribers to the necessary fund for carrying out this much-needed crusade against so scandalous a practice were requested "as soon as may be, to send their Names, with the Mention of what Sum they intend to subscribe, either to some of the above said Officers of the Town, or to Pearson and Rollason, Printers, or M. Swinney."

The contrast between the tradesmen of Birmingham, wilfully encouraging the circulation of base coinage, of which half a crown's worth (if the word "worth" can be used at all of such stuff) was in reality only *worth* threepence, — and Matthew Boulton, honestly producing at Soho, coinage of the most genuine character, and at the same time unrivalled as to excellence of workmanship,—must strike every reader of the history of our town, as it did our worthy poet Collins; who wrote respecting the latter the following

EXTEMPORARY STANZAS,

On seeing the inimitable Copper Coin of Mr. BOULTON'S *Mint, at* SOHO.

WHEN Bacchus to Midas a patent bequeath'd
(For so by the Poets we're told,)
For turning, as long as on earth here he breath'd,
Whatsoever he touch'd, into gold;

No license he gave to the Phrygian Old Drone,
On the bullion a STAMP to bestow;
But the hoard a dead heap to the muckworm was grown,
As no doit of it CURRENT would go.

But had Bacchus to BOULTON imparted the power,
To 'ply the philosopher's stone;
That grant, though confin'd to the lapse of an hour,
Had honor'd his Thyrsus and Throne!

For the bright rosy God had been blazon'd in gold,
In such rare combination and form,
And his brethren above might with envy behold,
And with jealous emotions grow warm.

Each exclaiming—"Who dares thus our likenesses ape,
"In such guise as may copies be reckon'd,
"And Gods thus epitomize, ought not to 'scape,
"But be deem'd a Prometheus the Second!"

And yet if desert should be paid in due COIN;
Modern works, which the ancients surpass,
The Gods, in full synod, should lib'rally join,
To applaud, though on COPPER or BRASS.

And when, LIKE Celestials, with justice they aim,
To discharge debts of honor below;—
To give merit, but CURRENT and STERLING, its claim,
"Twine a wreath for the Man of SOHO."

The influence of the disastrous war with America during the eighth decade of the century, was felt in Birmingham as well as elsewhere. The press gang—the system which wrought almost as much suffering in England as did the slave-trade in other lands—was rife everywhere. On August 25, 1777, the following paragraph in the local *Gazette* must have caused considerable terror and excitement in many an artizan's home in Birmingham:

The Press is now very warm here and in the Neighbourhood. We hear a Gang is stationed at Gloucester, but they procure so few Men that the Expense of each is esteemed at no less than Fifty Pounds a Man to Government.

At the commencement of 1778 certain of the inhabitants of Birmingham met, at the Coffee House in the Cherry Orchard, Jan. 18th, to take into consideration the situation of public affairs, the embarrassment of the Government consequent on the defeat of the British forces under General Burgoyne, and the necessity for a public subscription in the town in support of the Government. Upwards of £1200, according to the *Gazette* of Jan. 21st in that year, was "instantly and most cheerfully subscribed;" and another meeting appointed to be held at the Hotel on the following Monday afternoon, Jan. 21st, the amount raised by that date being over two thousand pounds. A county regiment of volunteers for the King's service was immediately raised; and the following announcement was made respecting the movement in the *Gazette* of the following week :

Birmingham, January 26th.—We hear that an Express arrived at Warwick on Thursday last, from the Earl of Warwick, with Information, that his Majesty highly approves of the Plan his Lordship laid before the County of Warwick, on the 14th Instant, for raising a Regiment for the Service of Government. From another Correspondent we are assured, that when his Majesty signified his Royal Approbation of the Zeal and Affection manifested by the County of Warwick, in their Intentions of raising a Regiment for the Public Service, he was graciously pleased to inform Lord Warwick :—that the Men which the County may raise shall be formed into a Regiment and agreeably to their own Request, be called The Warwickshire Regiment. The Choice to be left to the County of either the 14th or 6th Regiment, and that the men shall either be entirely drafted, in order to leave the whole of one of those Regiments entirely vacant for the Warwickshire Levies, or that some Men shall be sent down with the Officers of the Regiment they chuse, as shall be most agreeable to the County.

The next week further particulars were given :

February 2nd, 1778.—We have the Pleasure to inform our Readers that the Subscription set on Foot in this Place to raise Men for the support of Government will now be prosecuted with the utmost Vigour, his Majesty having most graciously accepted the offer of a Regiment, which is to take the name of the Warwickshire Regiment, and the several companies raised here to take the Name of the Birmingham Companies ; for which Purpose the Officers of the Sixth Regiment will be ordered to march into the County to recruit and receive the Men. And we have the further Pleasure to assure our Readers, that a Meeting of the County will soon be called by the Lord Lieutenant, to promote this laudable measure ; of course, the Report so industriously propagated, that his Lordship disapproved of it, was totally without foundation.

Objection was taken by Lord Abingdon, in the House of Lords, to this method of raising troops as unconstitutional and illegal, but his motion to that effect was rejected, and "the work went on," says Dr. Langford, "with increased enthusiasm." On the 23rd of February the *Gazette* contained the following welcome statement :

We have unquestionable Authority to assert, that the Lord Lieutenant of the County of Warwick has subscribed the Sum of Five Hundred Pounds, toward the Warwickshire Regiment ; and in a few Days Places will be appointed where Books will be lodged in this Town, for raising a Fund to enlist Men into the said Regiment, who are to be formed into Companies, and called the Birmingham Companies.

The volunteer movement was now most popular in the town; and "Poet Freeth" encouraged the work of recruiting with a song entitled

The VOLUNTEER'S ROUSE, on the call for arming.
Tune—Hark the echoing Horn.

HARK to liberty's call—how it echoes around,
To arms ye bold Britons with speed ;
With courage unitedly cherish the sound,
To EXERCISE quickly proceed :
Your much injured kingdom calls loudly for aid,
Surrounded by numerous foes ;
When danger is near, be the Summons obey'd,
A sin 'twere a moment to lose.

With heart and with hand in the cause we'll unite,
Britannia applauds the design ;
We've long been oppress'd, and to do ourselves right
Together must freely combine :
'Tis liberty's call—can a Britain refrain,
His generous assistance to lend ;
Our country commands, and our utmost we'll strain,
So glorious a cause to defend.

With envious distinction—of party away,
And all be united and free ;
Than who should seem foremost his zeal to display,
Let no other strife ever be :
The SONS of HIBERNIA to danger awake,
Redress by such means did insure ;
Pursue the example, ye BRITONS, and make
Your liberties ever secure.

CHORUS—*Tune*, The Belle Isle March.
Then quickly away,
Manly zeal to display,
Haste, haste, where the standard of Freedom appears ;
In defence of your land
Join the free martial band,
'Tis an honour to rank with the brave Volunteers.

The last paragraphs relating to this subject, in the *Gazette*, tell how on Saturday, the 14th of March, a party of the 6th Regiment on Foot, into which the Warwickshire Levies are to be incorporated, arrived in Birmingham ; and that, "when compleated that Corps is to be called the Warwickshire Regiment, in Honour of the Loyalty and Zeal manifested by the County in Support of Government, at this critical and important Junction of public Affairs." And that during the week ending April 25, "the Officers of the 6th Regiment, into which the Warwickshire Levies are to be incorporated, at the Head of the Division of that Corps stationed here, made a public Procession through the

Town, to encourage Volunteers to enlist. They were preceded by a blue Flag, a Band of martial Music, a large Piece of Roast Beef, several Loaves of Bread, and a Barrel of Beer, and were attended by a great Concourse of People. In the Course of the Week, we are told, many promising young Fellows offered themselves and were enlisted."

From records of wars, and of the gallant patriotism of our townswen, we must turn now to other and less honourable doings of certain of the "Sons of Mars." For, among the events of this period, it is our duty to chronicle the first known commission of the dreadful crime of murder in the town. Several recruiting parties of soldiers were in the town in November, 1780; and among them a young man named Thomas Pitmore, a native of Cheshire, who, having recklessly squandered a small fortune of about £700, had enlisted in the 2nd regiment of foot, and was at that time a corporal. There was also, belonging to the 36th regiment, a young drummer, John Hammond, an American by birth. An acquaintance had sprung up between these two daring spirits, and, having procured a brace of pistols, they endeavoured to while away the tedium of their enforced sojourn in the town by playing at highway robbery. During one of these moonlight expeditions on the Coleshill road, about four miles out of town, they met three Birmingham butchers,—Scholefield, Barwick, and Rose,—who were returning from Rugby Fair, and rode closely behind each other. One of the robbers attempted to seize the bridle of the first, but the horse, being young, started out of the road, and ran away. Hammond then attacked the second, Wilfred Barwick, crying, "Stop your horse," and at the same time, "through the agitation of a timorous mind," says Hutton—discharged a pistol at the unfortunate Barwick, who immediately fell dead. Both the robbers then retreated; the younger, who had fired the fatal shot, hid in Ward End field, and was soon afterwards captured by a fourth butcher of the company, named Rann, and taken to Birmingham. The culprit at once impeached his elder companion, and both were lodged that night in the dungeon. They were tried March 31, 1781; and, on the second of April, were executed and hung in chains at Washwood Heath. Effigies of the two men are still to be seen on either end of Ward End House, the old residence of William Hutton.

The growth of the town since 1751—when Bradford's Plan was published—had been so rapid and extensive that it became desirable to provide a new map. The only modern one in existence knew no buildings, save the house of John Baskerville, west of "Swinford Street" and "Bewdley Street." It knew not "Paradise Row," except as the road to Stourbridge and Bewdley. Where, at the period referred to in the present chapter, the grimy, heavily-laden barge yielded up its freight of "black diamonds," was known only on Samuel Bradford's Plan as the "Old Brickiln Close." It was therefore necessary that a new map should be prepared with all speed. The projectors of that much needed publication seem, however, while desirous of presenting a correct map, unwilling to incur the trouble and expense of a new survey. Hence the following curious advertisement:—

"August 31, 1770.—Any Person well acquainted with the additional new Buildings erected in this Town since the year 1751, and capable of inserting them into the Plan of Birmingham, are desired to send their Terms sealed in a Letter directed to T. J. to the Printer of this Paper, where may be seen a Specimen of Part of the Plan already done."

We cannot tell whether this proposal to amend Bradford's Plan really emanated from the publishers of the next plan of the town which made its appearance, but certainly "The Plan of Birmingham, survey'd by Thos. Hanson, 1778," has every appearance of having been taken, in part at least, from its predecessor. It was "Published according to Act of Parliament by Pearson and Rollason," in the above year, and measures 43in. by 31in. As the changes in the appearance and extent of the town, and in the names of the streets, as marked on this old map, are numerous, a brief description may not be uninteresting. If the reader will refer for a few moments to the facsimile of Bradford's, he will be the better able to mark the points of difference.

Beginning with the New Hall estate, we notice that the town has now thoroughly surrounded the house itself, and streets are cut across the land

BIRMINGHAM OLD LIBRARY, UNION STREET.

in every direction. Great Charles Street crosses about twenty or thirty yards in front of the house; and parallel with it run other and shorter streets; viz., Bread Street, [Little] Charles Street, Edmund Street, (called on Bradford's Plan *Harlow Street*,) and Lionel Street. Between Great Charles Street and Bread Street, (on the site of the present New Market Street,) is an open square called the "New Hall Market." *Conegreve Street* is now marked where the "Conygree-stile-close" formerly stood. "Paradise Row" (the present Paradise Street) passes through an area now thickly covered with buildings. On the pleasant close which, in 1751, skirted that thoroughfare, as well as "Meredith's Bowling Green," (how our ancestors enjoyed the healthful sport of bowling—there were bowling-greens everywhere!) there is now quite a new settlement. From the Charles Street and "Harlow Street" of the old map, down to Smallbrook Street, there is a broad fringe of new buildings and streets; Hill Street and Suffolk Street are now both made and built upon, along their entire length, as well as the several short streets lying between the two, to wit, Swallow Street, Navigation Street, (the "canal frenzy" has to answer for that name,) and Princes Street, now called Cross Street. There are now "New Hinkleys" and "Old Hinkleys;" and the road leading out from Smallbrook Street to Bromsgrove and Worcester bears the names of Exeter Row and Holloway Head.* Close by the latter thoroughfare the old wind-mill (which most of our readers doubtless remember), appears on the map for the first time. An engraving of this old landmark, from a drawing in the possession of the publishers, appears on page 187.

In the south-eastern corner of the Plan, we notice that a portion of Bradford Street is formed, and partly built upon. It commences at the banks of the Rea, and runs outward from the town, in the direction of Camp Hill.

Coming to the centre of the town, we notice with regret that New Street and Temple Street have lost their pleasant rows of trees. As we have already said, "Bewdley Street" and "Swinford Street" are now no more; the former has taken the name of "Ann Street, or Mount Pleasant," and the latter is merged into New Street. The names of "High Street" and the 'Bull Ring" now appear on the map for the first time, and Walmer Lane has now the name of "Lancaster Street" appended. The two new Episcopal Chapels appear, St. Mary's, bounded by Catherine Street, (Whittall Street,) St. Mary's Row, Loveday Street, and Weaman Row; and St. Paul's, out in the fields, away from the town, but bearing evidence in the outlined streets that it is not destined long to remain in solitude.

On the right hand side of the plan are the engravings of St. Martin's and St. Philip's, exactly as in Bradford's, but the adornments on the left materially differ from those of the older plan. The title is surrounded by emblems of manufactures and commerce,—machinery, shipping, merchandise, etc. The upper half of the left border is occupied with a description of the town similar to that which we have previously quoted from Bradford's; the lower part contains views of the chapels of St. Mary, St. Paul, St. Bartholomew, and St. John the Baptist, Deritend, the Workhouse, the Hospital, the Blue Coat School, the Hotel, (Temple Row,) the New Meeting, and

"Mr. Green's House." The latter will be remembered by most of our readers as the Old Inland Revenue Office, which was demolished, with the Post Office, in 1874. In the small engraving on Hanson's Plan, which we copy here, it is represented as having two small wings, or out-offices, each connected with the main building by a low wall. A pleasant garden appears to have surrounded this desirable residence, rendering it almost equal to a country house, although in the middle of a busy manufacturing town. A portion of the house is visible in the old print of the Theatre Royal, of which an engraving is given on page 123.

In 1782 a project was set on foot for making a second canal, "from the collieries of Wednesbury to the lower part of the Town of Birmingham." The growing profits of the older undertaking, and the greatly increased value of the shares, (which had risen, Hutton tells us, from £140 to £400,) induced the projectors to take up the new scheme for establishing a rival company, in the hope of making an equally profitable speculation.

* Hutton's explanation of this name is as follows:—

"Where any of these roads [that proceed from Birmingham] lead up an eminence, they were worn by the long practice of ages into holloways, some of them twelve or fourteen yards below the surface of the banks, with which they were once even, and so narrow as to admit only of one passenger.

"Though modern industry, assisted by various turnpike acts, has widened the upper parts, and filled up the lower, yet they were all visible in the days of our fathers, and are even traceable in ours. . . .

"One of these subterranean passages, in part filled up, will convey its name to posterity in that of a street called *Holloway Head.*"
—History of Birmingham, sixth ed., pp. 21—2.

Accordingly, a meeting was called, at the Swan Inn, for the 8th of January 1782, of those "Gentlemen and Tradesmen of the Town of Birmingham and its Environs, who are desirous of encouraging the Scheme now in Agitation" for the purpose above stated, "where the Plan of a late and improved survey will be produced for their approbation." On the 4th of February the *Gazette* announced that "A Petition was presented on Monday last for Leave to bring in a Bill to make and maintain a Navigable Shaft or Canal from Wednesbury to Birmingham, and from thence to join the Coventry Canal at Fazeley;" and further that "since the subscription for carrying the same into execution was closed, sums to a very large amount have been offered." "The new company," says Hutton, "urged 'the necessity of another canal, lest the old should not perform the business of the town; that twenty per cent. are unreasonable returns; that they could afford coals under the present price; that the south country teams would procure a readier supply from Digbeth, than from the present wharf, and not passing through the streets, would be prevented from injuring the pavement; and that the goods from the Trent would come to their wharf by a run of ighteen miles nearer than the other.'"

"The old company," he continues—"alledged 'that they ventured their property in an uncertain pursuit, which, had it not succeeded, would have ruined many individuals; therefore the present gains were only a recompense for former hazard; that this property was expended upon the faith of Parliament, who were obliged in honour to protect it, otherwise no man would risk his fortune upon a public undertaking; for should they allow a second canal, why not a third; which would become a wanton destruction of right, without benefit; that although the profit of the original subscribers might seem large, those subscribers are but few; many have bought at subsequent price, which barely pays common interest, and this is all their s therefore a reduction would be barbarous on one side, and sensibly felt on the other; and, as the present canal amply supplies the town and country, it would be ridiculous to cut away good land to make another, which would ruin both." *

The battle would appear to have been waged fiercely on both sides. "Both parties," continues our witty historian, "beat up for volunteers in the town, to strengthen their forces; from words of acrimony, they came to those of violence; then the powerful batteries of hand-bills and newspapers were opened; every town within fifty miles, interested on either side, was moved to petition, and both prepared for a grand attack, confident of victory. . . . Each party possessed that activity of spirit for which Birmingham is famous, and seemed to divide between them the legislative strength of the nation; every corner of the two houses was ransacked for a vote; the throne was the only power unsolicited. Perhaps at the reading, when both parties had marshalled their forces, their was the fullest House of Commons ever remembered on a private bill." †

Taking into consideration the fact that the existing company had been first in the field, and had adventured their capital in a new and somewhat hazardous speculation, the House "gave them the option to perform this Herculean labour," and this they accepted. "Thus," concludes Hutton, "the new proprietors, by losing, will save £50,000, and the old, by winning, become sufferers."

In 1791, a new canal project was started; a meeting being held in February, to consider the desirability of constructing a Canal from Birmingham to Worcester. It was considered, as pointed out by a correspondent in the *Gazette*, that this undertaking "would give the Town almost every advantage of a Sea-Port, and pour into it the Produce of all Countries, at the easiest and cheapest Rate; and at the same Time take

* History of Birmingham, third edition, pp. 407-8.

† Ib. pp. 408-9.

off its Manufactured Produce by the readiest and cheapest Conveyance." The bill received the sanction of both Houses of Parliament during the session of 1791; it would appear however, from a song printed in Freeth's *Political Songster*, entitled "The Bishops turned Navigators," that it met with considerable opposition from the episcopal bench, in the House of Peers. Several lines will be recognised as having appeared in one of the old ballad-writer's invitation verses:

NAVIGATION'S a lottery frequently had,
And some it makes chearful and some it makes sad;
STOURPORT and HAMPTON rejoicing have been,
Whilst others elsewhere have been deeply took in;
CANALS pay so well, can it wonder excite,
Why some to get fresh ones so fondly unite?
For why, tell me why! should a few private elves
Engross the good things of the world to themselves?

That PIT-COAL's a blessing will not be deny'd,
For ever with us may that blessing abide,
But whilst we have plenty, and plenty to spare,
Is it right that our neighbours should not have a share?*
But think with what strange apprehensions it fills,
The owners of lands and the owners of mills!
Whose anger was raised to a very high pitch,
At what many said would have been a DRY DITCH.

Delays on the Severn for commerce make bad,
There should, and there must be a regular trade,
But if I'm not greatly deceived in my aim,
The Marquis of Staffordshire played a sly game;
Spectators might well with amazement be filled,
When heaps of lawn sleeves in the House they beheld;
The scene was alarming, for all of us know,
The *lumber troop* always with ministry go.

A contest so great on a mere private bill,
With wonder must many undoubtedly fill;
A dozen RIGHT REV'RENDS object to the plan,
And strong NAVIGATORS commence to a man;
Providing a war very soon should take place,
Our monarch I hope will consider the case,
Think, think GRACIOUS GEORGE of the BISHOPS I pray,
One half keep at home—let the rest go to SEA.

LANDAFF'S learned prelate, as public prints tell,
In chymics and nautics but few can excel,
Instead of the MITRE—of many the jest,
Let the ANCHOR or COMPASS appear for his CREST;
But think not the CLOTH I would wish to disgrace,
Not one should have less than a COMMODORE's place,
And why not, to figure in KEPPEL'S next *wake*,
The PRIMATE OF YORK a VICE-ADMIRAL make.

Int'rest the bill through the lower House bears,
And int'rest 'tis said threw it out of the PEERS;
Our hopes tho' once baffled again shall revive,
A fig for the calls, keep the spirit alive;
Rouse, rouse! ye COMMITTEE MEN every one,
Fear not in the end but the work will be done,
And if you compleatly would manage affairs,
Take care that the BISHOPS are furnished with SHARES.

We have extended the history of inland navigation in this neighbourhood somewhat beyond the period covered by the present chapter; and must now return to the year 1785, in which a change was made in the mode of conveying the mails to Birmingham, which indicates the growing importance of the town. Previous to 1784 the mails of the whole country had been conveyed by post bags on horse back, at an average rate, including stoppages, of from three to four miles an hour; but in that year one of the greatest reforms ever made in the Post Office was effected by the introduction of the plan of John Palmer, —the manager of the theatres of Bristol and Bath, and an intimate friend of our local poet Collins, —by which these important despatches were conveyed by stage-coaches, which were henceforth designated *mail-coaches*. Mr. Palmer, in his scheme submitted to Mr. Pitt in 1783, describes the then existing system as follows, "The Post, at present, instead of being the swiftest, is almost the slowest conveyance in the country; and though, from the great improvement in our roads, other carriers have proportionably mended their speed, the post is as slow as ever. It is likewise very unsafe, as the frequent robberies of it testify; and to avoid a loss of this nature people generally cut bank bills or bills at sight in two, and send the bills by different posts. The mails are generally entrusted to some idle boy, without character, on a worn-out hack, and who, so far from being able to defend himself or escape from a robber, is much more likely to be in league with him." And the observant manager had furthermore noticed that, when tradesmen of the city of Bath wished to have a letter conveyed with speed and safety, they were in the habit of wrapping it in brown paper, as a parcel, and sending it by the

* One of the principal objections urged against the project was that by giving increased facilities for the conveyance of coal to Worcester and the district, the supply would speedily be exhausted.

stage-coach, although at greater expense than by the post. But the new mode was not adopted for conveying the Birmingham mails until August, 1785. The *Gazette* of July 4th, announced the proposed reform in the following paragraph:

We hear that the new regulations for conveying more expeditiously the mails will begin the latter end of this month, or beginning of next, and that mail carriages are preparing to convey the mails from London through Oxford, Birmingham, Wolverhampton, Shrewsbury, and along the new road through Oswestry, Llangollen, Corwen, and Llanrwst, to Holyhead; which road, by avoiding the delay and danger of Conway Ferry, and being the shortest and best, will enable the proprietors of the coaches to deliver the mail at Holyhead with greater expedition and more certainty, than can be done on any other road.

John (or Thomas) Collins—for the conjectures as to our finest local poet's christian name are by no means unanimous—celebrated the adoption of his friend Palmer's project for the conveyance of the mails, in the following verses:

OLD SMITHY AND OPEN FORGE IN DIGBETH.
Taken down early in the Nineteenth Century.

MAIL COACHES.

IT was ever the Case, ere Desert cou'd take Place,
That Envy threw Rubs in its Way;
Yet the Day-light we prize, tho' we know that weak Eyes
Feel pain at bright Phœbus's Ray.

When Noah in Ark, with his Sons did embark,
Prediluvians, uplifted and pompous,
Deem'd his nautical Scheme a fantastical Dream,
And pronounc'd the Projector *non compos*.

And Columbus the bold, when the World we call *old*,
He first quitted in Search of the *new*;
In the wide swelling Ocean, found far less Commotion,
Than 'midst his own murmuring Crew.

Historians well know, that some Ages ago,
The Horse drew the Plough with his Tail;
And the Grain, there's no Doubt, from the Chaff was *trod* out,
Long before we made use of a Flail.

Time's Parts to divide, and to shew how they glide,
Men invented the Sand-Glass and Dial;
And was thought nothing more cou'd be done on that Score,
Till a Clock-Maker ventur'd the Trial.

Who strikes out new Lights, fell Derision excites,
If not Persecution to boot;
Gallileo so found, when he prov'd the World *round*,
And that Men walk'd *upright*, UNDER-FOOT.

'Twas at first thought a Bull, but a Pontiff's thick Scull,
Who wou'd suffer no Bulls but his own,
Hurl'd Vatican Thunder at Heretic Blunder,
And prov'd an old Wife, like Pope Joan.

Thus the Conclave of Fools, Tony Todd and his Tools,
Their Anathemas deal at Mail Coaches;
And like Zealots of Yore, trump up Lies by the Score,
Which their Proselytes swallow like Loaches.

Here a Wheel lost a Spoke, there an Axle Tree broke,
At a third Place the Perch snapt in two;
One Man lost an eye, a poor Girl smash'd her Thigh,
And the rest were all beat black and blue.

Then the Horses one night, with hard Driving took fright,
And ran down a Hill, Helter Skelter,
When the Passengers all, were thrown out great and small,
And left in Duck's Puddle to welter.

Yet, wond'rous to tell, after all that befel,
Old Time, that developing Smoaker,
Has prov'd all those Flams are but Bugbears and Bams,
Like Wilding's "Cat, Pistol, and oker."*

And the Lies Envy broaches, to run down Mail Coaches,
(Though fraught with Mischance and Disaster)
Like the Grease on each Axis, their speed not relaxes,
But only just makes them run faster.

For Life to secure, and Life's Means to ensure,
In a Land where Freebooter's abound,
Must engage ev'ry Mind, to its Int'rest not blind,
And the Plan with Success must be crown'd.

Nay, each hungry Cur, that now makes such a Stir,
To his Yelping wou'd soon put a Stop,
And be one of the Host, that Mail Coaches now toast,
If he had but a Share of the Sop.

Then Palmer, whose Brain can alone guide the Rein,
Like Apollo, thy Course daily run;
And never let Fear slack thy noble Career,
Till the Dog Star eclipses the Sun!

The first mails were conveyed to Birmingham by the new mode on the 23rd of August, 1785.

In the beginning of November, 1788, we find our townsmen preparing to celebrate, with every token of rejoicing, the centenary of the glorious revolution of 1688. The principal inhabitants were to dine together at the Hotel; and illuminations, bonfires, and other popular manifestations of joy were intended. But on the day previous to the celebration a notice was issued by the officers of the town, in which they "respectfully inform the Public that no Illuminations, Bonfires, or Fireworks will take place on the Celebration of the above Days, [the Revolution Jubilee and Gunpowder Plot,] on Tuesday and Wednesday Next, [Nov. 4th and 5th,] and hereby give Notice that proper People will be stationed in different Parts of the Town to apprehend all Persons letting off Serpents, Rockets, &c.; and such as are found offending will be prosecuted to the utmost Rigour of the Law."

Notwithstanding, however, the "proper people" and the threatened rigorous prosecutions, we read in the very interesting account of the celebration, quoted by Dr. Langford, from the *Gazette*, that "At night the principal streets of the town were illuminated; and that "the transparencies and ornamental lights at the Hotel were very beautiful; over the door was a transparent Portrait of King William;" in the windows on either side were large transparencies inscribed "to the Immortal Memory of the Great and Glorious King William III.;" also that on the Wednesday night there were fireworks, and that "there was not the least rioting in the streets, or accident of any consequence" therefrom. The bells rang out a merry peal; the assembly at the Hotel was "more numerous and respectable than any ever known in the town," and the majority of the guests were appropriately "dressed in blue coats, with orange capes, having on beautiful emblematical buttons," and wore also elegant silver medals, suspended by orange ribbons; a large quantity of medals of the same design, but in inferior metal, were distributed among the populace; an appropriate ode, set to music by Mr. Clark, was performed at the dinner; and the entire celebration appears to have been carried

* *Vide* Foote's Farce of The Liar.

out in a spirited manner, and to have passed successfully and harmoniously.

The next year saw the town rejoicing over the happy recovery of the King from that illness which threatened to incapacitate him from taking any further part in the affairs of the realm. Already a proposal had been made to transfer the executive Government to the Prince of Wales, and Birmingham had loyally expressed her adherence to the Regent elect; but by the end of February more hopeful news came of the state of the King's health, and as soon as certain intelligence arrived as to his Majesty's Message to that effect having been delivered to the Houses of Parliament, "the inhabitants were assiduously occupied in furnishing their windows with lights," the bells in all the churches were rung," and with the evening a more general and brilliant illumination commenced than was ever known in this place." The streets were thronged, (notwithstanding the inclemency of the weather,) brilliant transparencies and emblematical devices appeared on most of the public buildings. A huge bonfire, at which three tons of coals were consumed, was kindled in front of the Navigation Office, fireworks were displayed in various parts of the town, and at Soho the manufactory, house, and grounds of Mr. Boulton were "completely and grandly illuminated with many thousand lamps of various colours, most judiciously displayed.

Again, on the appointed Day of public Thanksgiving for the King's recovery, a similar display took place, and in addition to the usual illuminations, bonfires, and fireworks, a townsman who had thus early been smitten with the balloon mania, "gratified the populace by letting off, from St. Paul's Square, a Mongolfier balloon of 50 feet in circumference, which from the favourable direction of the wind glided over the town in a very majestic and pleasing manner." Our second local laureate, Collins, celebrated the event in a poem; services were held in nearly all the places of worship; a special form of prayer and psalms composed for the occasion, were read and sung at the Jews' synagogue; and everybody, both rich and poor, joined in expressing, each in his own particular way, the universal joy that the good and kindhearted "Farmer George" was once more enabled to take the reigns of Government, and to preside over a happy and, on the whole, contented people.

And with this public expression of loyalty and gratitude we close the present record of the life and doings of our townsmen during the ninth decade of the eighteenth century.

CHAPTER XXXI.

THE BIRMINGHAM LIBRARY.

Books—Intellectual Penury—Small Beginnings—Aims and Objects of the founders—Increased Subscription—History of the Library, to 1800.

"BOOKS," says Milton,—in his noble defence of the liberty of the press,—"are not absolutely dead things, but do contain a potency of life in them, to be as active as that soul was whose progeny they are; nay, they do preserve, as in a vial, the purest efficacy and extraction of that living intellect that bred them. . . . A good book," he continues, "is the precious life-blood of a master-spirit, embalmed and treasured up on purpose to a life beyond life." And if, as John Ruskin has said, for the individual to be without books of his own be "the abyss of penury," how much more so must it be for the community to be without a *public* library; and we are not surprised to find that our townsmen, as early as the year 1779, resolved that they would no longer endure *such* "penury." In that year the Birmingham Library—afterwards and still known as "the *Old Library*"—was founded. It is unfortunately impossible, at the present time, to discover the names of the founders of this excellent institution, as its early records are now lost. The first home of the library was in Snow Hill, where it was open *only one hour each morning*, for the delivery and return of books. Hutton tells us simply that "it originated in 1779, and, like many important things, from exceedingly minute beginnings;" that "each member paid a guinea entrance, and six shillings per annum;" and that "their number was so small, that they could scarcely have quarrelled had they been inclined, and their whole stock might have been laid in a handkerchief." The present librarian, Mr. Scarse, has very courteously informed us that the entire collection of books was originally kept in a small old-fashioned "corner-cupboard," which is still in existence.

The only notice of the new institution in the *Gazette*, during 1780, is an announcement of the general meeting of the Subscribers to be held at the Hotel, June 13th; and this is signed "J. L., Steward," *i.e.*, John Lee, jun., "steward" or librarian.

The first statement as to the library and the aims and objects of its proprietors, so far as can be discovered, appeared in the *Gazette* of June 11th, 1781, in an announcement of the general meeting:—

"BIRMINGHAM LIBRARY.—A general meeting of the subscribers to this institution is appointed to be held on Wednesday, the 13th of June, at the Castle Inn, in High Street, at three o'clock in the afternoon, when every subscriber is desired to attend, to consider of some laws relative to the government of the society. This Library is formed upon the plan of one that was first established at Liverpool, and which has been adopted at Manchester, Leeds, and many other considerable towns in this kingdom. The books are never to be sold or distributed; and, from the nature of the institution, the Library must increase till it contains all the most valuable publications in the English language; and, from the easy terms of admission (viz., one guinea for entrance, and six shillings annually), it will be a treasure of knowledge both to the present and succeeding ages. As all books are bought by a committee, of persons annually chosen by a majority of the subscribers, and every vote is by ballot, this institution can never answer the purpose of any party, civil or religious, but, on the contrary, may be expected to promote a spirit of liberality and friendship among all classes of men without distinction. The library in this town is at present in its very infancy, but it already contains a valuable collection of books, catalogues of which may always be seen at Messrs. Pearson and Rollason's; and when the Library Room (which is already engaged in the most central part of the town) shall be opened for the reception of it, and the constant accommodation of all the subscribers, the advantages arising from the institution will be greatly increased."

On December 12th the annual meeting was held at the Castle Inn, at which officers were to be elected for the ensuing year. Each person was "desired to bring a list of 20 names, consisting of those whom he would recommend to be of the committee for the year ensuing, as they are to be chosen by ballot; and as it will take some time to settle this list, the members are requested to attend and deliver them, as early as possible; as no list can be received after half-past three o'clock" It was also announced that "in consequence of the additional expense in which the society will be involved, it will be proper to propose some addition to the annual subscription;" but that "the subscribers may rely on the proposition never exceeding the sum of 10s., which is the limit prescribed by those who first formed the society, and for which they pledged themselves." It is hoped, however, "that, notwithstanding the additional expense, the annual subscription of 7s. 6d. or 8s. may suffice."

The annual subscription was ultimately fixed at eight shillings; and "a Librarian entered the service at 10*l*. per Annum."

The next announcement tells us the whereabouts of the new library premises:—

January 20, 1782.—BIRMINGHAM LIBRARY.—The Subscribers to the Birmingham Library are hereby informed that the Library Room, adjoining to Messrs. Pearson's and Rollason's House, in the Swan Yard, will be opened on Thursday Next; and that the Librarian will attend there to deliver the Books, &c., every Day (Sundays excepted) from Two o'Clock in the Afternoon to Five. Within those Hours any Subscriber may see the Books, read, and make Extracts, &c. at his Pleasure. A Fire will be kept in the Room, and the last Reviews will always lie on the Table. At the same Time the Tickets will be ready to be delivered to the Subscribers, signed and sealed by the President, and numbered according to the Order of each Person's Admission.

a notice announcing a general meeting to be held December 11th, 1782, we learn that the library then contained "near 500 vols." At a meeting held January 5th, 1783, the question of novel

"OLD TRIPE HOUSE" IN DIGBETH.

In 1780, as we have stated in a previous chapter, Dr. Priestley came to reside in Birmingham, and it was from him, Hutton tells us, that the society received "that stability and method, without which no institution can prosper." From

reading occupied the attention of the committee, but only as regards the number of volumes to be allowed out at once. It was resolved "that when a Novel consists of more Volumes than One, a Subscriber may be allowed to take Two Volumes or more; but he is to observe not to keep them longer than the Time allowed for One only, under the Penalty of forfeiting for each Volumne separately."

We next find the subscribers considering "a proposal of some of the Members to form themselves into a separate Society, for the Purchase of Books of Science, and especially Foreign Publications of that Class, to be under the same Regulations with those of the present Library, and to be accessible to all the Subscribers to it, but not to be taken out of the Library except by the new Subscribers." It is added that "if this proposal be approved, a Number of Persons intend to make a Deposit of a considerable Collection of scientifical Books, in order to begin the Establishment to more Advantage."

On the 14th of June we learn, from an announcement in the *Gazette*, that

> The Subscribers to the Birmingham Library having, at a Special Meeting, held this Day, given Leave to any of their Body to form themselves into a separate Society for the Purchase of Books of Science, and especially foreign Publications of that Class, and having granted them the Use of their Room and their Librarian; a Number of them have thought proper to propose an Annual Subscription of One Guinea for that Purpose: And Notice is hereby given, that a List of the new Subscribers is in the Library Room, and will continue there, in order to receive the Names of more Subscribers till Monday the 21st Instant, when all the new Subscribers are desired to meet in the Library Room, at five o'Clock in the Evening, to make proper Regulations for the Execution of their Plan.

By 1786 the library had grown from "near 500" to 1,600 volumes, and the annual subscription had more than kept pace with the growth of the library, being now a guinea and a half.

The librarian in 1786, was, as appears from the advertisement announcing the increased rate of subscription, William Horne, who, "in consequence of an Advance in Salary," now "attends to the Business of the Library an additional Hour in the Day, viz.: from Ten to Eleven o'clock in the morning." The growth of the library makes it necessary for the committee to remind subscribers, at the same time, "that the room which they rent at present will very soon be too small to answer the purpose for which it was taken."

In 1787 there arose a fierce and bitter dispute as to the non-admission of works on theological controversy. A motion for their expulsion being made by Mr. Charles Cooke, Dr. Priestley replied in a pamphlet, the profits of which were to be given to the funds of the Library. On the 3rd of September another pamphlet was announced to be issued the next day, "by a Subscriber," who expresses his apprehension lest the appearance of opposition among the subscribers should deter the outsiders from availing themselves of the many advantages offered by that excellent institution. He is persuaded that "the joint efforts of Dr. Priestley and himself" will contribute to promote peace and to dispel the bitter strife in which they are engaged. Following the doctor's example, "he also intends applying whatever gain may arise from the sale of this Address, to the Funds of the Library."

The peaceable endeavours of the two pamphleteers, were, however, unsuccessful, and a month later a pamphlet appeared on the other side, written by an outsider, who was in no way concerned in the discussion, and who proposed to devote the profits of his venomous little publication—which has been styled "one of the most uncharitable and unchristian tracts ever written"—"to the Funds of the Sunday Schools." The object of the author in joining in the controversy was obviously that of bespattering Dr. Priestley with his virulent abuse. The reader will not care to know more of this pamphlet than its title, which was as follows:—

> A Letter to Dr. Joseph Priestley, occasioned by his late Address to the Subscribers to the Birmingham Library.
>
> By Somebody, M.S.
>
> "Thou com'st in such a questionable shape that I will speak to thee."—*Shakespeare.*
>
> "Gloriam, honorem, imperium, BONUS, IGNAVUS, æquè sibi exoptant; sed ILLE, VERA viâ nititur, HIC quia BONÆ artes desunt, DOLIS atque FALLACIIS contendit."—*Sallust.*

Mr. Cooke's reasons for his proposal were given in the *Gazette* of December 10th, as follows:—

December 10, 1787.

TO THE SUBSCRIBERS OF THE BIRMINGHAM LIBRARY.

GENTLEMEN,—My Motion for a Law to exclude Books relating merely to controversial Divinity, having occasioned some Party Animosity, and the Motive being greatly misunderstood, I beg Leave, before the General Meeting, to assure the Subscribers the Motion was brought forward solely with a view to extinguish, and in future prevent, uneasiness occasioned by the late Mode of introducing them. Dr. Priestley, in his Address to the Subscribers upon my Motion, declares that he had always opposed their Admission; and I have often in conversation heard several of the Dr.'s Friends mention their own ideas of the Impropriety of their Introduction; and it was from one of these Gentlemen I learned these Words, "after the present moment, mere Lumber." I have heard Books relating to the two learned Professions objected to in the Committee, merely because they were professional, I mean Law and Physic, but never heard the same objection to those of Theology. The principal end of all public Libraries should be, to collect a Fund of Literature, both entertaining and useful, not only for the advantage of present, but future generations, but more especially for the purchase of the books of History, Science and Profession, whose Prices are in general too high for the Majority of Private purses, as the Philosophical Transactions, Moreri's Dictionary, Grose's Antiquities, &c., &c. The proposal which I wished to bring forward of a separate Subscription, on the Plan of the Scientific, for the Purchase of Books appertaining to the three sister Professions, sets aside every possible Idea of my Fears or Alarms relating to controversy. I have been told repeatedly, and with Warmth and Acrimony, that my Motion was originally intended as a personal attack on Dr. Priestley, and that the Subscribers who are of the established Church were angry because the Dissenters in general were better read, and consequently more liberal than them. I am sure that the Doctor will Laugh at the former idea, and as for the latter, I think every one should Laugh at it. The Society are under many and great Obligations to the learned Doctor; it was him who altered its original Plan, and put it on a more extensive scale; he amended and enlargened the Laws, and has paid a great Attention to its Welfare and growing Interests; it is now becoming a very valuable and useful Library, and promises fair to be a most capital one. Considering the future Consequence this Institution is likely to be of to this Neighbourhood, it were to be wished that any Mode likely to create Misunderstanding amongst its Members was exploded; it was therefore my Motion was put up, and not only with the Approbation, but at the Request of many Respectable Subscribers, with the prospect of preventing in future the Bickerings occasioned by the Introduction of these controversial Books, and at the same time to establish Unanimity and Concord in the Society, and to explode the idea of Party influence.—I am Gentlemen, Your most obedient and most humble Servant,

CHARLES COOKE.

Hagley Road, Birmingham, Dec., 1787.

This motion was carried, and controversial divinity was excluded from the Library. At the same meeting (held December 12th, 1787) it was resolved unanimously "that those Subscribers who live One Mile from the Town be allowed one Day extra for the return of a Book, and those who live at the distance of Two Miles be allowed two days extra." It was also resolved that the hours of the librarian's attendance be from three o'clock to six in the afternoon between the first of September and the first of May, and from three to eight between the first of May and the first of September. Again there arose difficulties as to the library accommodation; the larger room was all too small, and although the munificent sum of £25 per annum had been offered for a suitable room, with a promise to expend £50 in improvements, the subscribers were still unable to find a room which would meet their requirements. It was the day of Tontines; almost every undertaking was carried out on the Tontine principle; and the friends of the Library decided upon using this popular method of raising sufficient money to erect a suitable building for themselves, as will be seen from the following announcement:—

BIRMINGHAM LIBRARY.—A Subscription is open in the Library for two hundred names, to raise one thousand guineas for the purpose of building a new and complete Library, to be let to the Society at £25. per annum, on a Tontine plan. Those gentlemen who wish to subscribe for one or more shares, not exceeding ten, are desired to send their names to the Librarian immediately. Any person having a freehold spot of land in a centrical situation to dispose of, is requested to send his terms, in writing, to Mr. Horne, at the Library:—And any builder wishing to undertake the building, may send their plan and estimate to the same. The land must be at least two hundred, and from that to three hundred square yards."

Meanwhile it was still necessary to obtain a larger room pending the erection of the tontine building, (the Library having now increased to 3,400 volumes); and temporary premises were length secured in the Upper Priory, hitherto known as "Mr. Payton's Repository," which were opened to the subscribers as a Library and Reading Room on Wednesday, May 5th, 1790. In 1791, the librarian's hours of attendance were again lengthened, it being decided at a general meeting of subscribers, Dec. 19th, that he should in future attend from eleven o'clock in the morning till one, from three in the afternoon till six, and again from seven till eight in the evening.

STAINED WINDOW, BY FRANCIS EGINTON, IN ST. PAUL'S CHAPEL.

By the end of the year 1792, the tontine building subscriptions had reached a sufficient amount to enable the promoters of the undertaking to enter upon the work of erection; and a meeting was held on the 7th of January, 1793, at the Shakespear Tavern, in New Street, "in order to take into consideration and adopt proper measures for carrying the same into effect." The land selected was that with which our readers are now familiar, (from the facsimiles of old plans of the town), which had previously been known as "Corbett's Bowling Green," adjoining the pleasant Cherry-Orchard, and fronting "a certain Passage there, called Corbett's Alley," now better known as Union Street. The Tontine-Deed is dated March 25th, 1798, and sets forth the several particulars as to the exact position of the land, which was obtained on a lease from the celebrated Dr. Withering, whose house adjoined the said property on the north-west side thereof. The lease was granted for 120 years, dating from June 24, 1793, at a ground-rent of £11 15s. per annum. The older portion of the present library building was erected thereon, at a cost of £905, which sum was advanced by the several parties included in the tontine trust, (comprising 181 persons, varying in ages from five months to twenty-one years), equally in proportion to the number of shares of the value of £5 each. The proprietors of the Birmingham Library were to pay an annual rent of £22 12s. 6d., subject in addition to the ground-rent of £11 15s. The building was completed in 1797, being erected of stone, from designs by Mr. William Hollins; the exterior consisted of the present covered portico, supported by two pairs of coupled Doric columns, surmounted by an Ionic story of the same form, with one window only on either side of the entrance in each story. This latter particular will enable the reader, from the engraving given on page 191, to form an idea of the size of the original building, as well as of the later extension. Over the entrance is the following inscription, from the pen of the celebrated Dr. Samuel Parr:—

> "Ad mercaturam bonarum artium profectus, et tibi et omnibus ditesces,"

which has been thus translated:—

> "Resorting to the Mart of the Sciences, you will grow rich both for yourself and others."

And thus, the library being firmly established in a permanent building suited to the requirements of its members, its history comes to an end, for the present.

CHAPTER XXXII.

APPEARANCE OF BIRMINGHAM IN 1790.

Deritend—Bridges over the Rea—Old houses in Digbeth—St. Martin's Church—The Bull Ring—The Old Cross—William Hutton—Ashted—New Hall—"Hockley Abbey" and its founder—The Crescent—Foot-path to the Five-Ways.

Those who have with exemplary patience followed the course of our story thus far, may perhaps be desirous of learning something of the appearance of the town after the provisions of the several improvement acts, which we have duly chronicled, had been carried into effect, as well as the other private improvements of which we have taken note in the foregoing chapters.

In surveying the town once more, therefore, to note the improvements of the last twenty years, we will suppose our readers to start with us from Camp Hill, as in the seventeenth century.

As we pass the end of Coventry Road, we enter the domain of brick and timber. The old gaol of the parish of Aston first attracts our notice, with its grim-looking irons hanging outside and the old-fashioned, bulk-windowed alehouse in front, kept by the gaoler. The half-timbered houses are now becoming fewer, but there are still a few remaining to give picturesqueness to the old "street called Dirtey." The chapel of St. John the Baptist, with its square heavy tower, does not harmonise ill with the quaint surroundings, now that the newness of its red brick has been toned down by the smoke; and the entrance to the town of Birmingham may still be said to be through a "pretty strete."

Reaching the banks of the Rea, in Deritend, we come to the first noticeable improvement, in the erection of a new bridge over that stream. In early times, before the water was dammed up to supply Cooper's Mill, which was about four hundred yards below the present bridge, Hutton is of opinion that the stream must have been so shallow as to admit of its being crossed, between Deritend and Digbeth, with the aid of a few stepping stones. But when it became necessary to dam up the water, several "paltry bridges" were erected in succession, chiefly of timber, to connect the two streets; the cost of making and maintaining the said bridges being provided for out of the property bequeathed for such good works by that worthy townsman, William Lench, the pious founder of "the Gild called 'Lench's Trust.'" These old bridges were barred, and kept chained and locked, and had an attendant bar-keeper. In the seventeenth century, these rude wooden bridges—which were so easily washed away by the winter floods—gave place to one of stone, as shown in Westley's Prospect, with recesses in which foot passengers might take refuge during the passage of large and heavy vehicles over the bridge. This was removed in 1750, and another erected by Henry Bradford and John Collins, (overseers of the highway,) consisting of five arches; "but the homely style, the steep ascent, and the circumscribed width, prevented encomium."* This was also demolished in 1789, to make way for the present bridge, the first stone of which was laid by Mr. James Yates, August 5th, 1789. This was not, however, completed until 1813, the Act under which it was erected having expired before the work was accomplished, and the trustees being opposed by the inhabitants and frustrated in their attempt to obtain an extension of the term. The works, therefore, remained incomplete until a new Act was obtained, in 1813, enabling the trustees to complete the improvements.

* Hutton.

As we pass along Digbeth we notice that the spirit of improvement has influenced private inhabitants, as well as public commissioners, and that many of the old gabled, half-timbered houses have given place to newer buildings; the music of the anvil has departed from the street of "manie smithes," along with their quaint old shops, half open to the street, of which only one yet remains (1790); where dwells a hale and hearty old blacksmith, John Roberts by name, whose health the smoke of the town and the lack of an "improved dwelling" has failed to injure, and who lived to the good old age of a hundred and three years.* Of this old smithy we are enabled to give an illustration from a small pen and ink drawing by W. Hamper, on page 195. †

Another of the quaint and picturesque old houses which has escaped the ravages of time and of modern improvements, is that now (1878) known as "The Old Digbeth Tripe House."

At St. Martin's Church considerable alterations have been made since our last notice of it. In 1781 the spire was found to be in a decayed and exceedingly unsafe condition. From the Parish Books we learn that a Vestry Meeting was held February 5th, and it was agreed by the inhabitants present, "that John Chesshire ‡ be employed to raise scaffolding to examine more minutely the Condition the said Spire is now in, and that he shall be allowed Ten Pounds for raising such scaffolding if he shall not be employed in repairing the Spire. If he is employed the expense for raising it is to be looked upon as included in the estimate

* In the *Universal Magazine*, 1792, is the following paragraph respecting this old Birmingham centenarian :—

"AUGUST 4.—Lately died in Digbeth *near Birmingham*, in the 103d year of his age, John Roberts, who retained his faculties to the last, and followed his employment within a few weeks of his death. This extraordinary old man married three wives, by whom he had 28 children; he was nearly 80 when he married his last and had six of the children by her."

The old smithy was taken down in April 1804.

† In his interleaved copy of Hutton's History of Birmingham now in the possession of Mr. Alderman Avery.

‡ John Chesshire was an ingenious, self-taught architect, a native of Over-Whitacre. *See* "Gentleman's Magazine," 1789, part 1, p. 214.

he has delivered to the Churchwardens. N.B. The Ladders to be the property of Mr. Chesshire when the repairs are complete."* On the thirteenth of the same month another meeting was held, at which it was decided to give the work to Mr. Chesshire. Thirty-three feet of the spire were to be taken down, and the remainder repaired; an iron spindle of 105 feet long was to be brought through its centre, and secured to the side walls every ten feet by braces; the material to be used in the repairs to be Attleborough stone. It was subsequently found necessary to rebuild an additional seven feet, making forty feet in all; the entire cost of the repairs being £166 9s.

The portion of the churchyard which was now opened to the street (by the demolition of the house of Francis Moles,) at the gateway opposite Moor Street, was now fenced in with "iron palisadoes." In the interior of the church great alterations had been made. "The seats," says Hutton, "would have disgraced a meaner parish than that of Birmingham; one would be tempted to think they were the first ever erected on the spot, without taste or order; the timber was become hard with age, and to the honour of the inhabitants, bright with use. Each sitting was a private freehold, and was further disgraced, like the coffin of a pauper, with the paltry initials of the owner's name. These divine abodes were secured with the coarse padlocks of a field gate. . . . As the town increased, gallery after gallery was erected, till no conveniency was found for more. Invention was afterwards exerted to augment the number of sittings; every recess capable only of admitting the body of an infant, was converted into a seat."

To remedy this undesirable state of affairs it was resolved by the Vestry, in December, 1784, that application should be made to the Chancellor of the Diocese, for a faculty to empower them to take down "all and singular the pews, Seats, and Sitting Places, together with the Pulpit and reading Desk, and the several galleries within the parish Church of St. Martin in Birmingham, and totally to remove the same, and re-erect new Seats, Pews, and Sitting Places, with a pulpit and reading desk upon the ground floor of the said parish Church together with large and spacious galleries with seats, pews, and sitting Places therein," according to certain plans furnished by Mr. Richard Dicken, "the surveyor of the architect intended to be employed in the alteration of the Church."

Here was an opportunity for the churchwardens to redeem all the follies and blunders of their predecessors, and to restore the interior of the church to something like its original appearance. But alas for the want of taste which characterised that period in our history, the new "Pews, seats, and sitting Places," which the restorer designed "to remain for ever hereafter" were quite as bad as, if not even worse than, those which they superseded. Happily, however, the "for ever hereafter" came to an end earlier than the perpetrators of the restoration intended, being doomed to destruction, with the old building, in 1872.

During the alterations in 1785-6, (which included not merely the erection of new pews and sittings, but also the new roofing of "the north and south side," an 'improvement' which entirely hid from view the clerestory windows), the amount of damage done to the interior of the church can scarcely be estimated. "The vast number of grave-stones, which nearly covered the floor," says Hutton, "and the names of the defunct, with their concise funeral memoirs, were committed to the same oblivion as themselves. The arms, monuments, pews, pulpit, roof, and charities,* fell in one general ruin. Nothing was left of this venerable edifice but part of the walls. Even the fine old monuments of the ancient lords, the pride of the church, could barely find a place above ground, and that in the last stage of

* J. T. Bunce: History of Old St. Martin's, p. 49.

* A list of the charities of the town is frequently to be met with in old parish churches, painted on a board, which is set up in some conspicuous place. Modern "restorers" have, in too many instances, caused these interesting memorials to be removed.

existence, the stair-hole. With all my powers I pleaded for the lords and their arms; but although I pleaded without a fee, I was no more regarded than some who plead with one."*

The following entry in the town accounts, under date Oct. 18, 1786, probably has reference to the sale of some of these venerable remains :—

"recd. for Old Lead	...	246	11	10¾
"do. Old Material	...	17	8	4"

The entrance to the churchyard is now open, the house at the gateway opposite Moor Street having been cleared away. But there still remain certain of the old houses crowding around the sacred edifice, as did the mercenary traders around the temple of old; the Commissioners have still much to do, for the shambles and the Roundabout Houses still crowd up the market-place, notwithstanding the acts of 1769 and 1773. The Old Market Cross has gone, however, having been demolished in August, 1784. The materials were sold by auction by T. Sketchley, August 7th, for £60, and the clock and bell for £10; that course having been sanctioned by a Town's Meeting held at the Public Office in Dale End, July 21st, to consider the ruinous state of that venerable structure. The event called forth from some local versifier the following epigram, which appeared in the *Gazette*, August 16th :—

"EPIGRAM.

On the Sale of Birmingham Old Cross.

"Conscience's Court by auction goes,
Bidders, though few, the hammer does
The business in a trice;
At sixty pounds the blow is struck,
Ten more knocks down the bell and clock;
Commissioners—no price."

Passing a little further up the High Street we notice the most improvement yet effected under the Lamp Acts, viz., the opening of the end of New Street. The old houses blocking up the end of the street which is in future years to become the principal thoroughfare of Birmingham, are now removed, and we no longer pass under a narrow gateway to reach it. The old houses of William Hutton have passed away, and now we behold our friend's newer place of business on the other side of the street, opposite the end of New Street. Little does he think, as he stands amid his valuable collection of books and prints, or chats with a friendly customer over his new literary undertakings, his *History*, his *Court of Requests*, and *Battle of Bosworth Field*, his *Journey to London*, and *Description of Blackpool*,—smiling to think of his having entered upon a busy literary career at the age when most men leave off,—of the evil days which are so near at hand. As he receives the friendly word and the nod of recognition from the many townsmen who have learned to respect and admire the old bookseller who has proved himself so worthy a citizen, he dreams not of the surging mob of enemies, eager to destroy his home and his property, and ready even to take his life, if he should fall in their way,—yet the hour of terror is not far distant!

But we must pass on our way. The Welsh Cross still stands, and the Beast Market still hinders the traffic in Dale End. The horse-fair has been removed to what has hitherto been known as Brickiln Lane, near the end of Smallbrook Street, but which is hereafter to bear the new name of the Horse Fair. As we pass along Coleshill Street we come upon an entirely new suburb. The fair estate of Dr. Ash has already begun to be built upon, and is cut up into broad, well-made streets. The doctor's house is undergoing considerable internal alteration, and the building will be ready for opening as a Chapel of the Establishment before the end of 1791. The first announcement of the break-up of the estate appeared in the *Gazette* of October 29th, 1787, the house and land having been previously offered for sale as a single lot without success. On the 13th of February, 1788, a more detailed announcement appeared as follows :—

Building Land in the parish of Aston, near Birmingham, late the estate of Dr. Ash, to be Let in parcels, for the residue of a term of ninety-nine years, about eighty-eight of which are unexpired. This estate, so peculiarly

* History of Birmingham, 3rd edition, p. 340.

John Wilkes. Richard Webster. Jeremiah Vaux. James Bisset. James Sketchley.

James Murray. John Freeth. John Collard. John Miles. John Toy. Joseph Fearon. Joseph Blunt.

THE FREETH CIRCLE: FROM THE TONTINE PICTURE BY ECKSTEIN.

eligible in its vicinity to the town, and not likely to be surrounded with buildings, having lately been laid out into streets well adapted to secure the benefit of a free and healthful air, has sufficiently proved the desirableness of its situation, as well as the essential advantages arising to the tenants who have already been fortunate enough to take part of it for building. The quantity now let and the preparations making, promise a rapid progress in the buildings intended to form the Hamlet of Ashted, which is planned with more regularity and uniformity than has usually been attended to in laying out Land for building in Birmingham. To render the streets spacious they are made from sixteen to upwards of twenty yards wide, and levels are taken to make proper falls for carrying off the the water, to prevent similar inconveniences to those which have been so generally experienced from the want of attention to so necessary a precaution.

The valuable articles of clay and sand upon the premises afford a very beneficial accommodation to the tenants; to which may be added, the convenience of plentiful springs of fine soft water, and a considerable saving in parochial payments; the levies being two-thirds less in the parish of Aston than in Birmingham.

As the season for building is approaching, it is hoped that those who are inclined to secure a situation so replete with advantageous inducements, will not lose the present opportunity of availing themselves of it.

A plan of the estate may be seen, and every other information and satisfaction that can possibly be required respecting the same, may be had by applying to Mr. Brooke, attorney, Temple Row; or to Mr. Kempson, surveyor, Bath-street, Birmingham.

N. B. A quantity of Thorns, growing Quick, and young Trees of various sorts upon the above estate, to be disposed of.

A difficulty appears to have been placed in the way of intending speculators, by statements to the effect that Sir Charles Holte had not power to grant leases for the term of ninety-nine years; these statements called forth the following announcement from the lessee of the land:—

Mr. Brooke having discovered that a number of persons are prevented taking the land for building which he bought of Dr. Ash, in consequence of a report being circulated that Sir Charles Holte had not power to grant leases for the term of ninety nine years, and of other futile insinuations; respectfully assures the public, that he made the purchase *with the concurrence of Mr. Legge and Mr. Digby*, and took the title under the direction of Counsel, which is perfectly clear, and may be perused by applying to him.

Whether envy of the success which has attended the purchase, or self-interest has stirred up the vicious minds of the authors of a report equally false as malicious, Mr. Brooke flatters himself they will not remain long undiscovered, that he may have an opportunity of seeking redress for the unwarrantable injury he has sustained, and hereby gives notice, that if any person in future shall slander his title to the above-mentioned estate, an action will be commenced against them.

Thus did the estate of Dr. Ash suffer invasion by the busy town; the cattle being "turned out of their pasture, to make room for man; and the arts planted where the daisy grew." * And while this great change was taking place on the one side of the town, the last vestiges were being removed of an old estate on the other. On the 2nd of July, 1787, we read in the *Gazette* an announcement of the sale by auction, "upon the premises, in Birmingham," on Tuesday, July 24th, "if not sooner disposed of by private contract," of "that well-known Mansion, called New Hall, with all the Offices and Out-buildings, except the Barn." The whole of this old Birmingham homestead is to be cleared away within a month from the time of sale. And so passes away, to become one of the grimiest districts of the grimy town, the pleasant, park-like estate of the Colmore family, and New Hall is known no more save in the names of two of the streets into which the land has been cut. We cross the estate, and reach the foot of Snow Hill, but the town has now grown beyond the "Salutation," and it is not until we have reached the crest of the hill beyond that we leave the buildings behind us, and obtain a delightful view over the valley at our feet,—across to the right towards Aston, where, behind the lofty trees in the park, we discern the graceful spire of the church, and the minarets of the old hall of the Holtes; and beyond these we get a view of Barr-beacon and the adjacent country. In the valley, to the left, we notice a curious and picturesque ruin of some apparently very ancient monastic building; but old as it seems, it was not in existence when Boulton founded his great manufactory at Soho. As we approach nearer to it the mystery seems to increase. What is the material of which it is built; how came it here, and who was the builder? are the questions we are immediately

* Hutton.

prompted to ask respecting this strange ruin. The story is as follows: An ingenious mechanic, Richard Ford by name, noticing the wasteful expenditure of his companions at the alehouse, conceived the idea of laying aside two shillings a day in order to build for himself a picturesque and apparently ruinous dwelling on a piece of waste, boggy land at Hockley, the material to be used in the deception being the large masses of scoriæ, usually termed slag or dross, that lay round about the Aston furnace, not far away, in great abundance. When his horse and cart (which his small business required him to keep) were at leisure, he sent them over to the furnace, to bring away the scoriæ to be used in his "ruined abbey," until he had collected a sufficient quantity, and then began to erect the building to represent ruins. In front of the house, to add to the deception, is the date 1473, in small pebble stones; but the real date of the building is probably about 1780. When overgrown with ivy it presented a picturesque appearance, as may be seen from our illustration on page 183, which is taken from a little sketch in Bisset's "Magnificent Directory." The builder, Richard Ford, is said by Pye to have invented a "one-wheel carriage," constructed entirely of iron, and to have received a gold medal from the Society of Arts for the invention.

Returning to the town we visit next the charming breezy site of the intended Crescent, commanding a view of the pleasant district surrounding St. Paul's, a part of the New Hall estate, which is, as yet, little built upon. Away to the left lies the north-western portion of Edgbaston, with Perrot's tower rising in the distance, and directly before us a view over fields and gardens to the Summer Hill estate, the prospect being bounded by the Icknield Street, lined on either side by a row of pleasant shady trees; truly a charming prospect, and one of which we fain would hope the projector's prophecy might be verified, namely, that it "cannot ever be interrupted." Alas for human hopes! Let the reader stand to-day, in the year of grace eighteen hundred and seventy-eight, on the plateau in front of the Crescent and mark the contrast! But certainly in 1788, when the project was first laid before the readers of the *Birmingham Gazette*, no better site could possibly have been chosen within anything like the same distance from the town, and it is not a matter of surprise to find that the proposed Crescent was looked upon with great favour. It is frequently mentioned during 1788 and 1789 in the journal referred to; the "extensive prospect that cannot ever be interrupted by other buildings," being more than once held out as an inducement to subscribers, and the "elegant" and "handsome" design continually meeting with the highest commendation. Perhaps the most interesting of these notices are the following:—

"November, 17, 1788.—A Correspondent who has seen the design for the elegant Crescent intended to be built in this town, remarks, that the houses will be very convenient, and the situation excellent in every respect, either for a winter or summer residence, as the houses will have both a southerly and northerly aspect. A reservoir will be formed in order to supply them with good water, without the trouble and danger of wells or pumps. *And it is an additional recommendation of the plan in this growing town, that there is not the least probability of any future buildings ever excluding the inhabitants of the crescent from a most agreeable prospect of the country.* The range of buildings undoubtedly will be the greatest ornament to the town, and pay the subscribers a good interest for their money."

"We are happy to hear that the Governors of the Free Grammar School of King Edward the Sixth, in this Town, have let on Lease, to Mr. Charles Norton, a large Plot of ground behind Mr. Ryland's house and garden, facing Summer-hill, whereupon he has engaged to build the handsome Crescent that we have before spoken of, and which will be a great ornament to the town. The prospect it will command will be most extensive and delightful."

Passing from the pleasant site of the Crescent, we come to the road leading to the Five-Ways, which afterwards became "Broad Street," but was at that time merely a foot-way, (marked on Hanson's Plan, 1778), along which there were scarcely half-a-dozen houses. At the Five-Ways a little village had sprung up; and so the handsome modern thoroughfare leading to Birmingham's most beautiful suburb was commenced at the end farthest from the town. About half-way between the Five-Ways and the town was an enclosed piece of land used as the Jews' Burial Ground.

The following advertisement, which appeared in the *Gazette* in December, 1783, will, however, give the reader a better idea of the rural appearance of this part of the town at that period than any mere description :—

"December 22, 1783.—Land near Birmingham.—To be LET three very convenient and desirable Inclosures, well supplied with water, and generally known by *the Name of Farmer Smith's Lands,* whereon are two Tenements, inhabited, and a third erecting and nearly compleated, *situate by the Foot Way from Pinfold Street to the Five Ways, at a very Little Distance from the Navigation Wharf, and one Part of which Land is contiguous to the Jew's Burial Ground.*—For Particulars and to view the Premises enquire of JOHN PHILLIPS, either at No. 4, Queen-Street, or of him at the Bull's Head, in Dale-End."

With this extract we close our notice of the appearance of Birmingham in 1790.

CHAPTER XXXIII.

A FEW OLD BIRMINGHAM WORTHIES.

John Freeth and his Friends—"The Twelve Apostles"—A warm reception—Biographical Notes on the Freeth Circle—Freeth's Poetical Writings—More Invitation verses—Later Publications—Death—John Taylor—Henry Clay—Dr. Withering, etc.

THE history of our town seems naturally to divide itself into four periods: that of its infancy, which ends at the time of the Restoration; the period of transition, from the village to the large manufacturing town, which is temporarily checked in its further growth by the riots of 1791 and the dismal and disastrous decade which closed the eighteenth century; the third period is one of manful struggle for political freedom and better local government, and may be considered as closing, as the fourth period commences, with the incorporation of the town.

We have now brought the history of the second period to the calamitous event with which it closes, (with the exception of a brief chapter on the religious history of the few years which preceded that event), and may, perhaps, be excused for pausing in our story in order to recall a few of the local worthies of that time.

As we have already made mention of John Freeth, in our chapter on his invitation cards, it will be well for us to place him first in our chapter of worthies, in order to complete our former notice. As we then stated, he was the son of Charles Freeth, who kept the Leicester Arms, in Bell Street, and after the death of his father, succeeded to the position and duty of host of that establishment. The exercise of his poetical faculties was not confined to the inditing of invitation-verses to sundry feasts and social gatherings, as our readers are doubtless aware, from the examples of his songs and ballads already quoted. In 1780 he collected his earlier effusions into a small volume, which he entitled, *The Warwickshire Medley, or Convivial Songster. By John Free.* His next publication was entitled, *A Touch on the Times, or the Modern Songster. By John Free.* This volume was published in 1783. In his preface he says :

"It is a very common, and not an untrue saying, that every man has his hobby-horse. Sometimes indeed it is a profitable one; more frequently it is otherwise. My hobby-horse and practice for thirty years past have been to write songs upon the occurrence of remarkable events, and nature having supplied me with a voice somewhat suitable to my stile of composition, to sing them also, while their subjects were fresh upon every man's mind; and being a

Publican, this faculty, or rather *knack* of singing my own songs, has been profitable to me; it has in an evening crowded my house with customers, and led me to friendships which I might not otherwise have experienced. Success naturally encouraged me to pursue the trade of *ballad-making*, for without it, it is not probable I should have written a tenth part of what this volume contains.

"My songs are principally adapted to the particular times in which they were written. I now lament I did not go more upon general topics; but engaged in many contested elections, I was obliged to turn them upon such temporary and local subjects, as might best serve the cause of the party I had espoused. During the American war, it will be perceived, I was no well-wisher to the Ministry that conducted it. When the *Coalition* took place, I went with the popular tide, and joined in sentiment with those who reprobated that extraordinary measure (for measures, not men, have always claimed my principal attention). Since that period I have viewed with a smile and indifference, political wranglings, being fully convinced that the contest of most politicians is only for power and for favours.

JOSEPH PRIESTLEY, LL.D.
From an engraved portrait after Fuseli, in the possession of W. Bates, Esq., B.A

"The present minister came idolized into office; and I have made songs in his praise, though I cannot but allow, that many of his taxes bear too hard upon the commercial interests of the kingdom, and that his extension of the Excise Laws has justly robbed him of much of his popularity.

"If I had no other motives, the requests of travellers in the mercantile line from every county, who pay me such frequent and friendly visits, for copies of my songs, would be a sufficient reason for the publication of this *three Shilling and Six-penny* Volume. I cannot expect it will please all parties; but I mean offence to none, and liberal minds will not be angry with me for freely expressing my sentiments."

Among the friends whom the genial good-natured host gathered around him were eleven of his townsmen, who, with himself, constituted themselves into a social club or convivial party; and it has been well said that "the nightly debates and clever productions of these worthies gave birth to and assisted in diffusing those great and glorious principles which in after years resulted in the passing of the Reform Bill, the Catholic Emancipation Bill, together with other progressive measures, and mainly contributed towards diffusing into the hearts of 'the people' those sentiments of liberalism and loyalty which experience has proved to have been productive of highly beneficial effects."

By their political opponents they were nick-named "the Twelve Apostles," and "the Jacobin Club," and a rival society was formed, which met at "Joe Lindon's," in Peck Lane; and over the fireplace of the room in which they assembled was printed, "*No Jacobin admitted here.*" Party feeling ran high, and on one occasion, when one of the twelve—the well-known James Bisset, of Museum and "Magnificient Directory" fame—called in at the Tory house, one of the company puffed a volume of smoke into his face. Bisset had already suffered many petty annoyances and insolent remarks aimed *at* him, but this direct and gross insult roused his indignation, and with one blow he felled the offender to the ground. There then ensued a general *mêlée*, in which most of the jugs and glasses came to grief, and Bisset was forcibly ejected from the house; the unlucky "apostle" was sued in the Court of Requests for breakages,—amounting to nearly £5,—and doubtless learned by bitter experience to abstain from putting in an appearance at "Joe Lindon's" in future.

The society at Poet Freeth's consisted, as we have said, of twelve members, including the host. A picture of the group engaged in debate around the board at Freeth's tavern, was painted by John Eckstein in 1792, and paid for by subscription on the popular Tontine principle, the picture becoming eventually the property of the last survivor of the twelve, who proved to be no other than the hero of the episode of "Joe Lindon's,"—James Bisset. A few biographical notes as to the other members of the club may interest our readers. Turning to our engraving of the Tontine Picture, the first portrait (beginning from the left hand side) is that of Mr. James Murray, a linen and woollen draper, who resided in Moor Street, and was known by the title of "Cheap John." He was a member of the Antiquarian Society of Scotland, and ultimately emigrated to America. Above him, in a cocked hat, is Mr. John Wilkes, a cheese-factor, who had a shop at the corner of Carr's Lane and High Street. He subsequently held a commission as Captain in the Militia. The third portrait is that of the worthy host himself; and immediately above him is that of Mr. Richard Webster, a brass-founder, in Moor Street. Next to him, snuff-box in hand, is the inveterate snuff-taker Mr. Jeremia Vaux, a surgeon who resided in Moor Street, and held a very high position in the town as a professional man, being both clever and experienced. Mr. John Collard is the next in the group; a hatter and tailor in High Street, and a very able logician. He wrote and published treatises on the "Essentials of Logic," "Praxis of Logic," and other kindred subjects. The next portrait, at the further end of the table, is that of Mr. John Miles, patent lamp manufacturer, of Edgbaston Street. The next is that of Mr. Samuel Toy, Newhall Street, in earlier years a "steel toy" manufacturer; but in after life, being reduced in circumstances, he became landlord of the Mitre Inn, where he died, after a brief illness. The next figure, wearing a tall hat of the most approved shape, is that of our friend James Bisset, of whom we purpose giving a more detailed notice in a future chapter. Below him is Mr. Joseph Fearon, a tin-merchant, in Digbeth, who was for many years constable of the town. He was considered the ablest and most fluent orator of the club, and is represented by the artist in the act of addressing his confrères. Behind him, in the background, is Mr. James Sketchley, an auctioneer, of Moor Street, who was for several years the senior member of the club. The last of the twelve, in the right hand corner of the picture, is Mr. Joseph Blunt, brazier, of High Street.*

We now return to "Poet Freeth." He re-published his second volume of ballads and songs, with his full name, under the title of "The Political Songster, or a Touch on the Times" in 1790, and called it *the sixth edition, with additions*, though, it must be confessed, the intervening editions between 1783 and 1790 have never seen the light of modern days, and, it is to be feared, were even unknown in Freeth's own. We have already quoted several of these songs, many of which,—says "Este,"—"possess the merit and sterling animus peculiar to Dibdin's popular songs, whose style they closely resemble." A congenial subject for Freeth's muse was that of the

BIRMINGHAM ALE-TASTERS.

Tune—How happy a State does a Miller possess.

Of all civil officers annually chose,
There's none in the Kingdom are equal to those,
Whose duty requires little more than to rove,
And taste at their pleasure, what Englishmen love.

From Bord'sley to Hockley our Province extends,
I wish we had time to address all our friends;
Of houses all free-cost, to visit, 'tis clear,
The number is more than are days in the year.

We carry no Truncheons our power to shew,
With Government matters have nothing to do;
We drink with the common, yet rank with the best,
And like Aldermen live at a *Low* Bailiff's *Feast*.

Our good Brother Officers strangers must be,
When beating our rounds to the pleasures we see;
From Office of Constable troubles ensue,
But that of a Taster is joy the year through.

For when upon duty, as custom has taught,
We call for a Tankard, 'tis instantly brought,
And how pleasing it is for a Landlord to say,
"You're welcome kind Sir—there is nothing to pay."

We visit the Markets and traverse the Streets,
Our Chief to assist in adjusting the weights;
And wish 'twere the practice in all kind of Sales,
To down with the Steelyards and up with the Scales.

The Butchers may throw out their Marrow-bone spite,
But reason informs us 'tis nothing but right;
For Justice relying on Truth as her guide,
When pictur'd has always the Scales by her side.

Fill a Bumper to Trade, 'tis the Tasters request,
With plenty may Britain, for ever be blest;
Where Discord abounds may true friendship commence,
And Birmingham "flourish a thousand years hence."

We have already alluded to the delight our ancestors took in the healthful sport of bowling; here is a poem by Freeth on this pastime:—

THE BOWLING-GREEN FESTIVAL.

Tune—The General Election.

In life's merry round—with hearts that are sound,
When subject to no innovations;
A Bowling-green feast—is surely the best,
And finest of all recreations;
On Worcestershire plains—where harmony reigns,
If truly inviting the weather,
For mirth all inclined—you'll frequently find,
Good soul's, a round hundred together.

On ven'son that's fine—how glorious to dine,
Will Shakespeare would thieve it, they tell us;
And doubtless the Bard—paid a special regard,
To feasting with hearty good fellows;
Let niggards hum-drum—keep glouting at home,
Themselves and their families starving,
Whilst open and free—the lovers of glee,
The good things of nature are carving.

Pleasure in horse-racing often is found,
None will deny the assertion;
To see the bold Rockingham sweep o'er the ground,
To many gives noble diversion;
But when on the green—a party is seen,
To festive enjoyments invited,
Tho' rubs will ensue—when bowling's in view,
All—all with the sport are delighted.

Come, throw off the Jack—nor of playing be slack,
And mark well its different traces;

*We are indebted for these particulars, to the Notes of "Este" in "The Buildings of Birmingham, Past and Present."

Flee, flee, and *beware—rub, rub*, and *forbear*,
Are bowling-green jocular phrases ;
LEIGH SINTON's the village, where every year,
We meet to be friendly and joyous,
From feasting, my worthies, there's nothing to fear,
So the HEAD's not too much on the BIAS.

Tho' strange it may seem, not to look at the cost,
In WOR'STER 'tis roundly asserted ;
To a poor WIDOW's grief, that a bowling-green must,
To a *Vinegar-yard* be converted :
The DEAN in his mind—tho' worldly inclined,
In a *spiritual* light may review it,
But a VINEGAR SAINT—what language can paint,
'Twould puzzle a BISHOP to do it.

When the heart's blithe and gay—old sages will say,
Time's precious—let no one misuse it,
And as freedom's our boast—I'll offer a TOAST,
And I think not a soul will refuse it ;
"To those hearty cheer—for each other each year,
"Whose friendship grows warmer and warmer,
"And a good roll-about—in a tub of SOUR crout,
"To every notorious INFORMER."

Leaving the Ballads for a few moments, we return to the invitation verses, of which, being so seldom seen, our readers will doubtless be glad to possess a few more examples.

The "hard times" appear to have borne hardly on the poet; in the preface to one of his volumes he defends its publication on the ground of necessity :

"In fact, each day, when children nine,
In perfect health sit down to dine
Think not the whole can be maintain'd,
By what is from the ale-score gained :
Profits on BEER and BALLADS too,
In these hard times will barely do."

Still he bravely kept up heart, notwithstanding the commercial gloom, as appears from the following invitation :

IN these hard times, some people say,
MUM is the order of the day ;
Yet shamefully as things appear,
Before we close this pinching year,
If hearty cheer—which I presume,
Will chace away November's gloom,
Obey the summons, and make free,
Beyond a doubt you'll happy be ;
Come and a cheering glass partake,
My rooms are not yet hung with BLACK.

A good large Loaf for Sixpence will
Please better than P—T's TREASON BILL :
Much may be said, but words are vain,
When sore oppress'd, Men will complain ;
PEACE is my wish—but this I'll say,
In spite of ministerial sway,
No rigid laws ! can conscience bind,
No padlock cramp the liberal mind.

Birmingham, Nov. 25, 1795. J. FREETH.

Again "hard times" are the burden of his song, in the beginning 1796 :

HOWEVER hard the Times may be,
Lovers of Jocularity,
Will some few Moments set apart,
With wholesome Cheer to glad the Heart ;
Then mark the Summons, come away,
And make the most of PANCAKE Day.

The Meadows, as in Spring, look green,
And SHROVE-TIDE without Snow is seen ;
For tho' old Ocean BOREAS shakes,
Stern Winter no Appearance makes ;
The Wind sticks closely to one Point,
The Seasons are got out of Joint ;
The THROSTLE has his Nest erected,
Next Month the CUCKOO is expected,
Whose Voice will doubly glad the Spring,
If Peace comes seated on his Wing.

Birmingham, Feb. 5, 1796. J. FREETH.

In the glorious month of June, in the same year, he seems for a while to have forgotten his troubles :—

GEESE and Green Peas—luxurious Fare,
Always in June in Season are ;
Come to the Board where plenty reigns,
My Vault the best of Ale contains,
And Drinking's seen in high Perfection,
At every GENERAL ELECTION.

Howe'er the busy Scene may close,
But few warm Contests have arose,
And when the hurly-burly's o'er !
What better than we were before ?

From Germany for News we look
And though no Blow has yet been struck,
ITATY's gone, beyond all hope
Unless we Subsidize the Pope.

At CARLTON-HOUSE — old Tricks renewing,
Whatever mischief has been brewing ;
If Tales of Women and of Men,
Full Credit gain, not one in ten,
Would to the P——e shew any mercy,
If CAROLINE had *comb'd* his JERSEY ;
But Discord drown—may Plenty smile,
And Peace make happy BRITAIN's ISLE.

Birmingham, June 8, 1796. J. F.

In 1798 his song is blithe and cheerful, as befitted the "plentiful time" in which he wrote :

'TIS a plentiful time all allow,
And as there is nothing to fear ;

"OLD AND NEW BIRMINGHAM" PORTRAIT GALLERY.—No. 10.

S. WALLIKER,

POSTMASTER.

PHOTOGRAPHED BY WHITLOCK.

BIRMINGHAM: HOUGHTON & CO. SCOTLAND PASSAGE.

Richard Brinsley Sheridan. Dr. Priestley. Sir Cecil Wray. Charles James Fox. J. Horne Tooke. Dr. Theophilus Lindsey.

"A BIRMINGHAM TOAST, JULY 14, 1791."

From the original etching by JAMES GILLRAY: *Drawn on wood by G. H. Bernasconi.*

If at home you've but little to do,
Come away, and enjoy hearty cheer.

To-morrow be what will the text,
I wish—Foreign Trade to increase,
The THANKSGIVING DAY that's kept next,
May be for a general Peace.

One Toast let me offer whilst wetting
Our PIPES in our SNUG LITTLE ISLE,
"All true British Hearts—not forgetting
"Brave NELSON, the LORD of the NILE."

Birmingham, Nov. 28, 1798. J. FREETH.

He closes the eighteenth century with a doleful catalogue of ills, brightened at the end like the silver lining of a black and threatening cloud, with a hopeful anticipation for the coming year:

I MUCH the Word *Scarcity* hate,
And long as I find myself able,
More Cost tho' hard Times must create,
I Plenty will have on my Table.

Against the fond Wishes of some,
Though PEACE for a while is suspended;
Depend on't that BLESSING will come,
Before the next CENTURY's ended.

The greatest of Ills to remove,
Away with that MONSTER—*Starvation;*
For Thousands can *feelingly* prove,
They too much are plagu'd with Taxation.

My Wish correspond will with many,
That soon through the Land may be found
"Twelve Ounces of Bread for one Penny,
"And good Beef at Four-pence per Pound."

Birmingham, Nov. 24, 1800. J. FREETH.

War with the French, on the banks of the Nile, contrasted with the happy prospect of a rich harvest at home, forms his theme at the commencement of the present century:

IN Egypt the French whilst the English are banging,
Of Grain through the Land a fine Prospect we view;
But the Bulk of the People say nothing but hanging,
To lower the Price of Provision will do.

In the Mem'ry of Man, a more beautiful Season,
By all 'twill be granted did never appear;
SPECULATORS are puzzled to give any Reason,
Why all Things should still be enormously dear.

As Changes the World ever ringing will be,
Distress to away with, and Misery drown;
Let the TOAST be—that soon happy Days we may see,
And Peace be at Hand, a rich Harvest to crown.

Birmingham, July 27, 1801. J. FREETH.

We return now once more to his published works. The "sixth edition" of the *Political Songster* was followed, in 1793, by a little pamphlet of eighteen pages, entitled, *A Collection of New Songs on the Present Times, Adapted to Common Tunes*, printed by T. Chapman, in Bull Street, and sold at threepence. The principal subjects of the songs are, the "Canal Fever," Paper Credit, ("Less Paper Credit, and mcre Tower Guineas,") Blue and Orange United, National Convention, Lord Macartney's Embassy to China, and the disturbances on the Continent. Two stanzas of the song on Lord Macartney's Embassy are prophetic as to the opening up of that vast empire to British Commerce, and have a local interest:

"What pleasure here must tradesmen feel,
For toil how 'twill requite 'em,
When calls for goods of brass and steel,
Are brought *ad infinitum;*
With fancy buttons, soft or hard,
Gilt, silvered, or platina,
'Twill take an age to pattern-card
The vast empire of China.

"Should building ten more centuries
Keep rapidly increasing,
The land be blest with tranquil joys
And commerce never ceasing;
The town of Birmingham will reach
The banks of fair Sabrina,
And larger then than Pekin be,
The capital of China."

Most of these songs reappeared in his next publication, *The Annual Political Songster*, a pamphlet of 48 pages, printed by Thomas Pearson, in 1794, which consisted chiefly of old pieces, selected from the several volumes previously published. A copy of this pamphlet in the possession of Mr. John Bragg is inscribed, in the autograph of the old poet himself, "the gift of Poet Freeth to J. Clarke, by the Hands of J. Pool, April 6th, 1794."

In 1803 came a new volume bearing the same leading title as his second published work. *A Touch on the Times; a Collection of New Songs.* This was followed, two years later, by his last pamphlet, the *New Ballads to Old Familiar Tunes*, printed for the author at Knott and Lloyd's office, High Street. This is entirely of a political character, and the songs are new, as described, with one exception, viz.: "Whipcord, or, The Walking Stationers," which, being "appropriate to the present Times," is "now printed," the author tells us, "by particular request."

He died, September 29th, 1808, in the 78th year of his age; his death was recorded in the *Gazette* as follows:—

Oct. 3, 1808.—On Thursday in the 78th year of his age, Mr. John Freeth, of this town, commonly called Poet Freeth, a facetious bard of nature, forty-eight years proprietor of Freeth's Coffee-House, Bell Street, a house much frequented by strangers as well as the inhabitants, where the Poet used every evening to delight a large company with original songs, composed from subjects of a public nature, replete with wit and humour—

"Who when good news is brought to town,
Immediately to work sits down,
And business fairly to go through,
Writes songs, finds tunes, and sings them too."

His morals were unsullied, and his manner unaffected. Formed to enliven the social circle, possessing wit without acrimony, and independence of mind without pride, he was beloved by his friends, courted by strangers, and respected by all. The harmless, yet pointed sallies of his muse, will be remembered with pleasing pain by thousands who admired his talents and revere his virtues.

He was buried in the Old Meeting House burial ground, and on his tombstone are inscribed the following lines:—

"Free and easy through life 'twas his wish to proceed,
Good men he revered, be whatever their creed;
His pride was a sociable evening to spend,
For no man loved better his pipe and his friend."

There are several portraits of the jovial old ballad-maker extant. One appeared as the frontispiece to the *Political Songster*, and from this our engraving on page 159 is taken; another, in oil, is in the Corporation Art Gallery; a third is in the possession of Mr. Timmins; another, according to Dr. Langford, represents him as a comparatively young man; and a fifth is included in Eckstein's group, which is copied on page 207 of this volume.

The name of John Freeth will probably never appear in the roll of English poets; he knew little, if anything, of the "divine afflatus," and his effusions are hardly of that order which the world will not willingly let die;—but neither were those of the poet-laureate of his day,—Henry James Pye,—"a man eminently respectable," says Lord Byron, "in everything but his poetry." Freeth's muse was of the mechanical order, and needed not the "fine frenzy" of the poet; it could work to order, whenever the events of the time required a stirring ballad, fitted to a popular tune, which the people could sing. And perhaps, in the times in which they appeared, these homely songs and ballads, albeit not "fine poetry," may have done more to foster a love of freedom and toleration among Birmingham men, and were productive of more innocent enjoyment, than even infinitely nobler productions, less "understanded of the people."

As illustrative of our local history, and of the manners and customs of the people, Freeth's little volumes will ever be treasured by the Birmingham antiquary, and for his services in the cause of freedom the name of their author will be had in loving remembrance among generations of Birmingham men and women yet unborn.

From the merry circle at the tavern, and its ballad-making host, we turn now to the worthies of trade and commerce. First among these (after those to whom we have devoted special chapters) stands John Taylor. He was born in the early part of the eighteenth century, and commenced life as an operative—a cabinet-maker, we believe. "He possessed," says Hutton, "the singular powers of perceiving things as they really were," and did not long remain in the ranks of the artizan. "To this uncommon genius," continues our historian, "we owe the gilt button, the japanned and gilt snuff-boxes, with the numerous race of enamels. From the same fountain issued the painted snuff-box, at which one servant earned three pounds ten shillings per week, by painting them at a farthing each." His improvements in these various branches of trade procured for him a more than local fame. He became acquainted with Dr. Samuel Johnson during the latter's first sojourn with Edmund Hector, in 1731, and thus secured for himself a niche in that gallery of eighteenth-century worthies, the peerless *Life of Johnson*, by Boswell. "On one occasion," Hutton tells us, a noble visitor, "examining the works, with the master, purchased some of the articles; among others, a toy of eighty guineas value, and, while paying for them, observed, with a smile, 'he plainly saw he could not reside in Birmingham for less than two hundred pounds per day.'" "There was in his inventions," says Mr. W. Hawkes Smith, "a decisive elegance, and an obvious indication of good taste, that ensured a quick sale and large profits." It is said that the value of the weekly production of buttons alone (exclusive of other valuable productions) at his works was not less than £800 a week. He is styled by Hutton "the Shakespear or the Newton of his day;" rising, "from minute beginnings, to shine in the commercial hemisphere, as they in the poetical and philosophical;" and our historian justly estimates that no inconsiderable portion of the riches, extension, and importance of Birmingham in the eighteenth century, are owing to the industry and ingenuity of John Taylor. His share in the establishment of the first Birmingham Bank will be noticed in our chapter on those institutions. He died in 1775, at the comparatively early age of sixty-four, leaving behind him a fortune of not less than £200,000.

Another of the heroes of the workshop was Henry Clay, to whom we owe the invention of papier-mâché. He was in early life an apprentice to John Baskerville, who was at that time engaged in the japanning trade. A species of papier-mâché had been made long previous to Clay's invention, by reducing paper to pulp, and pressing it into dies. Clay's patent is dated November 20, 1772, and sets forth the uses of the new material, in "making high varnished pannels or roofs for coaches, and all sorts of wheel carriages and sedan chairs, pannels for rooms, doors, and cabins of ships, cabinets, book-cases, screens, chimney-pieces, tables, tea-trays, and waiters;" the material being produced "by pasting several papers upon boards or plates of regular thicknesses on each side the same" until the requisite thickness is attained; the edges are then cut off or planed "until the board or plate appears," and the papers taken off such boards or plates are screwed or fastened on boards or plates, and rendered inflexible by drying on a hot stove, while at the same time they are rubbed with or dipped in oil or varnish, which "drenches into them, and secures them from damp."* The inventor claimed for the new material that it could be sawn, planed or turned like wood, and that after being japanned it would be brought up to the highest polish by friction with the human hand.

In 1778 he took out a patent for manufacturing buttons in this material; and afterwards obtained an extension of the patent, on the ground of hi having invented a new method of securing the shanks. He also manufactured buttons of slate on a large scale.

He amassed a princely fortune by his manufactures, and was elevated in the year 1790 to the office of High Sheriff of Warwickshire. Like his master, Baskerville, he seems to have been fond of display, as will be seen from the following extract from the *Gazette* of March 29, 1790:—

"On Monday last Henry Clay, Esq., the High Sheriff of this County, proceeded from his house in New Hall Street in this town, to attend the Judge, Mr. Baron Thompson, during the Assize at Warwick, the commission for which was opened on Tuesday. Few gentlemen have made so brilliant an appearance, or been so numerously attended in the high office which he holds, as Mr. Clay. He was accompanied by the Magistrates, neighbouring Gentry, and principal inhabitants of the town, in their carriages, and on horseback. His javelin men and servants were numerous, and were clothed in rich liveries of white faced with red, silver epauletes, buttons and capes; his postillions were in jackets of scarlet and silver, with black caps and silver tassels. The whole formed a most splendid train of nearly half a mile in length; and we may venture to say, from the concourse from all parts, that the procession was beheld and cheered by upwards of forty thousand spectators. We have been favoured by a friend with the following lines on the day:

The day was delightful and brilliant the train,
  And thousands went tripping away;
'Twas harmony all, and may harmony reign,
  Nor Discord her Banners display.

* Abridgements of Patent Specifications: Paper, Pasteboard and Papier Mâché, p. 3.

In Europe's Grand Toyshop, with lovers of trade,
The scene what great pleasure must crown,
Deserved respect to the Arts has been paid,
And honour it does to the Town.

The Aged and Young—fondly mix'd in the throng,
And gaz'd with anxiety keen;
'Twas a crowded Spring Fair—and like mercantile ware,
All Sorts and all Sizes were seen."

Clay also effected an improvement in the construction of Canal Locks; his elegantly designed address card in Bisset's "Magnificent Directory" has a small vignette illustration of this invention.

Our next and last "worthy" of the present chapter is the well-known botanist and physician, William Withering. He was born at Wellington, Shropshire, March 17, 1741, and was educated by the Rev. Henry Wood, of Ercall; he matriculated at Edinburgh in 1762, paying special attention to the study of anatomy and chemistry. After having attained many distinctions, he finished his academical course in 1766, and shortly afterwards proceeded to Paris. We find him in 1769 at the famous Shakespeare Jubilee at Stratford-on-Avon, being a great lover of the drama. He had, two years previously, settled at Stafford, where he commenced those botanical researches from which he gathered the material for his great work on that subject. On the 12th of September, 1772, he married Helena, daughter of Mr. George Cookes, and remained at Stafford, until the spring of 1775, gaining considerable reputation in his profession, so that, on the death of Dr. Wm. Small in that year, he was invited by Dr. Ash to come to Birmingham, an invitation to which he speedily responded, and settled down in this town, taking possession of the house and practice of Dr. Small. The next year his *Botany* appeared, in two volumes, and he translated Bergman on the Analysis of Waters, giving special analyses of the celebrated local springs. In 1778 he published his *Account of Scarlet Fever and Sore Throat*, then very prevalent in the town. On the completion of the General Hospital, in 1779, (in the establishment of which had laboured earnestly during his residence among us, as had his predecessor Dr. Small,) he was elected one of the first physicians, and was connected with that institution about thirteen years. He passed several months of the year 1784 at Soho House, as the guest of Matthew Boulton, and was admitted a member of the famous Lunar Society, which comprised nearly every eminent scientific man of that period. In 1785 he published his valuable treatise on the Medical Uses of the Foxglove, and it is to this work that we owe the introduction of that powerful medicine into practice; it was greatly valued and praised by the profession, and its discoverer elected a Fellow of the Royal Society. In the April of the following year he went to live at Edgbaston Hall, which Sir Henry Gough had just left; and there prepared the second edition of his *Botany*. He suffered in the riots of 1791,—although a churchman himself—for receiving and sheltering one of the persecuted families; being threatened, forced to leave his house, and to carry away or hide his goods, as well as his most valuable books and specimens. His residence was only saved by the timely arrival of the military, otherwise Edgbaston Hall would have become, like many other houses of which we shall have to speak in the next and succeeding chapters, a mere heap of charred ruins. From that time his health began steadily to decline, and although he tried a brief sojourn in a warmer climate, every year left less of hope, and on the 6th of October 1799, he died, at the age of 58, and was buried at Edgbaston, in a vault beneath the church, on the 10th of the same month. He was borne to the grave by six peasants who had been employed by him at the Hall, and followed and mourned by all the most famous local worthies of that day. There is a very good monument, with a bust of him, in the Church.

We shall have to speak of other local worthies, including our two poets, Lloyd and Collins, in a future chapter, inasmuch as they belong more particularly to the early part of the nineteenth century, rather than to the eighteenth.

INDEX.

Act of Indemnity (The), 356
Adderley (C. B., Esq.), gift of a Park at Saltley, 504; a Library formed, 515
Adderley Park, Opening of, 505
Adullamites (Calvanists), 430
Adulteration Act, 515
Agricultural Show, *see* Royal
Albert, Prince Consort, visits of, to Birmingham, 552, 556, 590; Death of, 563; Inauguration of a Statue to his memory, 563; Engraving of the Statue, 514
Albert Street, 616
Ale Tasters (Birmingham), 213
All Saints,' *see* Churches
Allin's Cabinet of Curiosities, 292
Allotment Gardens, 318
Almshouses (Lench's), 75, 76
Almshouses (Mason's) at Erdington, 604
Almshouses (James's) at Nechells, 604
Amateur Dramatic Society, 599
Amphitheatre at the back of the Stork, in 1802, 327
Analyst (Borough) appointed, 515
Anchor Inn (The) 43
Angel and Hen and Chickens (The), 109
Anti-Corn-Law Meeting, 396
Anti-Corn-Law Agitation, 530, *et seq.*
Apollo Gardens, 313
Apollo Gardens (Bridgman's), 92
Appeaarance of the Town (12th century), 8; (16th century), 17; (1660-1700), 54; (1730-31), 64; (1741-50), 83; (1751), 145; (1760), 119; (1778), 191; (1790), 203; (1800-1803), 308; (1832), 425; (1841-1879), 616
Apprentices provided for out of Jackson's Charity, 79
Arcade (Great-Western), 573
Arcade (Great-Western) View in the, 551
Archæological Section, 592
Aris's Birmingham Gazette, 83, 316
Armitage (Jas.), Obituary Notice of, 480
Arms, Museum of, 520
Art Gallery, 504, 512
Art Gallery, Opening of, 517, 518, 519
Arthur (Prince) Visit of, to Birmingham, 524
Artisans' Dwellings Act adopted, 529
Artists, Society of, 600
Arts (Society of), 389-90
Arts (Academy of), 388; First Exhibition, 389
Ash (Dr.), 125, *et seq.*
Ash (Dr. John), Portrait of, 143
Ash (Dr.) and Ashted, 155
Ashford (Mary), supposed murder of; View of the fatal spot, 370; Narrative of the event, 373; Plan of the scene of her death, 374; Portraits of, 375, 378
Ashted Estate, Breaking-up of the, 206-8
"Assinder's" (old half-timbered house in Digbeth), 312
Aston Almshouses (Erection of), 31
Aston, Bridgman's Apollo Gardens at, 92
Aston Church, 618; Free Library, Board Schools, Churches, &c. of, 618
Aston Church (View of), 33
Aston Furnace, 51, 339; "Hockley Abbey," built from the scoriæ of, 209
Aston Gaol, Bordesley, 186
Aston Hall, Building of, 22; Description of the Hall, 23
Aston Hall (Siege of), 30
Aston Hall, First visit of the Queen to, when Princess Victoria, 417
Aston Hall (view of), 24
Great Staircase, view of,
Long Gallery, view of, 25
Aston Hall and Park, proposal to purchase by the Corporation, 505; extent of the Park in 1856, 505, purchase of the Park and Hall by a limited company, 506; visit of the Queen to open it, 508; fatal accident in the Park, 509; completion of the purchase of the estate by the Corporation, 511; description of the Museum, 512
Aston Hall Fêtes, 560
Aston Lower Grounds, Aquarium and Theatre, 611
Aston Lower Grounds, Views in, 575
Aston Lower Grounds, Royal Horticultural Show at, 524
Aston Park, the old avenue of, in 1832, 426
Aston, Royal Agricultural Show at, 573
Asylum (Borough Lunatic), Erection of, 500
Asylum (Licensed Victuallers'), 550
Athenic Institute, 599
Attwood (T.), 349, 350, 354, 397 *et seq.*, 451, 461, 478
Attwood (T.) Statue of, erected, 561
Attwood Statue, View of, 351
Austin (Mr.), Governor of the Borough Gaol, charged with cruelty, 502 *et seq.*
Avalanche (a novel theatrical) in *Frankenstein*, 432
Ayres (Sir William), 42
Balloon Ascent by Mr. Sadler, 436
Balsall Heath, 619
Balsall Heath Road, construction of, 420
Bank Note Forgeries, 373
Banks, Taylor and Lloyd's, 337-8; Wilkinson, Startin, and Smith's, 338; Galton's, 338; failure of Attwood, Spooner, and Marshall, 567-8; failure of the Penny Bank, 568; stoppage of the Birmingham Banking Co., 569; Modern Banks, 615
Baptists, early meetings held in High Street, 101
—— Bond Street Chapel, 221; attack on, 364
—— Cannon Street Chapel, 102, 173-4; 581
—— Circus Chapel, Bradford Street, 580-1
—— Freeman Street Meeting, 101
—— Graham Street Chapel, 395, 580
—— Wycliffe, Chapel, 581; View of, 562
—— Other chapels, 581
Barber (J. V.) 388
Barnett's (J. F.) " Ancient Mariner," 607
Barnum (P. T.) 612
Baroness Von Beck, *see* Von Beck
Barracks, erection of the, 297
Barrett (F. T.), 518
Barry's (Mr.) Design for the Grammar School, 445
Baskerville (John) 111; Life of, with notices of his productions, 114, *et seq.*, 164
—— Portrait of, 115
—— Will of, 117
Baskerville House, 372, *see also* Riots
Baskerville's types, 317
Baths (Public) 500, 512
Battle of Birmingham (1643) 32
Battle of Birmingham (Reprints of old tracts relating to) 35-6
Beast Market, 55
Bayly (T. H.), Poetical Address on the Re opening of the Theatre Royal, 433
Bear-baiting, 318
Beardsworth's Repository, 401, 403
Beethoven's " Mount of Olives," 607
Bellrope Croft, 76
Bellropes for St Martin's, provided out of Lench's Trust, 76
Bells (Peal of) provided for St. Phillips, 71
Bells (Peals of), increased at St. Martin's and St. Phillip's, 100
Bells, " Madras " School System, 443
Bennett's (D.S.) "Woman of Samaria," 607; "The Lay of St. Cecilia," 607; "St. Peter," 607
Bennett's Hill, site of, in 1800, 309
Berington (Rev. J.), and his works, 317
Bermingham Family: The Manor and its Lords, 3 *et seq*
Bermingham Family: Edward Bermingham in the Tower, 6.1
Bermingham Monuments in St. Martin's described, 10; Engravings of, 5
Betty (W.H.), " The Infant Roscius," 324-25
Billington (Mrs.), 178
Bingley Hall, 556
Bingley House, 420; view of, 274
Bird-in-hand (The), 481
Birmingham in Transition, 44
Birmingham Chronicle, 316
Birmingham Commercial Herald, 316
Birmingham Journal (Warren's), 80
Birmingham Journal, first issued, 418
Birmingham Register, 316
Birmingham (Origin of) a Poem, 122
Birmingham and Edgbaston Proprietary School, 446; View of 448
Birmingham and Midland Institute, 502; History of, 589 *et seq*
Birt (Rev. Isaiah), 363
Bishop Ryder's Church, *see* Churches
Bisset (J.), Memoir of, 289, his Magnificent Directory, 290; and the Minerva Club, 212-213
Black Boy Yard, 313
Blakemore (Thos.), A Centenarian, 481
Blick (F.), Editor of the *Gazette*, 334
Blind (General Institution for the) 603
Blue Coat Charity School, 74; View of, 81
Blunt (Joseph), 213
Bond (Major), 529
Book Club (Birmingham,) Poet Freeth's connection with, 163-169
Booth, the Coiner, arrest of, 379
Booth (Miss), 381
Bordesley Gaol, *see* Aston
Bordesley Hall, *see* Riots, 171
Boswell's (James), visit to Soho
Botanical Gardens established, 422, view in the Gardens, 439
Boulton (Matthew), 113, 121
Boulton (M.), prevents Eginton from obtaining a Pension, 288
—— *See also* Soho
Bourn (Rev. Samuel), Pamphlet by, 102
Bowling Green Festival, 213
Boxing at the Theatre Royal, 380
Bradford Street, 312
Bradford's Plan, Description of, 145, 118; Illustrations from, 157
Bragge (W.), His Gift of the Cervantes Collection to the Town, 519
Brandis (Joseph), 360
Brassworks, 341, 613
Bray (Soloman) 480
Bridgins (George), a centenarian, 175
Bridgman's Gardens, Aston, 92
Bright (J.) first elected for Birmingham, 538; his first speech after election, 540
Bright (J.), Portrait of, 510
Bristol Job Nott (The) 303
British Association, visits of, (in 1839) 481; (in 1849) 556; (in 1865) 568, 596
Broad Street (old name of Dale End) 55
Brewer (Rev. Jehoiada) 363
Brougham, Lord, Presentation of a Service of Plate to, 349
Brougham (Lord) visit of, 476
Brownell's Hole, 186
Bruch's (Max) " Lay of the Bell," 607
Buckle-making, 112
Bull-baiting at Chapel Wake (1798) 305
Bull-baiting, 486
Bull Lane, 119
Bull Ring, 311-12, 426
Bull Ring Riots, Narrative of the, 457-61
Bull Ring, Old View of, 322
Bunn (Alfred) 385, Portrait of, 432
Burn (Rev. E.) 359
Burritt (Elihu) 593
Busby (Mr.) and the Duke of Norfolk, 428
Button-making, 113, 613
Cadbury (R. T.), 429
Cambridge (the Duke of) visit of, 476
Camden (William), his description of the town, 18
Campbell (Thomas), his friendship with Gregory Watt, 285

Canal Navigation, the first Birmingham Canal, 48 *et seq.*
——— First boatload of Coals brought, Nov. 7, 1769, 149
——— from Wednesbury to Birmingham proposed, 193
——— the Worcester, 193
——— Office, view of, 151
Cannon Hill Park, 525
——— Street Meeting House, *see* Baptists
Caradori (Madame), 441
Careless (Mary), 101
Carlyle on Dr. Johnson, 79
Caroline (Trial of) defeated ; Rejoicings in Birmingham, 371
Cartwright (Major), 352, 356, 360
Cartwright's Musical Glasses, 387
Carr's Lane, Accidents in, 66
Castle Inn (The), 108
Catalani (Madame), 326, 431
Cathedral, *see* St. Chad's
Catholic Apostolic Church, 395, 587
——— Association, 425
——— Question, 534 *et seq.*
Catholics (Roman), first Church of (St. Marie Magdalen), in Birmingham, 53 ; Destruction of the Building, 53
——— Temporary Chapel in Water Street, 364
——— Chapel in Shadwell Street, 363
——— Conventual Institutions, 586
——— Oratory (The), 586
——— St. Chad's Cathedral, Building of, 464 ; Description of, 465
——— St. Chad's Cathedral, View of Interior, 458
——— Bishop's House, 469
——— St. Michael's, 586
——— St. Peter's, Broad Street, 221
——— Other Chapels, 587
Cattle Show (the first), 556
Celebration of Peace, 1749, 88
Cemetery (Borough) at Witton, 512
Centenarians, T. Blakemore, 481
——— Geo. Bridgins, 175
——— J. Roberts, 204
Central Literary Association, 599
Chamber of Commerce Established, 372
Chamberlain (J.), 525, 527, 529, 549
——— Portrait of, 506
Charity Collections (Early Local), 50
Charles I. (Letter of), to Sir Thomas Holte, 27 ; Portrait of, 29
Charlotte (Princess), Death of, 371
Chartist Movement, 454; the Convention meets in the Bull Ring, 456; the Bull Ring Riots, 457-61
Cheltenham Amateurs (The), 431
Cherry Orchard (Walker's), 67
Cherubini's *Coronation Service*, 442
Chesshire (J.), 204
Children's Hospital, 603-4
China, "Poet Freeth" on our Trade with, 216
Christ Church, *see* Churches
Christadelphians, 588
Church (Dr. W.), 565 ; his Steam Coach, 450
Church of the Saviour, 587
——— Building Society, for building ten new Churches, 463
——— Extension (Proposed), 169
——— Rate Question, 550, *et seq.*
Churches :—Bishop Ryder's, 462; View of, 455
——— All Saints', 462
——— Christ Church, Building of, 306
——— ——— Medal (showing the original design for the building), 299
——— ——— View of, 295
——— Holy Trinity, 363, 391 ; View of 392
——— Immanuel, 578
——— Oldknow Memorial (Small Heath), 579
——— St. Alban's, 579
——— St. Andrew's, 577
——— St, Anne, 579
——— St. Asaph, 578
——— St Barnabas, 578
——— St. Bartholomew's, building of, 100
——— ——— View of, 106
——— St. Catherine's, 579—80
——— St. Clement's, 578
——— St. Cuthbert s, 579
——— St. David's, 578
——— St. Gabriel's, 579
——— St. George's, 361 ; View of, 359
Churches :—St. George's, Edgbaston, 462
——— St. James's, Ashted, 393
——— ——— View of, 174
——— St. John's, Ladywood, 578
——— St. Jude's, Tonk Street, 577-8
——— St. Lawrence's, 578
——— St. Luke's, 577
——— St. Margaret's, 579
——— St. Matthias's, 578
——— St. Matthew's, 463
——— St. Mark's, 577
——— St. Mary's, Building of, 170
——— ——— View of, 131
——— St Nicholas, 578
——— St. Paul's, Building of, 171 ; Musical Festival in aid of, 171 ; stained window by Eginton in, 202 ; erection of the spire, 393
——— St. Paul's (Old View of) 162
——— St. Peter's, Erection of, 391-3 ; Fire at, 393 ; View of, 394 ; View of the Ruins after the Fire, 399
——— St. Saviour's, Hockley, 579
——— St. Stephen's, 577
——— St. Thomas's, 393
——— *See also under* Deritend, St. Martin's, St. Philip's, and the name of each suburb
Civil War Tracts ; a fourth Tract discovered, 43
Clarendon Hotel, 397
Clay, Henry, Memoir of, 218
Club (Union), *see* Union
Coaches (Early Birmingham), 103, 108
——— (Birmingham) in 1770 and 1820, 345 ; appearance of, 345 ; George Eliot on Coaching Experiences, 346
Coal-fields (South Staffordshire), Yield of, 343
Coates ("Romeo") in Birmingham, 382
——— Portrait of, 382
Cock Inn (The), 108
Cock-fighting, 318
Cock Match, 1747
Cock Street (Digbeth), 54
Coffee House Movement, 615
Coinage (Boulton's) Stanzas on, by Collins, 188
——— (Counterfeit), 187
Coining, 613
Cold Bath, 67
Coleridge (S. T.), Visit of, to Birmingham, 280
Collard (John), 212
Colleges :—Mason's College, 592
——— Oscott College, 586
——— Queen's College, 589
——— View of, 567
——— Spring Hill College, 468, 599
——— Training College, Saltley, 599
Collins, John, Memoirs of, 272 ; his *Scripscrapologia*, 273 ; *Elements of Modern Oratory*, 275 ; Examples of his Poetry, 179, 180, 186, 195, 275-8
——— His Monologue Entertainment, "The Brush," 262 ; Theatrical Anecdotes ; Garrick and the Stage-struck Barber, 262 ; Stage Slips, 263 ; Foote's performance in Hamlet, 263
Colmore (W.), 76
Colmore Row and Ann Street, 616
——— View of, 530
Commerce (Chamber of), established, 372
Commissioners (The), 492 ; Transfer of their Power to the Corporation, 499
Complete Suffrage Association, 531
Concert Booth, *see* Operas
Concert-giving Societies of Birmingham, 611-12
"Conegreve Street," 191
Consort (Prince), *see* Albert
Constitutional Association, 546
Conveyances (Local), 1775, 1819, 348
"Conygree-Stile-Close" (The), 119, 191
Cooke (Rev. Dr.), 428
Cooper (John) and his Love-day Bequest, 108
Cooper's Mills, 66
Cope (C. R.), 431
Copying Press (invention of the), 141
Corbet's Bowling Green, 67
Corn Cheaping (The), 54
——— Exchange, 555
——— Laws, Petition against, 351
Corn Laws, *see* Anti-Corn Law Agitation
Corporation Art Gallery, 517, 518
——— Buildings, 522 ; first stone laid, 525
——— *see also* Council House
——— (History of the), 492 ; Celebration of the Incorporation, 492 ; the Corporate Seal, 492 ; Transfer of the Power of the Commissioners to the Corporation, 499 ; Borough Improvement Rate, 503
Costa (Sir M.), his first appearance here as *Signor* Costa, 442
——— "Eli," 606 ; Presentation to the Composer, 606 ; his "Naaman," 607
Council House, first stone laid, 525
——— Description of, 616-17
——— Views of, 1, 583
Counterfeit Coinage in 1776, 187
County Court, 555
Court Lane (also called Moat Lane), 56
Court of Requests, view of,
——— *see also* Hutton
Cowen's (F.) "Corsair," 607
Cox (D.), Memoir of, 561
Cox (W. Sands), and the Queen's College, 589
——— and the Queen's Hospital, 600
Cross (The Market), Repair of, 59
——— (Chamber over) completed, 59
——— Removal of, 206
——— View of, 55
——— (Old), near Stafford Street, 56
——— *see also* Welsh Cross
Crown House, The Old, 15
Cotton-Spinning, Wyatt's Experiments in, 111
"Creation," (The). first Performance in Birmingham of, 437
Crescent, The, 209
Cruikshank, G,, 371, 373
Curtis, Rev. C., 443
Curzon Hall, 569
Daggett (Wm.), 52
Dale (R. W.), 582
Dawson (G.), 516, 517; his appointment to the pastorate of Graham Street Chapel, 580 ; Erection of the Church of the Saviour, 587 ; the "Von Beck" Case, 557 ; his connection with "our Shakespeare Club," 567 ; his death, 573
———Portrait of, 554
———Statue (The), 573
Deaf and Dumb Institution established, 366
Deafness, Institution for the Relief of, 601.
Debating Societies (Old), 313-316
Debating Society (Birmingham and Edgbaston), 600
DeLys (Dr.), 366
Demonstrations (Open-Air), on Newhall Hill, 353, 356, 357, 450
——— at Brookfields, 545
Denmark (The Prince and Princess of) visit Birmingham, 415
De Quincey (Thomas) at the *Hen and Chickens*, 347
Deritend in 1660-1700, 54 ; in 1760, 120
——— Bridge, 204
——— Bridge Turnpike abolished, 421-22
——— Chapel, erection of, 11 ; appointment of Chaplain, 12
——— View of (in the Fourteenth Century), 9
——— View of (as rebuilt in 1735), 89
Derra (Constant), 557
Devil (The Famous Little), at the Theatre Royal, 166
Diamond presented to the Council, 525
Dickens' (C.) Testimonial to, 558 ; his first Readings, 589, 90 ; appears with other *littérateurs* and artists at the Theatre Royal, 609 ; appears on behalf of the Guild of Literature and Art, 609 ; his later Readings, 612 ; his address before the members of the Midland Institute, 571—2
Digbeth and the Bull Ring, old appearance of, 70 ; appearance of in 1808, 312 ; old view of, 423 ; the old open forges in, 195, 204 ; old half timbered house in, (Assinder's) 199
Dining Hall (Public) opened, 566
Dispensary (General) established, 365
Distress in the Country (1829), 397
Dixon (G). 545, 549
Dobbs, (James, Comedian), 383, 431, 481

Dog Show (The) 569
Dogg Inn (The), 108
Dolphin (The) in Corn Cheaping, 108
Doomsday Survey, references in, to Birmingham, 3
Dramatic Society (Amateur), 599
"Drums and Colours" purchased for the Town, 59
Duddeston Hall, Cockfighting at, 88
——— Manor House, 21
"Duddeston Town," 421
Dufton (W.), 601
Dungeon, *see* Prison
"Dungeon Entry" (The), 110
Ear and Throat Infirmary, 601
Earl, Bookseller, 317
Earthquake felt in Birmingham (1795), 304
East (Rev. Timothy), 363, 468
East India Company's Charter, Proposed Renewal of, 349, 350
Edgbaston, 619
Edgbaston, The "*Masshouse*" at, 53
Edgbaston Old Church, View of, 607
Edinburgh (Duke of), his Visit to the Birmingham Festival, 607
Edmonds (G.) and the Hampden Club, 350, his political career, 353-4, 355, 356, 360, 398, *et seq.*, 455, 480, death of 571
———Portrait of, 354
Edmonds (Rev. Mr.), of Bond Street, 350
Edmund Street (New), 616
Education, 442
Education Act (Elementary), 547
Education Society (Birmingham), 597, *et seq*
——— League (National)
Edward the Sixth's (King) Elementary Schools, 446
Eginton (Francis), Memoir of, 287
——— His process for copying oil paintings, 141
——— Stained Window in St. Paul's Chapel, 172, engraving of, 202,
Egyptian Conduit in the Bull Ring, 310
Election, *see* Members of Parliament
Electro-Plate Trade, 613-14
Elementary Schools, *see* Edward VI.
"Elijah," *see* Mendelssohn
Elizabeth (Queen) at Kenilworth, 19
Eliot (George) on the old Coaching Days, 346
Elkington Challenge Shield, 518, 527
Elliston (R. W.) 323, 380; his *Bohemian* hoax, 385
Encroachments on the Streets, in 1812—332
Erdington Orphanage, 524, 604
——— Orphanage, View of, 591
Etymology of the name of Birmingham, 3 & 4
Exchange (The), 566
Exchange, View of, 511
Executions at Washwood Heath, 190, 330
Exhibition (Industrial) of 1839, 481
——— (Industrial) of 1849, 556
——— (Industrial) of 1865, 568
Explosion in St. Mary's Square, 417
Eye Infirmary, 604
Fairfax (Mrs.), 416
Fairs (Pleasure) abolished, 526
"Farmer Smith's Lands," (now Broad Street) 210
Farror (Joseph), his bequest for cleaning the Nelson Statue, 337
Fearon (Joseph), 213
Feeney, Mr., 419
Fellows (Joseph), arrested for sedition, 331
Fentham's Charity, 76
Ferrers (Family of) Tamworth Castle, 21
"Fine-Slapper" (The), 316
Fire Engine (Old), 59
Fire at the Free Library, 520, 21
——— in Digbeth, 574
Fish Market Hall, 524
Fisher (Samuel) First Puritan Minister in Birmingham, 52
Fleur-de-Lys (The), 108
Footpath to the Five Ways, 209, 10
Ford (Richard) Builder of "Hockley Abbey," 209
Free or Christ Church, *see* Churches
Free Libraries' Act, rejected by Birmingham, 500; its subsequent adoption, 512, 13
——— *see also* Libraries
Free (J.) *see* Freeth
Freeman (E. A.,) 594
Freeth (John), his poetical writings, 210, 217
——— (John) Ode to commemorate the first boat load of coals, by the Canal and the Stratford Jubilee, 150
——— (John) Poetical Invitations to the book club dinners, 163, 168
——— (John) Verses on the conversion of the Moor Street Theatre into a Wesleyan Meeting House, 145
——— Circle, portraits of the, 207
Freeth's Coffee House, 79
Frevill (Sir Baldwin) of Tamworth Castle, 6
Gade's (N.) "Zion" and "The Crusaders, 607
Gaol (Borough), Erection of, 500
——— (Borough), Cruelties at, 502 *et seq.*
Garbett, Rev. J., 463
Gardens, *see* Allotment Gardens
Garibaldi invited to Visit Birmingham, 566
Garland Inn, (The) 108
Gas Illumination, the First, 269
Gas Lighting. Invention of, 269
——— Introduction of, 368
Gas Works purchased by the Corporation, 526
General Hospital, *see* Hospitals
Geology of Birmingham, 495
George III., Rejoicings over the Recovery of, 197
"Gibson's Wharfs," 372-3
Gideon, a New Sacred Drama, 441
Gild Hall, 55; Engraving of old window, 72
Gild of the Holy Cross, 9, 10, 71
——— called "Lench's Trust," 10; *see also* Lench's Trust
Gladstone (W. E.), his early Recollections of Birmingham, 347
Gladstone (W. E.). Visit of, 549
Glass-making, 342, 614
Glass-painting, Revival of, by Eginton, 289
Globe Hotel, 397
Glover, Miss, 468
Glover's (H.), "Tam O'Shanter," 606
"*God in the Mount,*" (Vicars's) Extract from, 43
"Golden Dustmen," 342
Gosta Green, 120
Graham Street Chapel, 394; *see also* Baptists
Grammar School, the original, 55; rebuilding of the School in 1707, 71; View of the building, 73; further notices of, 309, 426; Reform of, 444; rebuilding of, in 1832, 445; description of the new building, 445; View of the new building, 443; further Reform, 593
Grand Junction Railway, 449
Graphic Illustrations of Warwickshire, 388
Gravelly Hill, Levelling of, 425
Great Charles Street, 191
Great Lister Street, construction of, 421
Great Western Arcade, *see* Arcade
Greatorex (Mr.) Conductor at the Festival (1805), 438
Grey (Earl) *see* Political History
Green's (Beau) House, 192
Grimaldi, Anecdote of, 431
Grubb (Edward), 74
Gun Trade (Early), 47, 48; Later notices, 340, 613
Haddock's Mechanic Theatre, 387
Hæser's Oratorio, "The Triumph of Faith," 605
Half-timbered Houses; Weston's in the Bull Ring, 314; Assinder's in Digbeth, 199
Hall ('Billy'), 429
Hamilton (Sir W and Lady) visit Birmingham in 1802, 327
Hammond executed at Washwood Heath, 190
Hampden Club (The), 350, 356
Hamper (William), 313, 352
Handel Commemoration Festival, 177
Handsworth, 618, 19
Handsworth Old Church, View of, 602
Handsworth Volunteer Cavalry, 331
Hanson's Plan of Birmingham, 191
Harborne, 619
Harlow Street (Edmund Street), 191
Haydon's (B. R.), proposed picture of the Gathering of the Unions, 410
Hayes, (E. J.), 524
Health of the Town (Mr Rawlinson s Report on), 495
Heaton's Steam Coach, 450
Hector (Edmund) and Dr. Johnson, 79-80
——— House of, in the Square, View of, 127
Hen and Chickens, High Street, 86; Removal to New Street, 109; 309, 426; Visit of De Quincey to, 347; Old View of, 307
Heslop (T. P.), 603
Highgate Park opened, 528
Highway Robberies committed near Birmingham, 107-8
Hill (A., M.D.), 515
——— (M.D.), 480
——— (Sir Rowland), Statue of, 571
Hiller's (Dr. F.), "Nala and Damayanti," 607
History of Birmingham (Hutton's), 181-5
Hockley Abbey, 208-9; View of, 183
Hodgetts (Mr. William), 315, 419
Hollier's Charity, Land purchased from, to form Highgate Park, 528
Hollins (G.), 550
——— (Peter) 463
——— (W.), 310, 365, 423, 552
Holloway Head, 192
Holte Family, Early History of the, 19; Justice Holte, 21; Sir Thomas Holte, 21; Edward Holte, 21
Holy Trinity Church, *see* Churches
Homœopathic Hospital, 603
Hook (The Very Rev. W. F., D.D.), 428; Portrait of, 427
Hooke (Chr.), Solicitor to Jackson's Charity, 78
Horse Fair (The), 367
Horse-shoe Inn (The), 108
Horticultural Show, *see* Royal
Hospital (Children's), 603-4
——— (Eye), 604
——— (General) Early History of, 125, *et seq*; Recent Notice, 600; Views of, 118, 175
——— (Homœopathic), 603
——— (Lying-In), 601
——— (Orthopædic), 365, 601
——— (Queen's), 600, 601
——— (Women's), 604
Howard (John) visits the old Birmingham Prison, 185; his description of the place, 185; the Aston gaol at Bordesley, 186
"Humble Petition of the Pump in the Bull Ring," 311
Hummel's "Alma Virgo," 606
Humphreys (Mr.), *see* Riots (1791)
Hungary (Sympathy with), 534
Huntingdon's (Lady) Connection, Chapel in Peck Lane, 221; Bartholomew St. Chapel, 221
Hutton (Catherine) 173; her Narrative of the riots (1791), 235, 244, 250; 390, Death of, 553
Hutton (Rev. Hugh), 410
——— (W.) Early Life of, 93; his first visit to Birmingham, 96—98; his second visit to Birmingham, 123; commences business, 132; his courtship and marriage, 133; his experience as a Miller, 133; the Transit of Venus in 1761, 134; Election as Overseer, 134; builds a House at Bennett's Hill, Saltley, 134; chosen a Commissioner of the Court of Requests, 134; his Description of the Court, 134, 135; cases decided by him, 136; the Lamp Act, 136; his action in reference to the Lamp Acts, 157, 162; his *History of Birmingham*, 181; the preface, 183; description of the volume, 183; the second Edition, 183; his juvenile correspondence *(with facsimile)*, 182, 185; 206; his resistance to the proposed rating of small houses, 293; reply to, 294; his writings, 317; his death, 369
——— Portrait of, 167
Huxley (Professor), 572
"I can't find Brummagem," 435
Ick (Dr. W.), 552
Illustrated Midland News, 595
Improvement Acts (Early), see Lamp Acts
Improvement Acts, 367, 515
Improvement Scheme (1875-9), 529; views of Insanitary Buildings, 495, 498, 499
Improvements undertaken by the Commissioners, 420
Incorporation (Charter of) sought for, 478; and obtained, 480

Independents, Carr's Lane Chapel, 102, 303, 363, 552
——— Ebenezer Chapel, 363, 552
——— Francis Road Chapel, 552
——— Highbury Chapel, 552
——— Livery Street Meeting, 363
——— Paradise Street meeting house, 221
——— Wheeler Street Chapel, 468, 618
——— Other Chapels, 584
——— See also, Spring Hill College
Industrial School (St. Philip's), 100
Industry and Genius, or the Origin of Birmingham, 123
Infant Roscius (The), 324-25
"Infant Roscius" at the Royal Hotel, 433
Ingleby, the Conjuror, 387
Inkleys (The), 67, 616
Inns (The old) of Birmingham, 108
Insanitary Buildings in the area of the new Improvement Scheme, 495, 498, 499
Invasion, Local Preparations Against, 333
Irish Coercion Bill, Opposition to, 450
Ironworks in Birmingham, 340
Irving (Washington), 425
Irvingites, see Catholic Apostolic Church
"Israel in Egypt," first performance in Birmingham of, 178
Jabet (G.), 599
Jabet (Mr. R.), 352
Jackson's Charity, 77
Jacobin Club (The) 212
Jaffray's (Jas.) Narrative of the Bull Ring Riots, 459-61
James (Rev. J. A.)—363, 425, 561, 582
——— Bust of, 362
James' Memorial Cottages at Nechells, 605
Jennings (John), 100
Jewellery Trade, 341
Jews' Burial Ground, 210
Jews' Synagogue in the Froggary, 176
——— Synagogue, Severn Street, 221; attacked (1813), 364; rebuilt, 395
——— Synagogue, Singer's Hill, 587
"Job Nott," *see* Nott (Job)
"Joe Lyndon's," *see* Lyndon's
"Joe Shrewd, the Die-Sinker," 359
Johnson, Michael (Father of Samuel Johnson) 46
——— (Samuel), in Birmingham, 79; his translation of Lobo's Abyssinia, 80; his marriage with Mrs. Porter, 82; his later visits to Edmund Hector and Mr. Lloyd, 152
——— Portrait of, 82
Johnstone (Dr. John), Obituary Notice of, 480
Kean (Edmund), 381
Kemble (J.P.), 323
Kendal (Mrs.), 599
Kennedy (Rev. Rann), 425, 557
Kentish (Rev. John), 308
King Edward's Schools, *see* Edward, *and* Grammar School
Kohl (J. G.), his description of Birmingham, 337
Knott (Jonathan), Death of, 369
Knott (Thomas), Death of, 481
Kossuth (L.), 534; Visit of, 558
Kylcuppe's Gift, 77
Kynnersley (T. C. S.), 593
Lady Well, 67
Lady Well Meeting House, Attack on, 364
Lamb (Charles), his friendship with Charles Lloyd, 280
Lamp Act (The), Preliminary Meeting (1765), 156; action postponed, 156; meeting in 1768, 156; Hutton's opposition, 157; illustrations from Bradford's plan, 157; continued opposition, 158; Epigram by Poet Freeth, 160; the Act passed, 160; names of the first Commissioners, 161; provisions of the Act, 161-2; Second Act passed (1773), 162; Hutton's defence of the Scheme, 162
Lamp-posts first erected, 426
Lancasterian School, 443
Land at corner of Worcester Street (Value of), in 1864, 516
Langford (J. A.) 84—5; 567, 593
Law (Rev. J. T.), 600
Leather Hall (The). 110; destruction of, 110
Leather Trade (Early) of Birmingham, 49
Lawley (Sir R.), 389-90
Lee (J.) First Librarian of the Old Library, 198
Lee (Thomas), 422
"Legislatorial Attorney," election of a, 356
Leipsic (Battle of), celebrated, 371
Leland's Description of Birmingham, 17
Lemon (Mark) and the Guild of Literature and Art, 609; Lectures at the Music Hall, 612; impersonation of *Falstaff*, 612
Lench's Trust, 75—6, 424, 623
Leslie's (H.) "Judith," 606
Lewis (W. G.) 360
Liberal Association, Formation of, 542
Libraries (Free) The Act rejected, 500; Grant of Patent Office Publications to the town, 503; the act adopted, 512-13; premises obtained in Constitution Hill, 513; the first Library opened, 514-15; Adderley Park Branch opened, 515; erection of the Central Libraries, 516; the Reference Library, 516; Mr. Dawson's Inaugural Address—516, 17; the Shakespeare Memorial Library. 517; opening of the Library on Sundays, 519; the Cervantes Collection, 519; the Stauton Collection and its Contents, 519; Bust of Mr. Timmins, 520; treasures of the Reference Library, 520; the Fire, 520-521; contents of the various Libraries, 521
——— *see also* Art Gallery, and Museum of Arms
Library (Birmingham New), 430
——— (Birmingham Old), History of, 197-203, 599
——— (Birmingham Old), View of, 191
Licensed Victuallers' Asylum, 552
Lifeboats (The Birmingham), 567
Lines (S.) Memoir of, 565
Literary Association (Central), 599
Literature of Birmingham (Modern), 593-4
Livery Street Amphitheatre, 261
——— Street Meeting House, *see* Union, *and* Unitarians
Lloyd (Charles, the elder), Portrait of, 278; Memoir of, 279—423
——— (Charles, the younger), Memoir of, 279-282
"Locked-up Meeting," (The), 356
Lodge's Portrait Gallery, 488
London and Birmingham Railway, 448, 449
Loudon (J. C.), 422
"Love Days," 108
Lovett (W.), 458
"Lowcells" (The), 426
"Loyal Association," Uniforms of, 291
Loyal and Constitutional Association, 451
Loyal and Patriotic Celebrations, 87 *et seq.*
"Loyal Declaration" (1819), 359
Loyal Volunteers, 333-4
Lozells, 426
Lozells, Independent Chapel at, 468, 618
Luckcock (James), in defence of the "Peterloo" Demonstration, 358
Lunar Society (The), 283
Lunatic Asylum (Borough), erection of, 500
Lying-in Charity first proposed, 365
Lying-in Hospital and the Lying-in Charity, 601
Lyndon's (Joe), 212, 315, 419
Lys, *see* De Lys
M'Cready (The elder), Anecdotes of, 319-20; his management of the Theatre Royal, 320-26
Macready (W. C.), First Appearance of, 326-27
Macfarren's (G. A.) "Leonora," 606; his "Resurrection," 607
Macklin, as *Shylock*, 257
Maddox (Charles), 360
Mail Coaches established, 195
Manor of Birmingham and its Lords, 3
Manorial Rights, purchased by the Commissioners, 419
Mansfield (G. S.), 468
——— (Miss), 468
Manufactures (Local), *see* Trades
Mara (Madame), 179, 180
Market Hall (Interior), View of, 466
——— Hall (New) for Fish, 524
——— (New Hall), 191
——— Description of, 475
Markets (The old), 68
Martin (R.), printer, 317
Martin and Hunter, printers, 317
Mason's (Sir J.) Orphanage, 524, 604
——— View of, 591
——— Science College, 592—3; View of, 570
Mathews (Charles) "at Home," 387
——— (C. E.), 603
Matsell (Philip) execution of, in Snow Hill, 329
Mechanical Exhibitions, 91, 92
Mayors (List of), *Appendix*
Medical Miscellany (The), 316
Meeting House (New), 53
——— (Old) Erection of, 52—3
——— Houses attacked in the Sacheverell Riots, 63; *see also* Riots
Members of Parliament, List of, *appendix*
Mendelssohn's "Lobgesang," 605; first performance of his "Elijah," 605-6; his "Walpurgis Night," etc., 606
Mercer Street, 54
Meredith's Bowling Green, 191
Methodists (Early) in Birmingham, 102-3
——— The First Chapel (Cherry Street), 220; rebuilt, 394; View of, 402.
——— Belmont Row Chapel, 364
——— Bradford Street Chapel, 220
——— St. Martin Street (Islington) Chapel, 394, 585
——— Other Chapels, in the order of their respective circuits, 585
Methodist New Connexion, 515-6
——— (United) Free Churches, 586
——— Primitive, 586
Midland Institute, *see* Birmingham and Midland, &c.
——— Railway, 449
Miles (John), 212
Military Guard House proposed, 68
Miller (Hugh) in Birmingham, 553
Minerva Tavern (The), 212, 315, 419
Minority Clause, Working of, in Birmingham, 546
Missen's (Alex.), Travels (1690), Reference to Birmingham in, 47
Moat (The), and Moat Lane, 56
Moat House for Sale (1768), 147
——— Destruction of, 367-8
——— (View of), 154
Mogridge (G.), 594
Monument (The) at Edgbaston, 129
Moor Street Theatre, 89
Moore (Mr.), 354
——— (Mr. Joseph) and the Birmingham Musical Festivals, 437
Moseley, 619
——— Hall, *see* Riots (1791)
Mudie (Miss), another "infant Roscius," 325
Mullins (J. D.), 516, 518, 519
Munden in Birmingham, 323, 382
Munden's *Reminiscences*, 428
Muntz (G. F.), 398 *et seq.*, 476, 530, 533
——— Caricature Print of, 493
——— (P.H.), 546
Murdoch (William), 268; his invention of gas-lighting, 269
Murdoch's (Wm.) Locomotive Engine, 447
"Murphy Riots" (1867), 569
Murray (James), 212
Mursell (Rev. A.), 581
Museum of Arms, 520
——— at Aston Hall, 512
Music Hall, Broad Street, 610
Musical Festival (The First), 128
——— Festival of 1778, 171
——— Festivals, History of, *first period* (1768—1799), 176-181
——— Festivals (The), *second period* (1802—1829), 437-442
——— Festivals, *third period* (1834—1879), 605 *et seq.*
——— Performances in aid of erection of St. Mary's, 170
"Musical Roscius" (The Young), 326
——— Societies of Birmingham, 611-12
——— Tastes of Birmingham, 553
Nag's Head, Navigation Street, 350
National Education League, 598
National School, Peck Lane, 429
Natural History and Microscopic Society, 600
Nechells, Almshouses at, 605

Nelson (Lord) his visit to Birmingham in 1802, 327
Nelson Statue, 335-6; Farror's bequest for cleaning it, 337
Neukomm's "David," 605; his "Ascension," 605
New Hall, 122; Demolition of, 208
New Hall Estate, 191
New Hall Lane, 64
New Hall Market (The), 191
New Jerusalem Church, *see* Swedenborgians
New Royal Hotel, New Street, 451
New Street, opening of the lower end of, 206; appearance of, in 1800, 308; in 1832, 427—8; old view of the upper end of, 383
Newdigate (Sir Richard) and the Birmingham Gun Trade, 47
Newhall Hill, First Meeting on, 353
Newman (J. H., D.D.) 586
News Room, Bennett's Hill, 430
Newspaper (The first local), 80; *Aris's Birmingham Gazette,* 84-5; later Newspapers, 316, 594.
Noble's Memoirs of the Cromwells, 317
Norfolk (The Duke of), Anecdotes of, 428
Nott (Job), his Addresses and Pamphlets, 303, 317, 359
O'Connor (Feargus), 455
Odd Fellow's Hall, 556
"Off to the Wars," 299
Oil-paintings, reproduction of, by Eginton, 287
Old Meeting House, *see* Unitarians
"Old Nell," a bear kept for baiting, 318
Old Square (The) From the Print by W. Westley, 1732, 85
O'Neil (Miss), 383
Onion Fair, alteration of the date of, 439
Operas performed in the Concert Booth, Moseley Road (1778), 260; burning of the building, 260; performances in aid of the burnt-out players, 260, 261
Orders in Council, Agitation against, 349
Organ (Town Hall), 472, 605
Orphanage, *see Mason's*
Orthopædic Hospital, 365, 601
Osborne (John), 360
Oscott College, 586
Oxford's attempt to shoot the Queen, 482
Palmer's Mail Coaches, 194-5
Pamphlet literature (Local), 317
Papier Mâchié, Invention of, 218
Paradise Row, 191
Paradise Street, 429
Parkes (Bessie Rayner), 312
——— (Joseph), 312, 409, 413
——— Scholefield, and Redfern (Messrs), 419
Parks (Public) Adderley, 504; Calthorpe, 504; Aston, 505, 12; Cannon Hill, 525; Highgate, 528; Summerfield, 528; Small Heath, 528; Burbury Street Recreation Ground, 528
Parliamentary Elections, Results of, *appendix*
Parr (Dr. S.) on the "Church and King" cry, 227 *(note)*
Parsonage House, *see* St. Martin's
Patent granted to the Theatre Royal, 326
Patent Office Publications (Grant of), 503
Patriotic fund, against threatened invasion, 333
Paul (Lewis), 111
Paving (Improvement in), 617
Paving, New experiment in, 525
Peace Celebrations (1802), 332; (1814), 371
Pearce (J.), 567
Pearson and Rollason, printers, 317
Peck Lane, The Old National Schools in, 429
Peel (Sir R.) Visits Birmingham, 415
Peel Statue (The), 558
Pemberton (C. Reece), Notice of, 473; his description of the Town Hall, 473-5; appears at the Theatre Royal, 484; lectures at the Philosophical Institution, 487
Pen-making, 614
Pennington (Mr.), Murder of, 379
Penn's Lane, View in, 370
People's Hall, 550
Periodicals (Local), 316, 594-7, and appendix
"Perrott's Folly," 120
Peterloo Massacre (The), 357
"Petition of Rights" (The), 403
Peyton (R.), 557
Philosophical Institution, 366, 387-8
Pickard's Flour Mill, Attacks on, 300, 302
Pickard's Rotary Crank, 267
Pickpockets at the Festival, 180
Picture Gallery Fund (Public), 519
Piercey, printer, 317
Pin-making, 615
Pitsford and Hammond executed at Washwood Heath, 190
Plague in Birmingham, 45
Players (Strolling) in Temple Street, 56
Plot against Edward Birmingham, 7
Poems by John Collins, 275
Poetical Dream: A Dialogue between the Hospital and New Street Play House, 129
Police Force (Birmingham), 499; appointment of Major Bond, 529
Political History—The East India Company's Charter, 349; the Orders in Council, 349; Success of the Birmingham opposition, 349; foundation of the Hampden Club, 350; opposition to the Corn Laws, 350; disturbance at Mr. Jabet's shop, 352; interposition of the Magistrates, 352; the first meeting on Newhall Hill, 353; the speeches and petitions, 354, 5; the Prince Regent insulted, 355; the Birmingham Loyal Requisition, and the Locked-up Meeting, 355-6; the Newhall Hill Meeting of 1819, 356, 8; the Peterloo Massacre, 358; loyal demonstration, 359-60; prosecution of the Birmingham radicals, 360; Anti-Corn Law Meeting (1826), 396; Beginning of the Reform Agitation, 396; the distress in 1829, 397; Birth of the Political Union, 397; Meeting in Beardsworth's Repository, 398; object of the Union, 398; Mr. Attwood's Declaration, 399; Great Demonstration, 400; the Union Medal, 401; first Annual Meeting, 402; Dinner at the Royal Hotel, 403; the "Petition of Rights," 403; the first Reform Bill, 404; Dissolution of Parliament, 404; great meeting on Newhall Hill, 405; Another defeat, 405; Address to the Country, 406; the third Reform Bill, 406; the Union Hymn, 408; defeat of the bill in the House of Lords, 409; exciting scenes in Birmingham, 409; the middle classes join the Union, 409; another meeting on Newhall Hill, 410; proposed great picture by Haydon, 410; the government counselled to arrest the Union leaders, 410; scene in the barracks, 411; proposed march of the Union to London, 411; the "Solemn Declaration," 412; Lord Grey again in power, 413; the good news brought to Birmingham, 413; a joyous meeting on Newhall Hill, 413; another reverse, 413; the Reform Bill carried at last, 414; the first Parliamentary election for the Borough, 414; Reaction after the Reform Agitation, 450; the Irish Coercion Bill, 450; Demonstration on Newhall Hill, 451; Resuscitation of the Loyal and Constitutional Association, 451; Conservative Activity, 452; the Election of 1835, 452; Conservative Banquet. 452; Reform Banquet, 453; Meeting on Newhall Hill, 453; a "Woman's Political Union," 453; General Election of 1837, 454; Riot in front of the Royal Hotel, 454; the Chartist movement, 454; physical force, 455; Feargus O'Conner in Birmingham, 455, the Chartist National Convention, 456; Removal of the Convention to Birmingham, 456, Turbulent Meetings, 457; the Bull Ring Riots, 457-461; Resignation of Mr. Attwood, 461; Liberal Victory at the Election, 461; The Anti-Corn Law agitation, 530-533; the Chartists, 531; the Complete Suffrage Association, 532; the points of the Charter admitted by the Town Council, 532; death of Mr. J. Scholefield, M.P., 532; Election of a Conservative in his place, 532; General Election (1847), 533; the Birmingham Political Council, 533 the Reform League, 533; Jewish Disabilities Bill, 534; Sympathy with Hungary, 534; the Catholic question, 53-47; Parliamentary Reform, 537, *et seq;* General Election (1852), 537; registration of North Warwickshire, objections raised by the Conservatives, 537; General Election (1857), 537; death of Mr. G. F. Muntz, M.P., 538; Election of Mr. John Bright, 538; Lord John Russell in Birmingham, 539; Reformer's Union formed, 540; letter from Mr. Bright, 540; his first speech after his election, 540; the Reform agitation, 541-545; General Election (1859), 541; Mr. Gladstone's fiscal reforms, 541; the Liberal Association formed, 542; General Election (1865), 542; Conservative banquet at the Exchange, 542; the Reform Demonstration of 1866-7, 544-5; the Reform Bill passed, 545; death of Mr. W. Scholefield, M.P., and return of Mr. G. Dixon, 545-6; the Constitutional Association, 546; General Election (1868), 546; Liberal triumph over the "minority clause," 546; the Elementary Education Act: Election of the first School Board for Birmingham, 547-8; work of the School Board, 548-9; General Election (1874), 549; Resignation of Mr. G. Dixon, M.P., and Election of Mr. J. Chamberlain, 549; visit of Mr. Gladstone, 549
Polytechnic Institution, 599
Portugal House, View of, 192
Post Office arrangements in 1793, 297
——— (the original), 309; Bennett's Hill, 429; New Street (New Royal Hotel premises), 617; Paradise Street, 617
Postgate (Mr. John), 515
Poultney's Shop, the first lighted with gas 369
Power (Mr.) as *Frankenstein,* anecdote of, 432
Pratchet (Richard), death of, 423
"Pratchet's Folly," 310
Prattye (John) and Edward Birmingham, 621
Presbyterians, Broad Street Church, 468, 588; Camp Hill Church, 588. *See also* Early History of the Old and New Meeting Houses
Pressgangs in Birmingham, 188
Prices, comparison of (1759–1800), 343
Priestley (Dr. J.), Earlier life of, 172–4; accepts the pastorate of the Old Meeting, 221; the Theological Controversy at the Old Library, 201; Controversy with the local clergy, 222; wilful misconstruction of his words, 222; sympathy with the French Revolution, 224; Gillray's Caricature, 215, 224; inflammatory handbill, 224; the "Revolutionary Dinner," 235; destruction of his house, 228; address to the people of Birmingham, after the riots, 248; description of his house, by M. Faujas-Saint-Fond, 284; continuation of Memoir 285; his writings, 317. *See also* Riots (1791)
——— Portrait of, 211
——— Statue, 572; view of, 523
Prince of Wales, *see* Wales
Prince of Wales' Theatre, *see* Theatre
Printers (Early) of Birmingham, 114
Priory of St. Thomas the Apostle, 86
Prison (the Old), Peck Lane, 109; view of, 104; description of, by John Howard, 185
Proof House Erected, 372
Proprietary School (Birmingham and Edgbaston), 446; view of, 448
Prospect of Birmingham in 1640, 20
——— (East) of the Town in 1730, by Westley 69
Protestant Dissenting School, 103
Public Offices, Erection of, 334; view of, 330
Publications (Local), 317
Pudding Brook, 313
Pugh, of the "Wheat Sheaf," 427
Pugin (E. W.,) 464-5
Pump, the Humble Petition of the, 311
Quadrant (The), 516

Quakers, 53, 103, 174, 588, 623
Queen's College, 589 ; view of, 567
Queen's Hospital, 600—601
Racidula, Wilhelmina, *alias* "Baroness von Beck," 557
"Radicals," the Reformers first called, 359
Ragg (George), 360
Railway Station (New St), 554—5
——— (Snow Hill), 616
Railways (The Birmingham), 447 ; Murdoch's and Trevithick's Engines, 447 ; an affrighted Toll-keeper, 448 ; the London and Birmingham Railway, 448 ; the Grand Junction Railway, 449 ; opening of the first line in Birmingham, 449 ; completion of the London and Birmingham Line, 449 ; the Midland Railway, 449 ; the South Stafford Railway, 555 ; the Stour Valley Railway, 557
Rating of small houses, 293, 372
——— Proposed increase of the Borough Rate, 526
Rawlinson's (Mr. R.) Report on the Health of Birmingham, 495 *et seq.*
Rea (The) in 1800, 313
Recreation Ground (Proposed), 486, *see also* Parks
Redd Lyon (The), in Digbeth, 108
Redfern (W.), 480
Reference Library, 516 *et seq.*
Reformation, Tercentenary Celebration, 469
Reform Agitation, *see* Political History
Reform Demonstration on Newhall Hill, view of, 407
Reformer's Medal, Engraving of the, 419
Regent (The Prince) insulted, 355, 370
Registration Society (Liberal), 537
Revolution of 1688, Centenary of, celebrated, 196
Rifle Corps, *see* Volunteer
Rigby (V.), first appearance of, at the Festival, 607
Riland (Rev. John), 51, 443
Riot (Sacheverell) in 1715 ; Riots of 1791, what led to the, 220 ; Riots of 1791 ; The "Revolutionary Dinner," 226 ; Spies bring out false reports of the proceedings, 227 ; "Church and King," 227 ; The riot commenced, 227 ; Attack on the Meeting Houses, 228 ; Dr. Priestley's house, 228 ; *The second day*, 232 ; Baskerville House sacked and burnt, 232 ; Attack on Bordesley Hall, 233 ; Hutton's Shop, High Street, 233 ; *The third day*, 235 ; Attack on Hutton's house at Bennett's Hill, 235 ; Catherine Hutton's narrative, 235 ; Mr. Humphreys' house at Sparkbrook, 238 ; Mr. Russell's, Showell Green, 238 ; Miss Russell's narrative, 238 ; Moseley Hall, 243 ; *The fourth day*, 244 ; Miss Hutton's narrative, *continued*, 244 ; Address of the Magistrates to the rioters, 245 ; End of the Riots, 246 ; Conclusion of Miss Russell's narrative, 247 ; Dr. Priestley's Address, 248 ; *Aris's Gazette* and the riots, 249 ; Conclusion of Miss Hutton's narrative, 250 ; Trials of the Rioters, 253 ; Claims of the Sufferers, 253 ; The Union Meeting House, 256 ; Rebuilding of the Meeting Houses, 256
——— "The Little Riot" (1793), 298 ; The Scarcity Riots, 300, 302
——— in the market-place and at Edgbaston, in 1810, 331
——— (Religious) in 1813, 364
——— in Moor Street (1816), 352
——— in front of the Royal Hotel (1837), 454
——— in the Bull Ring (1839), 457-61
——— at Snow Hill Flour Mills (1847), 556
——— "Murphy Riots" (1867), 569
Robberies from Carriages in Birmingham, 329
——— from the Coaches, 348
Roberts (John) A Centenarian, 204
Robin Hood Society (The), 314-315
Robinson (The Right Hon.) visits Birmingham, 15
Rodway (A.), 512
Roebuck Inn, Cox Street, 350
Rogers (John) Biography of, 12
——— Portrait of, 13
Roscius (The Infant), 324, 325 ; the "Young Musical Roscius," 326
Rossini's "Moses in Egypt," 607
Royal Agricultural Show at Aston, 573
——— Horticultural Show, 524
Royal Mail (The first) from Birmingham to to London, 345
Royal Touch, 59
Rupert (Prince) Portrait of, 37
Rupert's (Prince) Burning Love to Birmingham, 35
Russell (Lord John) in Birmingham, 589
——— (Lord John) Pen and Ink portrait of, 418
——— (Joseph), 360
——— (Miss) Narrative of the Riots (1791), 238, 247
Russell (Mr.) *see* Riots (1791)
Ryan's Amphitheatre, 437
Ryan's Circus on the Moat Grounds, 387
Ryder (Bishop) 462-3
Ryland (A.) 557
Ryland (Miss) 525
Ryland (Mr.) destruction of his Residence, (Baskerville House) in the riots of 1791, 232
Sacheverell (Dr.) visits Birmingham, 63
St. Chad's Cathedral, Interior of, 458
——— *see also* Catholics
St. Clair (G.), 587
St. David's Society, establishment of the, 423
St. Martin's Church, Early History and Description of, 8-10 ; during the Commonwealth, 51 ; first "restoration" of, 56 ; Traffic in Sittings in, 57 *et seq.* ; Utensils and Vessels belonging to, 58 ; new organ for, 70 ; further "improvements" in, 70, 120, 204-5 ; Restoration of, 574-6
——— View of, after its encasement with brick, 45
——— as restored (exterior), 543
——— ——— (interior), 547
——— Houses round, 70, removal of, 311, 332
St. Martin's Parsonage, 56, 313 ; View of, 338
——— District around (Section of Hanson's Map), 319
St. Mary's Schools, 446
——— Square, Explosion in, 417
St. Philip's Church, 59
——— (Restoration of), 577
——— (Interior) View of, 65
——— (North prospect of), 61
——— (Modern View of), 346
——— Illuminated to celebrate the marriage of the Prince of Wales, 539
——— Churchyard, attempt to close, 493-4
St. Thomas (Priory of), 86
Salt (T. C.), 560
Saltley, 619
——— Training College, 599
Salutation Inn, Snow Hill, 121
Saracen's Head (The), 108
——— Snow Hill, 350
Savings Bank (the first), 372
Scholefield (J.), 530, 532
——— (W.), 533 ; death of, 545
School Accommodation in 1827, 443
School Board (The), 547—9
Schools (Elementary), 597 *et seq.*
Science College, *see* Mason
Scott Trust, 175
——— (Sir F. E.), 565—6
Scripscrapologia, see Collins
Second (Mrs.), Impromptu on, by Collins, 179, 180
Sewage Difficulty, 526
Shakespeare Jubilee at Stratford, 142—4
——— Edition of, printed with Baskerville's type, 144
——— Jubilee Medal, 144
——— Memorial Library, 517
——— Tercentenary, 566
Shambles (The), 54
Ship Inn (The Old), 43 ; View of, 41
Shoe-strings, a protest against, 180
Siddons (Mrs.), 322, 323, 324 ; farewell visit of, 325
Simcox Family, 621
Simpson's (D.) Sacred Literature
Sketchley (James), 213
Skey (R. S.), 333
Slater (Samuel) and the Rectory of St. Martin's, 51
Slave Trade, Agitation against, 476
Small Heath, 619
Smart's (H.) "Bride of Dunkerron," 607
Smith (Albert,) 612
Smithfield Market, Construction of, 367
——— Proposed Enlargement of, 420
Smithy or Open Forge in Digbeth, 195
Snow Hill, Execution of Matsell in, 329
Social Science Association, 596
"Society for Free Debate," 315
"Soft-Tommy," 112
Soho, Story of—Boulton's Manufactory at Snow Hill, 138 ; his character, 138 ; he removes to Soho, 138 ; joined by Mr, Fothergill, 138 ; Assay Office, 139 ; Savery's Steam Engine, 139 ; Watt's Improvement, 139 ; Soho in 1774, 140 ; the Soho Mint, 140 ; Eginton's Process for Copying Oil Paintings, 141 ; the Copying Press, 141 ; Extension of Watt's Patent to 1800, 265 ; the first engine made at Soho, 265 ; erection of the engine at Wilkinson's Ironworks, Brosely, 265—6 ; Services rendered to Boulton and Watt by John Wilkinson, 266 ; difficulties with workmen, 267 ; first interview of Boulton with William Murdoch, 268 ; Murdoch's Locomotive, 268 ; the Invention of Gas-lighting, 269 ; Bisset's Description of Soho, 270 ; the Soho Foundry, 271 ; Death of the Founders of Soho, 271—2
Soho Manufactory, View of, 135
——— Illumination at, 197
Somerville's (Alex) Description of the Scene in the Birmingham Barracks, May 13, 1832, 411
Sothern (E. A.), 599
Soult (Marshal), Visit of, 476
Saint Saens (M.), "The Lyre and the Harp," 607
Salford Bridge, 426
Small Heath Park, 528—9
South Stafford Railway, 555
Spanish Armada (The), 18
Sparkbrook, 619
Spooner (R.), 349, 372 ; elected M.P. for Birmingham, 532
Spring Hill College, 468, 584
Standbridge (T.), 523
Starr Inn (The), 108
Stapenhill (Mrs.) shot by her husband, 551
Steam Coaches—Dr. Church's, 450 ; Messrs. Heaton's, 450
Sword-making, 111-112, 341
Statues ; Nelson, 335-7
Staunton Collection (The) 43, 519-20
Steam Canal Boat, 424
Steam engine, the first local, 339
——— *see also* Soho
Steam Power, use of, in Birmingham, 496
Stephens (Kitty), 320, 440
Steel Houses (Kettle's), 66
Steel Manufacture, 340
Steel Pen Trade, 614
Steel Toy Making, 113
Stimpson (J.), 550
Stipendiary Magistrate appointed, 503
Stour Valley Railway, 557
Stratford House, 54, 621 ; Views of, 49, 622
Street Acts, *see* Lamp Acts
——— Acts Amendment Act, 1801, passed, 331
——— Improvements, 1801, 332
——— Condition of the, in 1806, 348
Sturge (Joseph) opposition of, to the Musical Festivals, 441 ; visits the West Indies, 477 ; death of, 560
——— Statue, 564
——— Statue, View of, 479
Suburbs, 618 *et seq*
Suett (Richard), the Actor, 264, 323
Sullivan's (A.) "Kenilworth," 607 ; "The Light of the World," 607
Summerfield Park, 528
Sunday Schools, 442
Surveyor (A) of the old school, 497
Swan Hotel (The) 108, 426
Swan (Thomas), 441

Swedenborgians, 221, 395, 587
Swinney (W.), printer, 317; death of, 369
Talbot Inn (The), 108
Tavern Bill (Curious Old Birmingham), 168
Taylor (John, manufacturer), Memoir of, 218
——— (Mr. Joseph), 396
Temperance Society, the first, 395
Temple Row, 59
——————— West, Old View of, 343
Theatre (The)—Strolling Players pitch their tents near Temple Street, 56
——— (New Street), Earliest Notice of, 90; Congreve's "Mourning Bride" performed, 90; "The Siege of Damascus," 90; "Hamlet" and "Othello,' 91, 141; erection of the first Theatre, on the site of the present house, 144; attempt to obtain a license for, 257; Speech by Mr. Burke thereon, 258; Benefits in the Eighteenth Century, 260—61; a Playhouse Riot, 261; Burning of the Theatre, 264; Suett's wig, 264; the Theatre rebuilt, 318; Macready appointed manager, 319; Anecdotes of Macready, 319—20; "No Music," 320; Miss Kitty Stephens, 320; description of the new theatre, 321; Notes from the Playbills (1796—1810), 322—25; a Patent granted, 325—6
——— Royal—A curious Playbill, 380; reappearance of Macready, 380; R. W. Elliston's management, 380; his address, 380—81; his first appearance, 381; Miss Booth, 381; Edmund Kean's first appearance here, 381; Charles Mathews, 382; Munden, 382; "Romeo Coates," 382; Dobb's Reaping Machine, 383; Miss O'Neil, 383; Grimaldi, 384; Anecdotes of Elliston, 384-5; the *Bohemian* hoax, 385; Alfred Bunn, 385; burning of the Theatre, 385-6; Reopening of the Theatre, 387; Madame Catalani, 431; The *Theatrical Looker-on*, 431; Edmund Kean, Macready, etc., 431; Colonel Berkeley and the Cheltenham Amateurs, 431; Anecdote of Grimaldi, 431; Mr. Power in *Frankenstein*: a novel avalanche, 432; a change of management: Mr. Warde, 433; Opening Address by T. Haynes Bayly, 433; another "Infant Roscius," 434; "real water," 434; Ducrow, 434; Macready's visit to America, 434; Madame Vestris, 435; "I can't find Brummagem," 435; Paganini, 482; Sheridan Knowles, 482; Charles Mathews, 482; alteration of prices, 483; West's Equestrian Troupe, 484; Charles Reece Pemberton, 484; a combination of "Stars," 484; Mr. Armistead's failure as a manager, 484; Mr. Clarke's management, 484; reduction of prices, 485; the Gnome Fly, Hervio Nano, 485; a theatrical riot, 485; "Lady of Lyons" first performed here, 485; "Nicholas Nickleby," 485; Ducrow, 486; Taglioni, 486; Mr. Simpson's management, 486; Macready, 608; first appearance of Sims Reeves in Birmingham, 608; Hackett as Falstaff, 609; Charles Dickens and the Amateurs, 609; the Guild of Literature and Art, 609; Ristori in Birmingham, 610; J. L. Toole, 610
——————— View of (from an old print), 123
——————— (Interior), View of, 487
——— King Street, 141; "Comus" and "As You Like It" performed, 142; "King John," 142; Enlargement of the Theatre, 144, 251
——— "The Gentleman's Private Theatre," Livery Street, 261; performance of Collins's "Brush" thereat, 262
——— Moor Street, 89, 141
——————— (The Amphitheatre), 610
——— Smallbrook Street, 141
——— (Minor) in Worcester Street, 386
Theatre "Tonks's Colosseum," Bingley Hall, 610; G. V. Brooke, 610
——— (Prince of Wales's), 610; Mr. H. J. Byron's first local appearance, 610; Mr. Sothern, 611; Mr. J. Rodgers's Management, 611; Shakespearian and other revivals, 611
——— (Holte), Aston, 611
Theatrical Looker-on (The), 431
Thomason's (Sir E.) Show-rooms in Church Street, 415
Thornton (Abraham), Trial of, 373
——————— Portrait of, 375
To-Morrow (poem by John Collins), 275
Tony Lumpkin's Ramble through Birmingham 323
Toulmin (Joshua, D.D.), 308
Town Books (The Old), Curious extracts from, 50, 57
Town Hall, proposed erection of, 421
——— Barry's Original Designs for, 469; Messrs. Hansom and Welch's Design, 470; Description of the Building, 470; the Organ, 472; Charles Reece Pemberton's Description of the Building, 473
——— Old View of, from Hill Street, 471
——————— from Paradise Street, 435
——— Interior View of, 474
Toy (Samuel), 212
Trades (Local), 47, 111, 337, 496, 531, 613 *et seq.*
——— *See also* Soho
Tramways, G. F. Train's proposal to lay down, 515
——— laid down, 524
Trees (planting of) in the streets, 573
Trevithick's Locomotive Engine, amusing Story respecting, 447
"True Relation (A) of a Great and Cruell Battell fought neer Brumegum," 43
"True Relation of Inhuman Cruelties," 39
Tussaud (Madame), 387, 436
"Twelve Apostles" (The), 212
Twiford (Robert), Murder of, in Snow Hill, 329
Tyndall (H. W.) and the Von Beck Case, 557
Union Club House, View of, 535
Unitarians—New Meeting House (Digbeth), 53; New Meeting House, Moor Street, erected, 101; View of, 93; Old Meeting House, 52—3; View of, 52; Destruction of the Old and New Meeting Houses, 228; Opening of the Union Meeting House, Livery Street, 256; Rebuilding of the Meeting Houses, 256; Union Meeting House, Livery Street, opened, 256; Old and New Meeting Houses, 308; Church of the Messiah, 580; View of, 559; Fazeley Street Chapel, 580; Lawrence Street Chapel, 580; Newhall Hill Chapel 468, 580; Hurst Street Chapel, 580
Vaux (Jeremia), 212
Vauxhall, 129, 318, 379, 488
Victoria, Accession and Coronation of, celebrated, 477—8
——— (Queen), Marriage of, celebrated, 481
——— (Queen), first visit of, to Birmingham, when Princess Victoria, 416
——— Visit of, to open Aston Hall, 508
Vince (Rev. C.), 580
Vittoria (Battle of), celebrated, 370
Vocalists at the Later Musical Festivals, 608
Volunteer Cavalry (Handsworth), 331
——— Challenge Shield, engraving of, 527
——— Enrolment of, in 1795, 300, 306
——— *see also* "Loyal Association"
——— Loyal Birmingham, 333—4
——— Rouse (The) by Freeth, 189
——— Rifle Corps, formation of, 561
Von Beck (Baroness) 559
"Wager of Battle," 379
"Waggon and Horses," Handsworth, 267
Wagner's (R.) Holy Supper 607,
Wales (Prince of) celebration of the Marriage of, 564—5
Wales (Prince of) visits Birmingham, 527
Walker's Birmingham newspaper, 84
Walsh (J. W.) 560
Wards, Division of the Borough into, 492; new division, 525
Warneford (Rev. S. W.) 600, 601
Warren (Samuel) Publisher of Johnson's translation of Soho, 80; his *Birmingham Journal*, 80
Warwickshire Regiment raised for the defence of the country (1778), 188
Washwood Heath, Double Execution at, 190
——————— execution of eight men at, 330
Waterworks, purchased by the Corporation, 526
Watt, Gregory, Memoir of, 285
Watt (J.) Character of, 139; his connection with Boulton, 139 *et seq.*
——————— Chantrey's Statue of, 272
——— *see also* Soho
——— Statue, 571; View of, 522
Watt's House, Harper's Hill (View of), 139
Watt, (James, *the younger*) 417, 555
Waxworks, 91
Wealth (Local) 339
Weaman (Mary) 170
Webster (Richard) 212
Wedgwood (Josiah) purchases some of Eginton's reproductions of oil paintings, 288
Well Street (Digbeth), 54
Wellington (The Duke of) visits Birmingham, 415
Welsh Cross, taken down, 309
Welsh Cross (View of the), 58
Wesley (John) in Birmingham, 102, 174, 175, 220
——— (John), Portrait of, 101
Westley's East prospect of Birmingham in 1730-69
Weston (Thomas,) his early career, 494
Wheat Sheaf Inn, New Street, 427
White (Councillor), 529
White Hart (The), 108
Whitehall or Steelhouse Lane, 66
Whitworth (Chas.), 320
Wickins's (Sam.), 314
Wilkinson (John), services rendered to Boulton and Watt by, 266
Wilkes (John, a member of the Jacobin Club), 212
William (Prince) of Gloucester, visit of, to Birmingham, 328
Williams (Rev. Edward), 308
Williams (Edward Lloyd), 423
Wilson (Mr.) at the Theatre Royal, 380
Wilson, Starkey and Co., explosion on their premises, 417
Withering (Dr. William), memoir of, 219
Windmill, Holloway Head, View of, 187
Witton Cemetery, 512
Wollaston (W.), 72
Wolseley (Sir C.) elected "Legislatorial Attorney," 356
Women's Hospital, 604
Wood paving, 525
Wooler (T. J.), 356, 360
Workhouse (The old), 75, 426; View of, 77
——— (The new), erection of, 500
Working Men's Liberal-Conservative Association, 546
Wright (Daniel), death of, 481 *note.*
Wyatt's (John) Experiments in Cotton Spinning, 111
Wycliffe (John) and his new Doctrine, 11
Yainciez (Mr. and Mrs.), 431
Yates (Mr.) of the Theatre Royal, quarrels with the Festival Committee, 178
Yorke (Grantham M.), 416

PRICE 6d.

OLD AND NEW BIRMINGHAM.

AN ILLUSTRATED HISTORY OF THE TOWN AND ITS PEOPLE.

PRINTED AND PUBLISHED BY

HOUGHTON & HAMMOND, SCOTLAND PASSAGE,
BIRMINGHAM.

ROBOTHAM AND HORTON, WINE AND SPIRIT MERCHANTS,
LOWER TEMPLE ST.

BRITISH WORKMAN'S ASSURANCE COMPANY, LIMITED.

CHIEF OFFICES: BROAD STREET CORNER, BIRMINGHAM.

ESTABLISHED 1866.

The surpassing progress, and great acnievements of this Office are the best proofs of the public confidence, and the high esteem placed upon the Company's liberal dealings; especially its promptitude in settling Claims, and its peculiar feature of Surrender Value. Through the Agency of the BRITISH WORKMAN'S ASSURANCE COMPANY, the great Principles and Advantages of Life Assurance become universal in their application. THIS COMPANY EMBRACES ALL CLASSES, AND ALL AGES OF HEALTHY PEOPLE

FROM BIRTH TO 85 YEARS OF AGE.

OVER 80,000 PROPOSALS FOR ASSURANCE WERE RECEIVED IN THE PAST YEAR.

ANY PREMIUM IS NOW TAKEN, FROM 1D. PER WEEK TO £100 PER YEAR.

The Sums Assured increase with the age of the Policy, although the Premium paid must only be 1d. per Week. A person who has paid in 12 years, is justly and fairly entitled to more than a per on that has paid in 12 months, only.

THE COMPANY WILL RETURN ONE-FOURTH OF THE PREMIUMS PAID (in the Life Department) to any persons wishing to discontinue their payments after the first three years. Thus the Company not only engages to pay the Sum Assured at Death, or in Lifetime (as agreed upon at the date of entry); but Five Shillings out of every Pound paid in can be withdrawn at will, as stated upon the Policy,

£1,118 WERE RETURNED TO THE WORKING CLASSES

IN THE INDUSTRIAL DEPARTMENT, IN THE PAST YEAR.

Thousands can bear witness, to the Company's prompt and liberal manner, in settling just and proper Claims.

NEARLY £75,000 HAVE ALREADY BEEN PAID.

Claims of £50 and under are paid at once; upon satisfactory proof.

THE PRESENT ANNUAL INCOME EXCEEDS £60,000.

Send for Prospectus. The Table Payable at Death or a given Age should have particular attention.

Mr. WOOLHOUSE, the Actuary, reports that the Funds in hand are in excess of the amount really required to meet the liabilities of the Company.

HENRY PORT, F.S.A., Managing Director.
D. A. BECKETT, Secretary.

My 75s. English Silver Levers are Surpassed by none, Guaranteed for 2 Years, and will wear 50 Years. W. BROWN, 46, PARADE, BIRMINGHAM.

DR. ROOKE'S MEDICINES

THE

ORIENTAL PILLS AND SOLAR ELIXIR.

THESE WELL-KNOWN FAMILY MEDICINES have had a continually increasing Sale throughout the United Kingdom and the British Colonies since their introduction in 1836, and are especially noted for their STRENGTHENING and RESTORATIVE Properties. Hence their invariable success in the RELIEF and CURE of

INDIGESTION,
LIVER COMPLAINTS,
ASTHMA,
BRONCHITIS,
Pulmonary CONSUMPTION
RHEUMATISM,
GOUT,
SCROFULA,
General DEBILITY,

And all Diseases of the NERVOUS SYSTEM.

Whether arising from a Sedentary mode of life, unhealthy occupation, insalubrious climate, or other cause whatsoever.

THE ORIENTAL PILLS AND SOLAR ELIXIR

Are prepared only by **CHARLES ROOKE, M.D., SCARBOROUGH.** The **Pills** are sold in Boxes at **1s. 1½d.** and **4s. 6d.** each; the **ELIXIR** in Bottles at **4s. 6d.** and **11s.** each, duty included. Around each Box and Bottle are wrapped Directions for the guidance of Patients in all Diseases.

DR. ROOKE'S ANTI-LANCET.

All who wish to preserve health, and thus prolong life, should read

DR. ROOKE'S "ANTI-LANCET," or "HANDY GUIDE TO DOMESTIC MEDICINE,"

Which contains 172 pages, and is replete with anecdotes, sketches, biographical matter, portraits of eminent men, &c. It may be obtained GRATIS of any Chemist, or POST FREE from DR. ROOKE, Scarborough, England.

CONCERNING THIS BOOK, THE LATE EMINENT AUTHOR, SHERIDAN KNOWLES, OBSERVED:

"It will be an incalculable boon to every person who can read & think."

CROSBY'S

BALSAMIC

COUGH ELIXIR

Is the leading medicine of the day, and is specially recommended by several eminent Physicians. It has been used with the most signal success for Asthma, Bronchitis, Consumption, Coughs, Influenza, Consumptive Night Sweats, Spitting of Blood Shortness of Breath, &c.; and is a most valuable adjunct to Dr. Rooke's Medicines in all Affections of the Throat and Chest.

Crosby's Balsamic Cough Elixir is sold everywhere, by all Chemists and Medicine Vendors, at the following prices:— **1s. 9d., 4s. 6d.,** and **11s.** each Bottle. A saving of THREE SHILLINGS is effected by purchasing the large bottles. Full directions with each Bottle.

NOTICE TO INVALIDS.

A NEW EDITION of the **TREATISE** on **"DISEASES of the LUNGS and AIR-VESSELS,"** containing full and plain instructions for the relief and cure of those diseases, has just been printed, and may be had GRATIS from any Chemist, or *post free* from JAMES M. CROSBY, Chemist, Scarborough.

PRICE 6d.

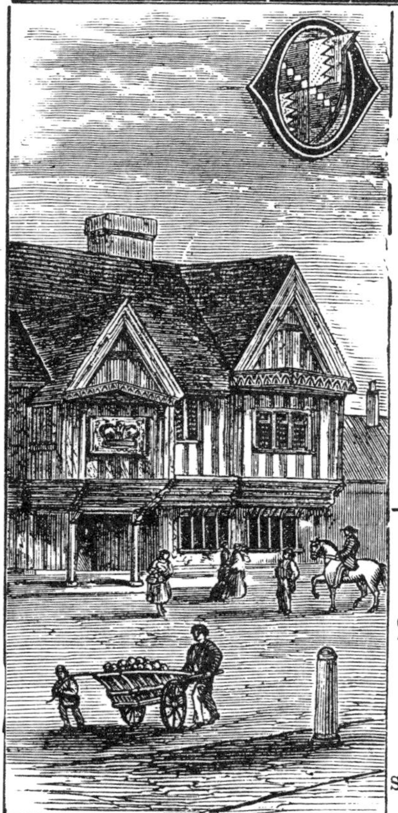

OLD AND NEW BIRMINGHAM.

AN ILLUSTRATED HISTORY OF THE TOWN AND ITS PEOPLE.

PRINTED AND PUBLISHED BY

HOUGHTON & HAMMOND, SCOTLAND PASSAGE,
BIRMINGHAM.

DR. ROOKE'S MEDICINES

THE

ORIENTAL PILLS AND SOLAR ELIXIR.

THESE WELL-KNOWN FAMILY MEDICINES have had a continually increasing Sale throughout the United Kingdom and the British Colonies since their introduction in 1836, and are especially noted for their STRENGTHENING and RESTORATIVE Properties. Hence their invariable success in the RELIEF and CURE of

INDIGESTION,
LIVER COMPLAINTS,
ASTHMA,
BRONCHITIS,
Pulmonary CONSUMPTION
RHEUMATISM,
GOUT,
SCROFULA,
General DEBILITY,

And all Diseases of the NERVOUS SYSTEM.

Whether arising from a Sedentary mode of life, unhealthy occupation, insalubrious climate, or other cause whatsoever.

THE ORIENTAL PILLS AND SOLAR ELIXIR

Are prepared only by **CHARLES ROOKE, M.D., SCARBOROUGH.** The **Pills** are sold in Boxes at **1s. 1½d.** and **4s. 6d.** each; the **ELIXIR** in Bottles at **4s. 6d.** and **11s.** each, duty included. Around each Box and Bottle are wrapped Directions for the guidance of Patients in all Diseases.

DR. ROOKE'S ANTI-LANCET.

All who wish to preserve health, and thus prolong life, should read

DR. ROOKE'S "ANTI-LANCET," or "HANDY GUIDE TO DOMESTIC MEDICINE,"

Which contains 172 pages, and is replete with anecdotes, sketches, biographical matter, portraits of eminent men, &c. It may be obtained GRATIS of any Chemist, or POST FREE from DR. ROOKE, Scarborough, England.

CONCERNING THIS BOOK, THE LATE EMINENT AUTHOR, SHERIDAN KNOWLES, OBSERVED:

'It will be an incalculable boon to every person who can read & think.'

CROSBY'S

BALSAMIC

COUGH ELIXIR

Is the leading medicine of the day, and is specially recommended by several eminent Physicians. It has been used with the most signal success for Asthma, Bronchitis, Consumption, Coughs, Influenza, Consumptive Night Sweats, Spitting of Blood, Shortness of Breath, &c.; and is a most valuable adjunct to Dr. Rooke's Medicines in all Affections of the Throat and Chest.

Crosby's Balsamic Cough Elixir is sold everywhere, by all Chemists and Medicine Vendors, at the following prices:— **1s. 9d.**, **4s. 6d.**, and **11s.** each Bottle. A saving of THREE SHILLINGS is affected by purchasing the large bottles. Full directions with each Bottle.

NOTICE TO INVALIDS.

A NEW EDITION of the TREATISE on "DISEASES of the LUNGS and AIR-VESSELS," containing full and plain instructions for the relief and cure of those diseases, has just been printed, and may be had GRATIS from any Chemist, or *post free* from JAMES M. CROSBY, Chemist, Scarborough.

My 75s. English Silver Levers are Surpassed by none, Guaranteed for 2 Years, and will wear 50 Years. W. BROWN, 46, PARADE, BIRMINGHAM.

PRICE 6d.

OLD AND NEW BIRMINGHAM.

AN ILLUSTRATED HISTORY OF THE TOWN AND ITS PEOPLE.

PRINTED AND PUBLISHED BY

HOUGHTON & HAMMOND, SCOTLAND PASSAGE,
BIRMINGHAM.

ROBOTHAM AND HORTON, WINE AND SPIRIT MERCHANTS,
LOWER TEMPLE ST.

BRITISH WORKMAN'S ASSURANCE COMPANY,

LIMITED.

CHIEF OFFICES:

BROAD STREET CORNER, BIRMINGHAM.

ESTABLISHED 1866.

The surpassing progress, and great acnievements of this Office are the best proofs of the public confidence, and the high esteem placed upon the Company's liberal dealings; especially its promptitude in settling Claims, and its peculiar feature of Surrender Value. Through the Agency of the British Workman's Assurance Company, the great Principles and Advantages of Life Assurance become universal in their application. This Company embraces all Classes, and all Ages of Healthy People

FROM BIRTH TO 85 YEARS OF AGE.

OVER 80,000 PROPOSALS FOR ASSURANCE WERE RECEIVED IN THE PAST YEAR.

ANY PREMIUM IS NOW TAKEN, FROM 1D. PER WEEK TO £100 PER YEAR.

The Sums Assured increase with the age of the Policy, although the Premium paid must only be 1d. per Week. A person who has paid in 12 years, is justly and fairly entitled to more than a person that has paid in 12 months, only.

THE COMPANY WILL RETURN ONE-FOURTH OF THE PREMIUMS PAID (in the Life Department) to any persons wishing to discontinue their payments after the first three years. Thus the Company not only engages to pay the Sum Assured at Death, or in Lifetime (as agreed upon at the date of entry); but Five Shillings out of every Pound paid in can be withdrawn at will, as stated upon the Policy,

£1,118 WERE RETURNED TO THE WORKING CLASSES

IN THE INDUSTRIAL DEPARTMENT, IN THE PAST YEAR.

Thousands can bear witness, to the Company's prompt and liberal manner, in settling just and proper Claims.

NEARLY £75,000 HAVE ALREADY BEEN PAID.

Claims of £50 and under are paid at once; upon satisfactory proof.

THE PRESENT ANNUAL INCOME EXCEEDS £60,000.

Send for Prospectus. The Table Payable at Death or a given Age should have particular attention.

Mr. WOOLHOUSE, the Actuary, reports that the Funds in hand are in excess of the amount really required to meet the liabilities of the Company.

HENRY PORT, F.S.A., Managing Director.
D. A. BECKETT, Secretary.

PIANOS, HARMONIUMS, AND AMERICAN ORGANS, At Low Prices for Cash, on the One, Two, or Three Year's System. **SAMES & SONS,** 5 & 6, SUFFOLK ST. Steam Works:—Exeter Row to Windmill St. Horse Fair, Birmingham.

INDIA-RUBBER STAMPS

ARE MADE FOR

HEADING NOTE PAPER,

ENDORSING ENVELOPES, CHEQUES, AND POSTAL CARDS.

MARKING LINEN,

STAMPING CRESTS, TRADE MARKS, FAC-SIMILES OF SIGNATURES.

MONOGRAMS,

AND A VARIETY OF OTHER PURPOSES TOO NUMEROUS TO MENTION.

THE PREMIER DATING STAMP, with Solid Rubber dates for 10 years, from 18/6 each.

Write for Pattern and Price List or call at

JOHN BERKLEY'S, 42, CHERRY STREET,

BIRMINGHAM.

ESTABLISHED 1837.

PRICE LISTS AND TESTIMONIALS ON APPLICATION.

THE AUCTION MART,

EAGLE FOUNDRY BUILDINGS, BROAD ST., BIRMINGHAM.

Two Minutes' Walk from the Town Hall.

Auctioneers, Valuers, Estate, Public-house, and Landlords' Agents.

Sales and Valuations of every description efficiently and economically conducted in Town or Country.

Cash Advanced on Property or Goods for absolute Sale.

SILVER MEDAL AT PARIS EXHIBITION, 1878.

THE PATENT "ECLIPSE" GAS ENGINE

(SIMON'S PATENTS.)

NEW FEATURES.

An internal, constant flame.

The intimate mixture, by compression, of the gas and air in a separate cylinder.

A gradual expansion, obtained by passing this mixture *through* the internal flame.

The utilisation of the surplus heat of the burning and burned gases to produce steam.

Admission of the steam into the working cylinder.

ADVANTAGES.

No Slide Valves, and, consequently, no delicate working parts, easily worn, and absorbing considerable power.

No explosion; no sudden shock or jar.

No waste of gas.

No expensive and elaborate lubrication.

Non-liability of cylinder and piston to wear.

No noise.

No constant circulation of cold water to prevent the destruction of the working parts by heat.

No danger of fire.

No foundation required. The engine may be placed on upper floors.

The use of Steam reduces the liability of the cylinder and piston to wear, and makes lubrication easy.

To the engineer the indicator diagram will be the best recommendation.

SOLE PATENTEE AND MANUFACTURER,

LOUIS SIMON, WILFORD ROAD WORKS, NOTTINGHAM

CANNOCK CHASE RAILWAY COLLIERY

COMPANY.

RETAIL DEPARTMENT:

Office—61, COLMORE ROW, Birmingham,

ADJOINING THE TOWN AND DISTRICT BANK.

Deep Coal, 16s.8d.; Deep Cobbles, 15s.10d.; Shallow Coal, 15s.10d.; Shallow Cobbles, 15s.; Old Park Coal, 13s.4d.; Small Shallow, 13s.4d.; Nuts, 12s.6d.; Screened Lumps, 12s.6d.; Household Coal, 12s.6d.; Rough Slack, 11s.6d.; Engine Slack, 10s.; Screenings, 7s.6d. per ton.; 1s.8d. per ton less at the Wharves. Delivery included within Two Miles of Vauxhall, Monument Lane, Perry Barr, Sutton, Erdington, and Soho Railway Stations.

For JOHN N. BROWN, Vendor,
F. BECK, Agent.

THE "OWL,"

A SATIRICAL JOURNAL.

—:o:—

PUBLISHED EVERY FRIDAY.

—:o:—

PRICE ONE PENNY.

—:o:—

BIRMINGHAM: HOUGHTON & HAMMOND, SCOTLAND PASSAGE.

DO YOUR OWN PRINTING. USE CLEMENT MALINS' "DEFIANCE" PRINTING & COPYING PRESS, With Type, Ink, Roller, &c., 25s. & 42s. A child can print with them. Type and Printers' Requisites supplied. MALINS' PURE RUBBER STAMPS, Linen Markers, from 2s. 6d. Monograms 2s. 6d., Rubber Stamps in all shapes and sizes, for all trades and professions. Cheapest House in Birmingham. AGENTS WANTED. Clement Malins' Cheap PRINTING OFFICE, 58 HILL ST., (Opposite the Post Office), Birmingham

PRICE 6d.

OLD AND NEW BIRMINGHAM.

AN ILLUSTRATED HISTORY OF THE TOWN AND ITS PEOPLE.

PRINTED AND PUBLISHED BY

HOUGHTON & HAMMOND, SCOTLAND PASSAGE,
BIRMINGHAM.

ROBOTHAM AND HORTON, WINE AND SPIRIT MERCHANTS,
LOWER TEMPLE ST.

BRITISH WORKMAN'S ASSURANCE COMPANY,

LIMITED.

CHIEF OFFICES:

BROAD STREET CORNER, BIRMINGHAM.

ESTABLISHED 1866.

The surpassing progress, and great acnievements of this Office are the best proofs of the public confidence, and the high esteem placed upon the Company's liberal dealings; especially its promptitude in settling Claims, and its peculiar feature of Surrender Value. Through the Agency of the BRITISH WORKMAN'S ASSURANCE COMPANY, the great Principles and Advantages of Life Assurance become universal in their application. THIS COMPANY EMBRACES ALL CLASSES, AND ALL AGES OF HEALTHY PEOPLE

FROM BIRTH TO 85 YEARS OF AGE.

OVER 80,000 PROPOSALS FOR ASSURANCE WERE RECEIVED IN THE PAST YEAR.

ANY PREMIUM IS NOW TAKEN, FROM 1D. PER WEEK TO £100 PER YEAR.

The Sums Assured increase with the age of the Policy, although the Premium paid must only be 1d. per Week. A person who has paid in 12 years, is justly and fairly entitled to more than a person that has paid in 12 months, only.

THE COMPANY WILL RETURN ONE-FOURTH OF THE PREMIUMS PAID (in the Life Department) to any persons wishing to discontinue their payments after the first three years. Thus the Company not only engages to pay the Sum Assured at Death, or in Lifetime (as agreed upon at the date of entry); but Five Shillings out of every Pound paid in can be withdrawn at will, as stated upon the Policy,

£1,118 WERE RETURNED TO THE WORKING CLASSES

IN THE INDUSTRIAL DEPARTMENT, IN THE PAST YEAR.

Thousands can bear witness, to the Company's prompt and liberal manner, in settling just and proper Claims.

NEARLY £75,000 HAVE ALREADY BEEN PAID.

Claims of £50 and under are paid at once; upon satisfactory proof.

THE PRESENT ANNUAL INCOME EXCEEDS £60,000.

Send for Prospectus. The Table Payable at Death or a given Age should have particular attention.

Mr. WOOLHOUSE, the Actuary, reports that the Funds in hand are in excess of the amount really required to meet the liabilities of the Company.

HENRY PORT, F.S.A., Managing Director.
D. A. BECKETT, Secretary.

DR. ROOKE'S MEDICINES

THE

ORIENTAL PILLS AND SOLAR ELIXIR.

THESE WELL-KNOWN FAMILY MEDICINES have had a continually increasing Sale throughout the United Kingdom and the British Colonies since their introduction in 1836, and are especially noted for their STRENGTHENING and RESTORATIVE Properties. Hence their invariable success in the RELIEF and CURE of

INDIGESTION,	BRONCHITIS,	GOUT,
LIVER COMPLAINTS,	Pulmonary CONSUMPTION	SCROFULA,
ASTHMA,	RHEUMATISM,	General DEBILITY,

And all Diseases of the NERVOUS SYSTEM.

Whether arising from a Sedentary mode of life, unhealthy occupation, insalubrious climate, or other cause whatsoever.

THE ORIENTAL PILLS AND SOLAR ELIXIR

Are prepared only by **CHARLES ROOKE, M.D., SCARBOROUGH.** The **Pills** are sold in Boxes at **1s. 1½d.** and **4s. 6d.** each; the **ELIXIR** in Bottles at **4s. 6d.** and **11s.** each, duty included. Around each Box and Bottle are wrapped Directions for the guidance of Patients in all Diseases.

DR. ROOKE'S ANTI-LANCET.

All who wish to preserve health, and thus prolong life, should read

DR. ROOKE'S "ANTI-LANCET," or "HANDY GUIDE TO DOMESTIC MEDICINE,"

Which contains 172 pages, and is replete with anecdotes, sketches, biographical matter, portraits of eminent men, &c. It may be obtained GRATIS of any Chemist, or POST FREE from Dr. Rooke, Scarborough, England.

Concerning this Book, the late eminent author, Sheridan Knowles, observed:

"It will be an incalculable boon to every person who can read & think."

CROSBY'S

BALSAMIC

COUGH ELIXIR

Is the leading medicine of the day, and is specially recommended by several eminent Physicians. It has been used with the most signal success for Asthma, Bronchitis, Consumption, Coughs, Influenza, Consumptive Night Sweats, Spitting of Blood, Shortness of Breath, &c.; and is a most valuable adjunct to Dr. Rooke's Medicines in all Affections of the Throat and Chest.

Crosby's Balsamic Cough Elixir is sold everywhere, by all Chemists and Medicine Vendors, at the following prices:—**1s. 9d.**, **4s. 6d.**, and **11s.** each Bottle. A saving of Three Shillings is affected by purchasing the large bottles. Full directions with each Bottle.

NOTICE TO INVALIDS.

A NEW EDITION of the TREATISE on "DISEASES of the LUNGS and AIR-VESSELS," containing full and plain instructions for the relief and cure of those diseases, has just been printed, and may be had GRATIS from any Chemist, or *post free* from JAMES M. CROSBY, Chemist, Scarborough.

PRICE 6d.

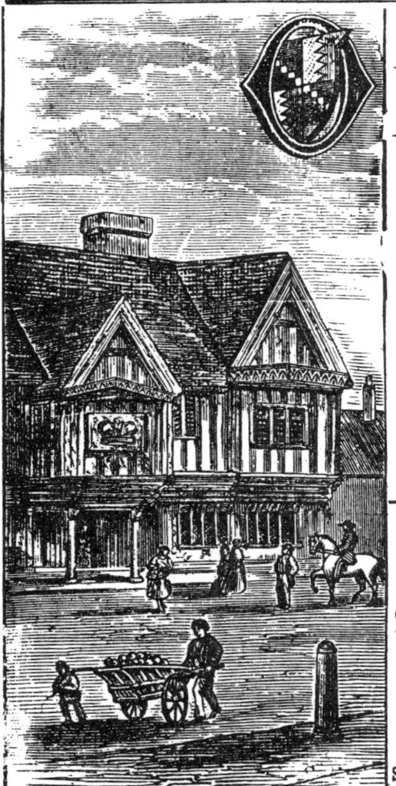

OLD AND NEW BIRMINGHAM.

AN ILLUSTRATED HISTORY OF THE TOWN AND ITS PEOPLE.

PRINTED AND PUBLISHED BY

HOUGHTON & HAMMOND, SCOTLAND PASSAGE,
BIRMINGHAM.

BRITISH WORKMAN'S ASSURANCE COMPANY,

LIMITED.

CHIEF OFFICES:

BROAD STREET CORNER, BIRMINGHAM.

ESTABLISHED 1866.

The surpassing progress, and great acnievements of this Office are the best proofs of the public confidence, and the high esteem placed upon the Company's liberal dealings; especially its promptitude in settling Claims, and its peculiar feature of Surrender Value. Through the Agency of the BRITISH WORKMAN'S ASSURANCE COMPANY, the great Principles and Advantages of Life Assurance become universal in their application. THIS COMPANY EMBRACES ALL CLASSES, AND ALL AGES OF HEALTHY PEOPLE

FROM BIRTH TO 85 YEARS OF AGE.

OVER 80,000 PROPOSALS FOR ASSURANCE WERE RECEIVED IN THE PAST YEAR.

ANY PREMIUM IS NOW TAKEN, FROM 1D. PER WEEK TO £100 PER YEAR.

The Sums Assured increase with the age of the Policy, although the Premium paid must only be 1d. per Week. A person who has paid in 12 years, is justly and fairly entitled to more than a per. on that has paid in 12 months, only.

THE COMPANY WILL RETURN ONE-FOURTH OF THE PREMIUMS PAID (in the Life Department) to any persons wishing to discontinue their payments after the first three years. Thus the Company not only engages to pay the Sum Assured at Death, or in Lifetime (as agreed upon at the date of entry); but Five Shillings out of every Pound paid in can be withdrawn at will, as stated upon the Policy,

£1,118 WERE RETURNED TO THE WORKING CLASSES

IN THE INDUSTRIAL DEPARTMENT, IN THE PAST YEAR.

Thousands can bear witness, to the Company's prompt and liberal manner, in settling just and proper Claims.

NEARLY £75,000 HAVE ALREADY BEEN PAID.

Claims of £50 and under are paid at once; upon satisfactory proof.

THE PRESENT ANNUAL INCOME EXCEEDS £60,000.

Send for Prospectus. The Table Payable at Death or a given Age should have particular attention.

Mr. WOOLHOUSE, the Actuary, reports that the Funds in hand are in excess of the amount really required to meet the liabilities of the Company.

HENRY PORT, F.S.A., Managing Director.
D. A. BECKETT, Secretary.

PRICE
6d.

OLD AND NEW BIRMINGHAM.

AN ILLUSTRATED HISTORY OF THE TOWN AND ITS PEOPLE.

PRINTED AND PUBLISHED BY

HOUGHTON & HAMMOND, SCOTLAND PASSAGE,
BIRMINGHAM.

ROBOTHAM AND HORTON, WINE AND SPIRIT MERCHANTS,
LOWER TEMPLE ST.

J. GOFFE'S
TRADE
GOFFE
MARK
BIRMINGHAM
DUKE St.
SODA WATER

PRICE
6d.

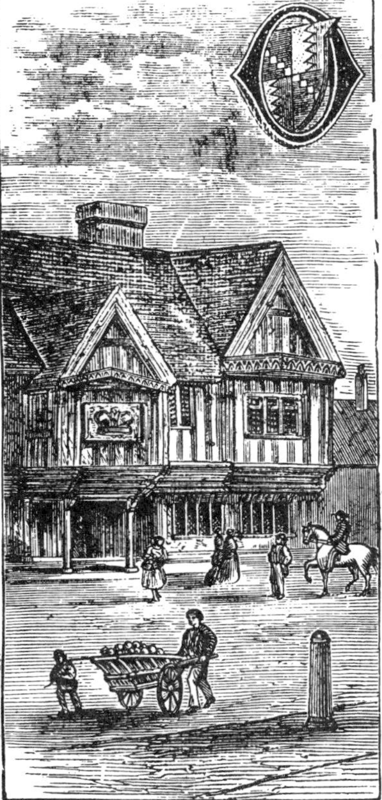

OLD AND NEW BIRMINGHAM.

AN ILLUSTRATED HISTORY OF THE TOWN AND ITS PEOPLE.

PRINTED AND PUBLISHED BY

HOUGHTON & HAMMOND, SCOTLAND PASSAGE,
BIRMINGHAM.

ROBOTHAM AND HORTON, WINE AND SPIRIT MERCHANTS,
LOWER TEMPLE ST.

BRITISH WORKMAN'S ASSURANCE COMPANY,

LIMITED.

CHIEF OFFICES:

BROAD STREET CORNER, BIRMINGHAM.

ESTABLISHED 1866.

The surpassing progress, and great achievements of this Office are the best proofs of the public confidence, and the high esteem placed upon the Company's liberal dealings; especially its promptitude in settling Claims, and its peculiar feature of Surrender Value. Through the Agency of the British Workman's Assurance Company, the great Principles and Advantages of Life Assurance become universal in their application. This Company embraces all Classes, and all Ages of Healthy People

FROM BIRTH TO 85 YEARS OF AGE.

OVER 80,000 PROPOSALS FOR ASSURANCE WERE RECEIVED IN THE PAST YEAR.

ANY PREMIUM IS NOW TAKEN, FROM 1D. PER WEEK TO £100 PER YEAR.

The Sums Assured increase with the age of the Policy, although the Premium paid must only be 1d. per Week. A person who has paid in 12 years, is justly and fairly entitled to more than a person that has paid in 12 months, only.

THE COMPANY WILL RETURN ONE-FOURTH OF THE PREMIUMS PAID (in the Life Department) to any persons wishing to discontinue their payments after the first three years. Thus the Company not only engages to pay the Sum Assured at Death, or in Lifetime (as agreed upon at the date of entry); but Five Shillings out of every Pound paid in can be withdrawn at will, as stated upon the Policy,

£1,118 WERE RETURNED TO THE WORKING CLASSES

IN THE INDUSTRIAL DEPARTMENT, IN THE PAST YEAR.

Thousands can bear witness, to the Company's prompt and liberal manner, in settling just and proper Claims.

NEARLY £75,000 HAVE ALREADY BEEN PAID.

Claims of £50 and under are paid at once; upon satisfactory proof.

THE PRESENT ANNUAL INCOME EXCEEDS £60,000.

Send for Prospectus. The Table Payable at Death or a given Age should have particular attention.

Mr. WOOLHOUSE, the Actuary, reports that the Funds in hand are in excess of the amount really required to meet the liabilities of the Company.

HENRY PORT, F.S.A., Managing Director.
D. A. BECKETT, Secretary.

PRICE
6d.

OLD AND NEW BIRMINGHAM.

AN ILLUSTRATED HISTORY OF THE TOWN AND ITS PEOPLE.

PRINTED AND PUBLISHED BY
HOUGHTON & HAMMOND, SCOTLAND PASSAGE,
BIRMINGHAM.

ROBOTHAM AND HORTON, WINE AND SPIRIT MERCHANTS,
LOWER TEMPLE ST.

DR. ROOKE'S MEDICINES

THE

ORIENTAL PILLS AND SOLAR ELIXIR.

THESE WELL-KNOWN FAMILY MEDICINES have had a continually increasing Sale throughout the United Kingdom and the British Colonies since their introduction in 1836, and are especially noted for their STRENGTHENING and RESTORATIVE Properties. Hence their invariable success in the RELIEF and CURE of

INDIGESTION,	BRONCHITIS,	GOUT,
LIVER COMPLAINTS,	Pulmonary CONSUMPTION	SCROFULA,
ASTHMA,	RHEUMATISM,	General DEBILITY,

And all Diseases of the NERVOUS SYSTEM.

Whether arising from a Sedentary mode of life, unhealthy occupation, insalubrious climate, or other cause whatsoever.

THE ORIENTAL PILLS AND SOLAR ELIXIR

Are prepared only by **CHARLES ROOKE, M.D., SCARBOROUGH.** The Pills are sold in Boxes at **1s.1½d.** and **4s.6d.** each; the **ELIXIR** in Bottles at **4s.6d.** and **11s.** each, duty included. Around each Box and Bottle are wrapped Directions for the guidance of Patients in all Diseases.

DR. ROOKE'S ANTI-LANCET.

All who wish to preserve health, and thus prolong life, should read

DR. ROOKE'S "ANTI-LANCET," or "HANDY GUIDE TO DOMESTIC MEDICINE,"

Which contains 172 pages, and is replete with anecdotes, sketches, biographical matter, portraits of eminent men, &c. It may be obtained GRATIS of any Chemist, or POST FREE from DR. ROOKE, Scarborough, England.

CONCERNING THIS BOOK, THE LATE EMINENT AUTHOR, SHERIDAN KNOWLES, OBSERVED:

"It will be an incalculable boon to every person who can read & think

CROSBY'S

BALSAMIC

COUGH ELIXIR

Is the leading medicine of the day, and is specially recommended by several eminent Physicians. It has been used with the most signal success for Asthma, Bronchitis, Consumption, Coughs, Influenza, Consumptive Night Sweats, Spitting of Blood, Shortness of Breath, &c.; and is a most valuable adjunct to Dr. Rooke's Medicines in all Affections of the Throat and Chest.

Crosby's Balsamic Cough Elixir is sold everywhere, by all Chemists and Medicine Vendors, at the following prices:—**1s.9d.**, **4s.6d.**, and **11s.** each Bottle. A saving of THREE SHILLINGS is affected by purchasing the large bottles. Full directions with each Bottle.

NOTICE TO INVALIDS.

A NEW EDITION of the TREATISE on "DISEASES of the LUNGS and AIR-VESSELS," containing full and plain instructions for the relief and cure of those diseases, has just been printed, and may be had GRATIS from any Chemist, or *post free* from JAMES M. CROSBY, Chemist, Scarborough.